CHICANO ART

FOR OUR MILLENNIUM

COLLECTED WORKS FROM THE ARIZONA STATE UNIVERSITY COMMUNITY

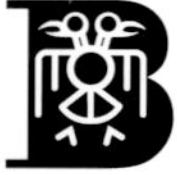

Bilingual Press/Editorial Bilingüe

General Editor
Gary D. Keller

Managing Editor
Karen S. Van Hooft

Associate Editors
Brian Ellis Cassity
Cristina de Isasi
Linda St. George Thurston

Project Team
Angelica Docog
Mary Erickson
Gary D. Keller
Melanie Magisos
Karen S. Van Hooft
Thomas H. Wilson

Additional Project Staff
Matt Anderson
Alexis R. Aten
Jo Ann Briseño
Sabrina Maldonado
Santiago A. Moratto
Amy Phillips
Roxann Ramos

Address
Bilingual Press
Hispanic Research Center
Arizona State University
PO Box 872702
Tempe, Arizona 85287-2702
(480) 965-3867

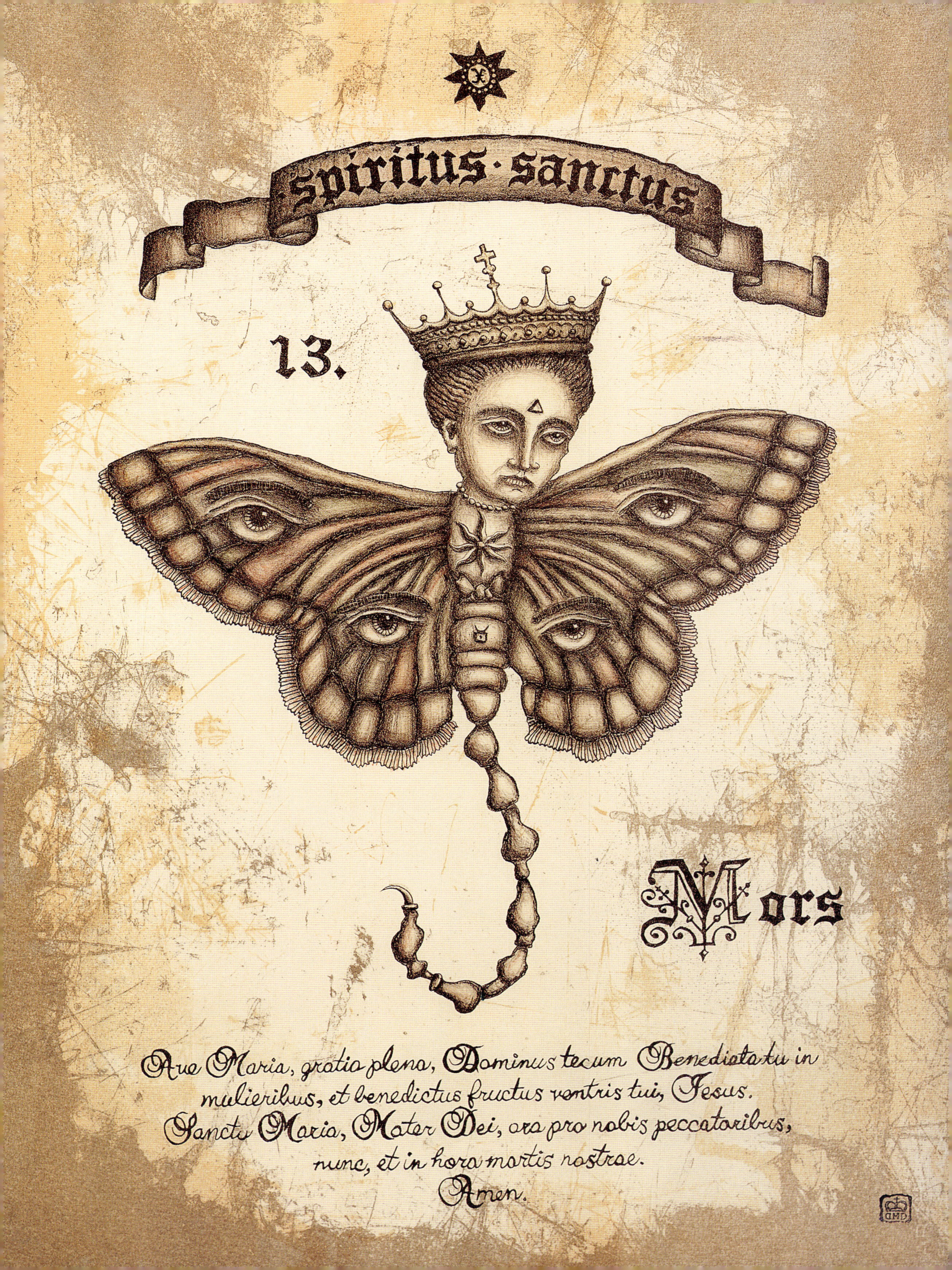

spiritus · sanctus
13.
Mors
Ave Maria, gratia plena, Dominus tecum Benedicta tu in
mulieribus, et benedictus fructus ventris tui, Jesus.
Sancta Maria, Mater Dei, ora pro nobis peccatoribus,
nunc, et in hora mortis nostrae.
Amen.

Overleaf: 1 Daniel Martín Díaz, *Magicus*, 2003, lithograph, 30" x 22.5"   2 Quintín González, *Spectre*, 2000, light jet print, 27" x 21"

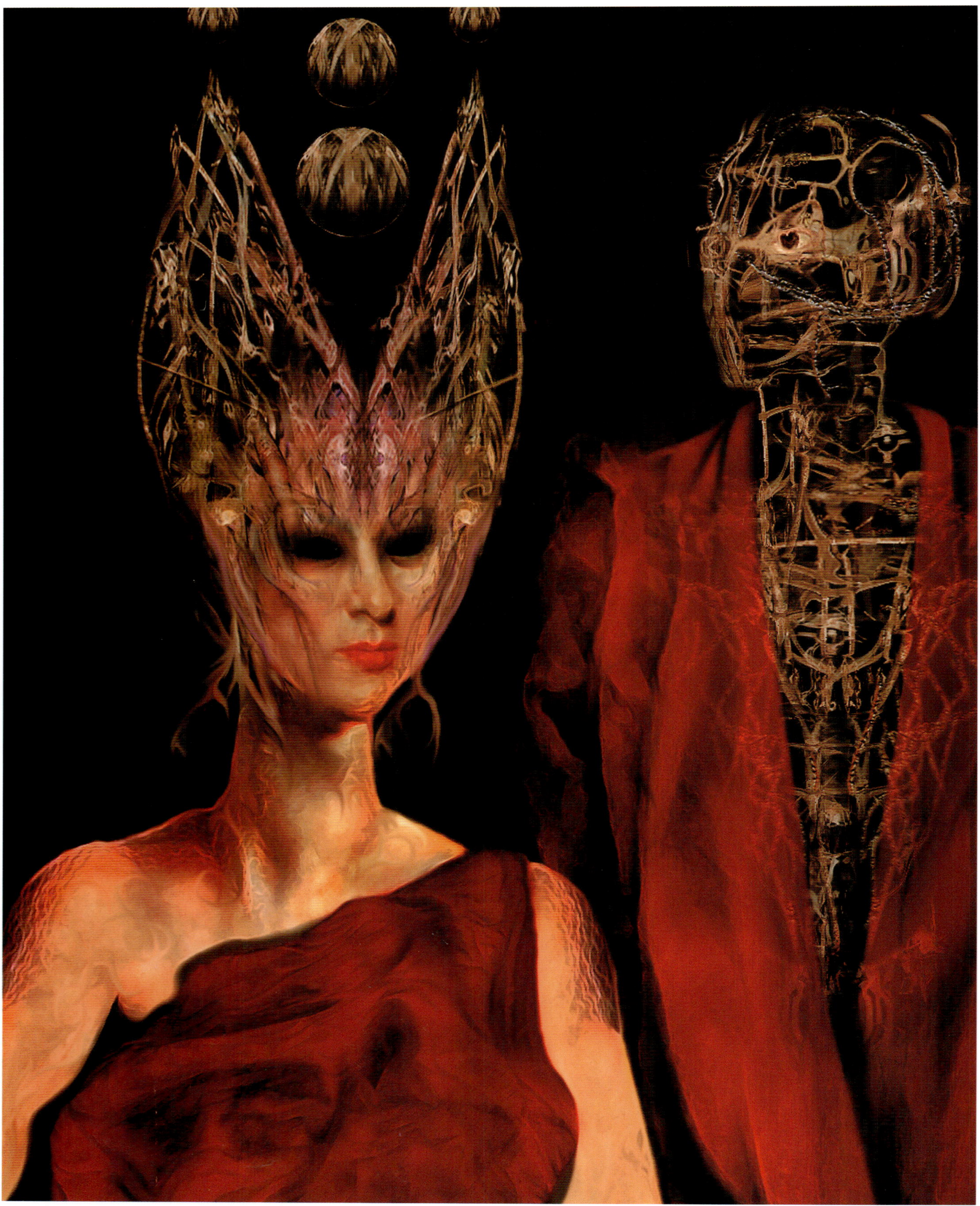

CHICANO ART
FOR OUR MILLENNIUM
COLLECTED WORKS FROM THE ARIZONA STATE UNIVERSITY COMMUNITY

Gary D. Keller • Mary Erickson • Pat Villeneuve

PRINCIPAL AUTHORS

Melanie Magisos • Amy Phillips • Angelica Docog • Thomas H. Wilson

CONTRIBUTORS

Gary D. Keller • Angelica Docog • Thomas H. Wilson

CURATORS

Craig Smith

PHOTOGRAPHER

Bilingual Press/Editorial Bilingüe

TEMPE, ARIZONA

ISBN 1-931010-25-0

Library of Congress Cataloging-in-Publication Data

Keller, Gary D.
    Chicano art for our millennium : collected works from the Arizona State University community / principal authors, Gary D. Keller, Mary Erickson, Pat Villeneuve ; contributors, Melanie Magisos ... [et al.] ; curators, Gary D. Keller, Angelica Docog, Tom Wilson ; photographer, Craig Smith.
        p. cm.
    Catalog accompanying a touring exhibition which was first held at the Mesa Southwest Museum, Mesa, Ariz., May 1-Sept. 19, 2004.
    Includes indexes.
    ISBN 1-931010-25-0
    1. Mexican American art--Themes, motives--21st century--Exhibitions. 2. Art--Arizona--Tempe--Exhibitions. 3. Arizona State University. University Art Collections--Exhibitions. I. Erickson, Mary (Mary Louise) II. Villeneuve, Pat, 1955- III. Magisos, Melanie. IV. Smith, Craig, 1959- V. Mesa Southwest Museum. VI. Title.

N6538.M4K45 2004
704.03'6872'007479173--dc22

                                                                              2004041061

PRINTED AND BOUND IN CHINA BY C&C OFFSET PRINTING CO., LTD.

Cover and interior design by John Wincek, Aerocraft Charter Art Service

Cover art: Front cover, Santiago Pérez, *First Aztec on the Moon*, 2002; back cover, Marion C. Martínez, *Madre querida*, 2002.

Acknowledgments

The Hispanic Research Center and the Bilingual Press would like to express their appreciation to the artists for permission to reproduce their works for this project.

We would also like to thank our institutional partners at Arizona State University, including Milton D. Glick, Executive Vice President and Provost of the University; Manuel Ávalos, Vice Provost for Research and Faculty Development, Office of the Vice Provost for Academic Affairs, Arizona State University West; Fernando Delgado, Associate Vice Provost for Academic Programs and Graduate Studies, Office of the Vice Provost for Academic Affairs, Arizona State University West; John M. Lincoln, Executive Director, Office of Youth Preparation, Office of Academic Affairs, Arizona State University Downtown Center; and Betty DeGraw, Dean, College of Extended Education, Arizona State University Downtown Center.

We especially thank our sister research unit, the Hispanic Border Leadership Institute, for its support, as well as its executive director, Leonard A. Valverde.

Finally, we would also like to acknowledge the contributions of Brian L. Foster, Provost and Vice President for Academic Affairs, Office of the Provost, University of New Mexico, and Marjorie Devon, Director, Tamarind Institute, University of New Mexico.

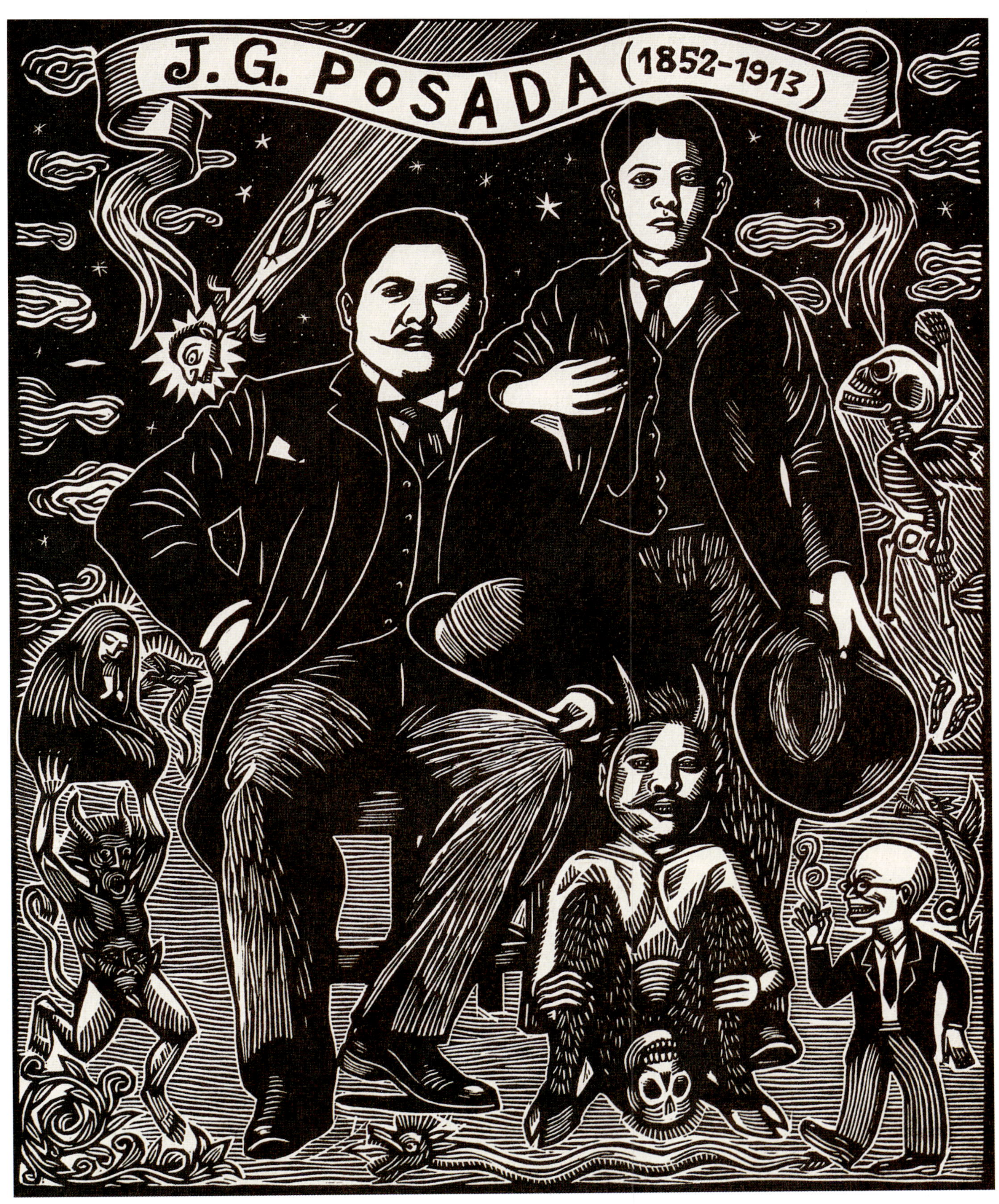

3 Artemio Rodríguez, *Posada y su hijo* (Posada and his son), 2002, linocut, 20" x 16"

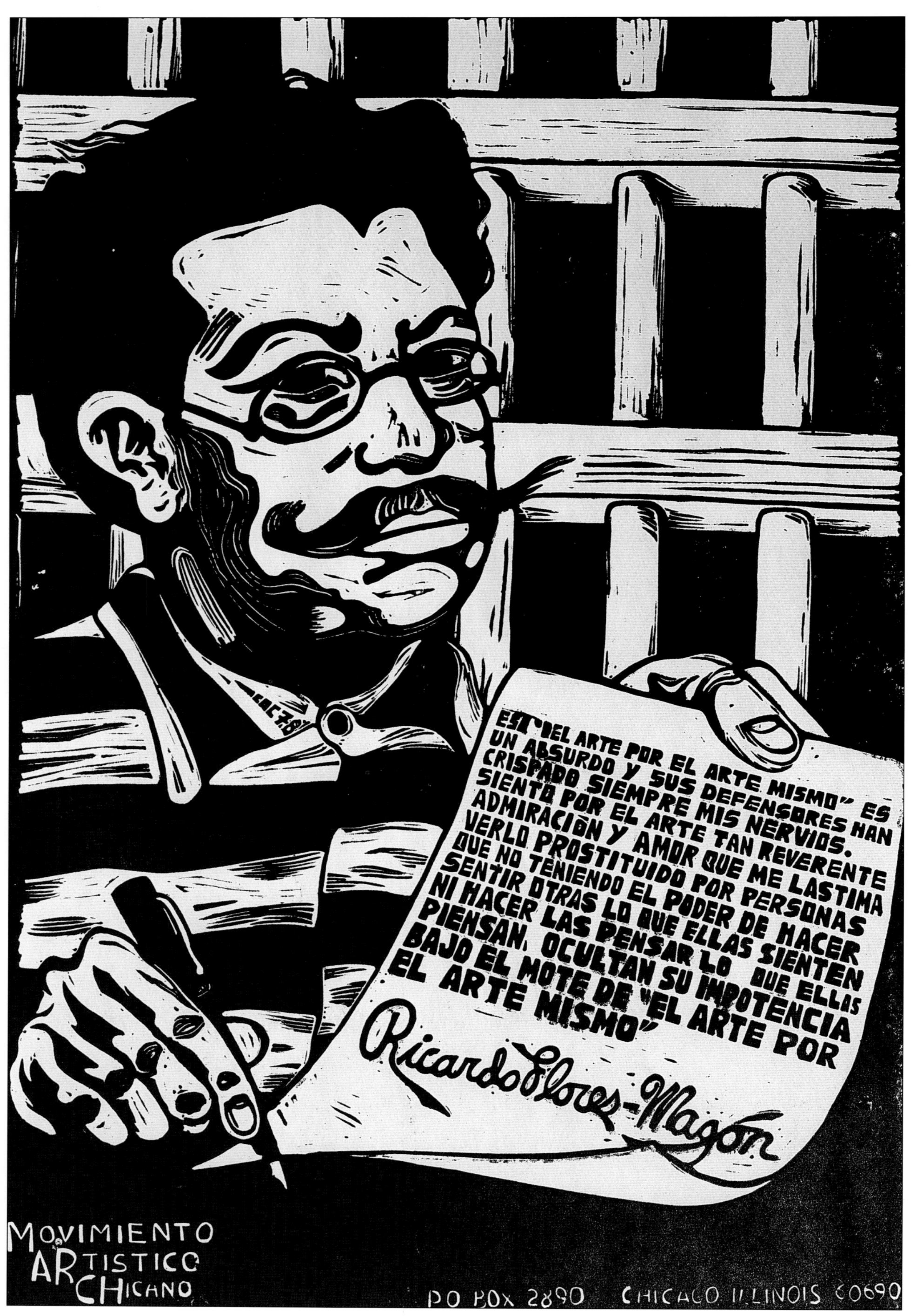

4 Carlos Cortez, *Ricardo Flores Magón*, 1977, linocut, 30" x 20"

contents

foreword

CHICANO ART: THREE ENCOUNTERS

Chicano Art for Our Millennium is my third major experience with Chicano art. The first was as program officer at the National Endowment for the Humanities (NEH) for the project *Chicano Art: Resistance and Affirmation* (CARA).[1] This project received a planning grant from NEH, and, upon its successful completion, the Wight Art Gallery at UCLA applied to the Endowment for implementation. The peer review panel, outside reviewers, and Endowment staff recommended the project for funding. In spite of this considerably positive evaluation, Lynne Cheney, Chairman of the Endowment, denied funding for the project. At NEH the chairman has final decision-making authority on all applications, and she was within her rights to reject *Chicano Art: Resistance and Affirmation*. During my five years at the Endowment, however, the chairman very rarely overturned the unified recommendations of the peer review panel, outside reviewers, and professional staff. Mrs. Cheney's decision on the CARA project was not based on the merits of the project as established by the professional review process. Instead, Endowment staff widely believed that it was primarily a political decision reflecting an unfavorable view of projects on minority, ethnic, or potentially controversial subjects.

My second major experience with Chicano art was as director of the Museum of New Mexico in Santa Fe, when the Museum of International Folk Art displayed Alma López's computer-generated collage *Our Lady* as part of the exhibition *Cyber Arte: Tradition Meets Technology*, curated by Dr. Tey Marianna Nunn. López's image, as portrayed by performance artist Raquel Salinas, is a Virgin with attitude.[2] Not the demure, unassertive, head-bowed Virgin of the traditional image, López's Virgin is a head-up, chin-out, hands-on-hips assertion of the power of women and womanhood. Otherwise unclothed, garlands of roses cover her breasts and hips, and a cloak of Aztec symbols surrounds her. The press immediately dubbed her "the bikini-clad Virgin," and the fight was on.

Our Lady offended certain traditionalist, conservative Hispanic male activists, who made their objections known to the media. Representatives of very powerful institutions demanded removal of *Our Lady* from display, including members of the museum's board of regents, the archbishop of Santa Fe, a group of influential, mostly Hispanic Democratic legislators, representatives of national Catholic organizations, and segments of the general public. I refused. For months, the museum was embroiled in highly public discord that fractured Hispanic and Catholic communities in New Mexico and reached national and even international proportions before the exhibition ended. By then, this one little image by a Chicana artist had engendered considerable heated debate and raised visceral issues such as the role of artists and museums in society; free speech versus respect for traditional religious images; the role of women in patriarchal Hispanic culture; who controls art; public funding of the arts; loss of cultural heritage; art and cultural change; the role of the church in such debate; and various us/them, insider/outsider, rich/poor, and white/brown dichotomies. *Our Lady* exposed all kinds of raw nerves and real issues.

My conclusion from these experiences: Chicano art is powerful indeed. It has the ability to reach across ethnic groups and class lines, to captivate

---

[1] *CARA Chicano Art: Resistance and Affirmation, 1965-1985*, edited by Richard Griswold del Castillo, Teresa McKenna, and Yvonne Yarbro-Bejarano. Los Angeles: UCLA Wight Art Gallery, 1991.

[2] *Contemporary Chicana and Chicano Art*, edited by Gary D. Keller et al., pp. 76-77, 131. Tempe: Bilingual Press/Editorial Bilingüe, 2002.

greatly diverse viewers, and to compel a large variety of intellectual and emotional responses. *Chicano Art for Our Millennium*, a collaborative project between the Mesa Southwest Museum and the Hispanic Research Center of Arizona State University, emphatically demonstrates this artistic power. No previous exhibition establishes the artistic range and thematic sweep of Chicano art more forcefully than *Chicano Art for Our Millennium*.

Much has been said of the origins of Chicano art in the barrios of East Los Angeles and San Antonio, the *campos* in between, the universities of the Southwest, political movements such as the United Farm Workers and the Brown Berets, and artistic traditions such as the Mexican muralists and pre-Hispanic art. Because of its geographical cohesiveness, ethnic associations, subject matter, and political and social edge, Chicano art has been variously labeled "ethnic art," "political art," "outsider art," and so forth. One encounters the well-known antecedents of Chicano art in *Chicano Art for Our Millennium*. But Chicano artists do not work in a vacuum; they are aware of the great traditions of art history. Looking at these works of art, one recognizes references to Goya, Sargent, Monet, Matisse, Gauguin, Picasso, Duchamp, and even Vermeer, to movements such as surrealism and German expressionism, and to pre-Hispanic, Spanish, Spanish colonial, and Mexican art. In Chicano art one sees references to the European pantheon from the Renaissance to impressionism and beyond.

Chicano art is a distinctly American art. The time has come to place Chicano art within the context of American art history. *Chicano Art for Our Millennium* is a major step toward making Chicano art better understood and appreciated by the mainstream art world and general public. As that occurs, the world will be much richer.

Thomas H. Wilson
DIRECTOR
MESA SOUTHWEST MUSEUM

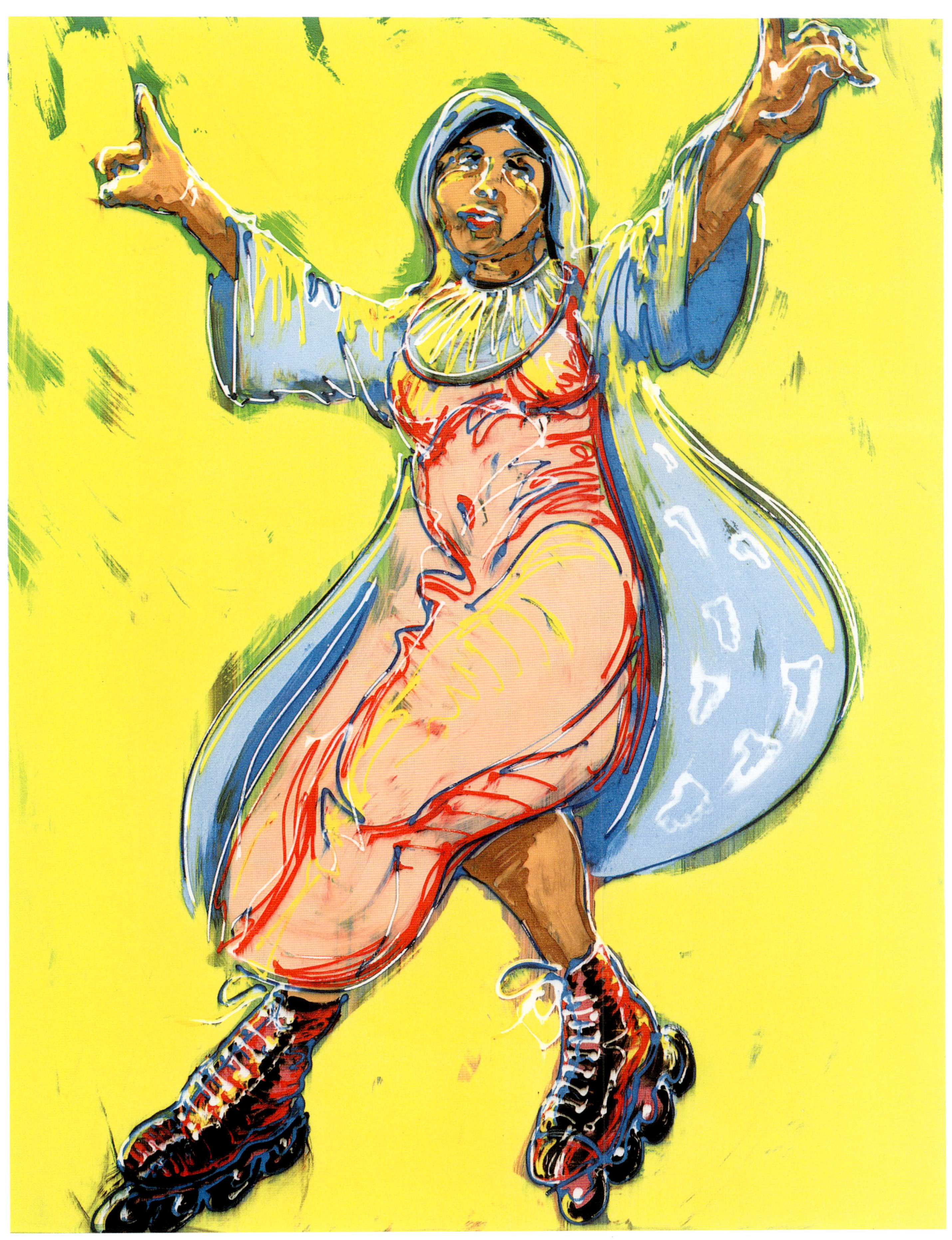

5 Wayne Alaniz Healy, *La Virgen de Venice*, 1995, serigraph, 43" x 30"

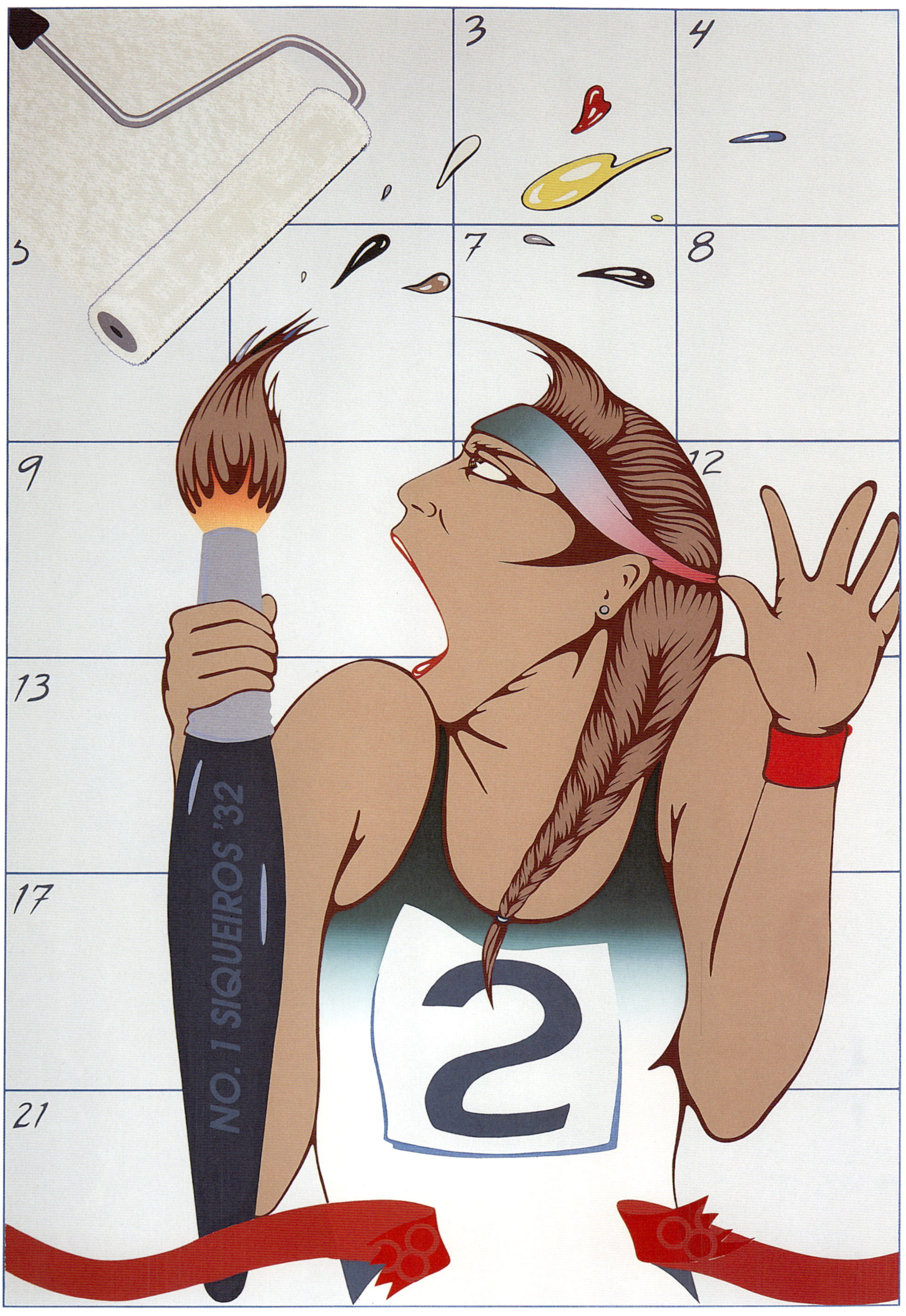

6 Barbara Carrasco, *Self-Portrait*, 1984, serigraph, 40" x 28"

on the creation of this exhibition...

eorge Rivera, professor and rhetor excelsior of Chicano art at the University of Colorado, Boulder, made his *pronunciamiento* at the Mexic-Arte celebration of the tenth anniversary of Sam Coronado's renowned Serie Project. On 26 July 2003 in Mexic-Arte's downtown Austin museum and community art space, Rivera proclaimed, "It's the new millennium." The millenarian topoi quickly took hold. "Right on," supported a Raza chorus of critics and curators including Gilberto Cárdenas, Amelia Malagamba, Tomás Benítez, y tu humilde servidor, Keller: " 'Tis the new millennium!" There were many artists present at the event including Sam Coronado, Celina Hinojosa, Carmen Lomas Garza, and Vincent Valdez, to name a few, and they seemed to like the new millennium, too. We came to Austin not to quibble with George. We came to bury old preconceptions, to surmount the barricades and celebrate the dawning of the new age. *Magister dixit!*

Later that night, we artists and critics reassembled at suitable watering holes in that veritable gown town of students that is downtown Austin, Texas, playing out the night and bringing in the dawn of the new millennium. I vividly recall Herr Doktor Professor George Rivera damning the "do not walk" signs and manically and maniacally rolling me in my wheelchair like Ben Hur straining against his evil antagonist, an anti-art Messala.

We enjoyed the ride. We enjoyed the buzz. The memories y la frasecita have stuck. We are determined to make this our millennium. There is no turning back for Chicana/Chicano and Latino art. We go forward in the dawning of our time, earning our stripes, step by steadfast step.

What is newly and nuestramente millenarian for Chicana and Chicano art? For one, the convergence of new exhibitions, new books, and new audience appreciation of nuestra casa of Chicana/o art. Particular reference must be made to several highly significant exhibitions as well as a number of new books on Chicana and Chicano art, several of them calibrated to the important art exhibitions mentioned here. (See references that follow.)

Just Another Poster? Chicano Graphic Arts in California opened the millennium not with a whimper, but a bang. This exhibition was a retrospective of decades of graphic art produced in association with each of six major Chicano art centers and cooperatives: Royal Chicano Air Force/RCAF (Sacramento), Galería de la Raza (San Francisco) and La Raza Silkscreen Center/La Raza Graphics (San Francisco), Self-Help Graphics and Art and the Mechicano Art Center (both in Los Angeles), and Centro Cultural de la Raza (San Diego). All but the Galería de La Raza were centers of poster production. These centers offered different ways of moving between cultural politics and fine art approaches to Chicano poster making. This diversity of approach was reflected in the forms and styles of the work itself, from silkscreen to digital and from traditional to postmodern pastiche. For the largely working-class communities marginal to the mainstream world of galleries and museums, these art centers were the first public places where Chicano artists could develop and showcase their talents. The works date from the 1960s through the present, including, for example, Andrew Zermeño's famous 1965 poster, *Huelga!*, which, in support of the United Farm Workers, introduces the UFW eagle that became a key symbol of the movement.

The exhibition ran from 2 June through 13 August 2000 at the Jack S. Blanton Museum of Art, University of Texas, Austin; 12 January-4 March 2001 at the University Art Museum, University of California, Santa Barbara; 16 June-9 December 2001 at the Fowler Museum, University of California, Los Angeles; 4 May-18 August 2002 at the Oakland Museum of California; 23 September 2002-4 January 2003 at the Merced (California) Multicultural Arts Center; and 14

March-31 May 2003 at the Jersey City Museum, New Jersey.

Just Another Poster? Chicano Graphic Arts in California was a comprehensive exploration of the critical role posters and other graphic materials played in the Chicano struggle for self-determination. The Chicana/Chicano story was told in the vivid art of its posters, which originally disseminated their messages from building walls, telephone poles, and other surfaces on the urban landscape. These powerful graphic works, created by artists to raise awareness and rouse conscience, were brought together in a groundbreaking exhibition of more than one hundred examples by fifty-seven Chicano/a artists, including Lalo Alcaraz, Leonard Castellanos, Yreina Cervántez, Richard Duardo, Ricardo Favela, Rupert García, Louie "The Foot" González, Ester Hernández, Ralph Maradiaga, José Montoya, Malaquías Montoya, Herbert Sigüenza, and John Valadez.

The exhibition examined not just the profound role art played as a part of the Chicano civil rights movement, but also the remarkable effectiveness of the poster medium itself. Chicano/a artists use the poster as a visual tool to articulate the goals and issues that are important to their communities. They build a communications network on the walls of homes, stores, and offices that allows people in different places to share the same symbols, to appreciate the same aesthetic forms, and to enjoy the same humor.

Just Another Poster? was organized by the University Art Museum, University of California, Santa Barbara (UCSB), in collaboration with the California Ethnic and Multicultural Archives, Department of Special Collections, Davidson Library, UCSB, and the Center for the Study of Political Graphics. The interdisciplinary curatorial team included Holly J. Barnet, Department of Art and Art History, University of New Mexico; C. Ondine Chavoya, Tufts University, Boston; Salvador Güereña, director, California Ethnic and Multicultural Archives, Davidson Library, UCSB; George Lipsitz, Department of Ethnic Studies, UC San Diego; Chon Noriega, Department of Film and Television, UCLA; Rafael Pérez-Torres, Department of English, UCLA; Tere Romo, at that time curator, The Mexican Museum, San Francisco; and Carol Wells, director, Center for the Study of Political Graphics, Los Angeles. The project was overseen by Marla C. Berns, director, University Art Museum, UCSB.

Alfredo Arreguín: Patterns of Dreams and Nature is a large-scale retrospective celebrating the work of Mexican-born Seattle painter Alfredo Arreguín. The exhibition includes key works from the major areas of the artist's production: Jungles series, Icons/Portraits, Patterns, and the Pacific Northwest. Arreguín's extraordinarily original art draws images from dreams, nature, and political and social events. The artist evokes the patterns that arise from the fusion of the real and the imaginary.

Alfredo Arreguín: Patterns of Dreams and Nature was organized by the Bellevue (Washington) Art Museum and curated by Brian Wallace in conjunction with an important book (authored by Lauro Flores, Arreguín himself, and poet and writer Tess Gallagher) published by the University of Washington Press treating the past thirty years of this foremost artist of the Pacific Northwest. The exhibition ran at the Bellevue Art Museum between 23 March and 16 June 2002. It also ran between 11 January and 6 April 2003 at the Museum of Northwest Art, La Conner, Washington, and between 14 June and 28 September 2003 at the National Hispanic Cultural Center in Albuquerque, New Mexico. It will appear between 13 November 2003 and 15 February 2004 at the Northwest Museum of Arts and Culture, Spokane, Washington.

Chicano Visions: American Painters on the Verge is an exhibition that features the art collection of actor Cheech Marín, owner of one of the finest and largest collections of Chicano art, as well as a few pieces owned by Nicholas Cage, Sean Penn, and others. This hugely influential exhibition made its national debut at the San Antonio Museum of Art from 15 December 2001 through 7 April 2002. It ran between 1 May 2002 and 5 January 2003 at the Smithsonian Institution Art and Industries building; at the National Hispanic Cultural Center (Albuquerque) between 1 February and 18 May 2003; and between 14 June and 21 September 2003 at the El Paso Museum of Art. The next stop for this exhibition, which is slated for a five-year tour, is the Indiana State Museum, Indianapolis, between 30 January and 2 May 2004.

The exhibition, curated by Rene Yáñez, consists of more than fifty works, mostly oil and acrylic paintings. It features more than twenty artists, including Carlos Almaraz, Frank Romero, GRONK, Patssi Valdez, George Yepes, Rupert García, Leo Limón, Margaret García, Eloy Torres, Adán Hernández, César Martínez, Jesse Treviño, Melesio Casas, Carmen Lomas Garza, Vincent Valdez, Gaspar Enríquez, and Alex Rubio. The works, which present images of urban life and the Chicano experience, date between 1969 and 2001.

For the Bilingual Press/Editorial Bilingüe, the dawning of the age, not of Aquarius, but of Cortázar's "Axolotl" surely came on 16 September 2002, the day we released the two-volume work *Contemporary Chicana and Chicano Art.* Since then, there has been no turning back.

How do a couple hundred Chicana and Chicano artists organize themselves? In our new millennium, apparently by spontaneous combustion. Initially, the Bilingual Press/Editorial Bilingüe had little to do with this conflagration of enthusiasm, except to monitor its mounting achievements with increasing awe.

Shortly after the appearance of *Contemporary Chicana and Chicano Art,* and certainly by November 2002, out of pure gutsy gusto, a troop of artists organized themselves around the book and established three huge book signings in metropolitan Los Angeles. Present were scores of artists, not only from Southern California but from everywhere around the state and from Arizona, Colorado, New Mexico, Washington state, Texas, Chicago, and even New York. These three book signings took place between December 4 and 8 at 18th Street Arts Complex in Santa Monica, California, and at Ave 50 Studio and Galería Mundo in Los Angeles. We owe a debt of gratitude to Jan Williamson, Kathy Gallegos, and Margaret García, respectively, for their role in organizing these events.

In my experience, these book signings were at that point the largest gatherings of Chicana/Chicano artists. In attendance, variously, were: Jack Álvarez, Richard Álvarez, José Antonio Aguirre, David Buenrostro, Mario Calvano, Silvia Capistrán, Irene Carranza, Martin Charlot, Alex Donis, Richard Duardo, Fidencio Durán, Susan Elizalde-Holder, Rudy Fernández, Ignacio Gómez, Yolanda González, Marilú Flores Gruben, Roberto Gutiérrez, Tlisza Jaurique, Alma López, Aydee López Martínez, Jacalyn López García, Gilbert Luján, Rosa M., Daniel P. Márquez, Max-Carlos Martínez, Oscar J. Martínez, Laura Molina, Martín Moreno, José Orozco, Eva Pérez, Antonio Rael, Ramón Ramírez, Jesús "Chuy" Rangel, Miguel Ángel Reyes, Robert Rivera, Augustine Romero, David Rosales, Arturo Urista, Linda Vallejo, Frank Ybarra, and Marcus Zilliox.

"Gary," the call came out from Los Angeles, "can you come out to the book signings? We want your presence, your voice, and your writing hand. Bring a few good pens, and while you're at it, ship a few hundred books to the site!"

To Los Angeles I came, I saw, and I was conquered! The book signing at 18th Street Arts Complex really sizzled. My dear colega, A.P. González—art connoisseur and longtime and incredibly effective head of the film director's program at the UCLA film school—and I arrived early at Santa Sushi Sobre el Sea. Well fortified with double Bombay Sapphire martinis and *shiro maguro, saba,* and *suzuki,* we headed on to the book signing. The rest, as they say, is Historia Hispanae, and I've got the rushes to prove it. The Hispanic Research Center of Arizona State University brought a camera crew to do this event justice, and at some future point we will be showing our professionally shot homemade movies, which include multihour interviews of Fidencio Durán, Richard Duardo, and Cheech Marín as well as interviews with Yolanda López, Daniel Martín Díaz, and others that were done in Arizona.

So many were accounting for themselves! Cheech was there and holding forth. Martin Charlot, the illustrious son of one of the greats of Mexican muralism—the brilliant mid-century professor at the University of Hawaii and analyst of twentieth-century art, Jean Charlot—was there, and he urged me to come with him the following day to see his murals at the Ventura County Discovery Center and at the Children's Dental Center in Los Angeles. Alma López told us we should have put her notorious *Our Lady* (Lupe and Sirena series) in the book, which had created puro pedo with traditionalists and the archbishop in Santa Fe (the two-volume book was still so new and so encompassing that even some of the artists hadn't digested it yet), and I promptly and gravely opened the second volume to the page with this enfant terrible's digital creation. Alex Donis, on the other hand, who was in residence at 18th Street Arts Complex, showed me his newest works and hailed the book's attention to the gay canon. Fidencio Durán, in his engaging, taciturn tejano way, told me more about his commission at the new Austin, Texas, airport. Gilberto "Magú" Luján, in his trademark cuate abrazo style, and with his customary salutation to me as "Dr. Gary," recounted the many splendors of *Contemporary Chicana and Chicano Art* and told me wondrous things about his new Pomona-centered artistic activities. My oldest son, el Randito, arrived from Pasadena (a Cal Tech computer-based spinoff) to share the experience, and we both had a long and exciting conversation with genial David Rosales of San Bernadoo about the subtext of his wonderful work "In Memory of a Rabbit."

The upshot of these memorable book signings was that the artists and Cheech, A.P., and numerous others urged the Bilingual Press/Editorial Bilingüe to do something special for the book, for Chicana and Chicano art, and for its practitioners. This was a homework assignment that has become something of a lifetime calling. The Press, in quick order, decided to have a reception for the artists on campus at Arizona State University during Cinco de Mayo weekend of the following year, 2003. This modest provision quickly expanded to an encompassing vision. Kirsten Hammer, bless her heart, head of Latin American art at Sotheby's, hopped aboard and promised to give a workshop, pro bono, on beginning and advanced theory and praxis of collecting Chicano/Latino art. Gilberto Cárdenas, obsessive art collector par excellence and gallery owner of Galería Sin Fronteras, promised to help. In short order, we received considerable support from Arizona State University's main campus and west campus (our accomplishments would not have been possible without the commitments of Provost Milton Glick, ASU Main, and Provost Elaine Maimon, ASU West; Manny Ávalos, associate vice provost for research and faculty development, ASU West; Fernando Delgado, associate vice provost for graduate studies and academic programs, ASU West; and David Young, dean of the College of Arts and Sciences, ASU Main) and, with no time at all to spare, by January 2003 we had become committed to mounting a full-fledged Chicano/ Latino art happening.

The events of 2 through 4 May 2003 represented another millenarian landmark that has led directly to this exhibition and its accompanying book. They consisted of a signal auction of over 200 works of Chicana/Chicano art both on-site and on the Internet in real time through eBay; a *mercado* where artists were able to staff their own tables and sell their own works of various types; a conference that featured presentations by artists, art historians, art educators, and critics; a workshop on collecting Chicano/Latino art run by Sotheby's Kirsten Hammer; several student-focused educational events; and digitally recorded interviews of numerous artists and critics by film director Jesús Salvador Treviño.

This event was successful in so many ways— with the artists, scholars, and students, financially through the numbers of works sold, and in terms of its coverage by the mass media—that we have been emboldened to do an expanded and enhanced version, the Arizona International Latina/Latino Arts Festival (AILAF). One of the less obvious but hugely significant successes of the 2003 event was in the area of acquisition of works of art by the Arizona State University community. Over the past twenty years the Hispanic Research Center, its affiliates, and other members of the ASU community have permitted the Center to become one of the largest repositories of images of Chicano/ Latino works of visual art (in the form of transparencies, slides, digital images) and film. Equally important, at ASU we have collected a critical mass of original art in the forms of paintings, sculptures, mixed media, works on paper, and the like. Similarly, we have had the opportunity to commission a number of original lithographs in cooperation with fine print publishers including Segura Publishing Company in Mesa, Arizona, the Tamarind Institute in Albuquerque, and Hare & Hound Press in San Antonio.

AILAF expands the scope of the previous event not only to the visual arts but also to film, literature, theater, and performance, and not only nationally, but internationally. Nevertheless, the key event of the 2004 AILAF is the 1 May 2004 opening of *Chicano Art for Our Millennium: Collected Works from the Arizona State University Community*. This exhibition and accompanying book, produced through the collaboration between Arizona State University and Mesa Southwest Museum, reflect the collection of the ASU community. We anticipate that the exhibition will travel extensively both nationally and internationally once it closes on 19 September 2004 in the Phoenix metropolitan area.

Gary D. Keller
14 FEBRUARY 2004

REFERENCES

The titles that follow illustrate the observation that there has been a surge since January 2000 of exhibitions and books (often affiliated with exhibitions) about Chicana and Chicano art.

Arreguín, Alfredo, Lauro Flores, and Tess Gallagher. *Alfredo Arreguín: Patterns of Dreams and Nature/Diseños, Sueños y Naturaleza.* Jacob Lawrence Series on American Artists. Seattle: University of Washington Press, 2002.

Dávalos, Karen Mary. *Exhibiting Mestizaje: Mexican (American) Museums in the Diaspora.* Albuquerque: University of New Mexico Press, 2001.

Keller, Gary D., Mary Erickson, Kaytie Johnson, and Joaquín Alvarado. *Contemporary Chicana and Chicano Art.* Tempe, AZ: Bilingual Press/Editorial Bilingüe, 2002.

Maciel, David, Isidro D. Ortiz, and María Herrera-Sobek, eds. *The Chicano Renaissance: Contemporary Cultural Trends.* Tucson: University of Arizona Press, 2000.

Marín, Cheech, Max Benavídez, Constance Cortez, and Tere Romo. *Chicano Visions: American Painters on the Verge.* New York: Bulfinch Press, 2002.

Noriega, Chon A., ed. *East of the River: Chicano Art Collectors Anonymous.* Santa Monica Museum of Art. Seattle: University of Washington Press, 2001.

———, ed. *Just Another Poster?* Berkeley: University of California Press, 2002.

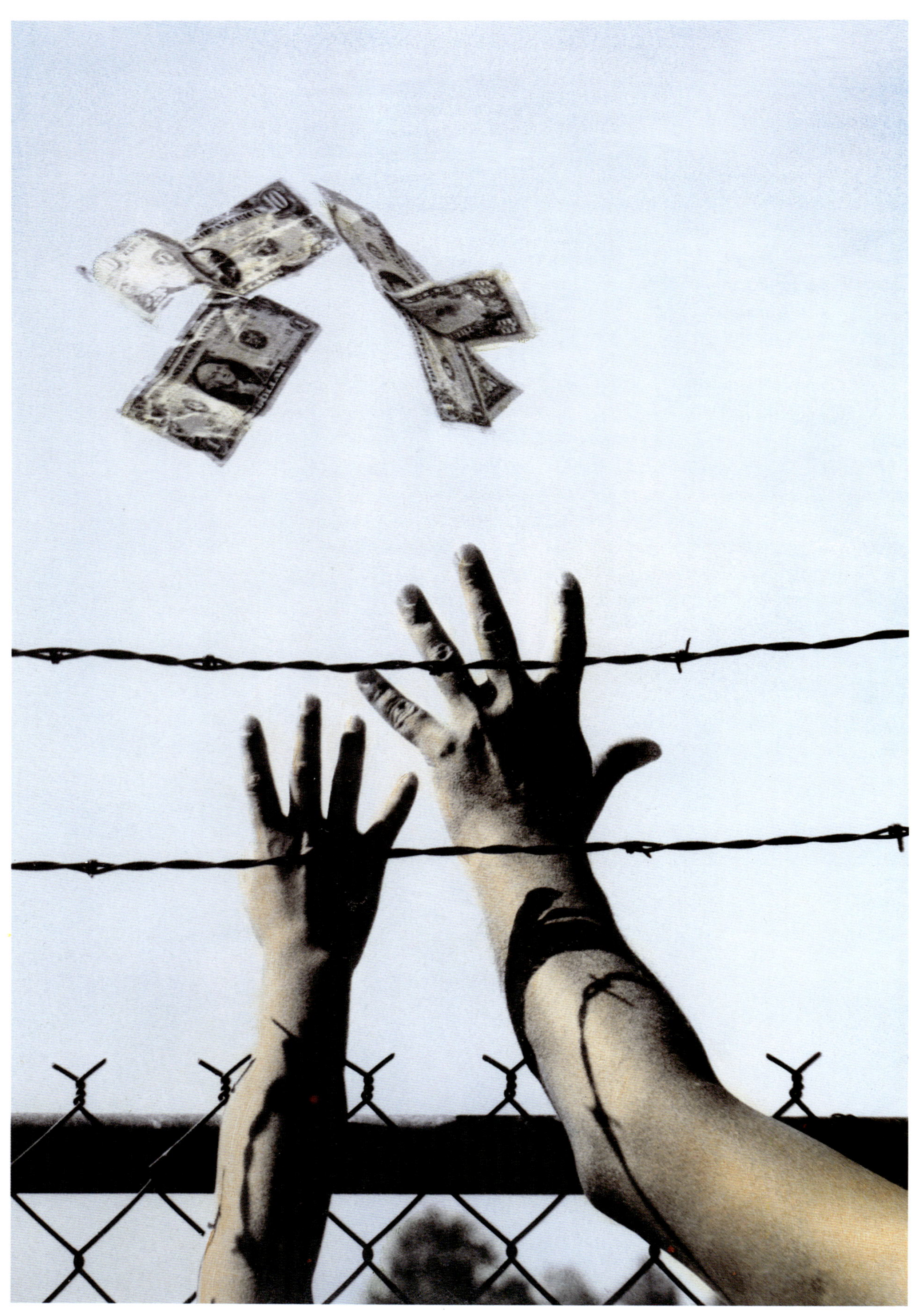

7 Jacalyn López García, *California Dreaming*, 1997, silver gelatin print, sepia toned, hand tinted, 20" x 16"

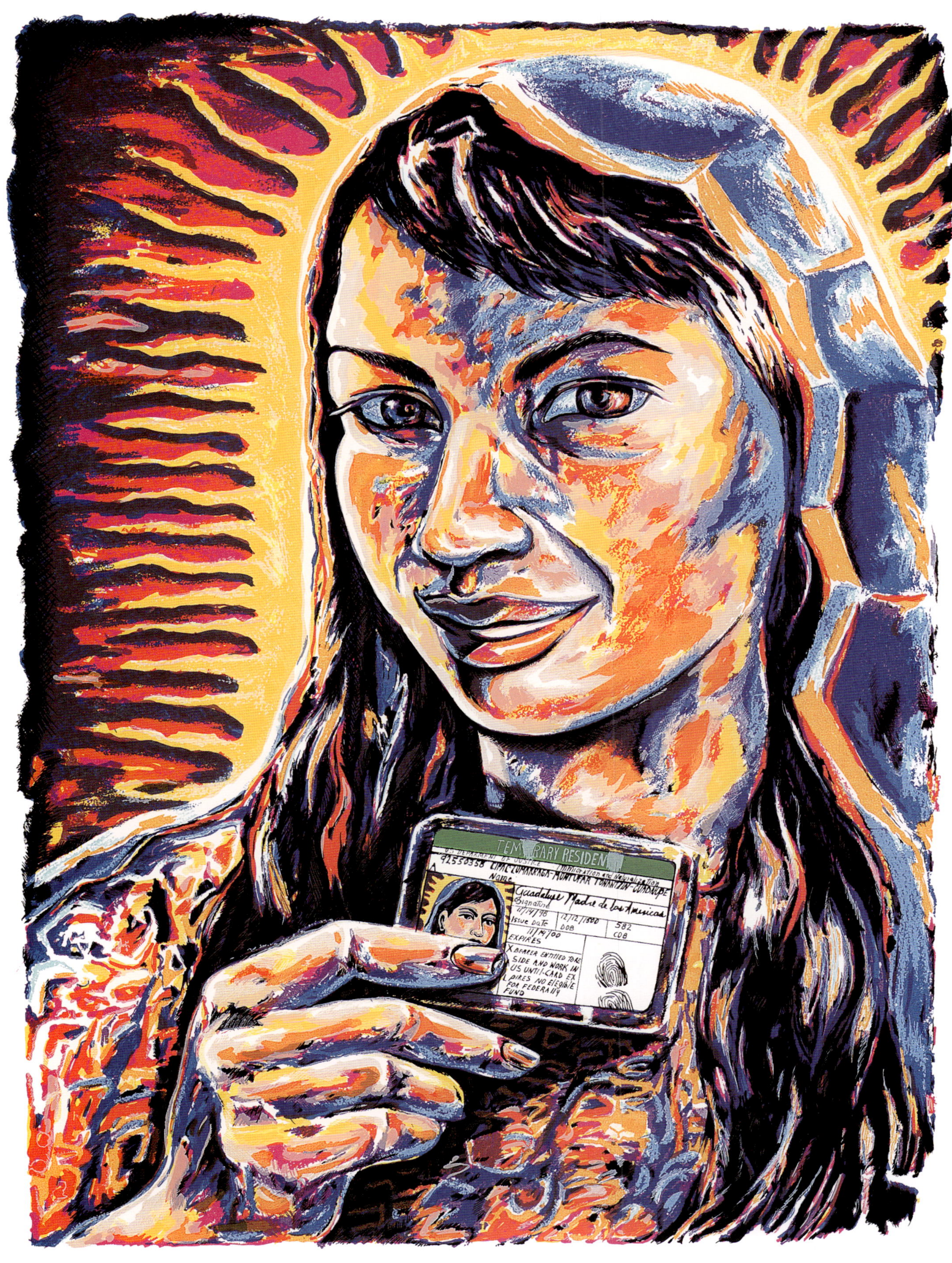

8 Isabel Martínez, *VG Got Her Green Card*, 2001, serigraph, 26" x 20"

a book of three parts . . .

Like Julius Caesar's ancient Gaul, this book has three parts. First, it is a lively, visually intensive trade book available at a moderate price (if not exactly *precios populares*) that we direct to the general Chicano/Latino audience and the general community of art devotees in the United States, Latin America, Europe, and around the globe. An interested reader and viewer will be able to experience a good representation of Chicana and Chicano art in a book that is notable for its superb production values.

Second, it is the catalog of the eponymously named exhibition, *Chicano Art for Our Millennium*, which opened on 1 May 2004 and runs through 19 September 2004 at the Mesa Southwest Museum and which will then embark on a multiyear tour. The book contains the images of the works of art that are exhibited plus a number of additional images in order to enhance the educational value of both the exhibit and this accompanying book.

Finally, *Chicano Art for Our Millennium* has been designed to serve as an educational resource for the teaching of Chicana and Chicano art both to Chicano/Latino students and the general student population beginning in elementary school and going through college and graduate school. We are confident that this educational component of the book can also be used profitably by the general public to gain unusual insights into contemporary art as a whole. We have used Chicana and Chicano art paradigmatically to teach elements of art of universal application.

organization of the exhibit and of the book

The exhibition, and hence this book, is organized thematically.

At the portal of the exhibit we have built a simple structure that represents an adobe house, to beckon and invite the attendee under the rubric of the well-known phrase *mi casa es su casa,* "my house is your house." The attendee passes through the adobe abode, stopping of course to view the unique work of Arizona artist Larry Yáñez, who has created—through a series of ingenious, innovative, and humorous serigraphs—a singular and, at the same time, archetypal Chicano/Latino house, a house with a comic yet endearing, bilingual-tricultural (Anglo-Hispanic-Amerindian) perspective that invites you in for further exploration. The artistic abode of Larry Yáñez is an ideal introduction to the Chicano palette, with its predominance of bright colors including hues of pink, blue, green, and red. It is also a good introduction to the traditional icons of Chicano art: the Virgin of Guadalupe, calendars featuring Aztec lovers turned into volcanoes, tacos and salsa, crucifixes, chiles, cacti and other flora of the Southwest, and family altars. However, sometimes these icons are transmuted comically or by artistic sleight of hand. Our *casa* features taco shell shower curtains, calavera magnets, a crucifix with Jesus suspended ethereally from the mirror above the bathroom sink, and desert landscapes that spring from ambiguous interior/exterior origins. Finally, the Yáñez works also make strategic use of Amerindian iconography as it is often found in traditional and current architecture (frequently with the designation of territorial design) and Navajo textiles.

It is but a short stop from my/your/our house to the theme of "Community Values/Lo que representa nuestra comunidad." Guided into this section through the mediation of the introspective self-portrait of Mario Calvano, in the book we find works dedicated to the family and to barrio and *campo* (urban and rural) ambiences and life. Here the viewer will find, among others, works dedicated to the care and development of children, to the traditional Chicana/o attention to ancestors and the deceased, to important dates ranging from birthdays to patriotic holidays, and to numerous enterprises, occupations, or *oficios* of the Chicano/Latino world. Some of the works in this section, such as Esperanza Gama's, expand outward and make connections both formal and cultural to the universal world of art in its depictions of the family and community.

"Across Borders and the Biculture/Atravesando fronteras y culturas" is a rich theme for Chicana and Chicano art. In this part of the exhibit and of the book, the viewer will be able to appreciate, thematically, dimensions of Chicano/Latino biculturalism and transculturalism as well as, on occasion, jarring juxtapositions of Chicano and mainstream culture, lifestyles, and values that are difficult to digest, synthesize, or transcend. From the vantage point of images and their analysis, in a manner analogous to the themes, the works have been divided into "Yuxtaposición" (where the images, like water and oil, do not mix), "Transición" (where there is the dimension of movement across culture and value systems, a sense of transculturalism in some cases), and "Nuevo milenio," which is the designation we have chosen to evoke the creation of new images, and sometimes, with those images, new identities that take from both Chicana/o and mainstream or other cultures in order to produce something that is both singular and transcendent of the sum of its parts.

"Spirituality/Espiritualidad" is a deeply felt component of Chicano culture, which has maintained its value system intact for hundreds of years and, after the Treaty of Guadalupe Hidalgo, has been forced to resist the periodic incursions of Anglo culture. This section has been divided into two subthemes, "Representación religiosa" and "Espíritu humano." The icons of many of these pieces are notable for their originality. They are sui generis since they are often not traditional icons of Hispanic religious or spiritual sensibility, although they often originate in those traditional icons. In some of these works the traditional predominates, but in a manner different from the home country of Mexico (or even Spain). In others there is a clear ironic or even iconoclastic quality. And in still others there is a significant departure from traditional norms of Hispanic society, a postmodern spirituality.

"Deeply Felt, Widely Known/Profundamente sentido, ampliamente reconocido" thematically juxtaposes certain feelings, intuitions, and events that individuate us all, Chicana/o and other populations alike, with other phenomena that are integral components of the social fabric. Thus, on the one hand, the viewer is exposed to self-identification through self-portrait, to grief, fantasy, reminiscence, and religious apprehension, and, on the other, to music, cinema, or pastimes that are characteristically Chicano/Latino such as the heroic, social-justice dimension of public wrestling, or the uniquely Hispanic *Lotería* game.

"Cultural Icons/Temas culturales" is divided into three subthemes. "Héroes" evokes many Chicano/Mexicano role models or individuals of renown including Pancho Villa, José Guadalupe Posada, Frida Kahlo, Sandra Cisneros, and César Chávez as well as legendary figures such as the Cisco Kid and Muffler Man, a Chicano everyman caped hero. "¡Venceremos!" borrows a slogan from Chicana/o militancy to evoke such icons as *zapatista* guerrillas; the revolutionary intellectual of the Mexican Revolution of 1910, Ricardo Flores Magón; a syncretized Virgin of Guadalupe/Statue of Liberty; a Statue of Liberty metamorphosing into a Hispanic woman; a lone Chicana struggling against conglomerated corporations; and another Latina who has arrogated the identity of the conventional *bandolero.* "Nuestros símbolos" develops a variety of notable icons from such sources as the pre-Hispanic world, traditional folklore, and the Southwestern environment with its notable fauna and flora.

"Beyond Conventional Themes/Sobrepasando lo convencional" expands the traditionally assumed dimensions and scope of Chicano/a art. Contradicting the notion that our art is exclusively a folk art rooted in Chicano culture and the figurative evocation of that culture, we are confronted here with nonfigurative work that is preoccupied with color, composition, line, the interplay of shadow and light, and the use of space. Additionally, those works that are figurative cultivate figures in novel ways when contrasted with the conventional appreciation of Chicano art. In our exhibited collection, for example, Jerry de la Cruz executes collage with superb results, Silvia Capistrán utilizes varied horizontal and vertical lines against a field of brilliant yet subtle red hues, Marcus Zilliox explores abstraction, countering verticality with rows of soft curves and sprinkling in a hint of cartoon, Mónica Martínez evokes a polyphony of shapes and bold lines that harkens to Paul Klee and Joan Miró, and Quintín González explores the intersect between myth, religion, and mass culture in his creation and transformation of popular images into implausible ones.

And finally, and with finality, Gabriel García communicates to us the open-ended nature of Chicana and Chicano art, subject to temporary or first defeats perhaps, yet alive with potential and capability for freshness and originality.

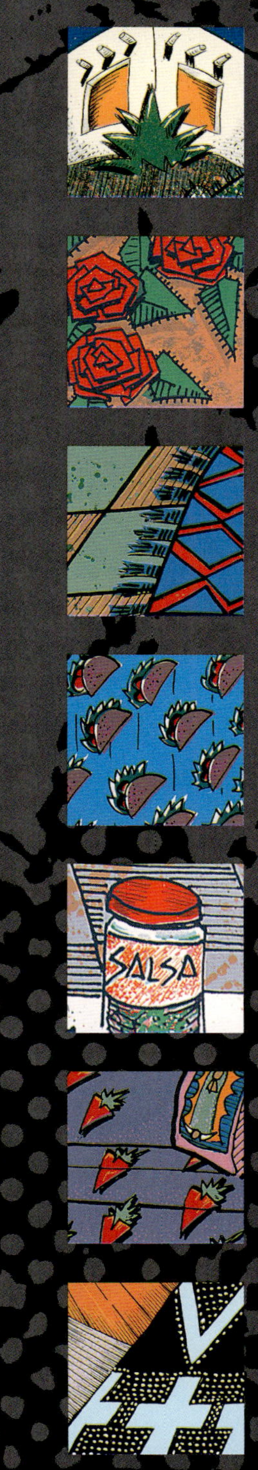

Mi casa es su casa

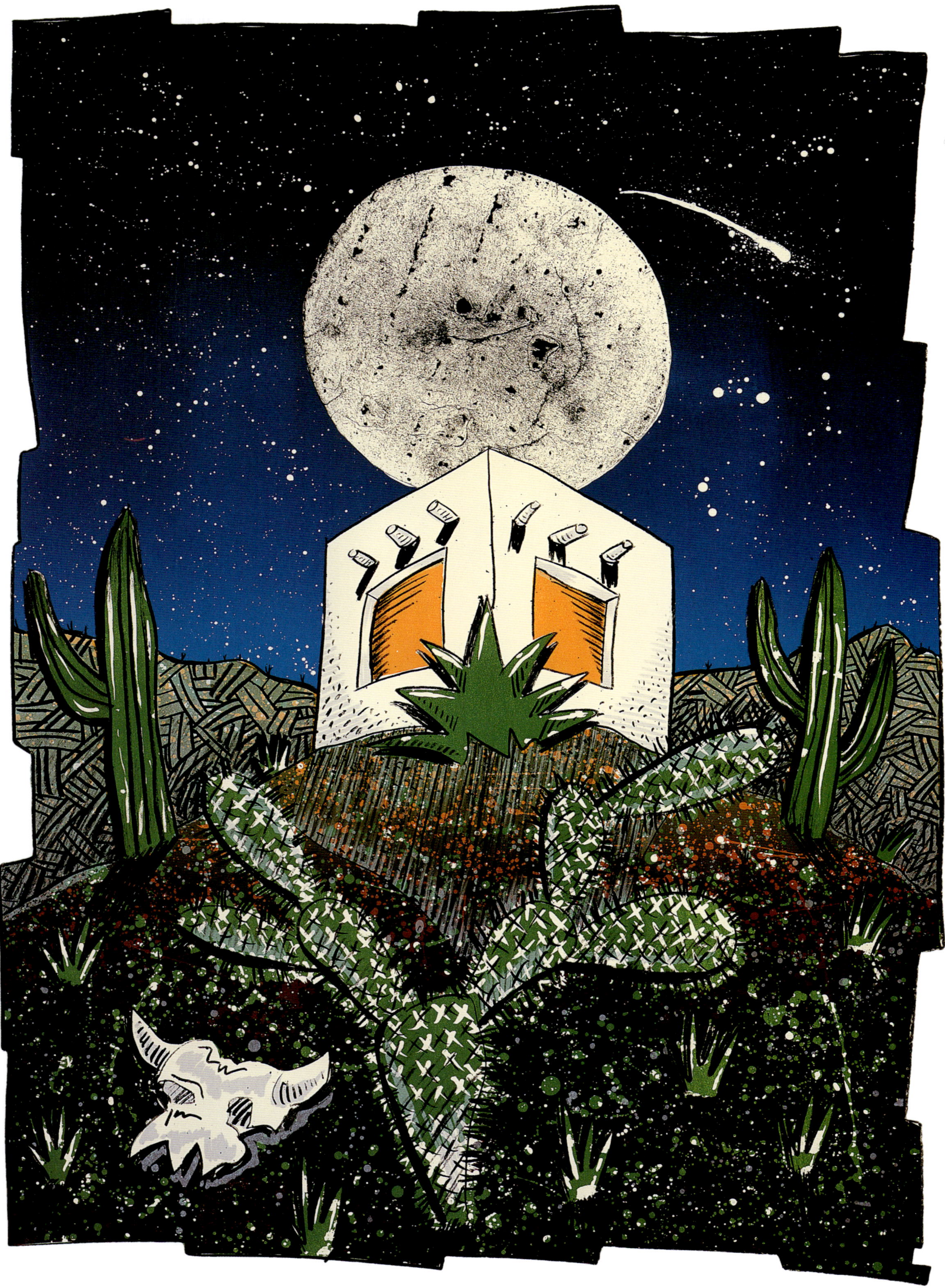

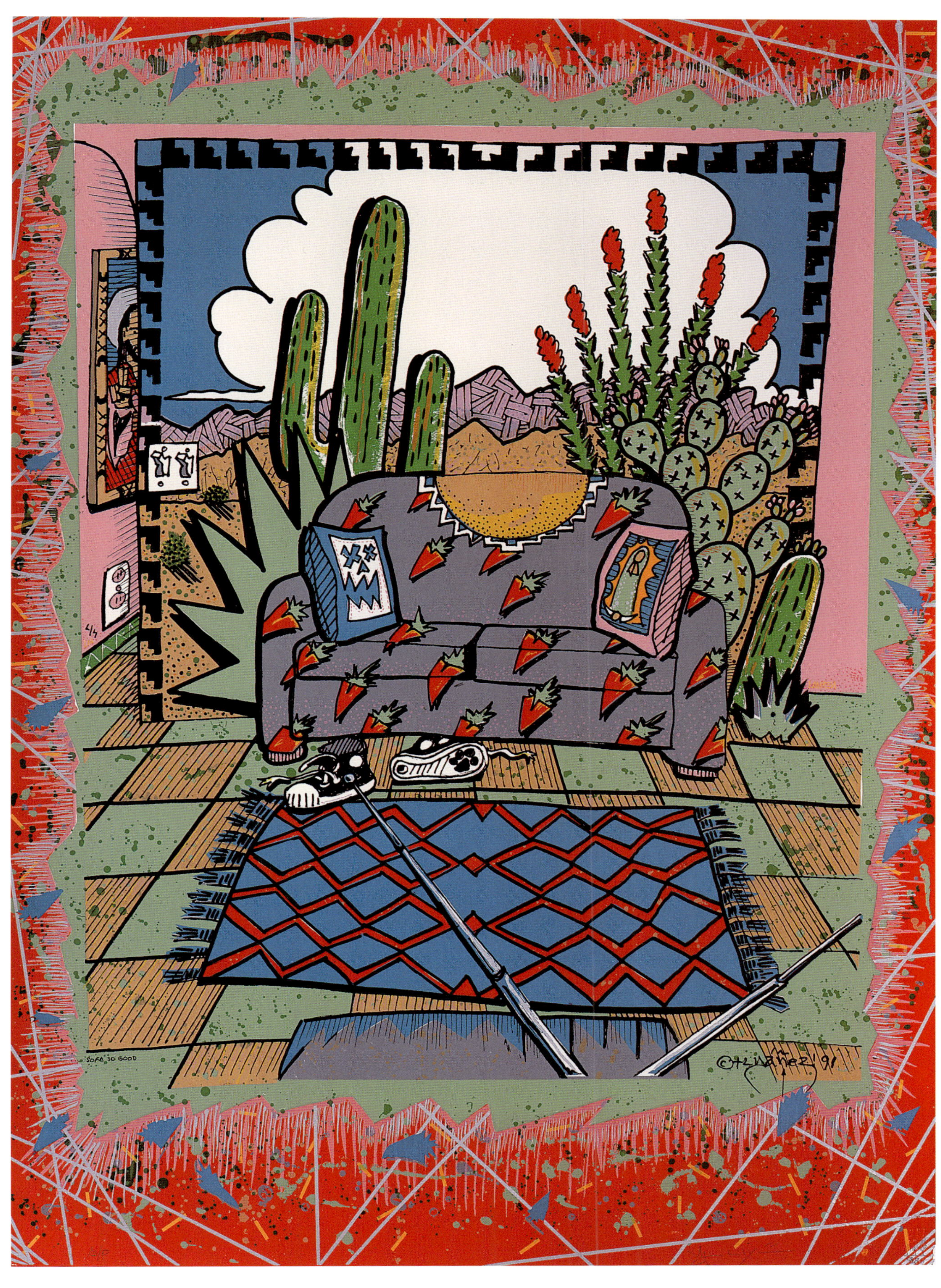

11 Larry Yáñez, *Sofá So Good*, 1991
Serigraph, 37" x 27"

12 Larry Yáñez, *Camana My House*, 1997
Serigraph, 34" x 30"

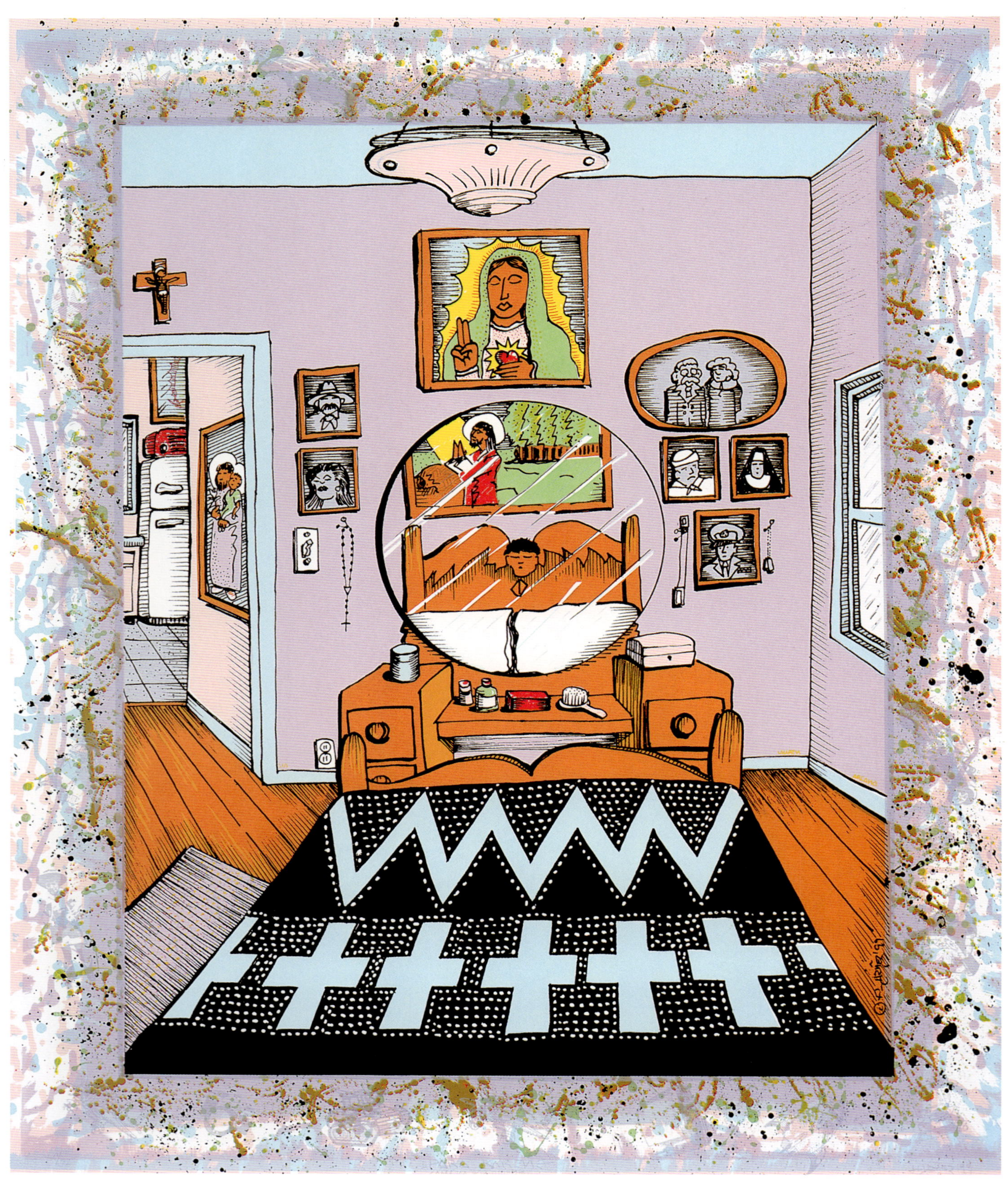

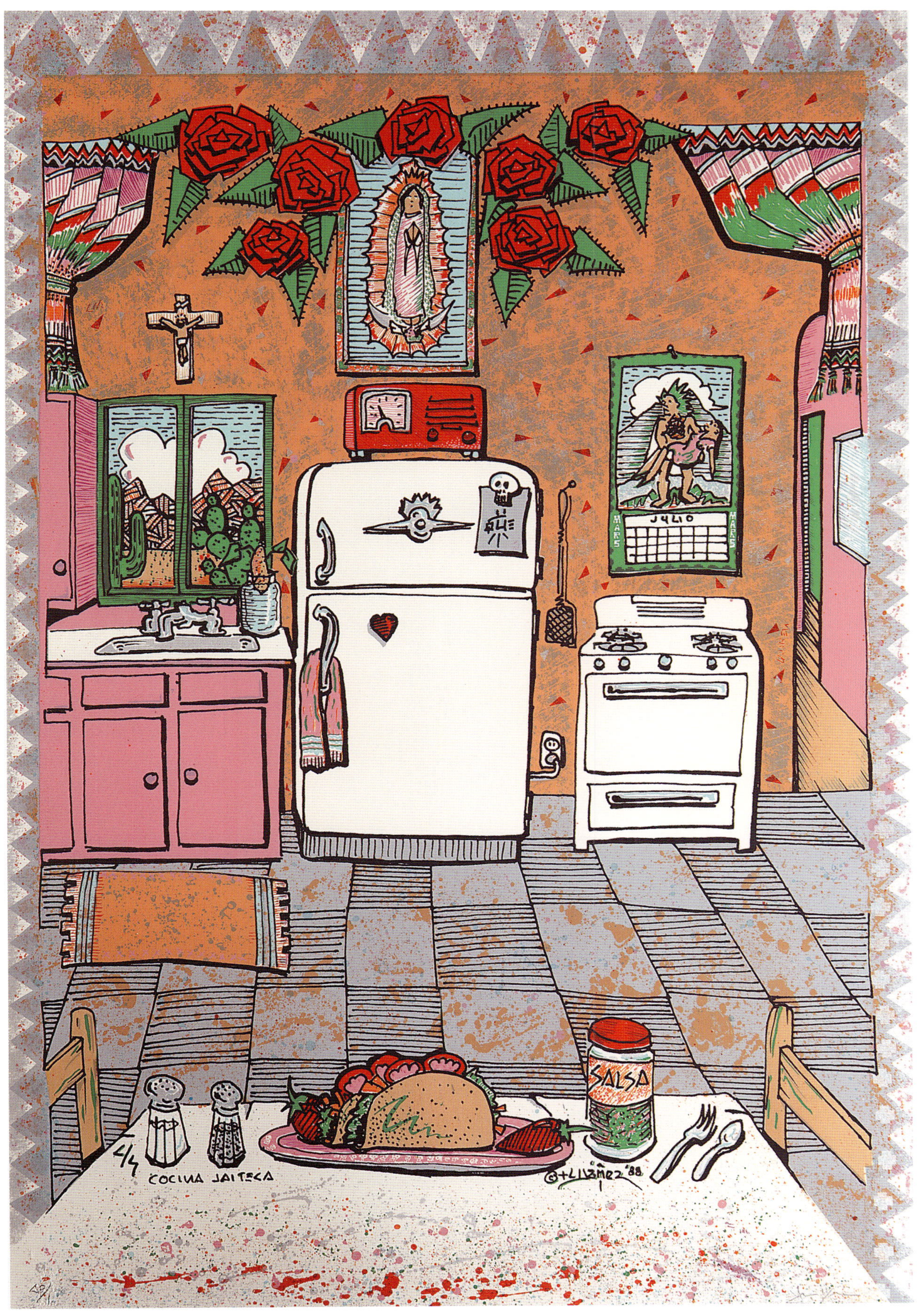

Left: 9 Larry Yáñez, *Ay Juana Cholla*, 1999
Lithograph, 29.5" x 22"

10 Larry Yáñez, *Cocina jaiteca*, 1988, serigraph, 47" x 34"

n this series of works by the renowned Arizona artist Larry Yáñez, one panoramic and overarching, the others of the various rooms of a unique yet simultaneously representative house, both the Chicano/Latino viewer and the general public are invited in to experience a family identity that is at the same time a community identity. This is not a grand house but a modest one, a comfortable home with a warm and welcome feeling where the archetypal comic rubber duck of mainstream culture cohabits naturally with the image of the Virgin of Guadalupe. Rooted in folk art, this group of works by Yáñez takes us to a new place where a cross-cultural imagination predominates, saturated with good humor, a friendly pulling of the leg, and camaraderie. Making full use of his repertoire of bilingual and bicultural artifices, both in the punning titles and in the combinations of images, the artist creates a *casa* that is at once beckoning, endearing, and a continual source of novelty, surprise, and, ultimately, revelation.

Ay Juana Cholla (a pun also read as "I want a cholla" or "I wanna show ya"). PLATE 9. We are introduced to the archetypal house on the hill. However, although it may be as square as a New England saltbox, this is no conventional house, but rather one evocative initially of a Pueblo Indian and subsequently a mestizo tradition that cumulatively has endured for hundreds, in fact thousands, of years. Lit by the light of a tortilla moon, punctuated by a sky filled with stars and the portent of a shooting star, this abode of Chicano-Amerindian provenance, with its adobe walls and its ceiling fortified by timbers of Ponderosa pine, invites entry and further inspection if only we can get past the daunting cacti with their needles and the augury of a steer's skeletal head of bleached, moonlit bone. Of course, we really do want a cholla, but we also need to be mindful of that lament encrypted by ¡Ay Juana! A cholla is a type of cactus that is very common in the Southwest, but in Spanish the word also stands, colloquially, for head, mind, or brain, and in fact it is a variation of the Chicano word *chola*, which stands for a street-savvy Chicana. The sense that cholla transcends mere shrubbery is height-

ened by the use of the capital *c*, so that it seems to indicate a person: Juana Cholla. The hip Chicano artist, in addition to evoking everything that is physically obvious in this landscape, appears to be lamenting ¡ay! that he seeks an equally hip Jane, an equally turned-on Juana soul mate.

Cocina jaiteca. PLATE 10. (*Cocina* is "kitchen"; read jaiteca as a made-up or macaronic Spanish word created through the English-language influence of the word "high-tech"). This is a jaiteca/high-tech kitchen that is overtly and paradoxically behind the times, on the lee side of modernity, with refrigerator and stove models of yesteryear punctuated by an old-fashioned flyswatter hanging from the wall between them and a large, vintage analog clock radio atop and encompassing almost the entire width of the refrigerator. On the walls are affixed traditional icons of Mexican American culture including a crucifix, an image of the Virgin of Guadalupe, and a calendar with the Aztec lovers who in the traditional Mexican folktale later are converted into the volcanoes Popocatepetl and Ixtaccihuatl. Framing the Virgin in an arc above the icon are huge naturalistic roses with equally large petals that seem to be suspended in air or magically attached to the wall. The walls are draped with what appear to be fringed, cactus-adorned serapes, an artistic flourish that goes beyond the conventional or the typical and takes us to the comical and the parodical. On the refrigerator, in a similar comic spirit, we find two magnets in the shape of a heart and a *calavera*. The refrigerator itself sports a front piece that is large and gaudy enough to adorn the hood of a lowrider, and from one of the two huge old-fashioned doors hangs a handy low-tech towel. Through the window we spy archetypal cacti, the saguaro and the nopal; occasionally, Mexicans and Chicanos harvest and prepare the latter in various ways as food, including prickly-pear ice cream. On the kitchen table beckons a meal for one. There is a cross-cultural, mildly ironic air to this meal, which features the hard taco shells usually associated with gringo versions of Mexican fare, together with two whole red hot chiles that would appear to have the poten-

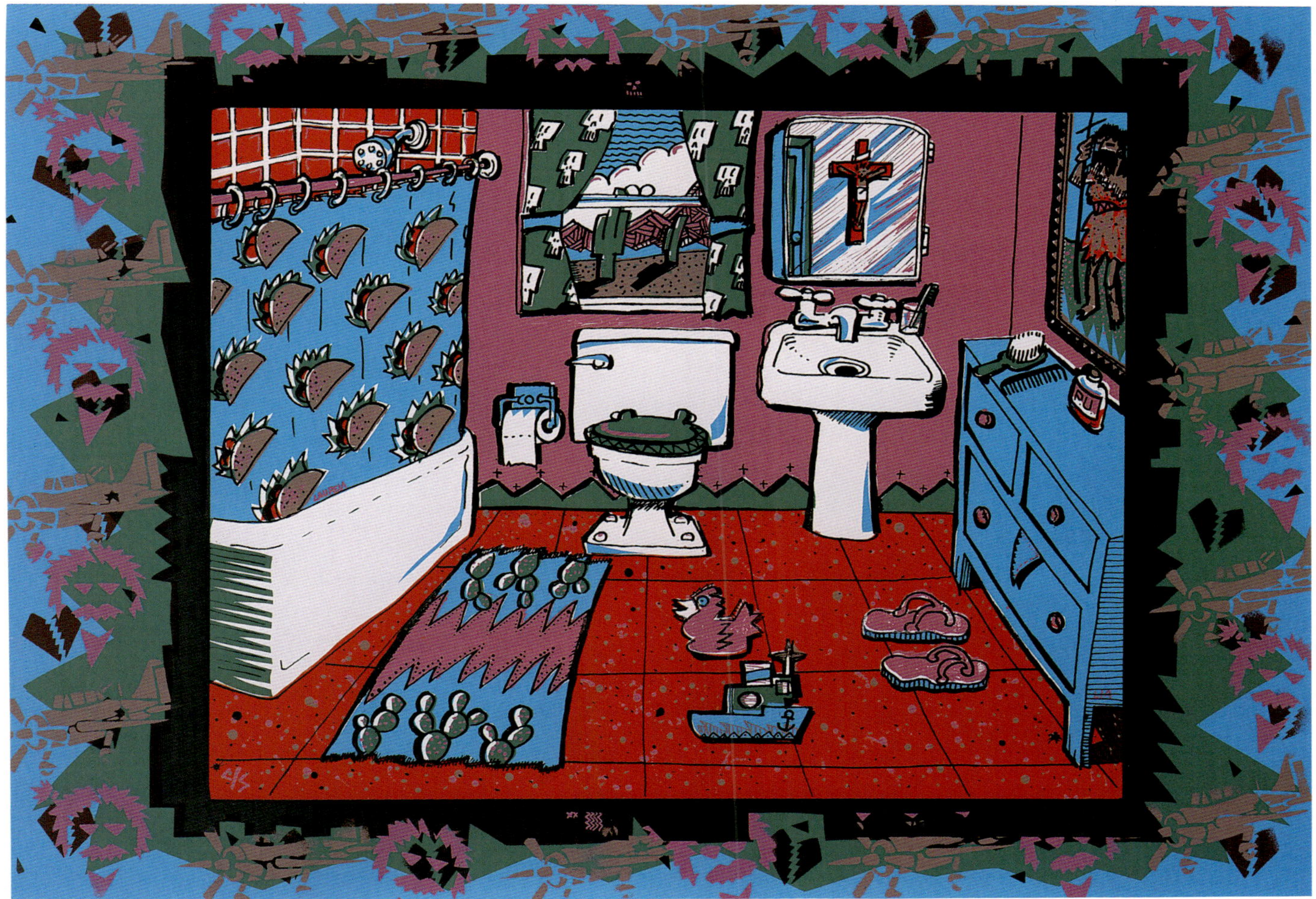

tial to create the conventional scene of a naive diner being smitten by piquant Mexican food. Who is this meal for? The home dweller? Or is it for you, the viewer? Is there an invitation here to partake of the conventions of Mexican Americanness and the comic transcendence of those conventions? An integral part of the answer to this probably unsolvable riddle is the outer stratum of this work of art. We note that it has an overt frame that the artist has painted. This is a work that calls attention to itself as such, and if we look at each of the other pieces in "Mi casa es su casa" we find that each in turn has a frame, some more overtly than others, of artistic self-appellation.

Sofá So Good (as in, "so far so good"). PLATE 11. We are inside the home now, although this work of art is also curiously inside out. Just as *Hamlet* is a play that within it contains a second, highly meaningful

play for the understanding of the drama, in this room, behind the sofa, there appears at first sight a glorious window to the outside world, with cacti, mountains, clouds, and blue sky. Closer inspection forces upon us the awareness that this cannot be a window but is instead a more "supportive" structure, inasmuch as there are two light switches, together with some electrical outlets in the adjoining room, affixed to it. They are jarring symbols, on the one hand, of modernity in a traditional milieu, and on the other (the light switches), of incongruity and the suspension of the physical order. And then there is a traditional Navajo meander design that frames the entire outside that is inside, giving us the sense that this is a Navajo rug. But now, that cannot be right either because of the light switches and because to the right of the sofa the cactus and the shrub come right into the house from the supposed "outside." Inside out and outside in, the image of the physical environment seems suspended in the imaginary, beyond the constraints of physics or construction technology. The sense of the imaginative that is at the same time imaginary in this seemingly traditional structure is further reinforced by the fact that there is no human physically present. There is a pair of tennis shoes casually fronting the homey sofa upholstered with a design that might be chiles or strawberries but that is primarily processed esthetically as hearts, and there is an echo of a Mexican revolutionary past in the work of art within this work of art on the wall further inside. This is a house inhabited or graced by the presence of humankind but one that journeys through time and culture by means of artifices of imagination.

Camana My House. PLATE 12. (There is a play here between "come on to my house" rendered colloquially and the Spanish word for bed, *cama*, which after all is the defining object of the bedroom). Framed in its own unique manner, we are offered a peek at the bedroom. Tellingly, the door to the kitchen is open on the other side in the background, on the left, and we are offered a glimpse of the refrigerator, which carries within it sustenance in the form of food. In center foreground there is a double image. On the one hand we see the vanity table, but through its mirror, almost as if revealed by a magnifying glass, we see the headboard and two pillows of the bed. It is a *cama matrimonial*, a double bed for man and wife. Even further foregrounded is a carpet with a bicultural Christian/Amerindian motif. The carpet features a row of crosses in a fashion consistent with a Navajo rug (the cross is a very familiar symbol in the folk art of Navajos, Pueblos, Zunis, and other Amerindians of Arizona and the Southwest), combined syncretically with the Navajo symbol of the bolt of lightening. This bed is indicated as functioning in the traditional ways, for a man and wife to sleep together and procreate in accordance with the laws of God—a multicultural deity in this instance, combining elements of both Western and Amerindian Christianity. In the middle, carved in the headboard, above the pillows of the magnified bed, is a winged cherub, symbol of the fruits of matrimony; surrounding the ensemble on the wall around the dressing table are the sanctioning icons of the Virgin of Guadalupe and the cross together with family images, presumably of the loving parents of the mother or father and family members who are or were a nun, a soldier, and a sports figure, among others. This is an empty bedroom but one that is symbolic of a family whose life has nothing to hide and who live in accordance with traditional norms, values, and practices.

Once Juan Won One. PLATE 13. The most bilingually and biculturally comic room in the house is punctuated by a title that plays havoc with the word *Juan*. This Spanish word translates as John in English, and then, by extension, although Juan does not have the same colloquial meaning in Spanish, connotes "the john." However, both Juan and John do indicate the "everyman," the male gender generally. Additionally all four words of the title are veiled or direct references to "one" (once, Juan, won, one), which admittedly is a number associated in English-speaking culture with a primary function of the bathroom and perhaps the most common occasion for a visit to this room. The room, the center of the work itself, is markedly framed, and beyond the overt frame there appears what may be interpreted as a wallpaper design with ethereal *calavera* figures. This design both contrasts with and provides counterpoint to the bathroom window curtain, which boasts a parodic *calavera* design that is over the top, quite beyond the pale of the typical Chicano house. This *calavera* curtain in turn contrasts sharply with the "life-giving" design of the hard-shell tacos on the shower curtain. However, both curtains at the same time reinforce each other because of the luridness and unlikely nature of each of the design choices, and all of this is further reinforced by an area rug contrastively featuring prickly pear cacti and an Amerindian lightning bolt design. Once again, archetypally gringo rubber duck and tugboat bathtub toys lie casually on the tile floor, contrasting markedly with the crucifix that is appended to the mirror without visible signs of physical support. We would normally expect the mirror to be bare in order to fulfill its function and reveal the likeness of any onlooker at the sink. Contrasts between life forces and death or spectral images and between comic and parodic renderings of both Anglo and Latino icons predominate in this work, which calls overt attention to itself as art framed within art. At center stage, fittingly, is set the toilet—Juan/John's throne, as it were.

The Guide

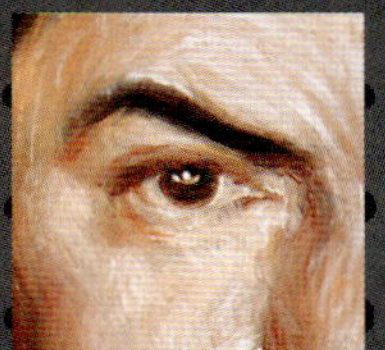

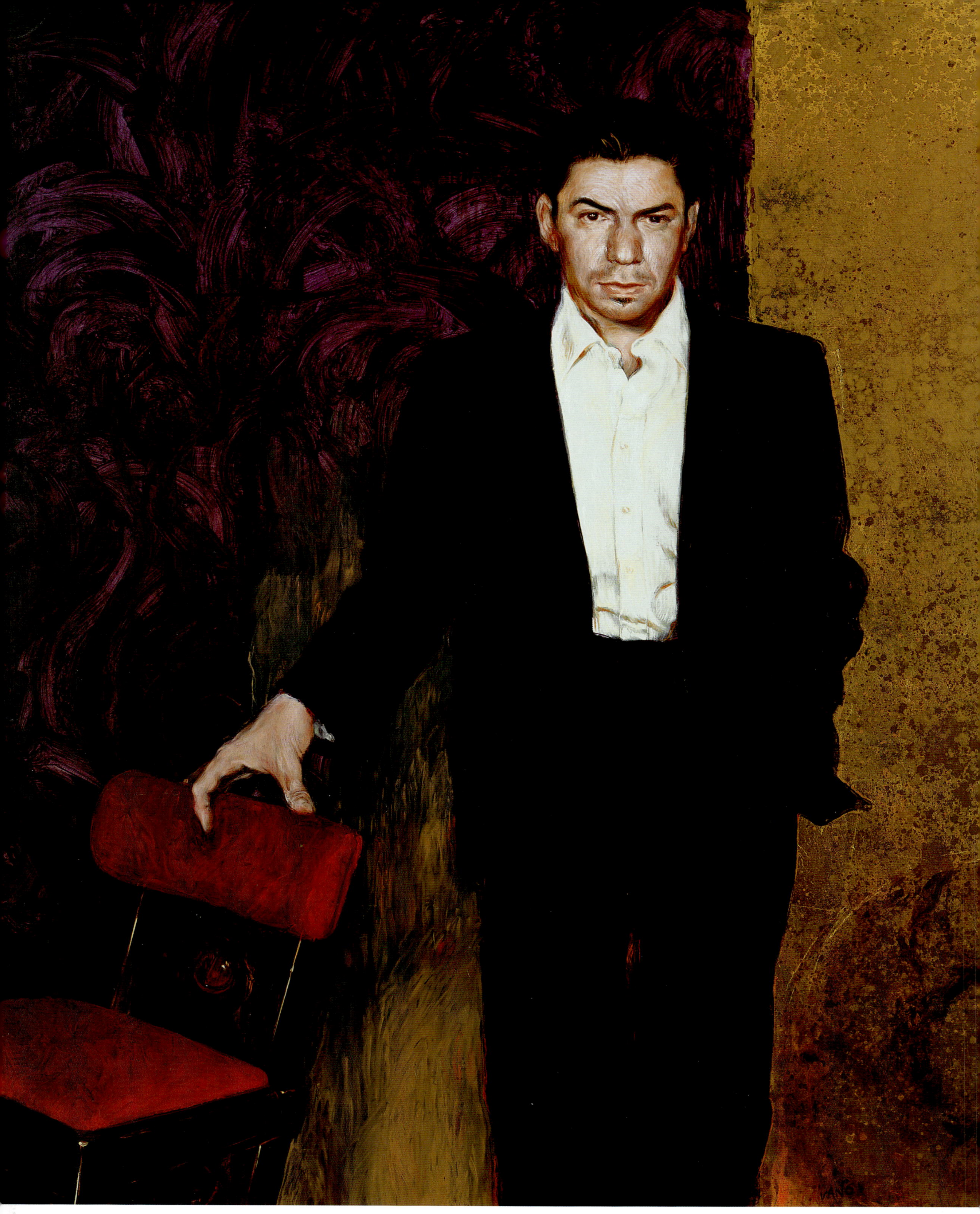

M**ario Calvano, *Self-Portrait*.** PLATE 14. This image is the first human presence that becomes available to us in the *Chicano Art for Our Millennium* exhibition. We have selected it to function partly as an artistic guide or human introducer to the exhibition. The work is in the tradition of Western portraiture as seen in the classical pose that connects it to both American and European art, such as the work of John Singer Sargent (1856-1925), who was prominent in both American and British art. The work depicts a Chicano artist who fixes the viewer with a very serious gaze as if to communicate, "I am a serious artist and my work is serious as well."

The work also carries with it a covert admonition not to make facile assumptions about what Chicano art is. This painting both underscores the diversity of Chicano art and contradicts the conventional interpretation of what it embodies. For example, the color tones are far removed from conventional expectations of Chicano art, as were well exemplified by the bright colors and pastel hues of the "Mi casa es su casa" suite of works by Larry Yáñez. Here the seriousness and severity of the gaze are reinforced by a posture that expresses, with subtle, dark tones contrasting with the artist's white shirt and his prominently lit head with its furrowed brows, the serious, intellectual side of Chicano art and an artistic project of international esthetic relevance.

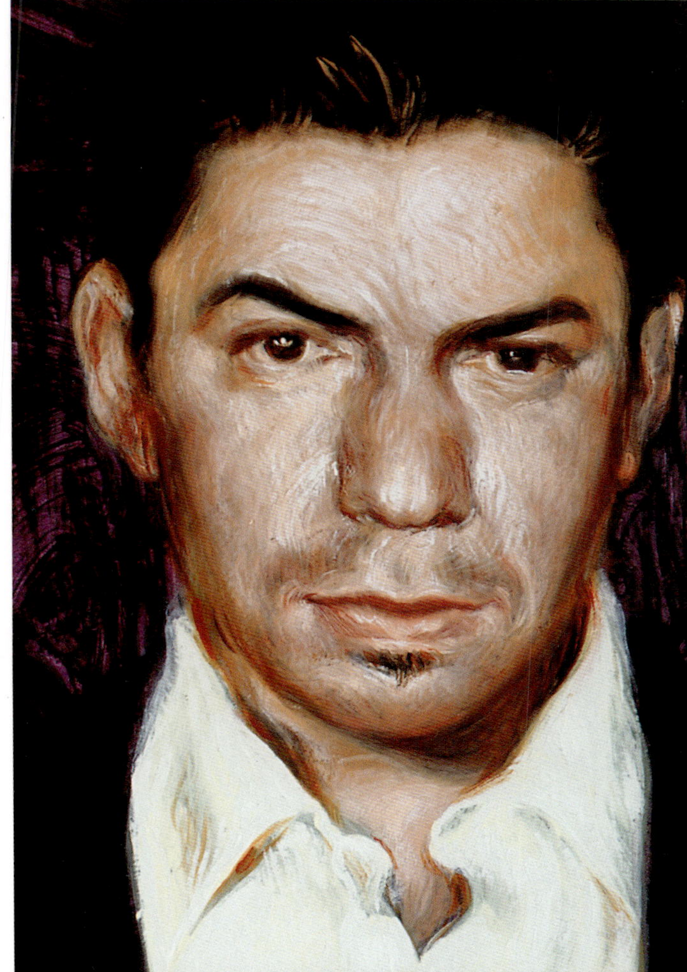

Left: 14 Mario Calvano, *Self-Portrait*, 1993
Oil on canvas, 60" x 48"

15 Celina Hinojosa, *Reyna's Cantina*, 1991, acrylic on canvas, 48" x 36". Collection of Dr. Marco and Sue Rubio Ardila.

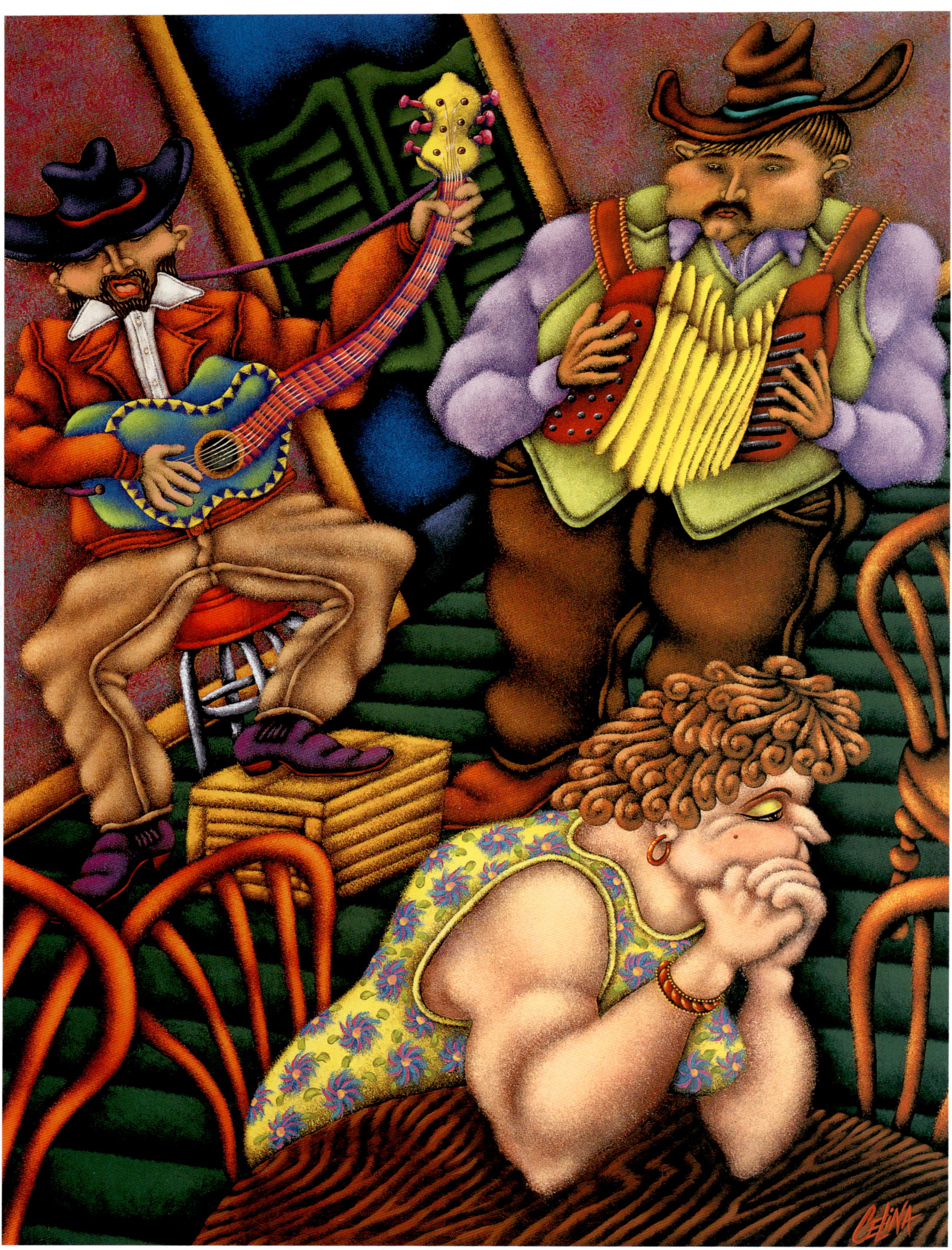

Lo que representa nuestra comunidad

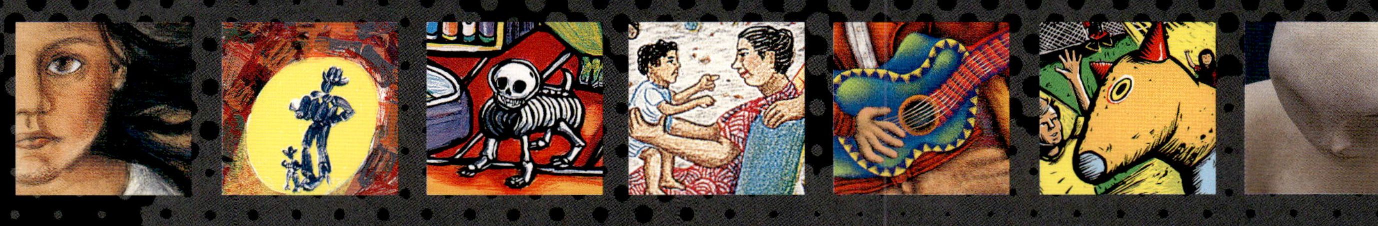

Community Values

he theme "Community Values/Lo que representa nuestra comunidad" moves us from that unique bicultural/bilingual house of Larry Yáñez and the individuated Chicano artistic identity of Mario Calvano's self-portrait to broader terrain, the Chicana/Chicano community. Here, in the section "Entre familia" we find a variety of works that represent both family life and family values. We are introduced to works that depict the development of children at choice moments, or their care by parents. We are presented with one work that evokes the traditional Chicana/o concern for ancestors and the deceased as well as the striving of Chicano-Mexicano culture to incorporate the deceased in the world of the living—to live with death as it were—in order to bridge that divide and attenuate or blur the finality of the distinction and, above all, to be at ease with death and accept it as an integral part of the life cycle. Other works in this section depict moments of family celebration such as a birthday or a Cinco de Mayo backyard party. In "Barrio y campo" we are introduced to the varied environments, lifestyles, and consequent mores and folkways that Chicanas and Chicanos practice in the barrio or urban neighborhoods, or on small farms in a rural setting. Naturally, education and mentorship are represented, as are a variety of musical or acrobatic diversions, distinctive or unique types of work, enterprises, or *oficios,* and community poses or social identities, such as that of the *vato loco* or the *cholo.*

ENTRE FAMILIA

Frank Ybarra, *Backyard Pachanga.* PLATE 16. (*Pachanga* is a colloquial Mexican/Chicano term for party or fiesta.) Commissioned to celebrate the Mexican holiday of Cinco de Mayo (the heroic defense of the city of Puebla on May 5, 1862, against the French expeditionary army of Napoleon III), which has assumed even greater importance for the expatriate Chicano communities than in the Mexican homeland, the artist has created a backyard fiesta of canonical proportions. All of the elements of

celebration are present. In the top left foreground the sun shines approvingly on the family in its backyard. Father and mother function in the role of idealized providers and nurturers. The only hint of patriotic observance is part of the Mexican flag on the father's apron; otherwise this could be the backyard of any modest tract home in the Southwest. The children, who range in size and age and are equally represented in gender, are paragons of youthful energy and enthusiasm. In the foreground above the model parents is the requisite piñata at the precise moment of eruption, disgorging not the blood and gore of a Cinco de Mayo battle but the fruits of liberty and family life—candies and other goodies. Clearly, all is well on Cinco de Mayo at the bicultural Mexican American community *celebración.*

Eva C. Pérez, *Little People Series #6.* PLATE 17. This sandstone clay sculpture harks back to one of the most cultivated themes of Western art, the Madonna and child. At the same time the work both greatly de-emphasizes the Western characteristics of this theme and imbues it with pre-Hispanic and contemporary Amerindian or mestizo characteristics. The nurturing of the child by the mother studiously avoids the elements of Christian care and compassion or the religious transcendence of the infant that we normally associate with this icon. On the other hand, Eva Pérez brings the pre-Hispanic element into the work. The piece, in part because it eliminates all elements, including even color, that are extraneous to the original sandstone, reminds us of a sculpture found at an archaeological site, possibly even a work of art recovered from the past and effaced of its original detail over centuries so that it is reduced to its formal essentials. Thus the work both recuperates pre-Hispanic sculpture and recreates it within a spare, even minimalist ambience. Similarly, we note in the work the influence of Francisco Zúñiga (1912-1998) and perhaps even more overtly, especially in the treatment of the feet of the mother, that of Native American artist R.C. Gorman (born 1932), who himself has asserted his artistic debt to Zúñiga.

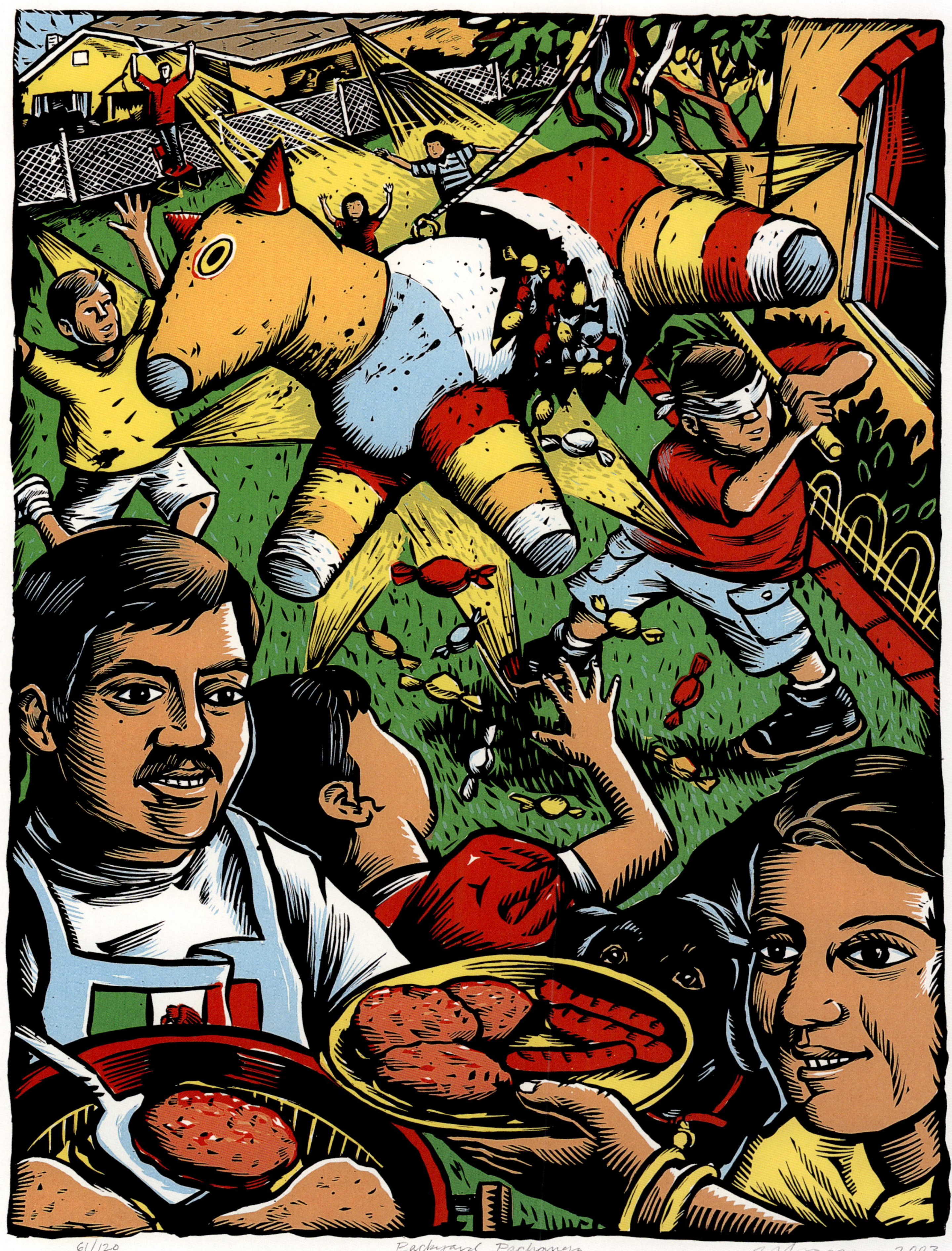

61/120   Backyard Pachanga   2003

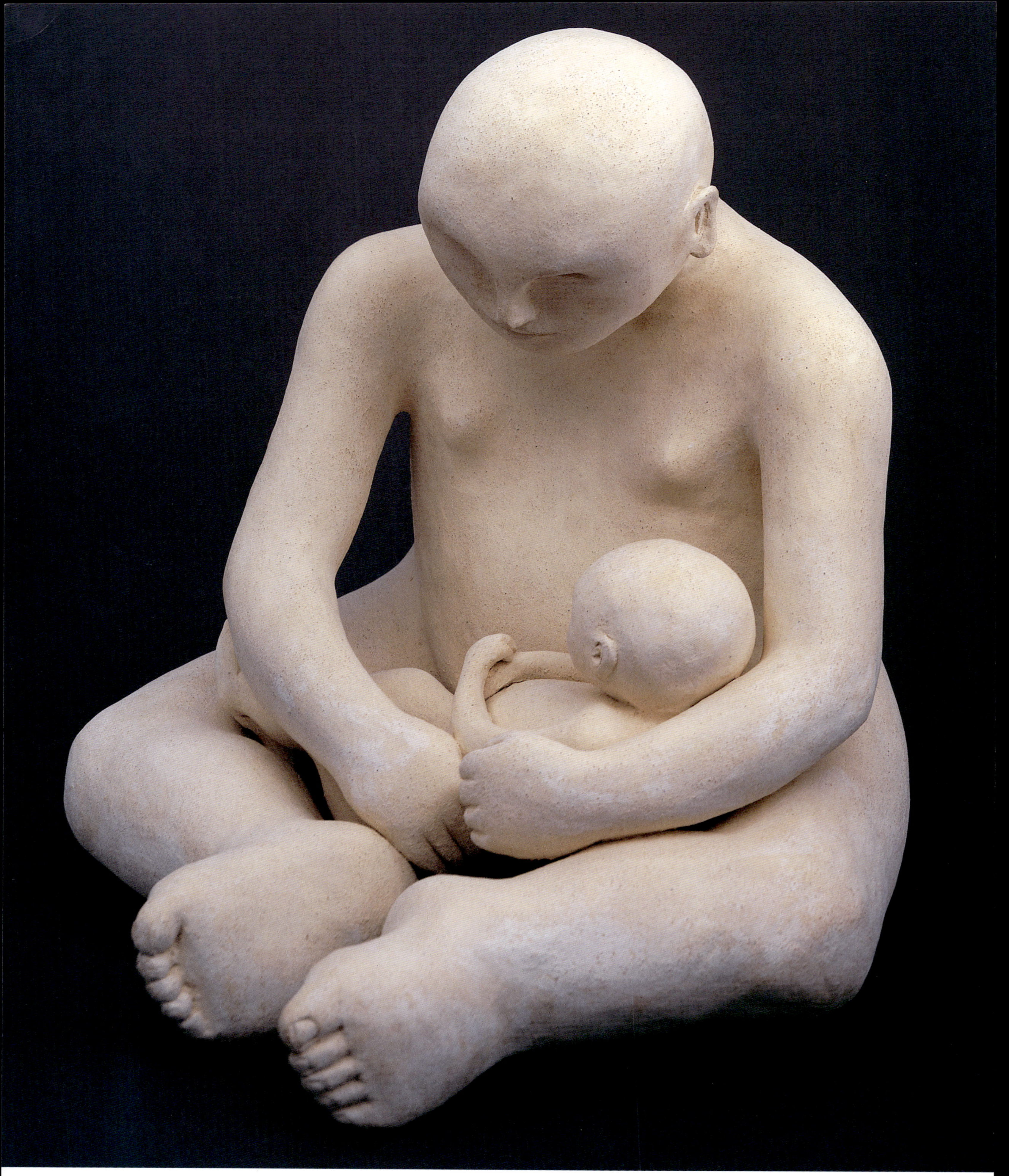

17 Eva C. Pérez, *Little People Series #6*, 1997, sandstone clay, 12.5" x 11" x 11.5"

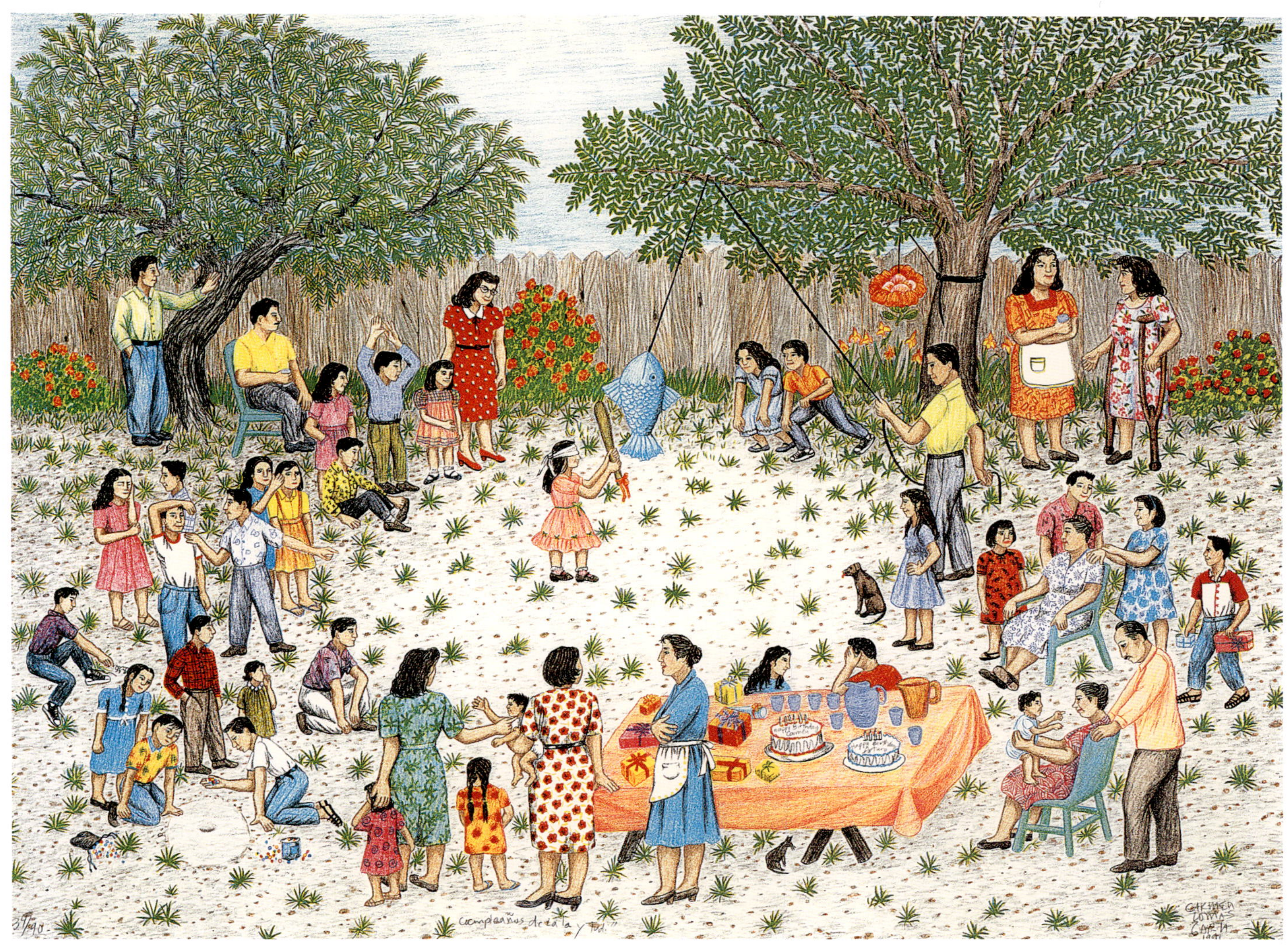

18 Carmen Lomas Garza, *Cumpleaños de Lala y Tudi* (Lala and Tudi's birthday), 1989, lithograph, 22" x 30"

Carmen Lomas Garza, *Cumpleaños de Lala y Tudi* (Lala and Tudi's birthday). PLATE 18. The subject of this work is the celebration of the birthday of two young girls by a Chicano community, probably in the Rio Grande Valley area along the United States-Mexico border. Inclusiveness within the community is one of the thematic hallmarks of this work, along generational lines certainly, and including both males and females, the able and disabled, and even pets. A characteristic work of Garza, *Cumpleaños* depicts a community event with all of the folk singularity of a specific small town or semi-rural community. Surrounded by adults and children with homemade cakes, refreshments, and gifts, one of the blindfolded birthday girls attempts to break a piñata in the form of a fish. Many of the children are looking attentively, ready to rush out and snatch the goodies and small presents that will tumble out of the piñata once it has been struck open. Bright colors predominate in this scene of an outdoor gathering. Carmen Lomas Garza is a highly trained artist and her work overtly recreates the drawing style, rudimentary execution of perspective, and compositional and formal components (such as numerous individual figures, high attention to details, varied colors, and abhorrence of space) that are characteristic of the naïve painter. The artist's recreation of the naïve style helps her to reinforce the evocation of simple and natural community folkways and values and the depiction of memorable events that transcend the vagaries of history and social or technological evolution and thus are fixed in eidetic memory for all time.

27

Antonio Rael, *Panchito y Tía Tita.* PLATE 19. (Little Pancho and Aunt Tita. Pancho is the endearing nickname for Francisco, and Tita is also an endearment, perhaps for Conchita). With masterful control over detail and a range of colors, Rael creates a comfortable, homey scene of life in the afterlife. The key to interpreting this painting is to set it within the context of the Mexican or Chicano tradition of living with death. This is most clearly expressed in the observance of *El Día de los Muertos,* the Day of the Dead, which takes place currently at the beginning of November during the Christian holidays of All Saints' Day and All Souls' Day (in Spanish, *Día de Todos los Santos* and *Día de Difuntos)* but in pre-Hispanic culture was celebrated roughly (in Western calendrical terms) at the end of July. This centuries-old Mexican/Chicano tradition emphasizes remembering the dead, realizing the cyclical continuity of life, and integrating death into the natural cycle. The family members spend some time with their ancestors, visiting the gravesites with food and ordinary small gifts or remembrances of their lives, living with them in the sense of bringing them back to the life of the family and the community. Using traditional hues of the Mexican/Chicano palette, pastel limes and pinks and earthen golds and browns, Rael recreates the aspect of living with the dead in Chicano culture in a comic but entirely endearing way. Here we find the "perfect" traditional home of everyday life; multiple images of the dog on the wall, a landscape scene, an icon of the Virgin of Guadalupe, food—a still life in artistic terms—on the table and in the pet bowl, a discarded bone on the rug that presumably the dog has been gnawing, books and knick-knacks in the bookcase, and so on. Perfectly integrated into this homey, common scene are the dear departed aunt, made up and reading a familiar book, and her alert companion dog in the form of skeletons. They are the living dead who at the same time are the dead living in the world of the caring family and community.

19 Antonio Rael, *Panchito y Tía Tita* (Little Pancho and Aunt Tita), 2002, acrylic on canvas, 18" x 24"

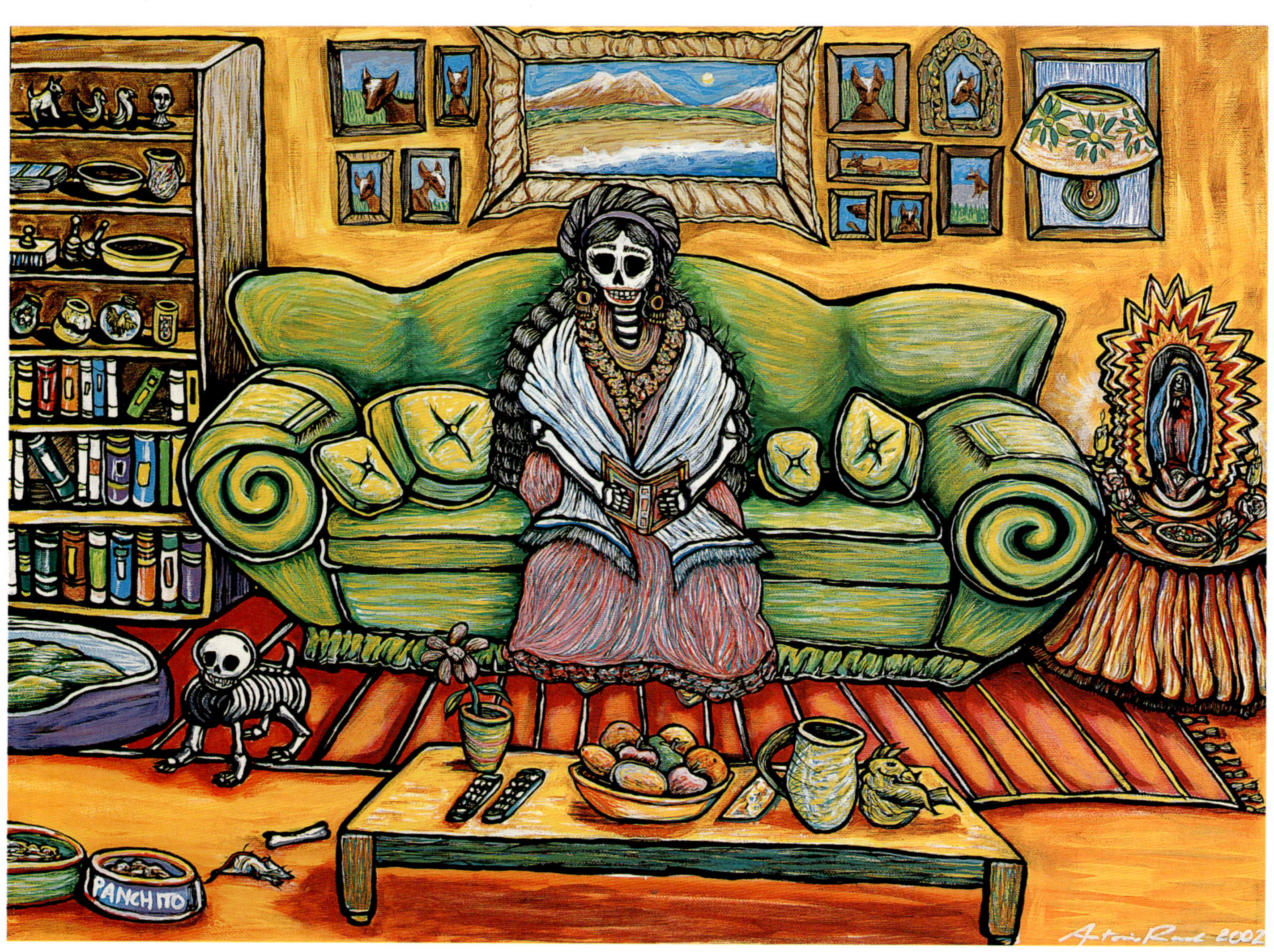

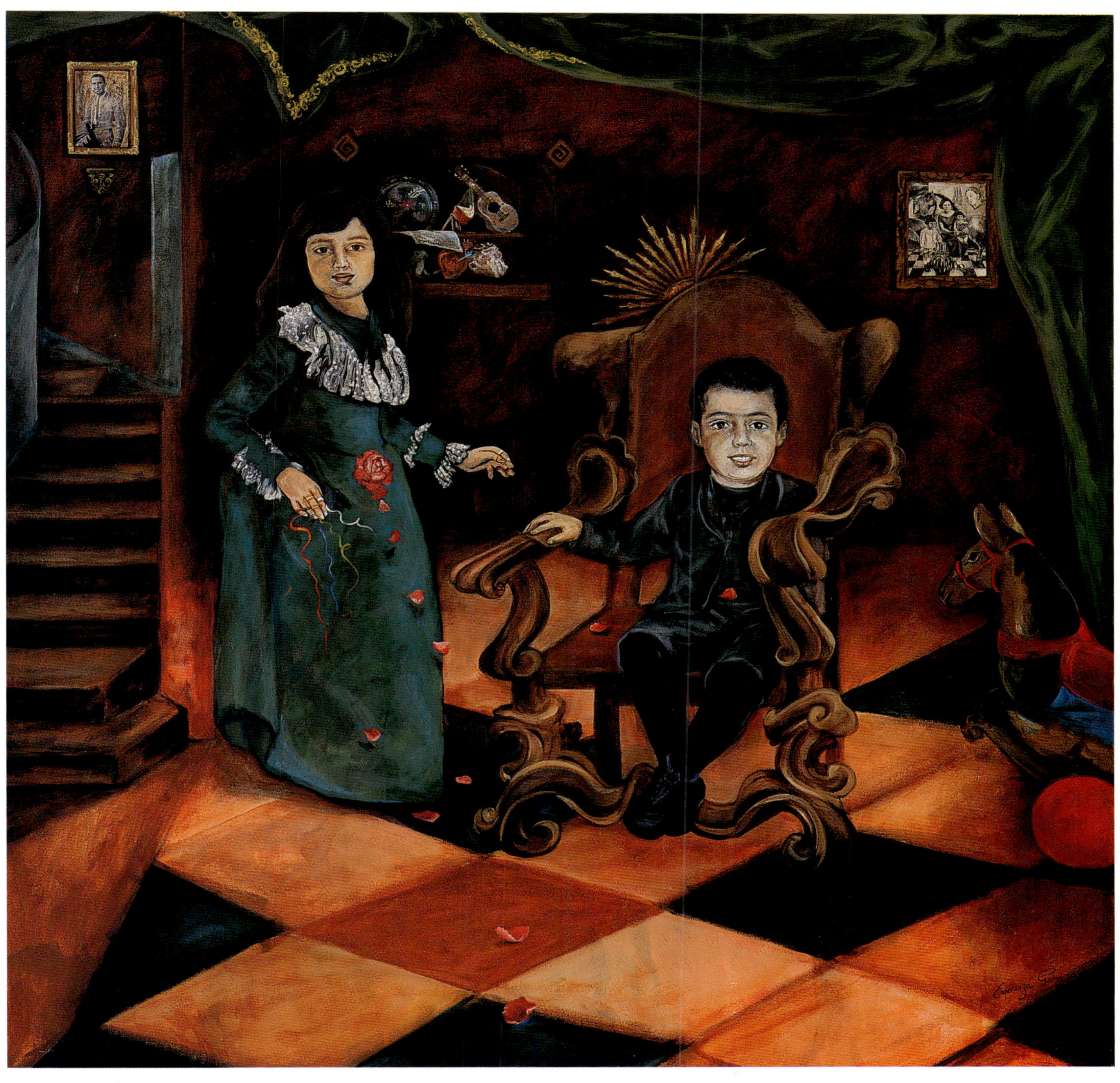

20 Esperanza Gama, *El amor rojo* (Red love), 2001, acrylic on canvas, 48" x 48"

Esperanza Gama's *El amor rojo* (Red love), PLATE 20, is a work within the surrealist tradition. There are parallels here with two artists, Leonora Carrington (born 1917), and Remedios Varo (1908-1963), the former English, the latter Spanish, who both fled France during World War II and lived for a long time in Mexico, and there is also some influence from the Dutch master Johannes Vermeer (1631-1675). Gama uses the artistic device of a foregrounded checkered floor to draw the viewer into the painting, as well as drapery to frame the scene, a device used with similar results in Vermeer's *The*

Allegory of Painting. As in Varos's *Useless Science or the Alchemist*, in *El amor rojo* the colors are subdued except for the checkered floor in the foreground. Gama has created a supposed scene from life, but it is highly symbolic, mannered, and cryptic. Part of the artistic purpose of surrealism, which emerged from the distinct psychoanalytic movements initiated by Sigmund Freud and Carl Jung, is to recreate the dream world and evoke its symbolism. The dreamlike and at the same time stagelike quality of this work is marked, especially in the postures of the boy and the female, the way they are lit (emerging

Right: 21 John Valadez, *Robert and Liz,* 1984,
Pastel on paper, 60" x 42". Collection of Glenna and Paloma Ávila.

out of surrounding darkness), and their presence at center stage. The boy's head is slightly out of proportion, larger than it would normally be, and he sits in the "grand manner" in a chair fit for a prince, a chair that itself seems to have a carved crown or rays of the sun growing out of it. At his side, seemingly in an attendant function, is a female who could be the boy's mother or perhaps his older sister, since her age is ambiguous. The symbols that abound in this work are suitably surrealistic. They defy easy decipherment, as would be customary for dreams and, consequently, for the challenge of dream interpretation. A rocking horse stands on the other side of the boy. The female carries a needle or a thorn, and from her waist, where a rose is affixed, petals are falling almost like drops of blood. Although the work has *rojo* in its title, this color is very sparingly used except for the rose and what it sheds, which, of course, is the principal icon that calls for deciphering. This scene is archetypal rather than stemming from a Chicano or even Latin tradition. The relationship of the male and female figures to each other and to their dreamlike environment is more easily interpreted in relationship to classical Western art, to the masters rather than anything else. An important element of this work that evokes the mystery of human relationships as presented in a surrealistic setting is the painting in the far right top background, a beacon of light in an otherwise dark and subdued interior. What is most compelling about that painting is the foregrounded checkered floor, which seems to reinforce the notion about the cyclical and repetitive nature of the dreaming out or enactment of archetypal human relationships (mother/son or nurturing sister/younger brother) that are part of the human condition.

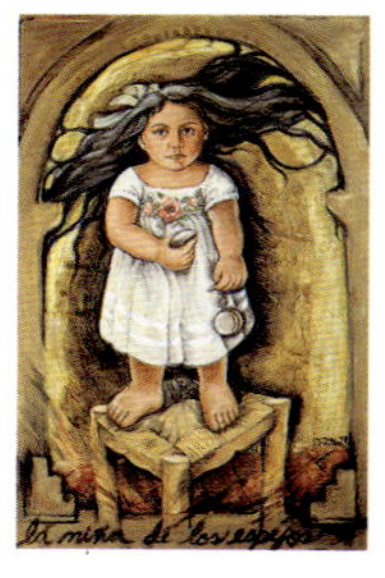

Cristina Cárdenas, *La niña de los espejos* (The looking glass girl). PLATE 25. We are faced with a young girl who, standing on what may be a family-fashioned stool, confronts us directly. This face-to-face quality establishes a relationship of heightened energy or tension between the subject and the viewer, a dimension that is further intensified by the confounding contrast between stillness and movement. At one extreme, the girl appears perfectly still and is possibly studying her image in a mirror. The mirror motif is strengthened by the way the

La niña de los espejos, see page 36

work is framed within the work, suggesting that the image of the girl herself is once removed, emanating from a mirror. She has a magnifying glass in her right hand and what is perhaps the case for this object in her other hand, which is placed across her chest. At the other extreme, her hair appears to defy the laws of physics because it is flowing wildly in an environment that seems totally secluded, private and inaccessible to the elements. Additional contrasts abound: for example, the girl is beautifully dressed in a hand-embroidered party gown of Mexican or Chicano tradition. Yet she is barefoot and her feet, which are large in a way that we associate with the unclad, together with her face provide the polar contrasts and centers of focus of this work. Another example is her hair ribbon, which is serenely set atop a full head of long hair, the strands of which flow wildly in each direction. The contrast between upbringing and secrecy, between stasis and kinesis, between a traditional status and a wild side replete with options is clearly present although at the same time it is somewhat covert and subtle. This *niña* appears to be standing in a santos niche, which reinforces the paradigmatic quality of the icon. Here is a young girl, both still and restless, traditionally and properly dressed and yet unclad. She is perhaps ready to burst out with energy and emotion but has a solemn, studious, and determined look on her face, and she is looking at us, the viewers, and at herself possibly in a mirror, with an additional utensil of identity magnification at the ready. The family and the greater community are present in their absence, present in the dressing, and grooming, and in apparent support for this determined young girl, who is reviewing her presence, countenance, and identity options and sharing them as well with us; in fact, she's genuinely "in our face." The browns and golds of the background, the indeterminate forms of the environment (more churchlike than homelike), the roses at the bottom right of the work (referent to the Virgin but also to romance, flowering, and love), the bannerlike textile at the bottom (empty so that she/we can fill in the identity choice), and the posture of a very young girl standing atop a stool and rising to future stature—to womanhood—all emphasize the emergence of life options and the initial formation of self-identity within an environment of tradition, family concern, and even propriety and obedience.

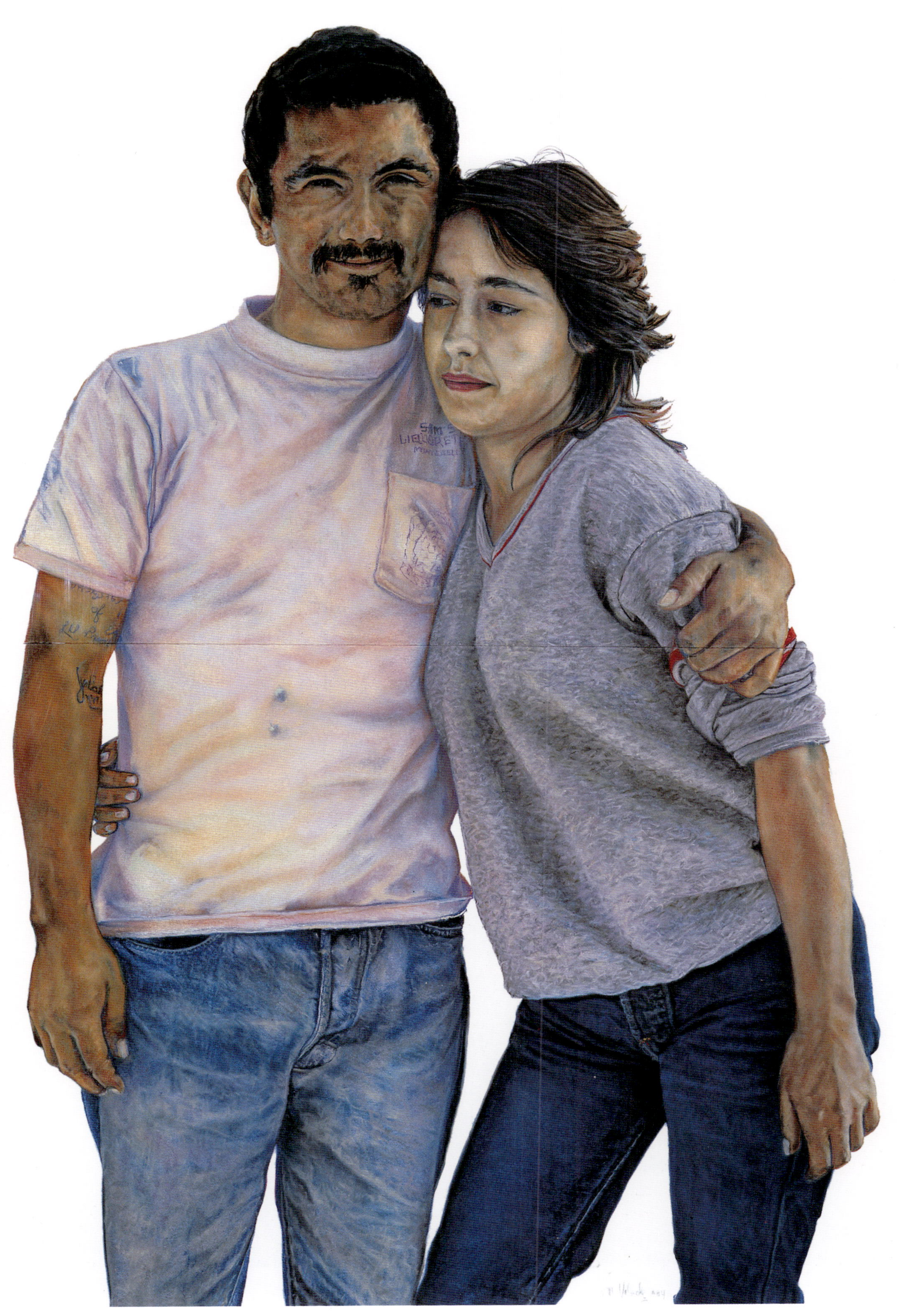

BARRIO Y CAMPO

John Valadez, *Robert and Liz.* PLATE 21.
Robert and Liz, clearly Latino but titled with the
Anglo versions of their names (not Roberto and
Isabel), are depicted with a hyperrealism that goes
beyond photorealism in that they are removed from
any contextual or distracting background and are
presented holding on to each other in firm, loving
support on a background of white space. These are
working-class people and Robert is wearing what
appear to be his work clothes, which have smudges
on them. Smudges also appear on his face and arm
together with tattoos in the form of what in Spanish are called *garabatos* or scribblings. Liz appears to
have no trepidation whatsoever about Robert's
after-work condition and, displaying incontrovert-
ible allegiance, leans into him, resting her head on
his shoulder, even as she holds him firmly around
the waist. The couple, rather than looking at each
other, appears to be looking outward, toward life and
its challenges and joys, which on this blank background are intensified and deepened. Liz has a more
enigmatic countenance, but she appears to have an
element of forbearance and satisfaction with her
man and perhaps just a hint of deep emotion in her
eyes. Robert, on the other hand, is an open book.
With his arms around his loved one, whose head is
crooked in his shoulder, he is a paradigm of pleasure.
A hard day's work and a well-earned, unqualified
reception tell us that all is good. Here is a couple
that has weathered life's storm together. In this pic-
torial slice of life, despite the fact that the context is
totally quotidian and nothing is out of the ordinary,
the conclusion is that this loving couple will prevail.

Ester Hernández, *Los Recyclers.* PLATE 22.
The use of a bilingual title in this work, combining
the Spanish *los* (the) with the English *recyclers*,
emphasizes the Chicano nature of these self-
employed itinerants who make their livelihood
with their truck from the transformation of the dis-
cards of mainstream culture into economically
valuable substances. The recyclers—one man and
two women wearing bracelets—may be working
with cans, bottles, and other refuse, their truck may
be old and old fashioned, their packaging may con-
sist of burlap sacks, but they are fastidiously neat

22 Ester Hernández, *Los Recyclers*, 1995, pastel on paper, 30" x 44"

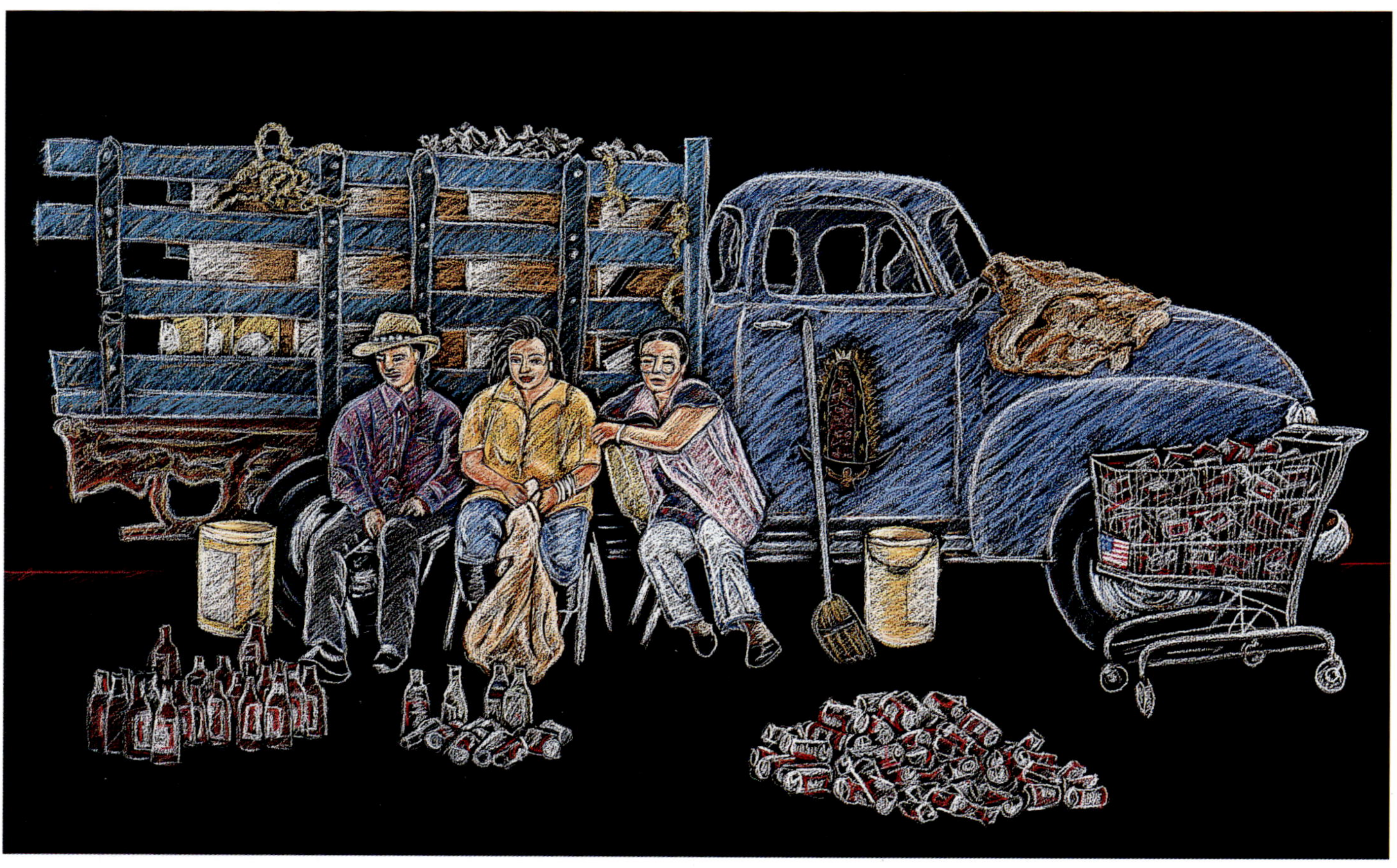

and organized. All of the objects are ordered and separately stacked or bagged. A broom, a bucket, and a receptacle, part of the tools of their trade, are standing at their sides. The figures appear tired but not discouraged and are sitting on chairs they brought with them, taking a breather. They provide for themselves in every conceivable way. Their condition as self-starters making a living at an acceptable albeit relatively low socioeconomic level is accentuated by the fact that they stand out apparently in the utter darkness of a remote locale. They appear before us against a black background (contrasting with the white background of *Robert and Liz* but fulfilling the same function) that eliminates any distracting or attenuating context from their human condition. These people invite moral appraisal and the conclusion is positive. Their life is set between two determining icons, the U.S. flag on the shopping cart and the Virgin of Guadalupe on the truck. It is a bicultural world and a difficult life, yet there is honesty, dignity, and freedom—the lower echelon freedom of self-employment and entrepreneurship evoked by the treasure of cans and bottles, and the freedom of wheels on the old but painstakingly maintained and honored truck, worthy of the emblem of the Virgin of Guadalupe.

Celina Hinojosa, *Reyna's Cantina*. PLATE 15. In contrast to *Still in Reverence*, which is depicted with naturalistic attention to detail, this work is heavily stylized. In the morphology of the accordion player (see comments on Treviño's *Sonido del barrio* about this instrument), not only the girth but also the rolling quality of the legs and arm make a nod to the achievements of renowned contemporary Colombian painter and sculptor Fernando Botero (born 1932). Set on a foundational green floor, the planks of which are established horizontally, the primary orientation of this work is diagonal. There are also very few straight lines in the composition and almost none in the depiction of the human body, its clothing, or the musicians' instruments. The function, in addition to the creation of a uniquely stylized compositional effect, is also partially thematic. We are bearing witness to a tipsy moment in the cantina, that moment of musical and emotional buzz when everyone, in contrast to the typical social jocularity, has turned sentimental or introspective. Even the musical instruments are partaking of this sinuous, overspirited affectation. Reinforced by the self-engaged musicians farther back in the composition, whose eyes have been either obscured by the cowboy hat or

which seem to have almost closed and turned inward, the foregrounded figure of a woman is caught at a moment of deep introspection with some implication of wistfulness and self-judgment. She is perfectly still, but her head of hair, truly validating the concept of "a mop of hair," evokes her inner turmoil, perhaps a moment of disbalance physically, emotionally, and cognitively. The colors are masterfully combined in this piece and work well to develop the theme of the work. On the one hand, we are treated to strong contrasts: the floor as opposed to the garments, flesh, hair, curvy chairs, and tipping walls. On the other hand, there is considerable subtlety and nuance at the micro level, for example in the tones of the skin and hair of the female and the browns and burnt orange colors of some of the garments of the musicians.

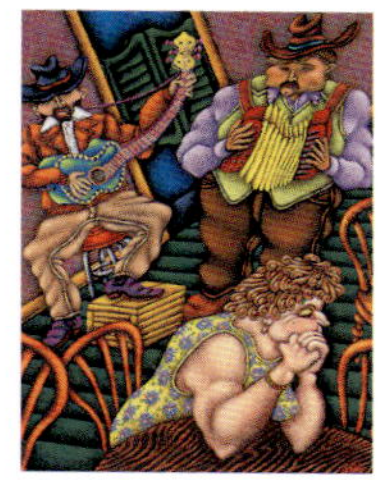

Reyna's Cantina,
see page 22

Larry Yáñez, *The Monthter What Ate the Thity*. PLATE 23. Combining folk art with a certain religious undertone (Jonah living in the stomach of the whale), the artist creates a miniature city that has been swallowed up by a polka-dotted cartoon monster. Although teeth are foregrounded here and the title indicates that a city has been eaten, the "reality" of this comic piece is that life appears to go on as always, and the blockheaded urban dwellers stand facing the viewer with an automaton-like rigidity that has been overtly created by the artist through his use of materials so they appear to have come out of a young child's toy box. There is a strong theatrical element to this work; it confronts us rather like a tableau vivant. What has mostly been suppressed is the element of fear. For example, the title takes the sting out of the supposed subject of having been eaten by reducing monster and city to a child's version of their spelling and pronunciation. Like the cartoon characters who are flattened or mashed but magically come back together, this is fear with a lisp, the artist with his tongue outside the mouth, creating not a monster, but a monthter. The sharp pointed teeth of the monthter have the aspect of a railing or a stage fronting more than the implication of disaster, and they are matched by the creature's triangular eyes and pointed outer scales. This work has clearly been fashioned to suggest that it has been crafted by a child out of the materials available to him or her and, by extension, that it reflects a child's dealing with postmodern apprehensions about the fate of humanity and its edifices in our dangerous times.

Fidencio Durán, *Stilts*. PLATE 24. This work features three young men engaged in three different but

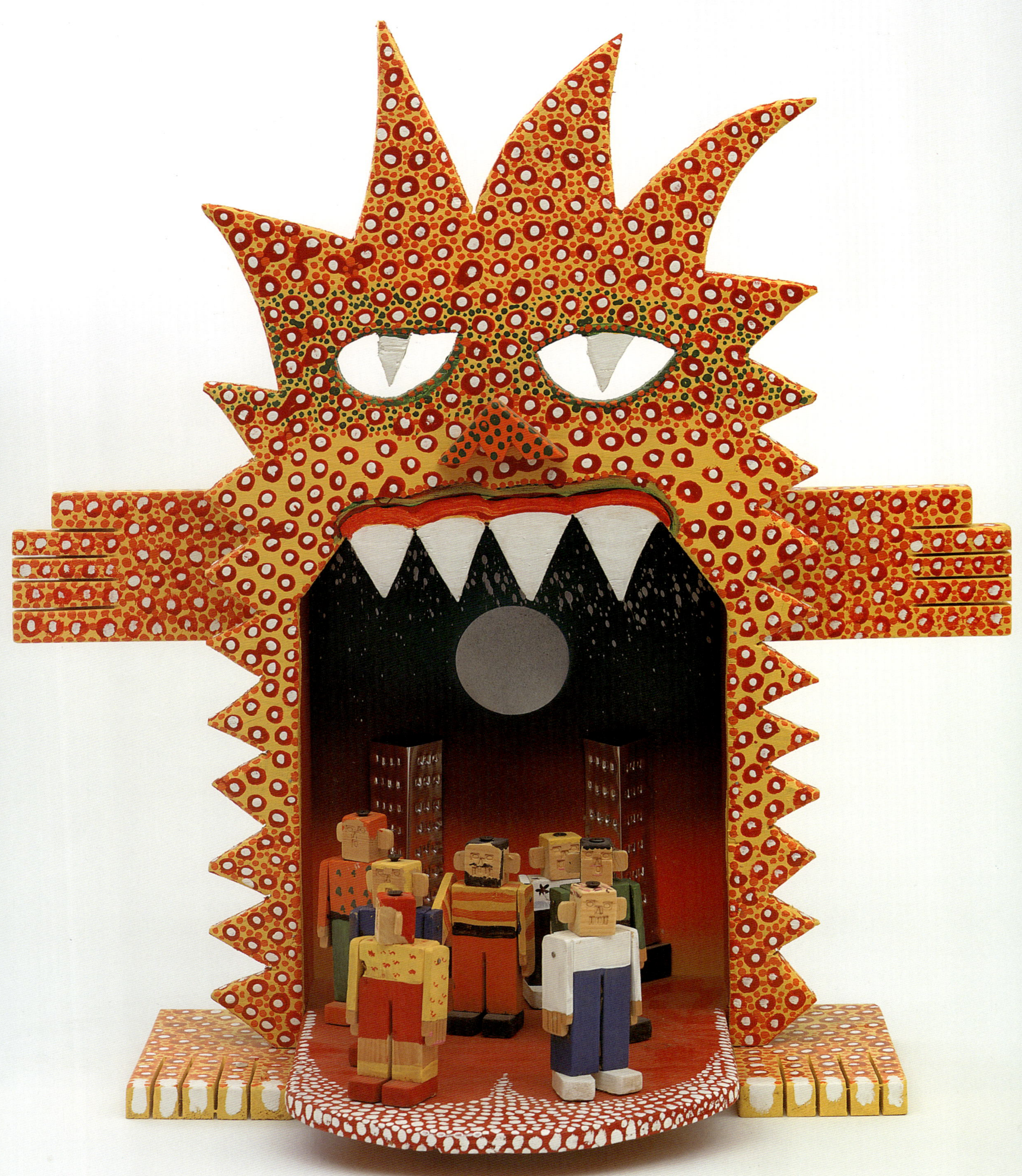

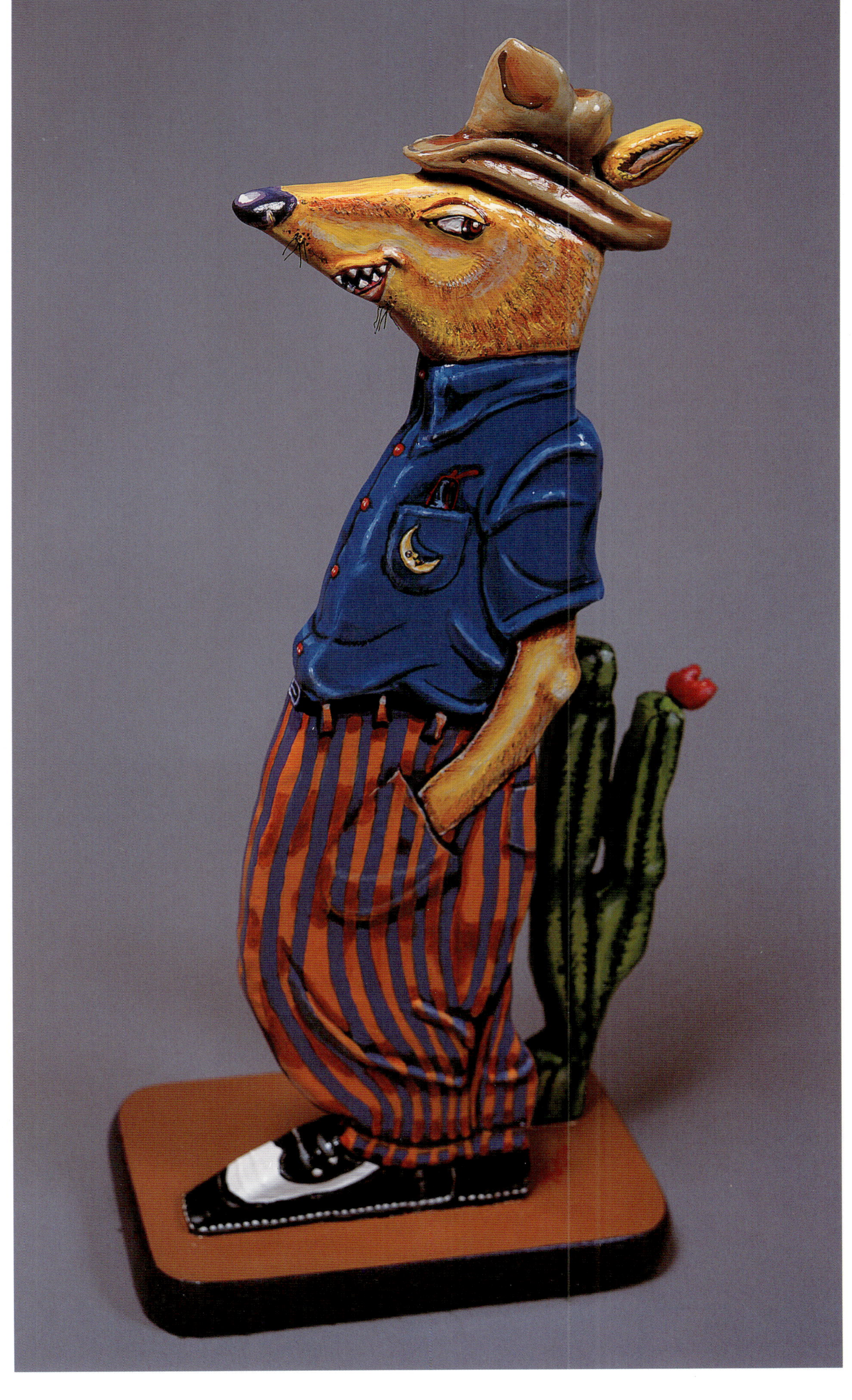

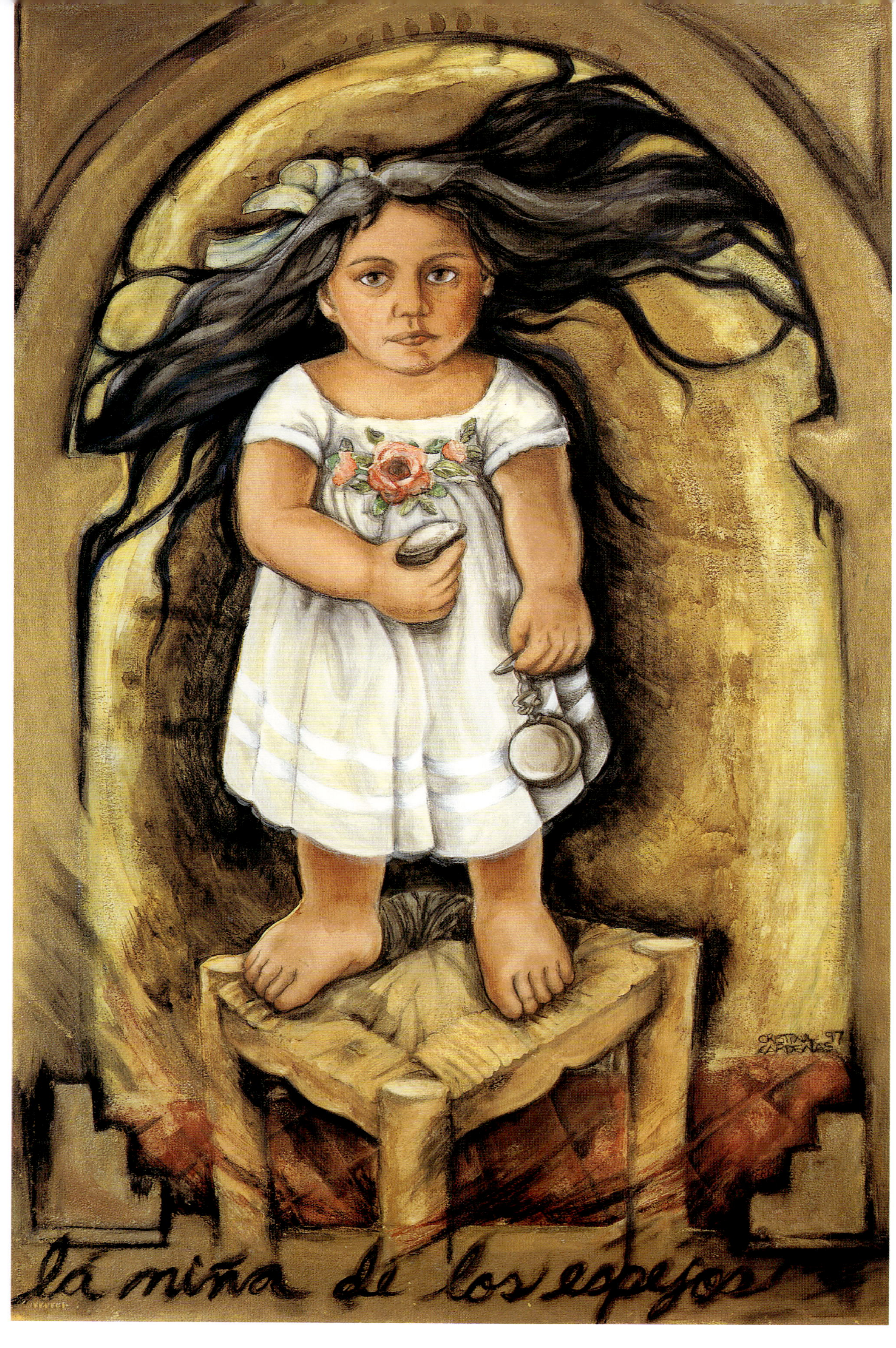

25 Cristina Cárdenas, *La niña de los espejos*
(The looking glass girl), 1997, gouache on paper, 40.5" x 26"

36

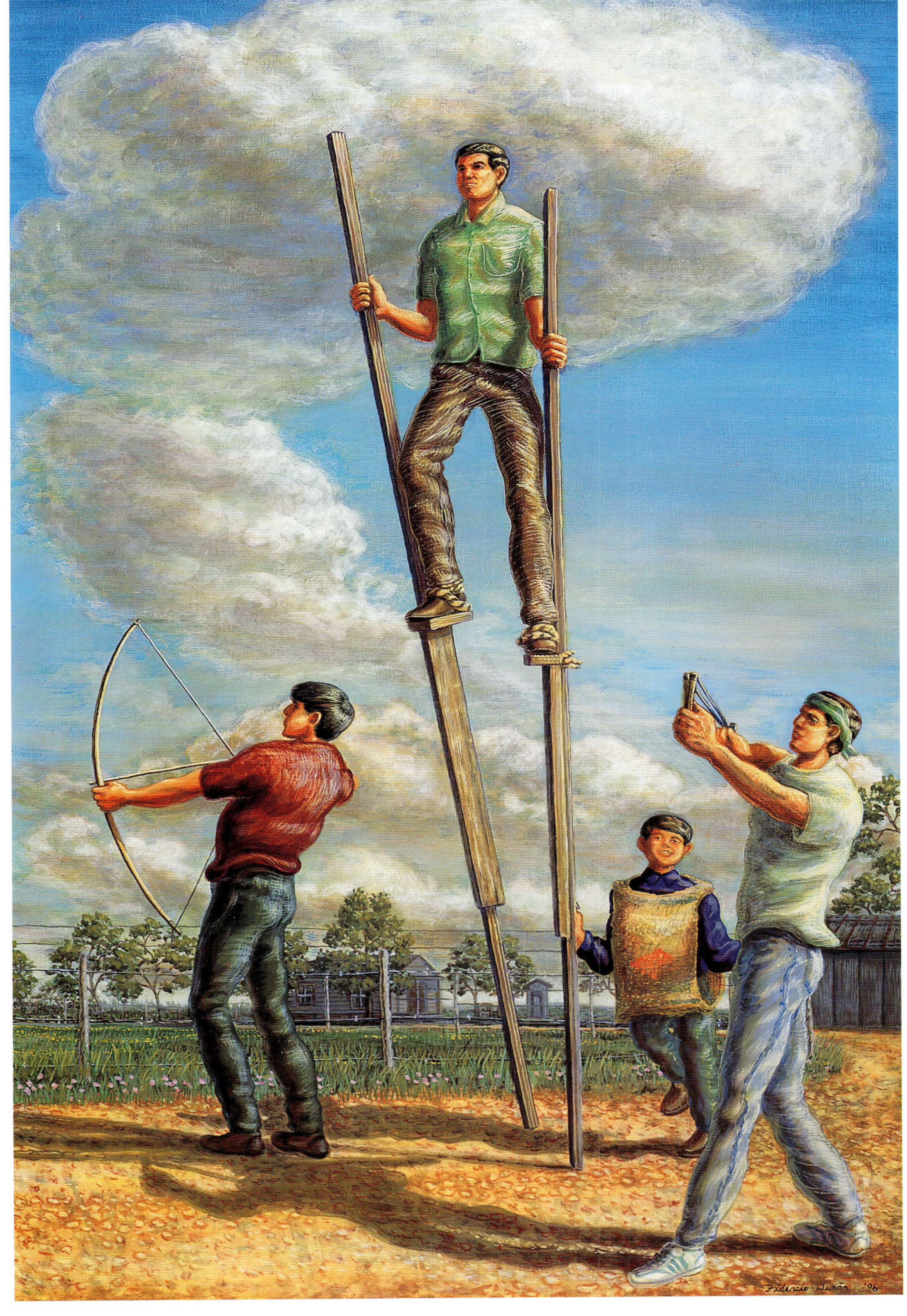

24 Fidencio Durán, *Stilts*, 1996, acrylic on canvas, 36" x 24"

Left: 23 Larry Yáñez, *The Monthter What Ate the Thity*, 1997, mixed media, 24.5" x 23.25" x 13.5"

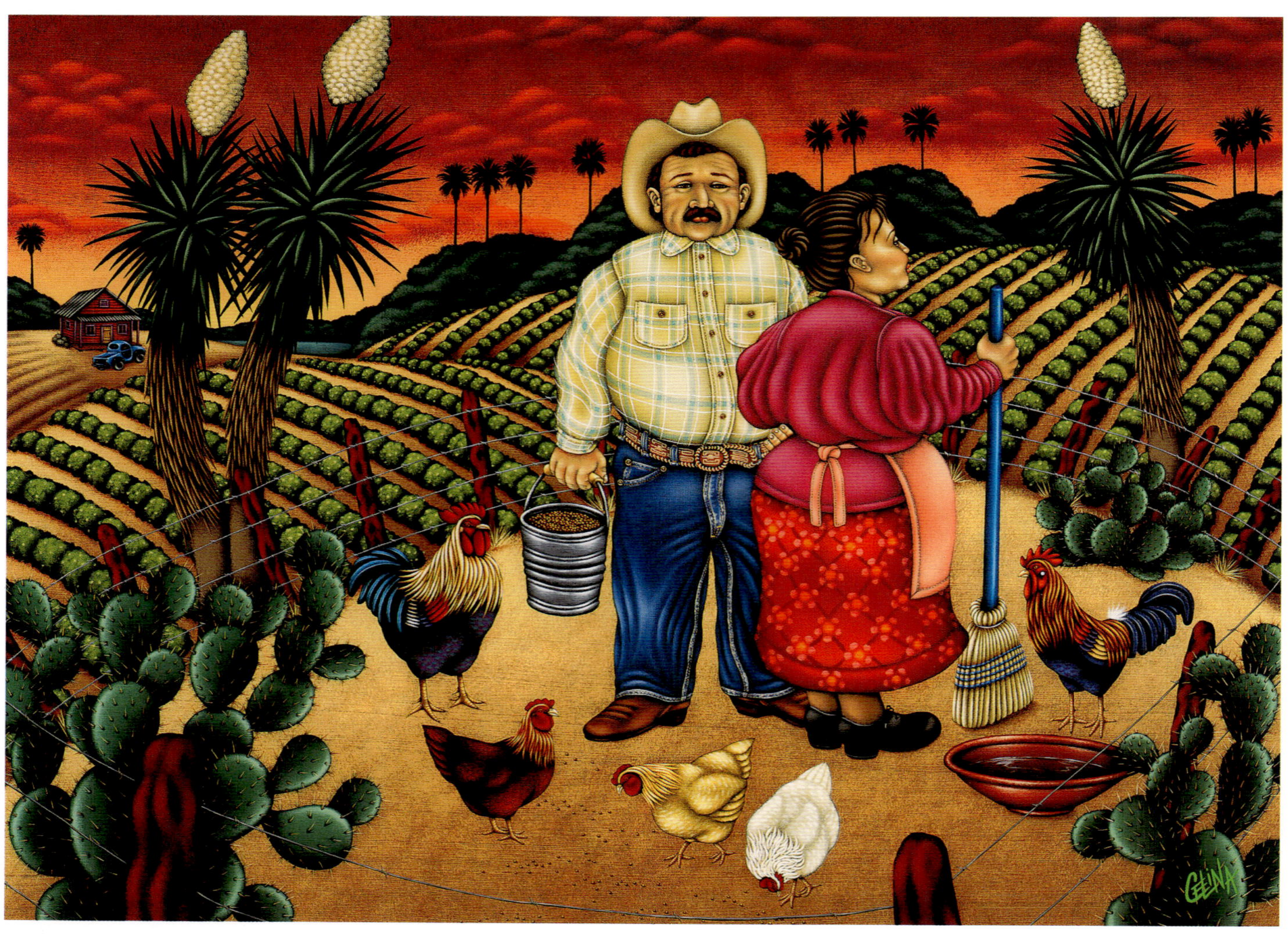

27 Celina Hinojosa, *Still in Reverence*, 1998, acrylic on canvas, 36" x 48". Collection of Rudy and Heather Ruiz.

similar pastimes. In the center, a young man on stilts dominates the composition. Behind the central figure is a fourth, younger boy, holding the stilts up supportively. To the left and to the right, respectively, are two youths engaged in more energetic sports, archery and working a slingshot. They are depicted in full sunlight toward the end of the day so that their elongated shadows slant to the left of the composition; above, set in an otherwise blue sky, is a robust swirl of clouds. The work seems naturalistic at first blush, but in fact the vertical element has been emphasized through a conscious and careful elongation of the three lean youths. This is a technique that the Renaissance master El Greco used with superb results to express the spiritual exaltation of his subjects. Fidencio Durán, on the other hand, is emphasizing the physical prowess, health, conditioning, and perhaps, in the case of the youth on stilts, the farsee-

ing quality of his subjects. In fact, even though this work seems initially to be entirely secular, the position of the central figure high above the two more aggressive males carries with it the hint of the crucifixion of Christ between the two thieves. However, this triadic grouping underpins the overt depiction of aggressiveness and supportive group behavior: there is a certain pagan quality in the composition, as if a special, intimate sort of Olympiad were being rehearsed by the trio and their younger supporter, or alternatively, as if scanning (the youth on stilts) and hunting were being rehearsed. The work is as colorful, sumptuous, and unbound as the great outdoors itself. Not only have the three figures been elongated to emphasize their physical prowess, but the stilts themselves have also undergone a marked vertical exaggeration to further endow this youthful rite of an outdoor afternoon with an exalted dimension (at the

Previous page: 26 Larry Portillo, *El Guapo "Ay te watcho"* (Handsome guy, see ya soon), 2003, mixed media, plaster, Styrofoam, acrylic, 33" x 9" x 14". Collection of the artist.

same time that it hints at the cross) that controverts and even subverts the naturalistic cast of the work.

Larry Portillo, *El Guapo "Ay te watcho"* (Handsome guy, see ya soon). PLATE 26. This sculpture features an anthropomorphically depicted animal, seemingly a composite but whose snout recalls a rat and whose dress, countenance, and posture are those of a stylish, somewhat zoot-suiter-like urban habitué. This work was produced in the San Antonio area, and the locale is signaled by placing a second, smaller sculpture of a flowering cactus directly behind the *guapo*. The flower itself recalls a red rose, and together with other components of the ensemble—a sliver of moon with a man's smiling face in it, the jauntily placed hat, the striped pachuco-style pants and two-toned patent leather shoes, the sly and attentive look of the eyes and comically menacing full set of razor-sharp teeth—it offers an image worthy of attention but certainly not of trust. This well-dressed rat, his ear popping through his unique hat that evokes the multicultural heritage of Texas (both the cowboy hat and the German Alpine type with the ear in the spot for the customary brush or feather), is about as fetching as a rodent can be, but he also seems on the prowl and ready for what opportunities a moonlit night might offer him, particularly of the amorous kind. A sweet-talking *guapo* on the hustle has been depicted here. The human masculine underpinnings of this piece are obvious, and creating an image of a *vato* (dude) dressed to kill in the form of a rat seems analogically appropriate. However, the ensemble is rooted in folk art and the overriding quality is the comical spoof emanating from this depiction of a recognizable macho human type as a rodentlike double. The color scheme, featuring a deep velvety blue shirt that sets off the rodent's fur and felt hat and that both contrasts and complements the blue and burnt-orange striped pants, is a strikingly vivid reprise of the Chicano mastery of color in its folk art.

Celina Hinojosa, *Still in Reverence.* PLATE 27. Somewhat similar in theme to Treviño's *Sonido del barrio,* this work also depicts a crepuscular transition

28 Diane Gamboa, *Little Gold Man*, 1990, serigraph, 24" x 36"

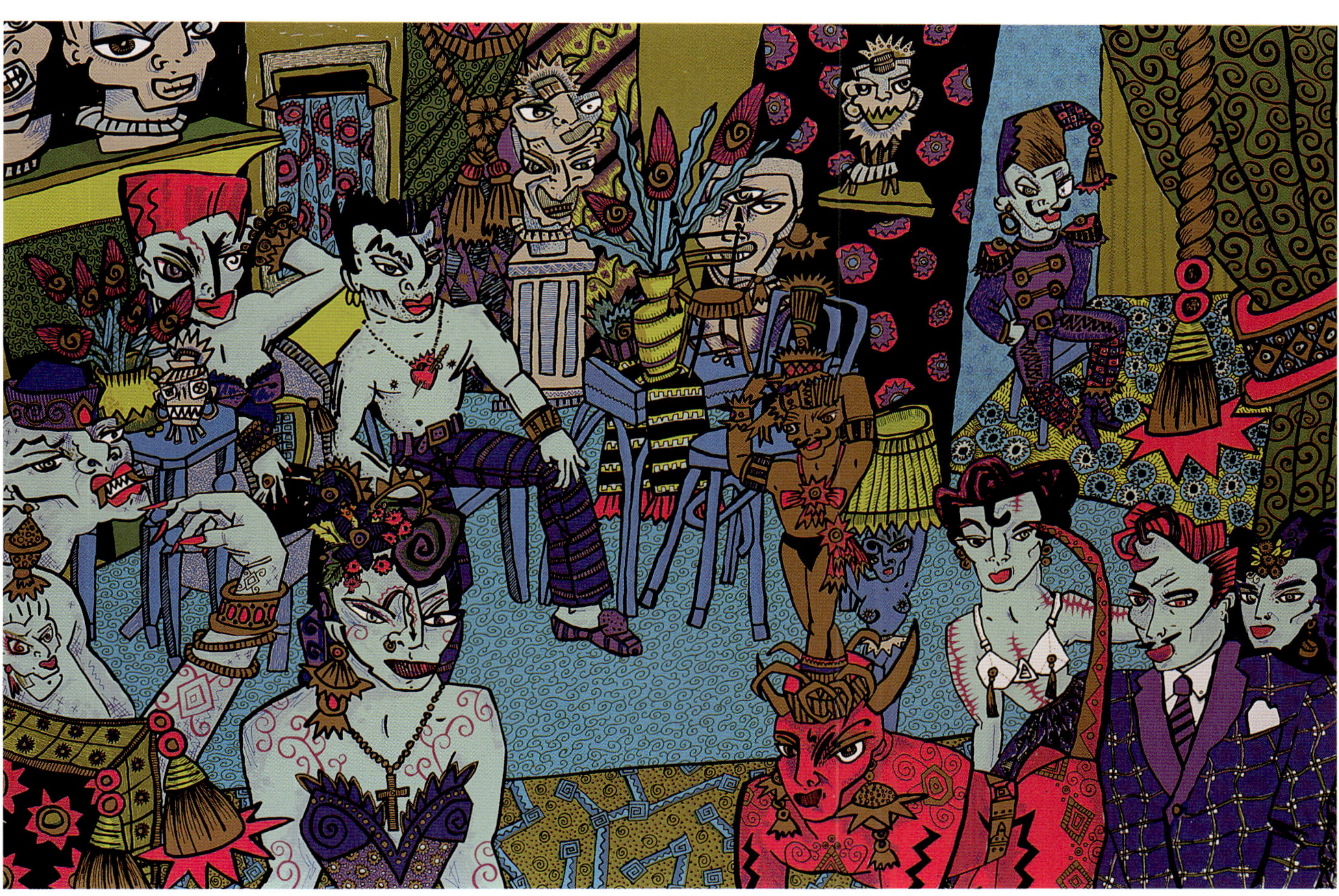

in the environment, perhaps in this case sunrise, given the farmer's activity of feeding the chickens. This is the border area of the Rio Grande, a highly fertile, well cultivated, and therefore uncharacteristic part of Texas. With two edible nopal cacti in the foreground, we see a married couple flanked by palm trees; there is also the outline of numerous palm trees in the distance as well as a homestead in the left background. This is a poignant matrimonial moment. Together, reinforcing each other, the middle-aged Chicano couple, one with broom in hand, the other with a pail of feed, have stopped their activities for a moment to experience the beauty of their land in the well-lit sky. The wife, apron-clad, looks out on the horizon with a countenance somewhat hidden but which hints at awe and esthetic pleasure. The husband, cowboy hat firmly on his head and stitched leather belt around his ample waist, looks directly but ambiguously at us. He would seem to beckon the viewer to glimpse emphatically and share vicariously his agrarian lifestyle and the positive feelings he derives from his environment and his work. With earthen tones complemented by a subtly toned sky, strong pure colors in the woman's dress and the man's blue jeans, and close attention to every detail of animal, plant, and human, Hinojosa has created a moving depiction of the pleasures of rural life in the fertile Rio Grande valley.

Diane Gamboa, *Little Gold Man.* PLATE 28. Diane Gamboa has been a member of ASCO (literally, loathing), a conceptual multimedia performance art group, and this work evokes the qualities of performance as well as visual art. All of the figures look out at the viewer and none at each other, emphasizing the solipsistic, self-centered quality of the personages and, at the same time, the sense that they are performing for us. The performance quality of the characters is further reinforced by their stylized dress and the patterning and stylization of their bodies, which evoke an ancient art. Some of these characters represent characteristic Chicano or Chicana types, such as the bare-chested man sitting on the left sporting a heart-shaped pendant with a sword through it, the character reminiscent of a zoot-suiter at the right front, and his *chola* counterpart with the crucifix at the left front. Other figures go far beyond the socially recognizable, such as the hot-pink Minotauran figure, part human and part animal. Within this "scene"

each figure is immersed in his or her own thing and the little gold man is only a minor novelty, a sort of logical extension of the milieu that has been created. The little gold man has more of the qualities of an ancient figurine than a creature of flesh and blood. But in this environment that mimics a social event but that is without social interaction, none of the other personages pays the little gold man the slightest attention. Interspersed with the characters are numerous works of art in the form of sculptures that cultivate the grotesque and perhaps extend it further, parodically in the case of the excessively cubistic head on a pedestal in the top central background.

Frank Romero, *California Plaza.* PLATE 29. Southern California is the center of the national and international film industry, and this work plays with that fact using the icon of the spotlight. California Plaza is in the heart of downtown Los Angeles. In that area one finds in close proximity urban landmarks as varied as the Cathedral of Our Lady of the Angels, the Pacific Stock Exchange, Great Performances, which features free concerts and the like, the criminal courthouse, the Los Angeles Music Center, and the Museum of Contemporary Art. In this work the spotlight penetrates into the heart of a "crowned" theater and fixes on a full-size performer with a cowboy hat and a guitar, and a diminutive cowboy. Center City is where much of the Chicano/Latino population lives. The spotlight on performers in a theater with a flamboyant crown surrounded by high-rise buildings seems to allude indirectly to the burgeoning presence and increasing control of the levers of power and prestige by Chicanos and other Latinos. On the surface, like Romero's *Frutas y verduras* or Yáñez's *Monthter,* this work seems to recreate the perspective and drawing style of a juvenile, but packaged in this polka-dotted and dreamy composition is a subtle reference to the passing of the mantle to a new world order.

Joe López, *Eggs for Sale.* PLATE 30. This work, with a theme similar to John Valadez's *Robert and Liz* and Ester Hernández's *Los Recyclers,* depicts an older couple functioning on the fringes of the standard economy. They are working out of their truck and have only one item to sell: eggs. The prominent sign next to their business indicating

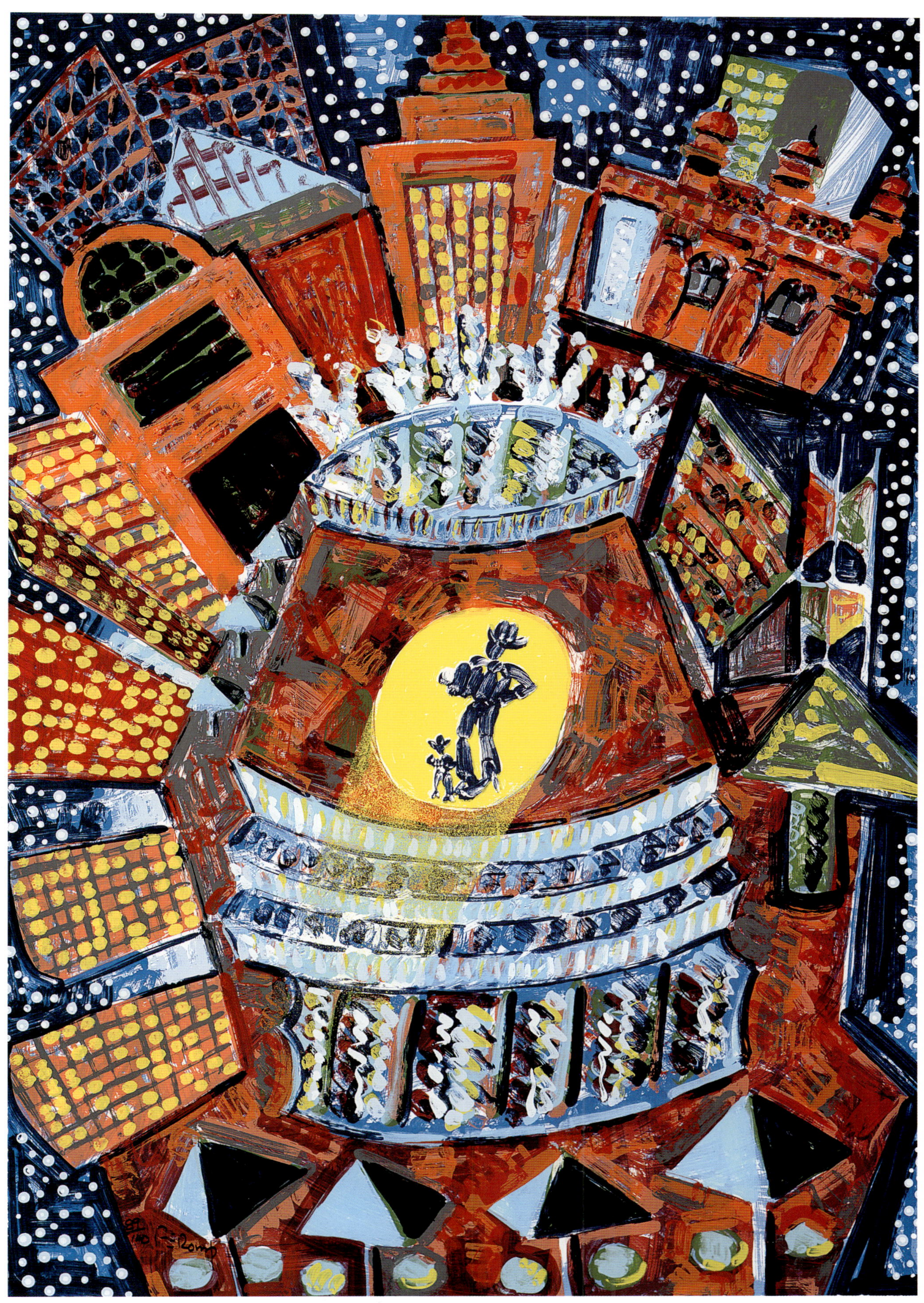

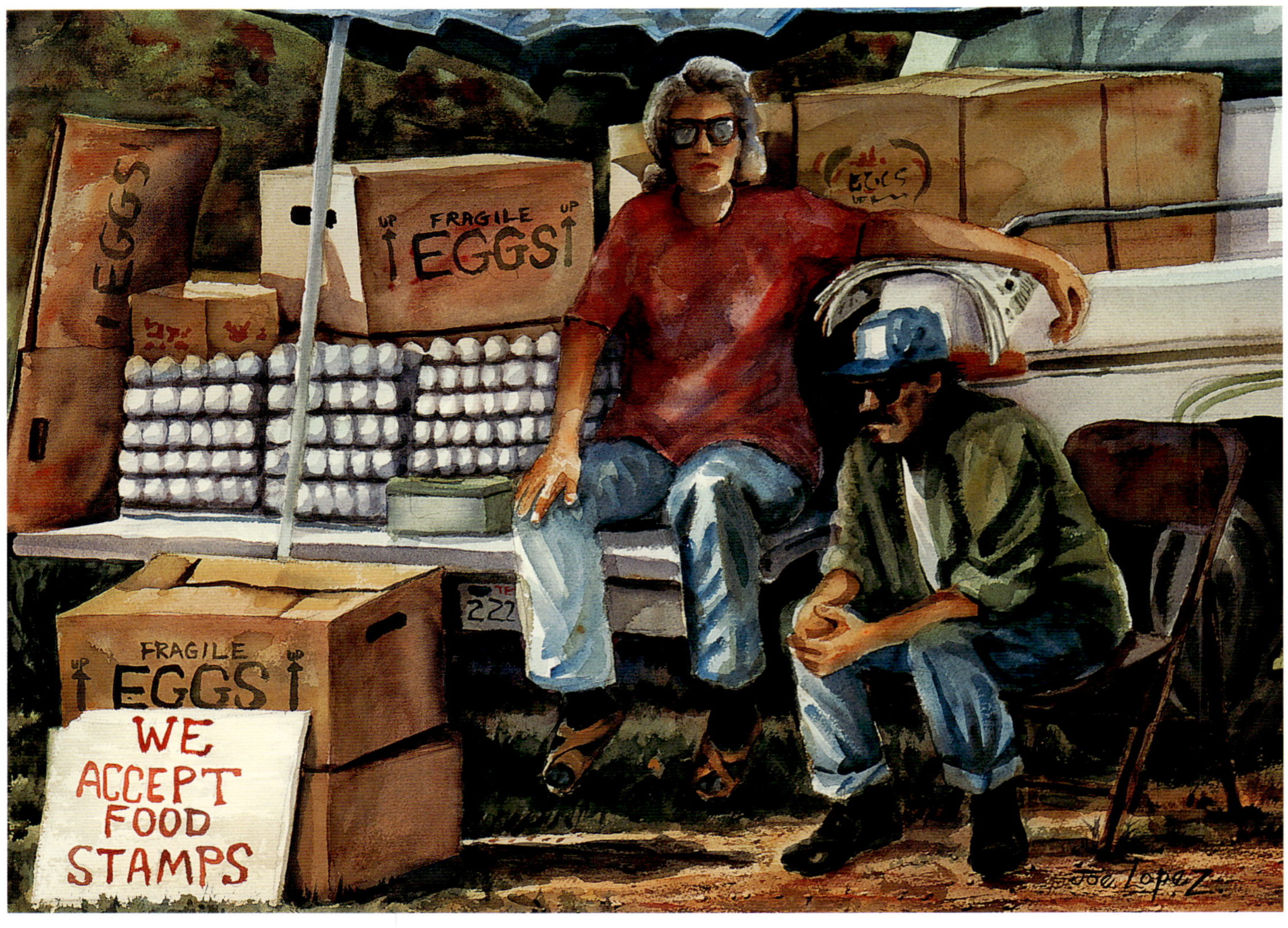

30 Joe López, *Eggs for Sale*, 1998, watercolor, 30" x 37.5"

that they will accept food stamps is a key element of the work, evoking an alternative, hardscrabble life that exists at the margins of the normal economy. While on the one hand the egg might be considered symbolic of a possible gestating future, in this work it functions in a more ironic role, expressing the mass commodification of life. These eggs that do not hatch but are eaten indifferently do not indicate the seed of the future, but rather express a sort of inertia and the harnessing of the forces of life. The sense of commodification is further reinforced by the expressions and posture of the couple and the flat, uncontrastive color scheme of the work. Tedium, getting by, a glum routine, marginalization from the core economy, and a somewhat itinerant lifestyle (as expressed by the truck) are the hallmarks of this work. Both this piece and Valadez's *Robert and Liz* depict aspects of lower socioeconomic lifestyles, but the emotional charges

evoked by each work are highly contrastive. Yet, while the emotional wellsprings place these two works at opposite poles, all three, *Eggs for Sale*, *Robert and Liz*, and *Los Recyclers* have in common images of togetherness, the bonds of family, the determination to make it on one's own without shirking, and a willingness to work hard and live up to responsibilities no matter what economic conditions or life in general offers.

Frank Romero, *Frutas y verduras* (Fruits and vegetables). PLATE 31. This work features colors that one might initially associate with a child's crayons, although upon further inspection we observe that in fact the work is executed in subtle pastels and that the color scheme travels a swathe of the color spectrum from blue on the left to a dusty rose on the right so that the colors simulate the motion of the truck. The choice of theme, the way it is composed, and the way it is executed also overtly echo the drawing style of a schoolboy. The selection of the archetypal moving truck, the creation of a frame for the truck within the bounds of the work, the flatness of the subject and lack of perspective, the rudimentary but gracefully childlike clouds above and what seems to be grass below, all suggest the re-creation of a school child's effort. As with several other works discussed here including *Eggs for Sale, Robert and Liz,* and *Los Recyclers,* the world of work is strongly evoked here, but in a manner that is unique to itself, highlighting both nostalgia for an earlier era and good humor. This is an early model truck equipped for the sale of fruits and vegetables from a time of family entrepreneurship before local supermarkets and especially the megastores of the contemporary Southwest. With its jaunty driver in a cowboy hat from which a conch brim gleams, and with a scale on one end and a hood ornament that is larger than life and as jocular as an exalted Christmas ornament on the other, this work exudes good feelings and the creative wellsprings of childhood.

Carmen Lomas Garza, ***Nopalitos frescos*** (Fresh nopal cactus pads or leaves). PLATE 32. Cactus leaves are an edible food and in certain parts of the Chicano community such as the Rio Grande Valley they are picked and prepared in various ways. For example, they may be used to make a marinated salad, as the flavoring of ice cream (prickly pear ice cream), or made into candy or jelly. The way this is usually done is to prune back a healthy plant by cutting off some of the newest growth, thus doing no harm to the living cactus as a whole, which will simply grow back the severed part. In this work, the artist depicts the procedure in a somewhat educational or clinical manner for both the edification and delight of the viewer. We are shown a close-up of the process so that what is displayed are just the cactus (which often grows quickly in the bright sunlight under good conditions)

31 Frank Romero, *Frutas y verduras* (Fruits and vegetables), 1989, serigraph, 24" x 36"

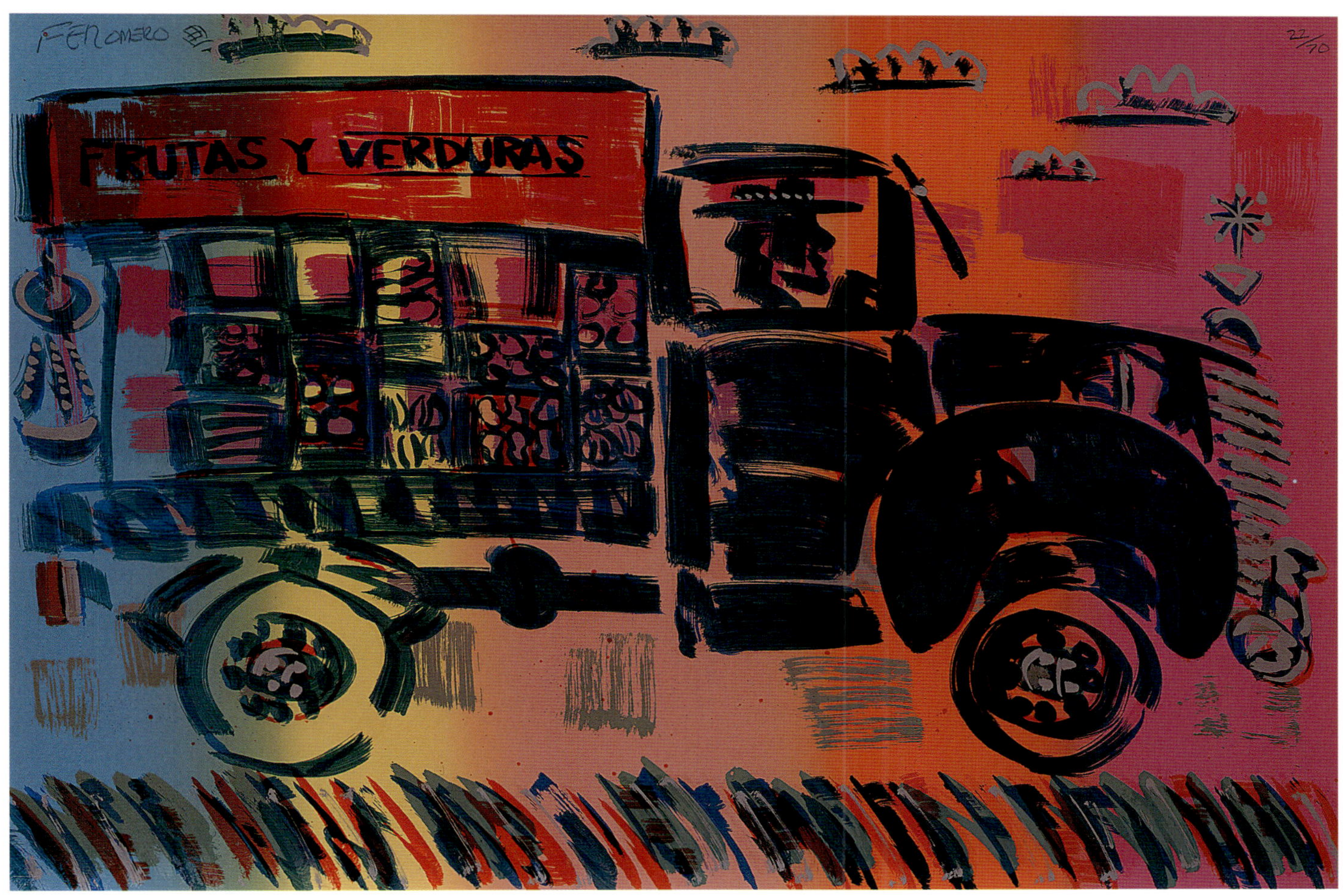

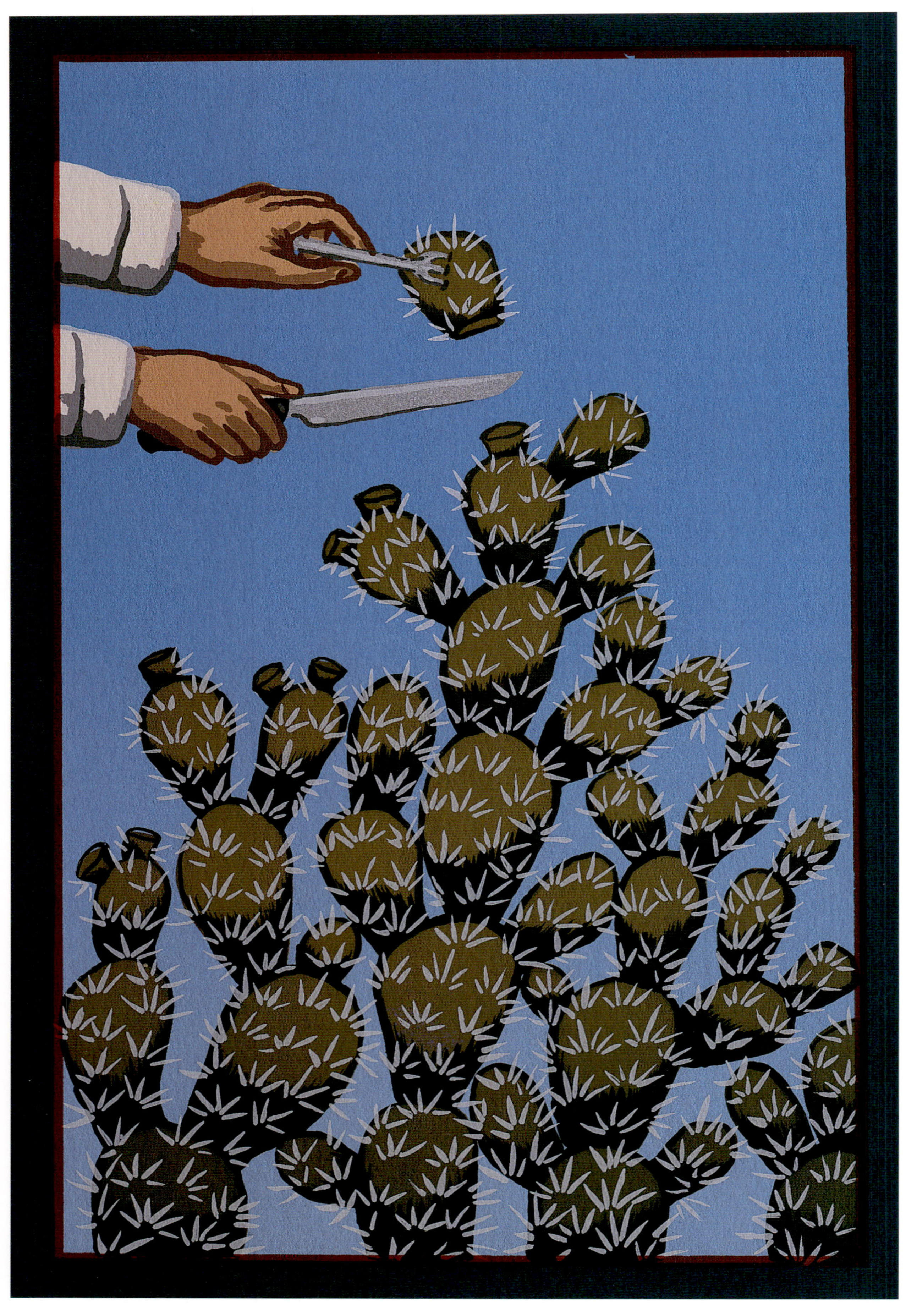

32 Carmen Lomas Garza, *Nopalitos frescos* (Fresh nopal cactus pads), 1979, lithograph, 17.5" x 14"

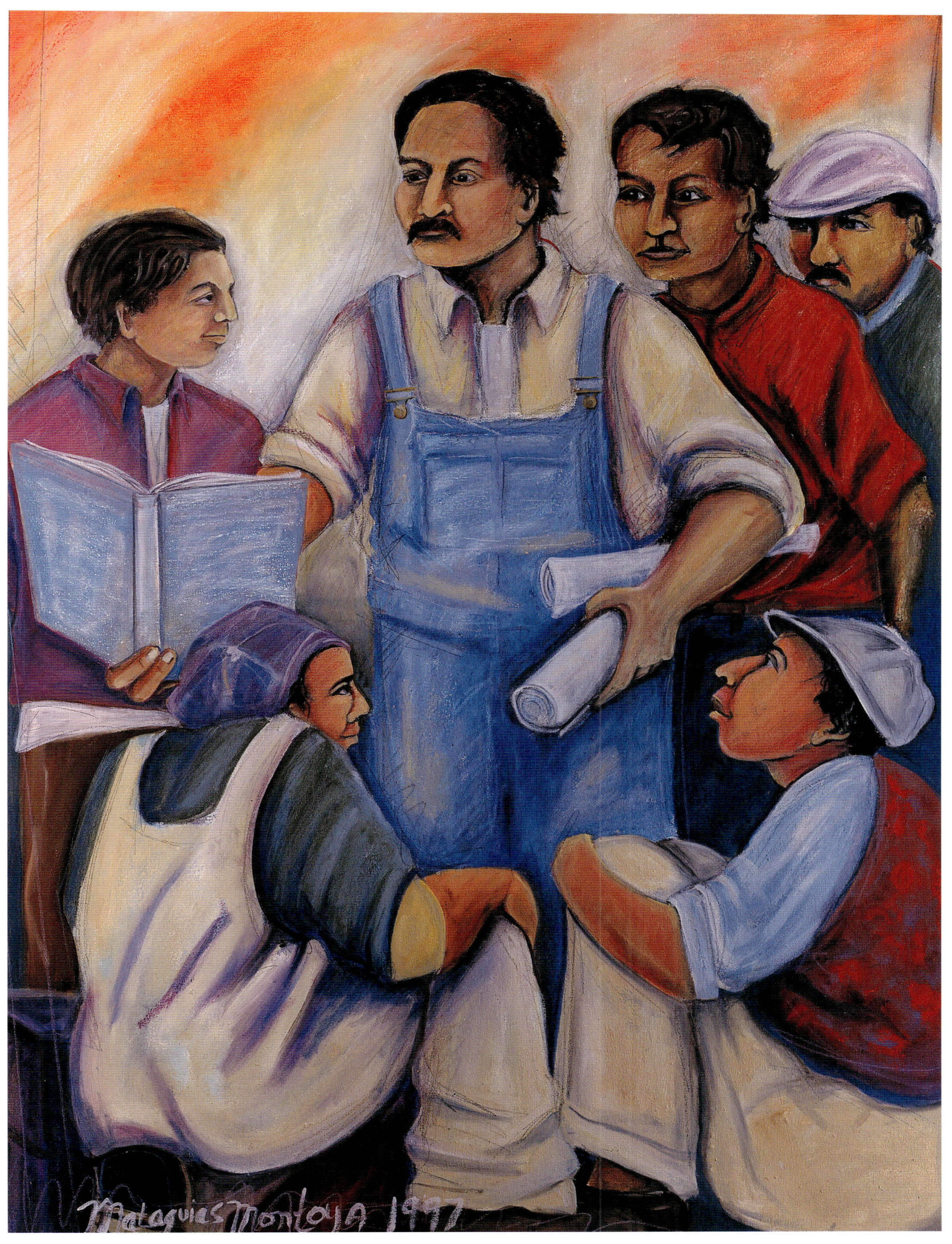

33 Malaquías Montoya, *Un maestro pa'l futuro* (A teacher for the future), 1997, oil on canvas, 48.5" x 36.5"

against a solid blue sky and a pair of outstretched hands with a knife and fork. A conflict is established between the cactus with its sharp, protective thorns and the anticipated succulence that will come of the harvested parts once they have been prepared. Thus the hands appear securely distanced from the thorns and a long knife and fork are used. The manner in which this is shown has such an immediacy that it implies that the cutter will be eating his or her bounty upon capturing it. But of course, that is not the case at all. Garza, who usually depicts life in the locale of her childhood and adult formation, the Rio Grande Valley (she now lives in San Francisco), has a very close rapport with her community, and her work is highly regarded for its fidelity to the folk reality of the area.

Malaquías Montoya, *Un maestro pa'l futuro* (A teacher for the future). PLATE 33. Montoya's depiction of a working-class hero and role model, the teacher, has close associations with the Mexican mural movement, especially as cultivated by Diego Rivera. This is a work that the working class can readily understand and empathize with. The central figure, as in a mural with its thematic "lesson," is in fact the teacher. However, in contrast to the conventional teacher of the classroom who is removed from his or her subject and students to a certain degree, this work breaks down barriers of all kinds. This is on-the-job teaching where no distinction is felt between the world of work and the world of learning. There are no class barriers, either. The teacher is clearly a working man who appears in his overalls, with his sleeves rolled up, but who also has assimilated bookish learning and what appear to be diagrams or perhaps construction or architectural plans. The teacher, with a countenance of utmost control, care, and authority, has in his outstretched arm an open book for all of his pupils—young working men including perhaps an adolescent or two—to study and learn from under his guidance. The esteem for the teacher among his working-class disciples is palpable. In front of the *maestro* are two young men who look up at their teacher. The three others look over his shoulder or his arm. The expressions range from rapt attention to pleasure to careful scrutiny of the open book. This work, executed in colors highly typical of the Mexican mural, is a fitting tribute to a working-class role model who at the same time fulfills the ambitions for learning and economic advancement that have characterized the Mexican and Chicano populations since the Mexican Revolution of 1910.

David Rosales, *San Bernardino Art Gallery.* PLATE 34. San Bernardino, a small city in the interior of Southern California, is not particularly known for its art scene, and this art gallery turns out to be nothing more than an outdoor wall and a moonlit turf that serve as a basis for imagination, posing, and various symbols, a sort of "Coney Island of the Mind," to quote Lawrence Ferlinghetti's celebrated poem. A creative exchange and tension is set up between the *vato loco* (the street dude), engaged in practicing or acting out his persona, and the artist with the face of a clown who is busy doing his own thing, completing a mural. Neither is facing the other or paying the other attention. The mural is purposely obscure and shrouded, as would be appropriate to the night and the lack of viewers. But we do know that it is replete with a riot of motifs. The entire wall has the feel of a gallery of icons that are now inert, dark, and in reserve but that could come out and be exposed and developed at some point. In contrast to the wall, but in a certain sense complementary to it, are the rehearsals of the *vato loco.* They are being perfected and have the potential of finding for themselves a proper, appreciative audience. The far left part of the outdoors appears rather like a science fiction environment, possibly with a flying saucer. *San Bernardino Art Gallery,* symbolic of a Chicano inventory of potential creativity, evokes a repertorial and iconic storage place that at some future time can be activated and emerge to be publicly viewed and esthetically judged.

José Treviño, *Sonido del barrio* (Sound of the barrio). PLATE 35. A solitary figure is sitting on a stool in a vast outdoor setting, accompanied by two attentive dogs (Chihuahuas perhaps) with their tails at attention. He has a bottle of soda pop and a working man's lunchbox at his side, and it is sunset—the crepuscular moment when the setting sun merges into eventide. In the background there is the outline of a few homes and what appears to be a cupola with a cross atop it, a hint of the architectural features of the Texas missions. The man plays his accordion, an instrument characteristic of Texas and

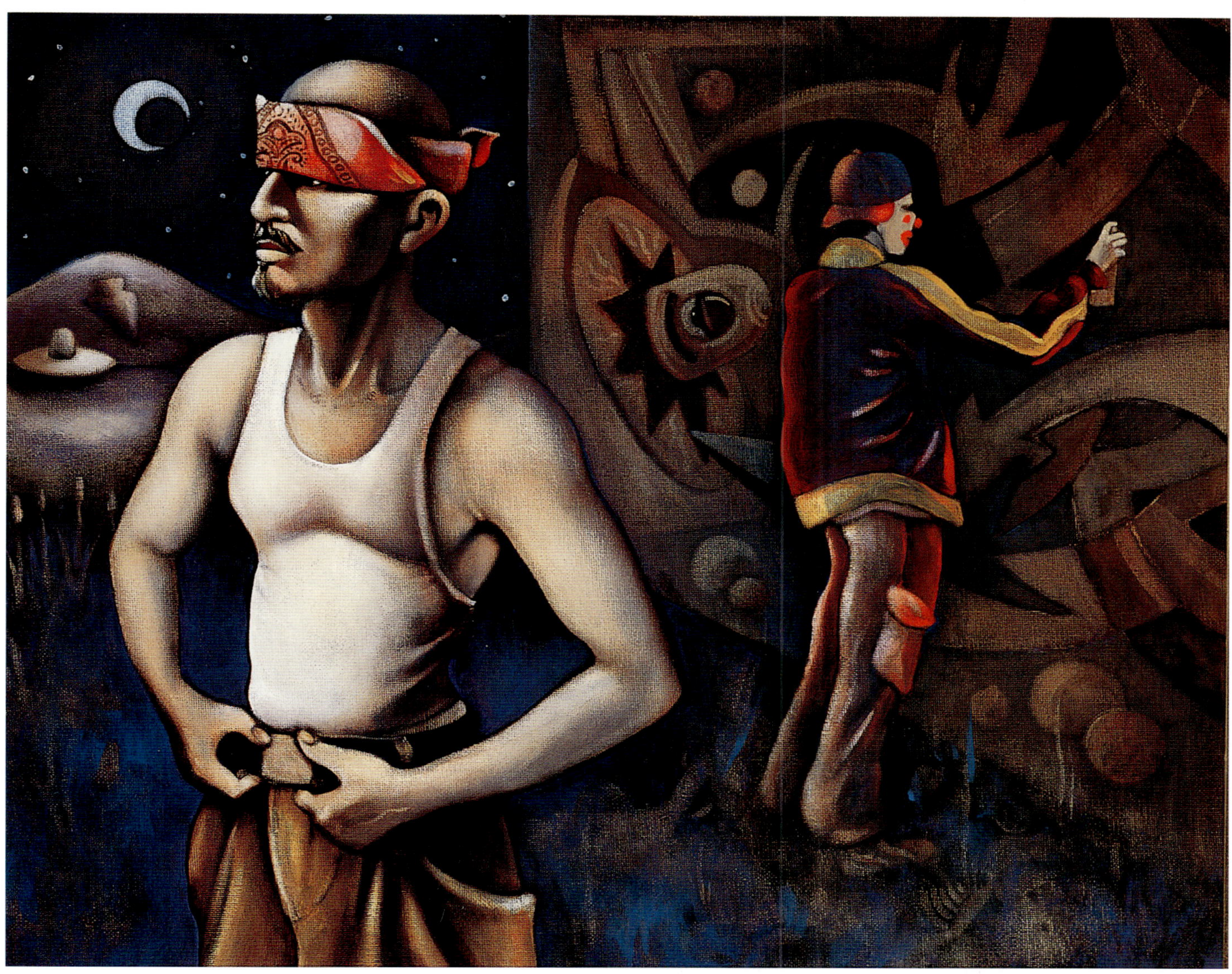

34 David Rosales, *San Bernardino Art Gallery*, 2003, oil on canvas, 16" x 20"

that portion of northern Mexico adjoining the state (before 1836 all of this land was part of Mexico) with its confluence of Bohemian German and Mexican culture. There is a cartoonlike quality in the image. Using the technique of the comic strip, the accordion-playing worker seems to be conjuring up from his mind and heart, through pixies and musical notes that rise from him, two majestic dancing figures, one male and one female, who bridge the waning sunlight and waxing starlight and dance in a characteristic contemporary style. Space bathed in the reds and oranges of sunset predominates but, also cartoonlike, immediately behind the accordion player are the imprints of two bare feet that from opposite orientations and therefore directions appear to meet behind his body. They would seem to point to the confluence of cultures once again, accentuating the bicultural accordion and the *norteño* music that it creates. The vastness of Texas and the musical and cultural sustenance that underpin it and make it habitable and palatable, the resources that the worker has at his disposal to make his life relevant, and the notion that we are more than our mere solitary entities and that our lives and enterprises are configured in the land and in the firmament are all implied in this work.

Overleaf: 35 José Treviño, *Sonido del barrio* (Sound of the barrio), 1995, serigraph, 30" x 22"

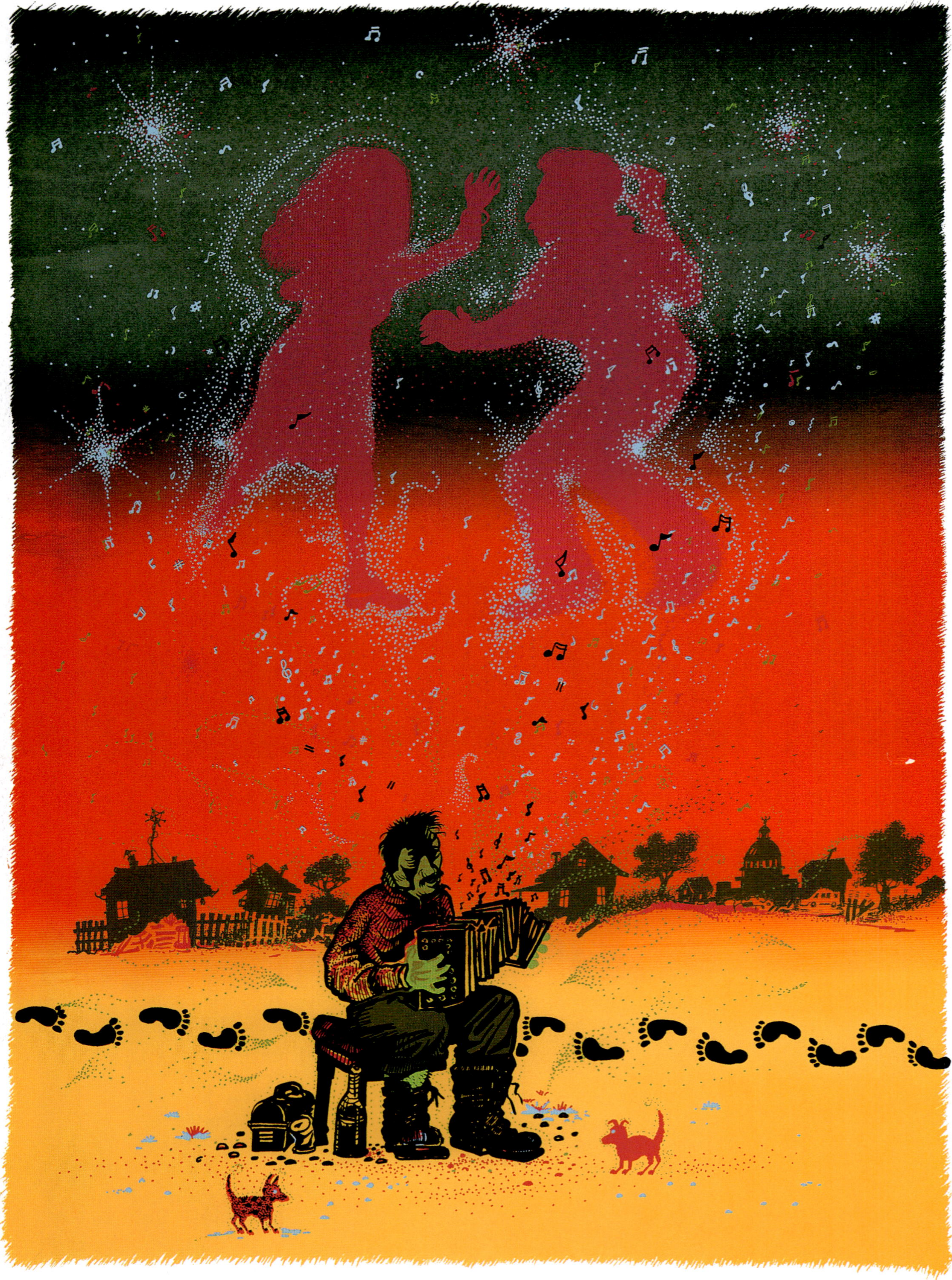

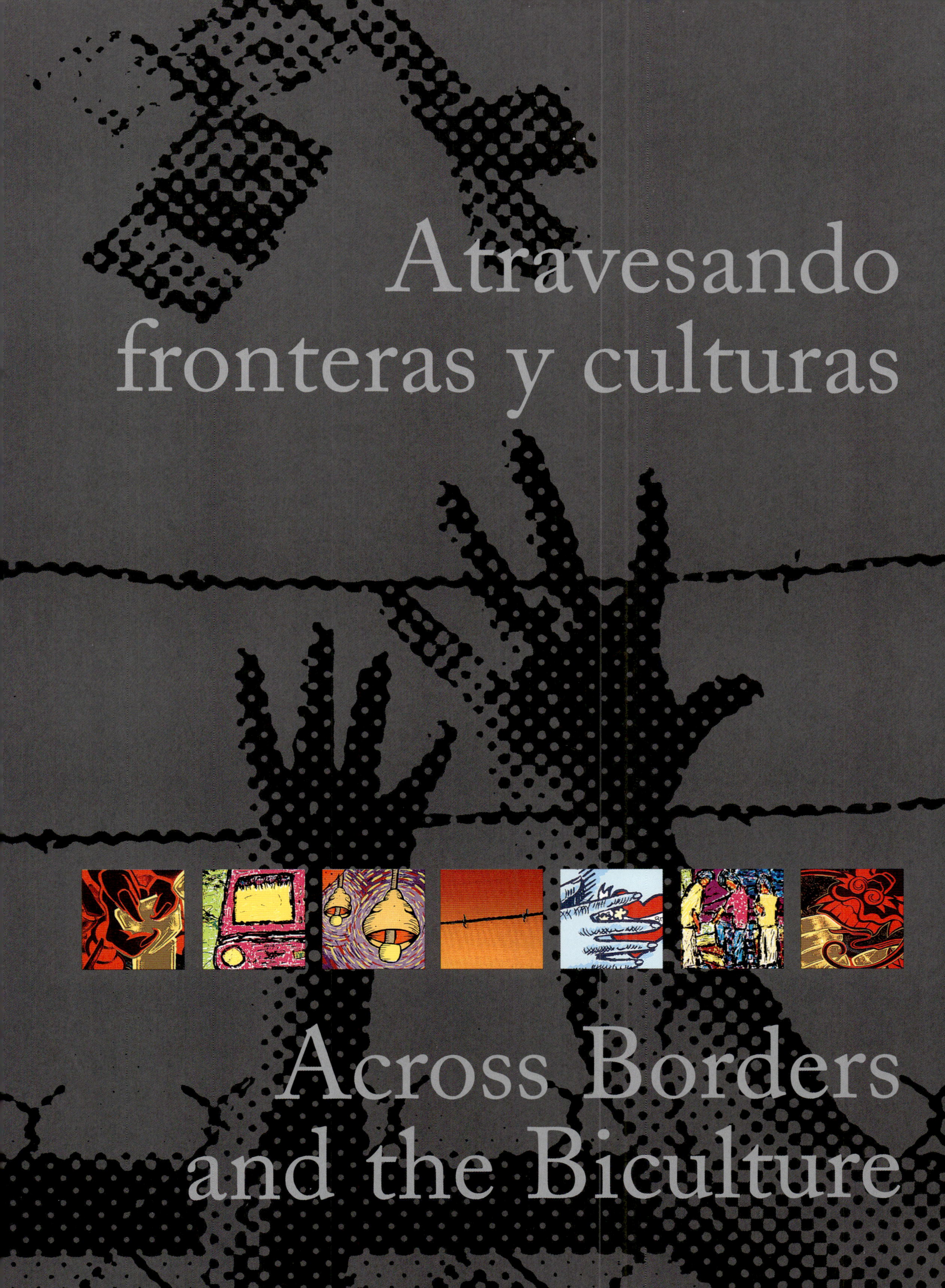
Atravesando
fronteras y culturas

Across Borders
and the Biculture

he term "border" (and by extension, "borderland" and "borderland studies" has assumed added dimensions in recent years, and this exhibition honors some of those additional resonances. In the case of this exhibition and the Chicana/o culture it evokes, the meaning of border in the usual demarked sense is used, and of course this denotation is clearly the United States-Mexican border, a "shatter zone" that paradoxically brings together—sometimes tensely, sometimes corruptly, but often ingeniously and imaginatively—the economic and cultural features of one of the wealthiest and most powerful nations in the world and those of a nation that is evolving from an underdeveloped status. Moreover, "border" has come to mean, more generally, a line drawn in various ways, the marking where adjacent jurisdictions meet. This combined conjunction and separation creates, in the domain of this exhibition, a zone in which diverse and sometimes seemingly incompatible cultural, linguistic, folk, attitudinal, and other social phenomena are regulated, hidden, examined, parodied, sublimated, modulated, fused, synthesized, and transcended.

Clearly, borderlands have historically often been the locale of major folk cultural achievements. The border often exposes a line of opportunity, although sometimes those opportunities are built upon covert features. People often express themselves artistically about themselves and others at the border: they regulate exchange and avoid regulation; they struggle to survive in an environment frequently shaped by the practices of superordinate structures or forces such as nation-states and a global economy. These human acts of exposure, disclosure, disguise, entrepreneurship, and the like are not unique to borders, but they occur there with a clarity and urgency that command our attention. This is an especially rich theme for Chicana and Chicano art, since the Chicano occupies a strange and unique place in the interface of both American and Mexican culture, sometimes not accepted by either and at other times signaled as a model of an evolving new world (b)order.

This theme is divided into three sections. "Yuxtaposición" favors artistic works that bring together in highly novel ways elements of Chicano and mainstream culture in lifestyles that are extraordinarily difficult to digest, synthesize, or transcend. Oil and water do not mix but they do coexist in various ways. Primary features of the works in this theme are novelty, surprise, and at times even cultural ambush. "Transición" depicts works in which there appears to be a sense of movement across culture and value systems and in some cases a trajectory of transculturalism. "Nuevo milenio" (new millennium) is the designation we have chosen to categorize a group of works that appear to take elements from both Mexican or Chicano and mainstream or other cultures and combine them artfully in such a way that the end product approaches a new identity that is more than the sum of its parts.

YUXTAPOSICIÓN

Charles "Chaz" Bojórquez, *ChinoLatino* (ChineseLatin). PLATE 36. Chaz Bojórquez is a graffiti artist, a street writer who has made the transition to painting on canvas and displaying his art in museums and galleries. His canvases and works on paper continue to explore the social and political uses of graffiti to mark the territory and give voice to the marginalized populations in Los Angeles, Bojórquez's home city. *ChinoLatino*, a serigraph based on a painting of the same title, is a comment on the cultural makeup of Los Angeles. Bojórquez believes that Latinos have more in common with Asians than with black or white cultures. In this piece he develops this view by juxtaposing the powerful Asian symbol of the dragon with the traditional Los Angeles style of graffiti, a form Bojórquez has studied and practiced extensively together with Asian calligraphy. This work, consistent with current artistic and intellectual practice, extends the concept of border beyond the narrow denotation of a line between adjoining territories and polities. In the current world of speedy travel and the nearly instantaneous transmission of visual, aural, and textual information, it is sensible to establish a zone of connection between east and west, especially in Los Angeles with its huge population clusters from both worlds. The Asian dragon is reminiscent of the Aztec feathered serpent god Quetzalcoatl, and the Los Angeles-style graffiti are compatible with traditional Asian calligraphy, further connecting Asian and Latino cultures in this piece.

Candace M. Briceño, *Las rosas de mi güelita* (My grandma's roses; *güelita* is a version of *abuelita*, grandmother). PLATE 37. Candace Briceño has in common with other artists in this exhibition such as Arreguín and Oropeza the use of patterning as a thematic or visual device (see the former's *La Malinche*

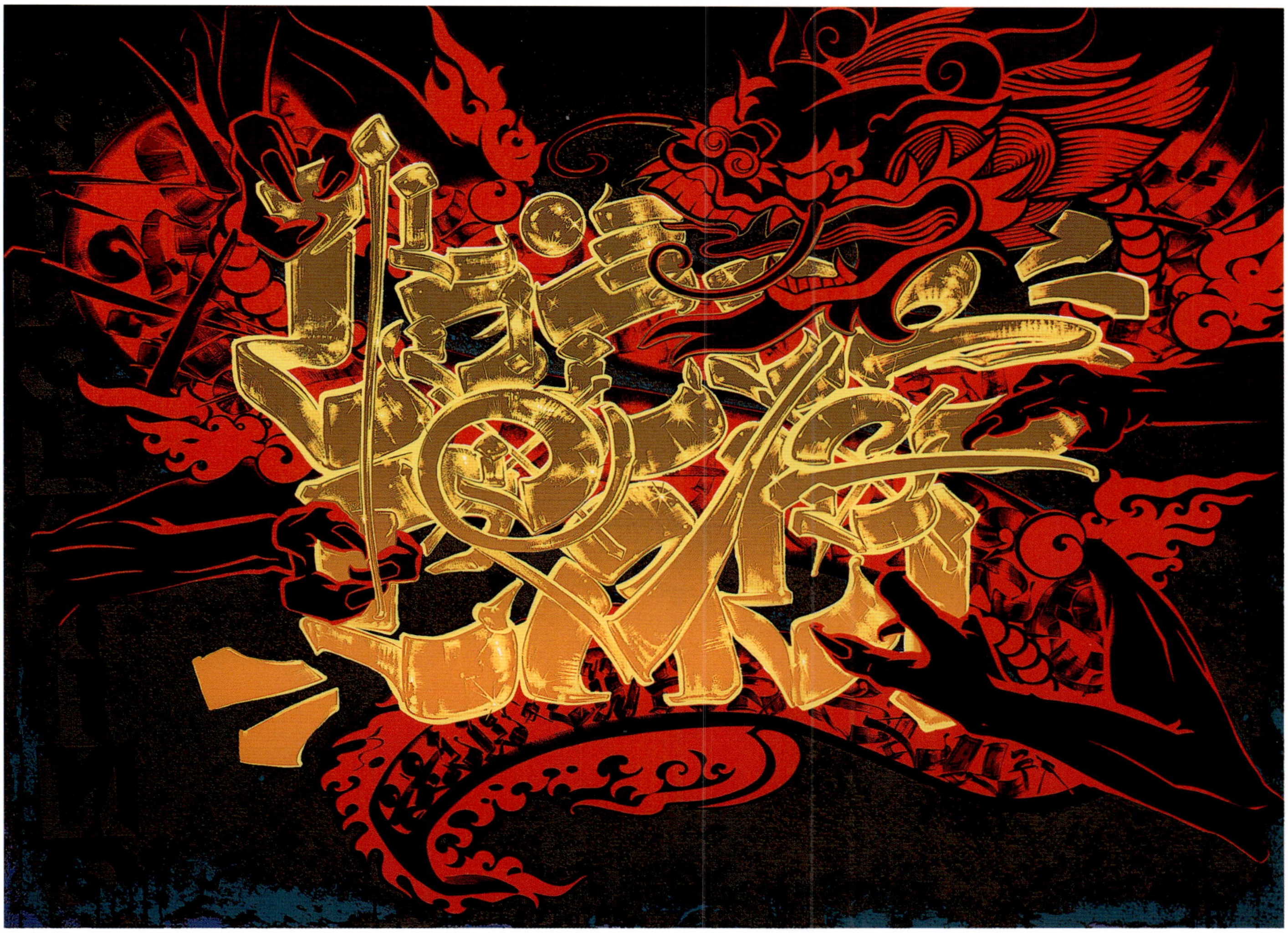

36 Charles "Chaz" Bojórquez, *ChinoLatino* (ChineseLatin), 2001, serigraph, 31" x 42"

and *Frida's Messengers* and the latter's *Héchale*). Flowers and family gardens were a constant presence as she grew up in San Antonio, and for the artist they symbolize life, growth, and the people she loves. She often uses flowers and floral patterns extensively in her art for thematic purposes. In this serigraph, Briceño uses a field of red roses to represent cherished memories of her grandmother. Briceño speaks only English, and her grandmother only Spanish. Roses became a point of connection and communication between the artist and her grandmother, something they both understood that required no words. Briceño depicts the red blooms on a sunny yellow bed of color. These are roses with no leaves, weeds, or thorns, nothing to distract or mar her memories of the time she and her grandmother spent together. Against the golden background the roses stand out prominently, pointing to indelible memories that are retained in the mind's eye.

Isabel Martínez, *VG Got Her Green Card.*
PLATE 8. Isabel Martínez came to California from Mexico in the early 1980s to pursue a better life for herself, and much of her artwork is an expression of her life as an immigrant. She is acutely aware of the difficulties faced by a Mexican trying to fit in with the majority culture without losing her soul. In this mixed media piece, she depicts the Virgin of Guadalupe's experiences as identical to those of so many immigrants who have come to this country. Martínez knows her well—well enough to call her by her initials. The composition is of the Virgin's face as she holds up her new green card documentation. VG looks directly at the viewer, smiling broadly and proudly displaying the proof of her acceptance as a legal resident in the United States. Martínez uses bright colors to establish a bold and upbeat atmosphere. Departing from the traditional, respectful, yet distant depiction of the Virgin,

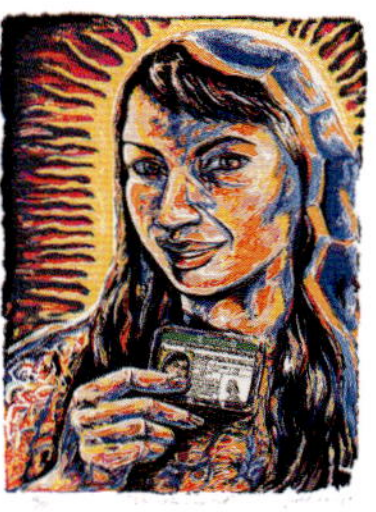

VG Got Her Green Card, see page 7

51

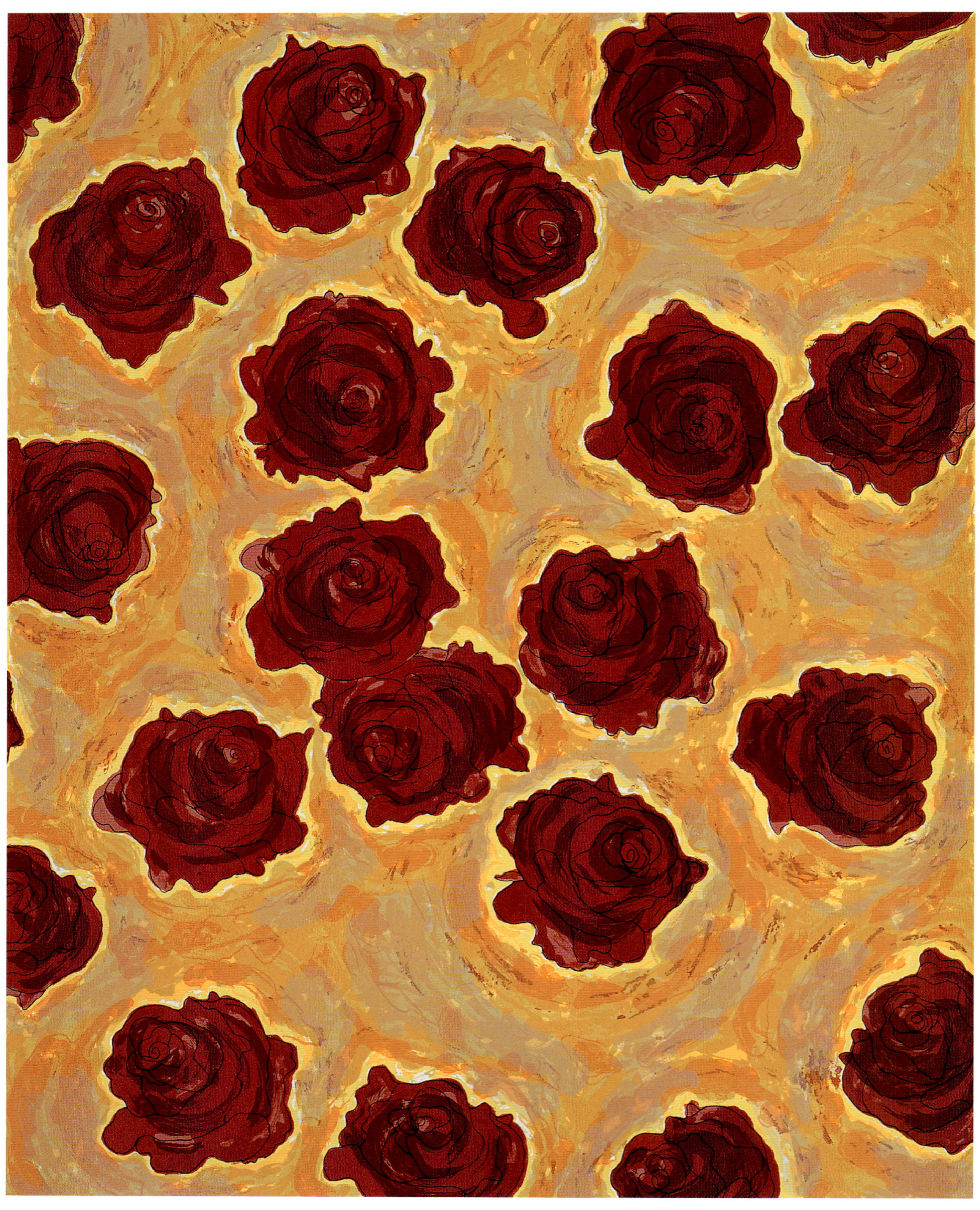

37 Candace M. Briceño, *Las rosas de mi güelita* (My grandma's roses), 1998
Serigraph, 28" x 22"

Martínez also establishes a humorous tone by connecting this religious icon with the contemporary world of Los Angeles and the daily cares of the average person. The Virgin of Guadalupe once functioned as a bridge between the Aztec and Hispanic belief systems. In Martínez's vision she now bridges the gap between traditional Mexican life and contemporary Chicano existence in the United States.

Rolando Briseño, *Bicultural Tablesetting.* PLATE 38. Food and the rituals of eating are experiences central to every culture. In this serigraph, Rolando Briseño uses the common ground of the mealtime table to suggest the divided nature of Chicano existence. The left half of the composition depicts a brightly flowered tablecloth similar to what might be used in a Mexican home. The right half shows the orderly pattern of a blue-and-white checked tablecloth commonly used in an American home. Two hands enter the frame from the opposite upper corners, an orange one from the left and a red one from the right. The orange hand points at the food on the plate. The red hand points at the orange hand. Almost literally, they point out the stark difference between the two halves of the composition and, by extension, of the Chicano self. The colors and pattern on the right side of the work are reminiscent of the American flag, and a TV remote control joins the table setting, as necessary an implement for an American meal as the knife, fork, and spoon. In the center of the composition is a dinner plate bearing a human figure and a swirl pattern, suggesting both the mixing of the two cultures and the confusion this can cause the bicultural individual.

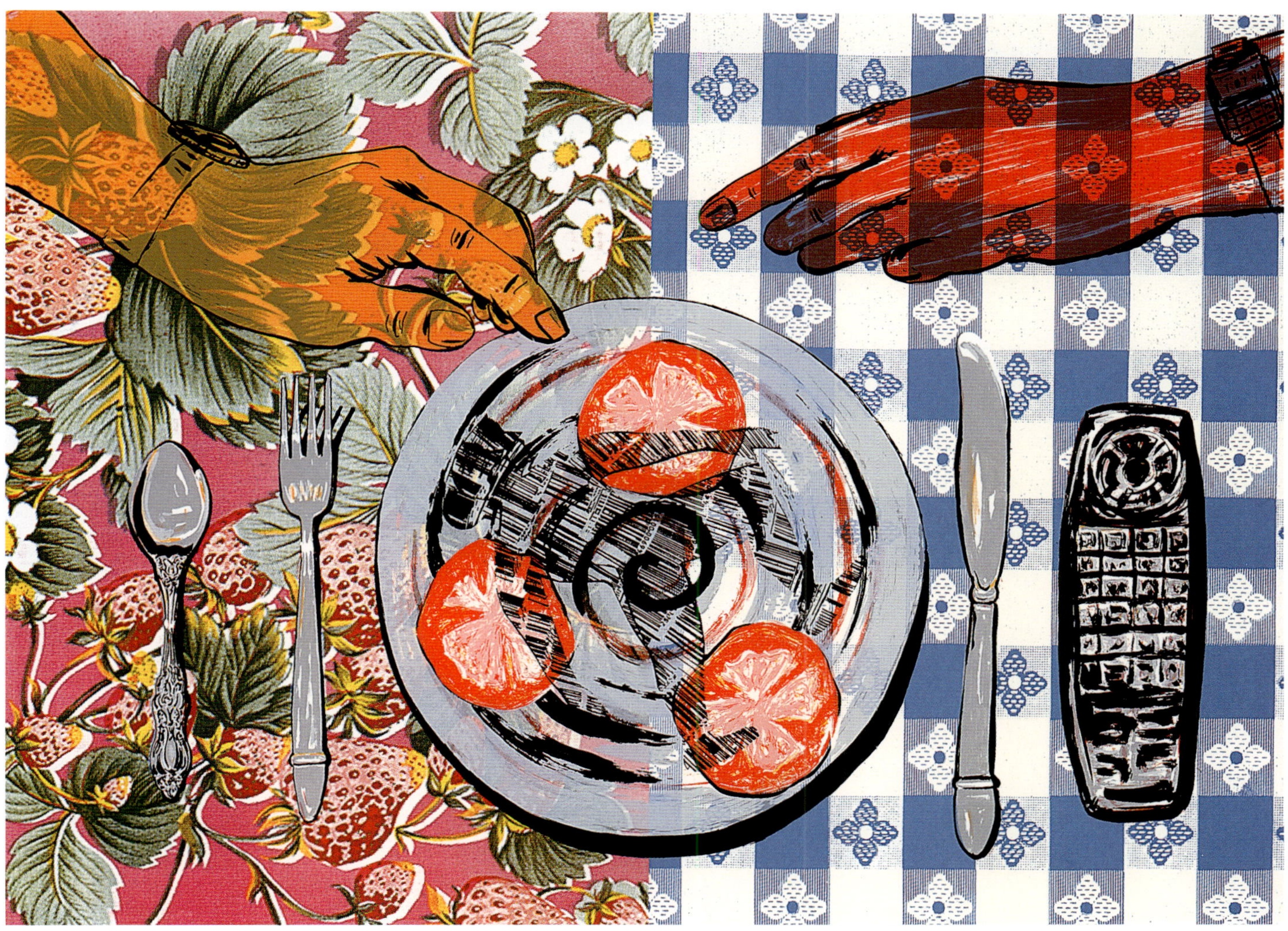

38 Rolando Briseño, *Bicultural Tablesetting*, 1998
Serigraph, 22" x 30"

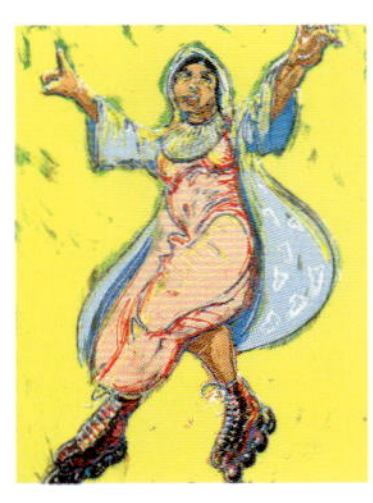

La Virgen de Venice,
see page xiii

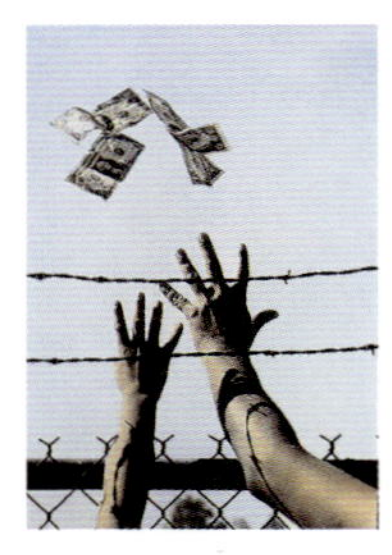

California Dreaming,
see page 6

Wayne Alaniz Healy, *La Virgen de Venice.* PLATE 5. Wayne Healy has been creating public art since the early 1970s and is widely known for his murals in East Los Angeles. This monoprint was made as part of a project in which artists explored the image of the Virgin of Guadalupe. Healy created a series of works that brought the Virgin into ordinary activities of everyday people, including the Virgin drinking at a bar, slam-dunking a basketball, and standing at a bus stop with a crying baby Jesus. The effect of desacralizing and bringing into urban contemporaneity an icon representing religious significance of the highest order that is usually situated in an age far removed in time is decidedly jarring, but in fact, Healy is following the precedent of other artists such as the Renaissance masters who portrayed the Virgin in European settings of the period. In this work he shows the Virgin on Rollerblades, engaged in one of the favorite recreations of people at Venice Beach. Healy shows her with her robes flowing, revealing the outline of her body with her arms and lower legs exposed. The colors are vibrant and the strong diagonal line created by the figure effectively creates the movement of an accomplished, dancing skater. This Virgin is a real person having a good time on a sunny day in contemporary American culture. Healy said about this series, "Although I'm Irish and Mexican, I'm not Catholic and so I guess I thought I could get away with my irreverence."

David Moreno, *Mona Maya.* PLATE 39. Leonardo Da Vinci's *Mona Lisa* is one of the best-known paintings in the world, and perhaps because of its notoriety, artists have often appropriated the image for their own purposes. For example, in 1919, when the world was celebrating the 400th anniversary of Leonardo's death and mass-producing cheap postcards of *La Gioconda,* Marcel Duchamp, one of the founders of the Dadaist movement, expressed the movement's revolt by taking one of the postcards and drawing a mustache and thin goatee on the face. David Moreno is not engaged in artistic provocation, but rather in synthesis and syncretism. *La Gioconda* was well known even in its own time for Leonardo's masterful technique and for the ideal female beauty expressed in the representation of the young woman. Moreno, a Texas artist who works as an illustrator and graphic designer, takes our knowledge of this classic European artwork and juxtapos-es it with the indigenous world of the Maya. The female figure is in the same pose as the Mona Lisa, with the same facial expression and position of the hands. The composition is also the same, with the figure in the foreground and a landscape in the background. In this version, however, the woman is wearing traditional Mayan dress and the landscape is a pastoral Yucatan setting. The bright colors are typical of Latin America and Mona herself is dark skinned. Moreno's juxtaposition of European and indigenous elements reminds us that not all classic beauty comes from Europe. It is worth noting that the Italian name Mona also means "cute" in Spanish.

TRANSICIÓN

Jacalyn López García, *California Dreaming.* PLATE 7. López García grew up in suburban California outside of Los Angeles. Her mother was an immigrant from Mexico who wanted her daughter to be an American girl and, because she was light-skinned and blonde, to pass for "white." Her mother's dream was that her child would have the privileges of being American that she herself never had, having grown up in poverty in Mexico. As a contrast, López García's dream, rather than being white, was to be like her mother. These conflicting dreams and desires led to confusion in López García and a belated understanding of herself as Chicana in her life and artwork. In *California Dreaming,* she depicts a foreboding barbed-wire fence and two hands frantically reaching to catch American dollars floating in the air above the fence. López García, who sees herself as primarily a digital media artist, created this piece as a sepia-toned, hand-tinted black-and-white photograph for use on a Web site exploring her upbringing. The piece functions as a metaphor for the desire of the Mexican poor to take part in some of the economic security believed to be across the border in the United States. The title, reminiscent of the 1960s pop song, suggests a deep longing to be in California instead of where one is now. López García says she created this piece in response to a part of her mother's life and, indeed, it reflects her thoughts on her mother's motivations in raising her as she did. She also sees it as a response to her memories of crossing the border with her mother as a young girl to visit poor relatives in Mexico.

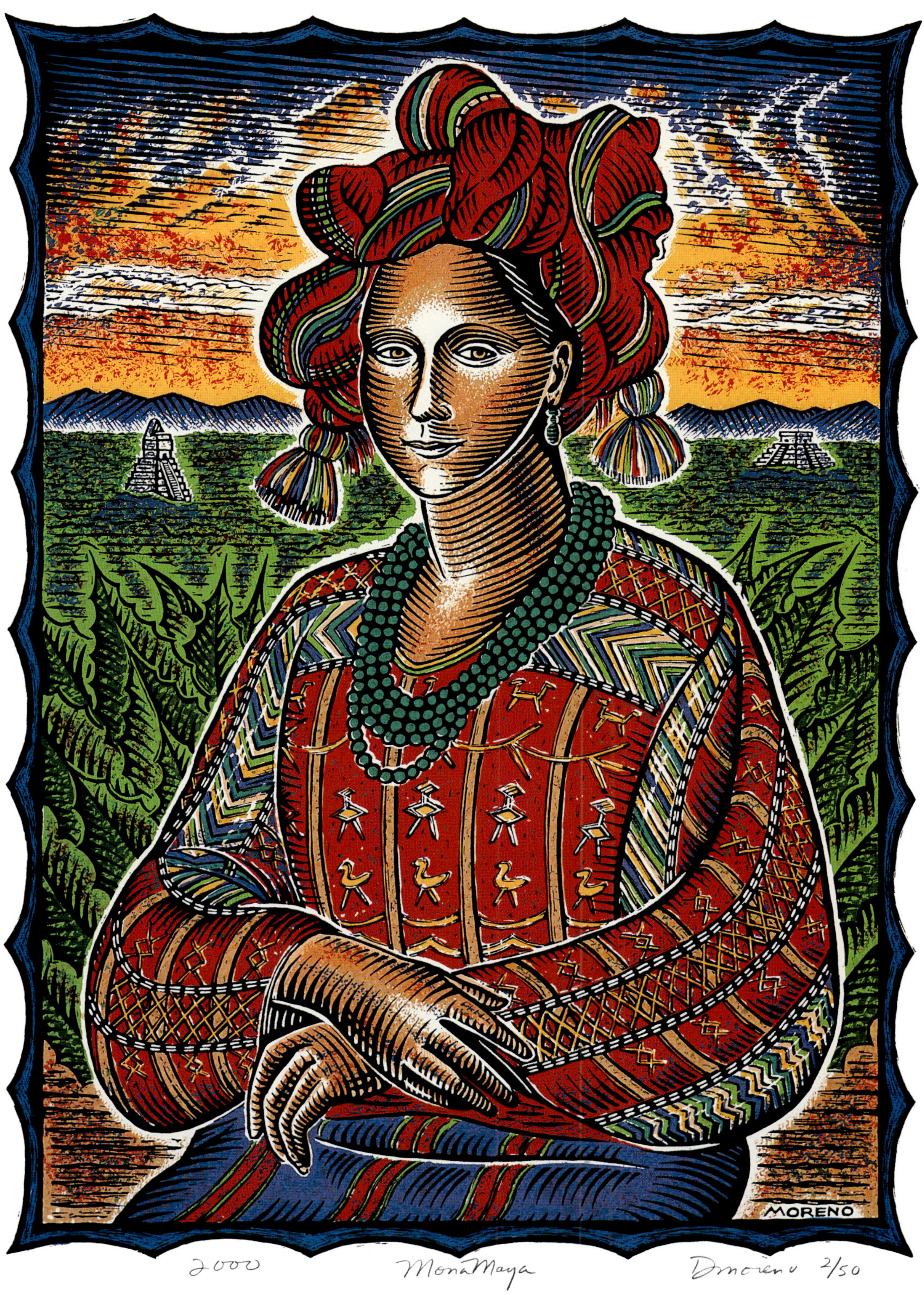
2000
MonaMaya
Dmoreno 2/50
MORENO

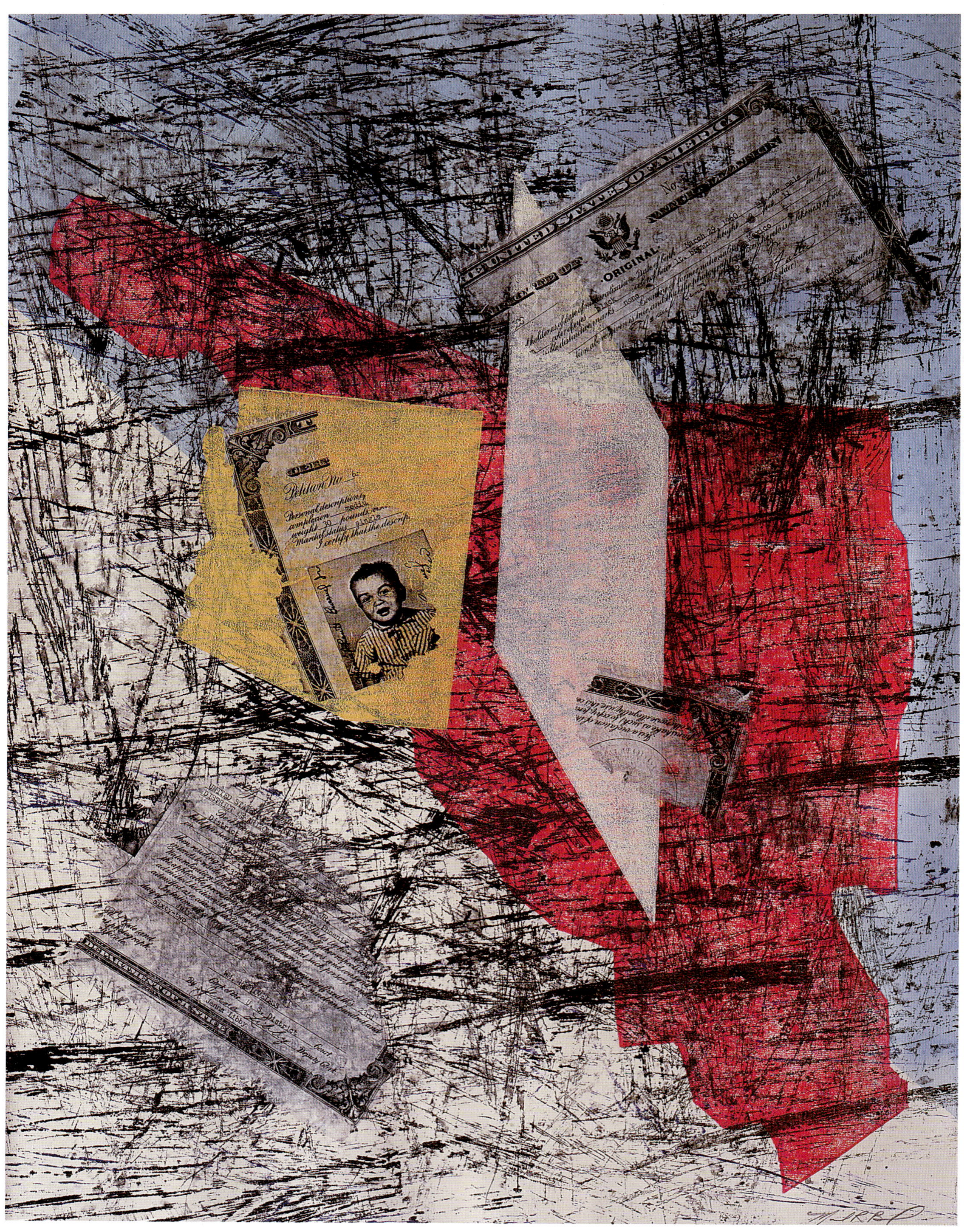

40 Manuel R. Burruel, *Self-Portrait: The Journey*, 1998, monotype with collage, 24" x 18.5"

Manuel R. Burruel, *Self-Portrait: The Journey.* PLATE 40. Burruel was born in Mexico, adopted by Mexican American parents, and brought to the United States as an infant when he was only a few weeks old. He grew up acutely aware of his cross-border background and his roots in Mexico. Growing up in a Mexican American family, he was surrounded by Mexican traditions but, at the same time, American culture was his norm. *Self-Portrait: The Journey* represents Burruel's exploration of these two sides of his personal history. In this monotype he uses layered images to contrast the geographic shapes of Arizona and Sonora. In the bottom layer, a diagonal line divides the composition, creating a literal border between the two halves. In the top layer, the artist's naturalization certificate is torn in pieces and scattered across the work, with the photograph of the baby Burruel resting squarely in the middle of the diagonal border. This composition suggests the parts that make up the whole of Burruel's life, their connection to Mexico and the United States, both of which he claims as his places of origin, and his intense feeling of being divided between the two. The maps represent the literal journey that Burruel took as a baby, from Sonora to Arizona, and the one he takes now in reverse as he explores his Mexican heritage and how the parts of his life fit together.

Ramón Ramírez, *No tocar la tierra.* PLATE 41. Horizontally composed to emphasize a wide panorama, this work depicts a calm, peaceful, astonishing sunset, the kind of sky so beautiful that we want to enjoy it together with family or friends. The brushstrokes are smooth, adding to the feeling of serenity. A section of barbed-wire fence cuts across the bottom of the work diagonally from the lower right corner, a violent contrast to the peace of nature's golden orange sky. Ramón Ramírez, trained as an architect and a painter, describes himself as an urban artist. Much of his work focuses on the built environment and the human perception of it. Ramírez has commented that this particular piece is open to a wide variety of interpretations. For example, the fence can be seen as the border between Mexico and the Unit-

41 Ramón Ramírez, *No tocar la tierra* (Do not touch the earth), 1991, acrylic on canvas, 24" x 36"

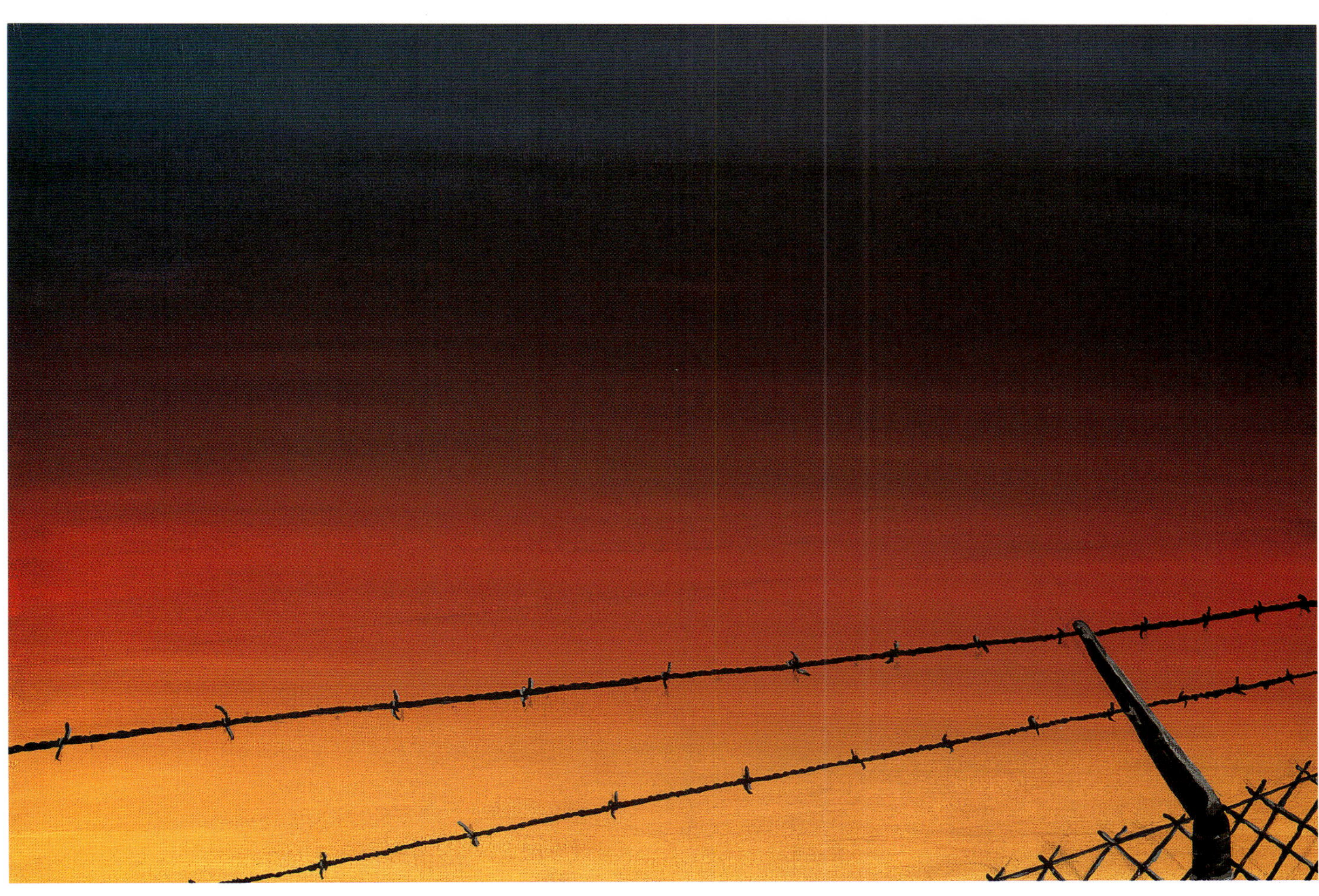

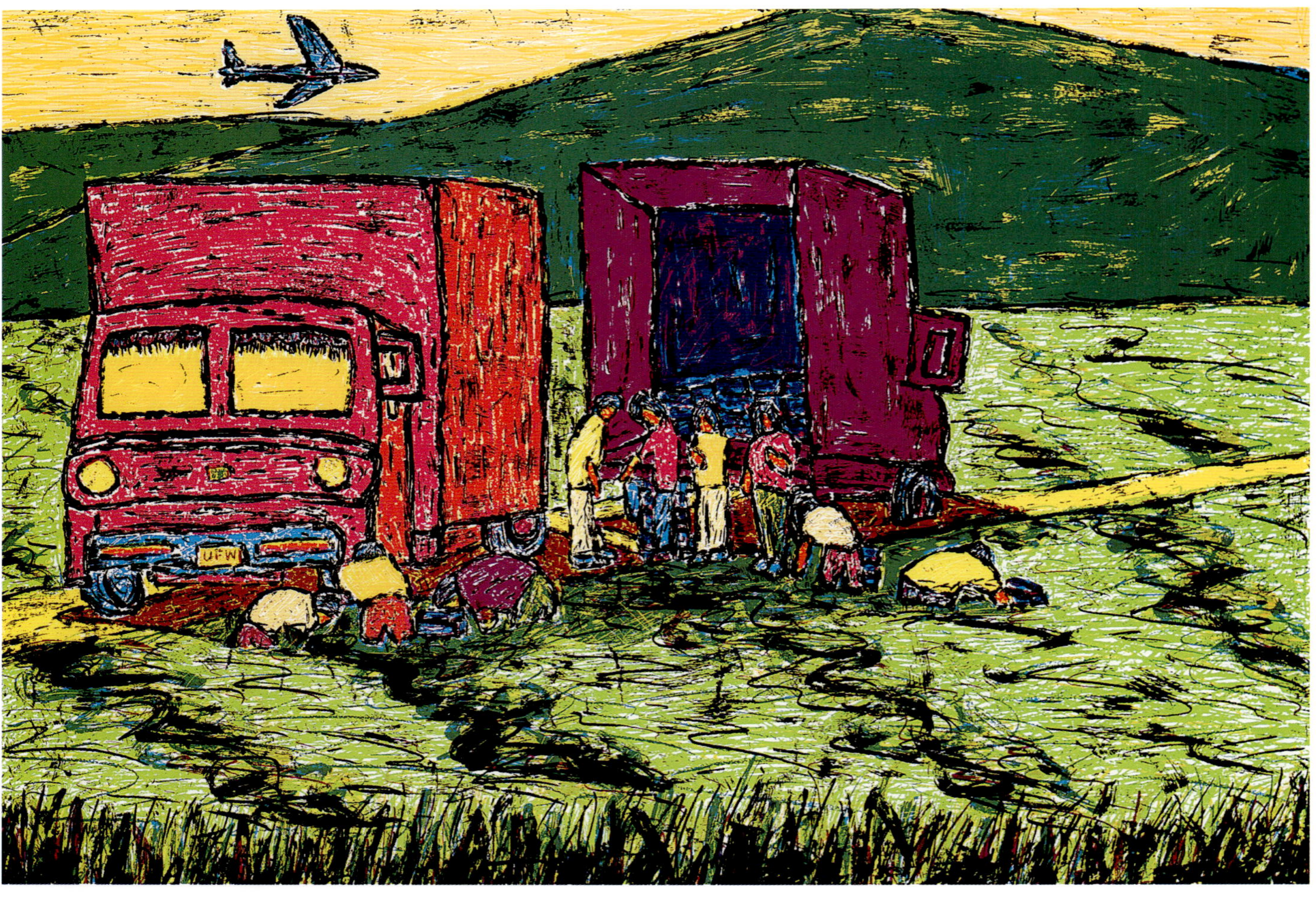

42 Tony Ortega, *Los de abajo* (The underdogs), 1993, serigraph, 25.25" x 36.6"

ed States, perhaps a view from the Mexican side looking at the promise to the north. But the fence is turned facing the other direction, designed to keep inside someone who is looking out from the other side. Perhaps this is a view from the United States looking south toward the beautiful traditions of Mexican life and away from the alienation of contemporary American culture. It can also be seen as an image juxtaposing the sky with the urban environment, a view of nature from within the city, reminding us that we are always a part of the natural world, even within our cities. The title, translated "Do not touch the earth," can be used to support any of these readings. The painting seems to suggest a border, a transition of sorts, but Ramírez does not intend to give us a single answer. Instead, he leaves it up to the viewer's own experience to supply an interpretation.

Tony Ortega, *Los de abajo.* PLATE 42. Tony Ortega's works of art often depict the activities of Mexican Americans in a variety of American locales. Chicanos are explicitly represented as a group and specific figures are drawn to represent types rather than individuals. Hence Ortega's figures do not have individual facial features but rather function to represent the group of which they are a part. *Los de abajo* (The underdogs) is typical of Ortega's style and a particularly good example of how he strives to show the Mexican American community in the larger context of American society. The title of the work is the same as one of the most enduring novels of the Mexican Revolution of 1910, Mariano Azuela's *Los de abajo,* the theme of which is not incompatible with this work since the book portrays Mexican country folk whom the Revolution has uprooted and forced into an itinerant form of life (not as migrant workers, however, but as a revolutionary band). This work also shows Ortega's characteristic use of the Western style of perspective as well as his use of light and shadow, blended with simplified geometric designs and the deployment of vivid colors that are often hallmarks of Mexican folk art. In this serigraph, a group of farmworkers toils in the vicinity of two panel trucks. Some are bent over, working the soil, perhaps picking a crop to be loaded into the truck. Their proximity to the truck suggests that they have just started their work. Others are gathered around the truck; perhaps they have not yet started. More than faceless, these figures are totally indistinct and anonymous as they gather the food that the rest of us count on finding in our supermarkets. The green field is vast; there is much work to be done. In the far distance we see purple mountains, and in the sky at the very top of the composition we see a passenger jet flying overhead. We are reminded that not everyone earns a living doing hard manual labor; some are able to leave their cares behind for a vacation, and from an airplane the workers are invisible. Back on the ground, these underdogs still have a long day's work to do.

Luis Valderas, *Bridge over the Rio Grande.* PLATE 43. Born in McAllen, Texas, which is a border town (Reynosa is its sister city) close to where the Rio Grande flows into the Gulf of Mexico, Valderas knows firsthand the culture of the border, which he has described as the "juxtaposition of festivity and misery." This work is mostly about misery, although it is dressed up in bright and festive colors; some of these, such as the red and white, have a highly satirical cast. The theme of the work is related to the commerce of the border, especially the maquiladoras, the foreign-owned manufacturing plants that have been built in Mexico to take advantage of low labor costs in order to maximize profits. On the American side of the border the more advanced technological forms of manufacturing are practiced, and on the Mexican side the jobs mostly involve manual labor. We look upon a naked worker stripped of identity or even clothes, whose only defining characteristic is a mechanical head. His companion in labor is an ox. Together they move a factory across the bridge, which actually undulates like a river and is colored in the manner of the stripes of the American flag. Side by side, naked man and dumb ox labor on the bridge, pulling a huge industrial burden the size of a factory, perhaps even a city. They pull with chains that are also those of their enslavement. They are wage slaves—at least the worker is—and no distinction of value is made between the man and the brute. Apparently, in the estimation of their overboss, they are essentially indistinguishable and interchangeable.

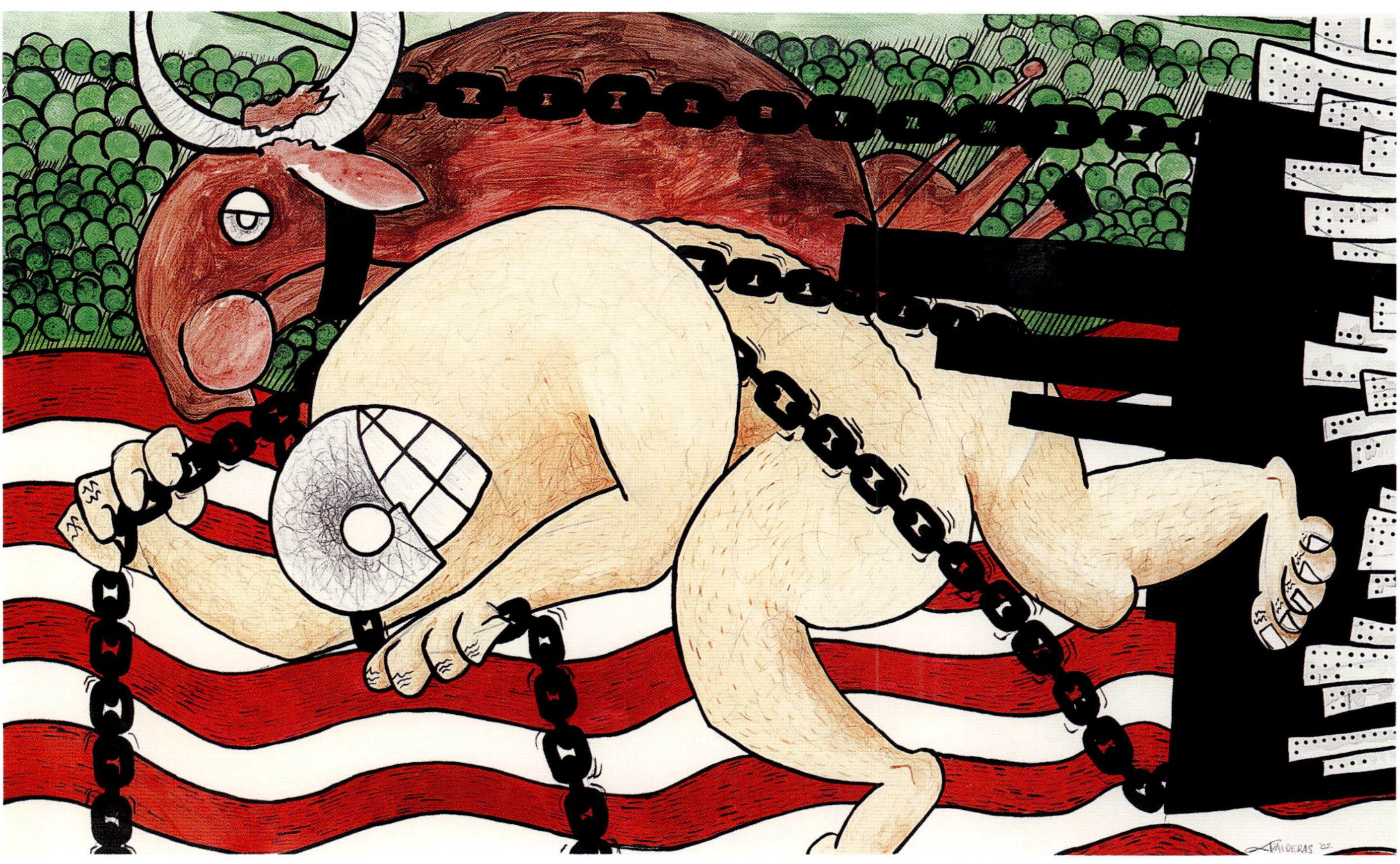

43 Luis Valderas, *Bridge over the Rio Grande*, 2002, acrylic, wax pencil, and India ink, 27.5" x 41.5"

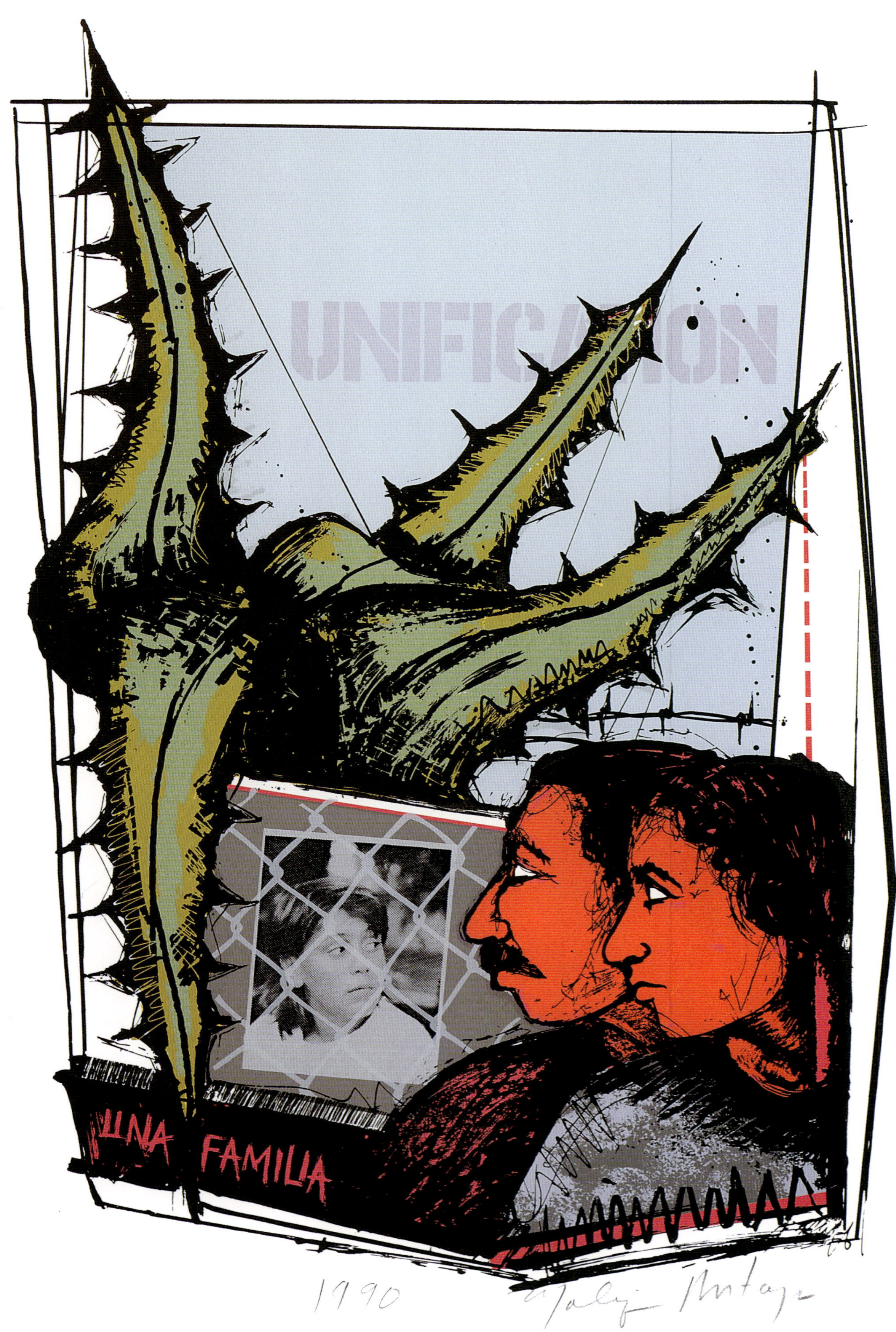

44 Malaquías Montoya, *Una familia* (A family), 1990, serigraph, 23" x 15.5"

Malaquías Montoya, *Una familia.* Plate 44. One of Malaquías Montoya's artistic goals is to give voice to the voiceless, disenfranchised Chicano, Mexican, and Central American working classes. He has worked extensively in the serigraph and poster forms, media accessible to the working classes that permit him to communicate directly to and awaken the consciousness of oppressed peoples and to actively work to transform their current reality. Montoya's art expresses protest and an aspiration for a better world. *Una familia* shows a dark-skinned indigenous mother and father at the right of the composition looking at a photograph of a child behind a pattern that resembles a chain-link fence. The composition includes a thorned agave plant and a strand of barbed wire, motifs that Montoya has used in other works to symbolize the forbidding nature of the border. In capital letters at the top there appears lightly written in red against a gray background the word "Unification" and at the bottom in dark red against a black background is "una familia" (a family), suggesting both a problem and a call to action for solving the untenable and cruel situation of a purely political boundary being used to separate parents from their children. It is notable that the parents are drawn in a generic fashion; they represent the many parents separated from their children. In contrast, the child is represented as an actual photograph, making the problem specific and immediate. While this piece refers to a contemporary problem, the viewer is reminded that families have been separated at other times by this and other borders. For example, in the Great Depression of the 1930s, many Mexican Americans were wrenched from their families and deported to Mexico by American authorities even though they were legal U.S. citizens and in some cases had been on the land that became part of the United States before it was taken from Mexico. The injustices of the border continue today and Montoya continues to struggle against them with his art.

NUEVO MILENIO

Laura Álvarez, *The Double Agent Sirvienta: Blow Up the Hard Drive.* Plate 45. Laura Álvarez explores themes of duality in this simple yet captivating work. Clean, simple design elements give *The Double Agent Sirvienta: Blow Up the Hard Drive* a cartoonlike quality. A maid appears to be seated at a desk, but the lack of any furniture gives the viewer a sense of intrigue and immediacy. She is inputting mysterious code—a virus, perhaps—into a laptop computer as she glances over her shoulder to see if danger lurks behind her. This woman is the Double Agent Sirvienta (or DAS), and she is on a mission. A background of fire atop a folder labeled File://translation.underdone gives the viewer a sense of emergency as well as simmering anger. In a playful fashion, Álvarez comments on the ignorance and social stigmas that conspire to make her character a successful double agent in a series of prints and watercolors. The unwitting homeowners think they have hired a meek and loyal domestic assistant, giving DAS open access to their home and never realizing that she is more than the subservient, loyal employee she appears to be. DAS is highly intelligent, subversive, and confident as she works to undermine an oppressive system. While her employers underestimate her ability, her technological savvy is apparent. A communication device is imbedded in her hat, and the viewer is invited to ponder the contents of the knapsack she sports. The blue of her dress is stereotypical of the uniforms worn by maids, whereas the white arrows remind viewers of a computer keyboard.

Daniel Maldonado, *Mi Tierra* (My turf). Plate 46. This is a work that combines an earthy, *rasquache* sensibility (see the entry on Luis Guerrero's *El Chuy* for a description of the concept) with a dimension of science fiction and fantasy. There is a famous restaurant in San Antonio called Mi Tierra, known locally by everyone, and perhaps this is a nod to that landmark. But here Mi Tierra (in contrast to the real restaurant which, although popular and casual, is also quite respectable) is a barrio bar of the lowest order, where sentient creatures mingle with barnyard fowl and a mangy dog. However, the sentient beings are green "people" from outer space (the boot of one proclaims that it is "made on Jupiter") and, simultaneously, they are also recognizable as 1910 Mexican revolutionary types with crisscrossing *cartucheras* (cartridge belts), revolution-style broad-brimmed hats, and guns and liquor to spare. In this comic fantasy that embroiders on the Mexican Revolution, known for its brawling and violent excesses, there is also a nod to the famous creature cantina of the *Star Wars* film series. Certain characteristic and caricaturistic features of the past have been projected out into a fictional future, all for fun.

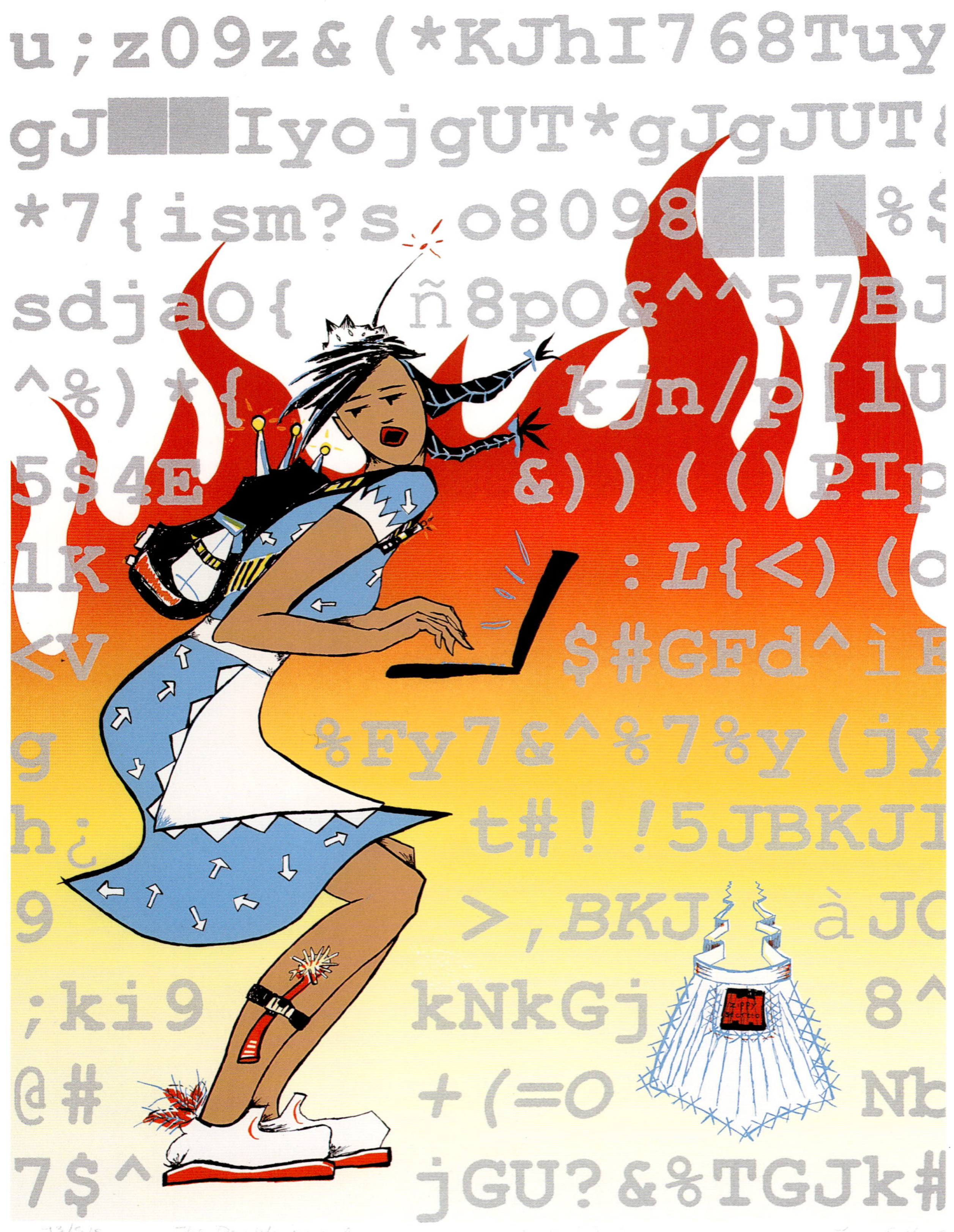

45 Laura Álvarez, *The Double Agent Sirvienta: Blow Up the Hard Drive*, 1999, serigraph, 30" x 22"

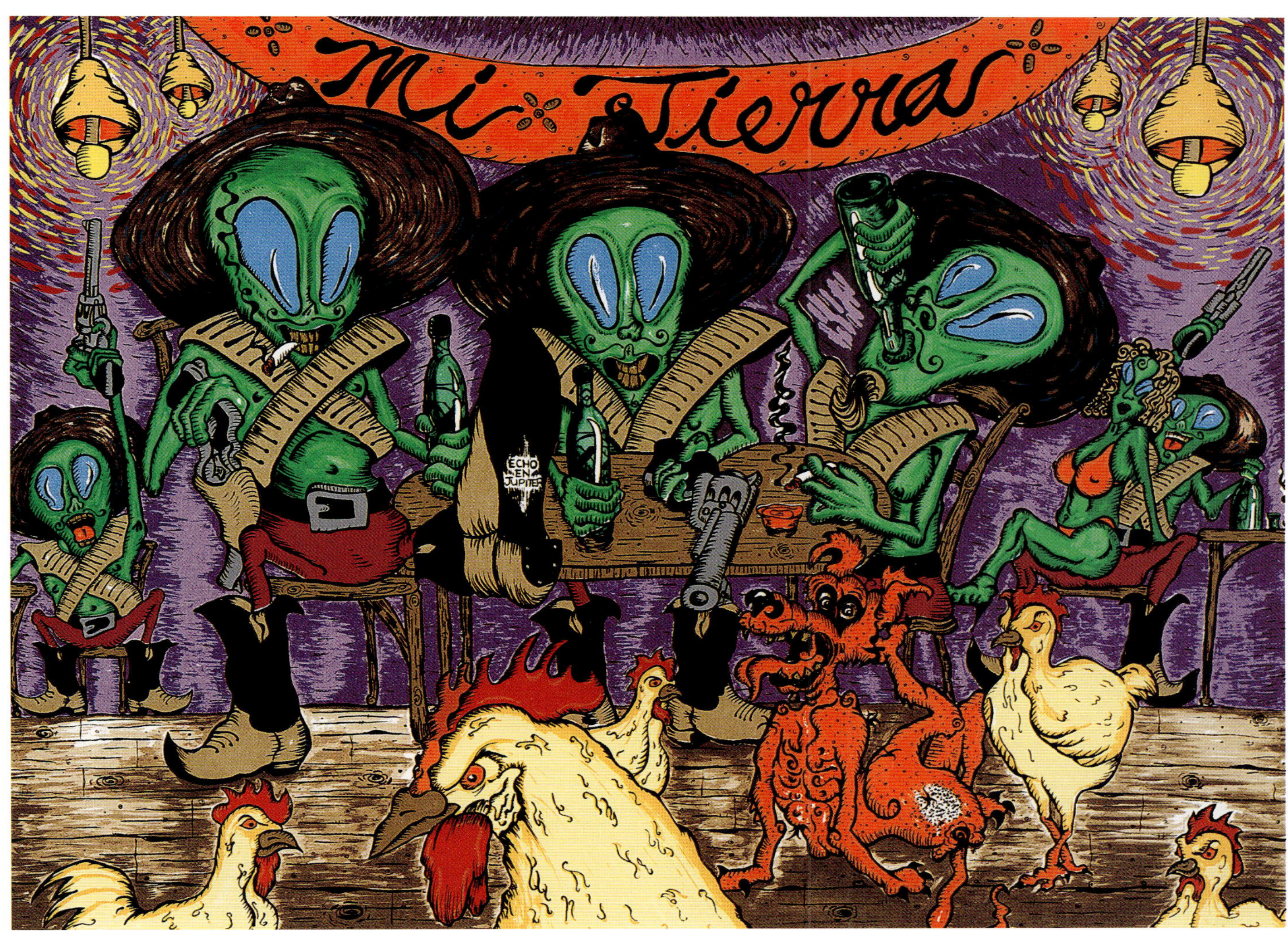

46 Daniel Maldonado, *Mi Tierra* (My turf), 2001, serigraph, 22" x 28"

**Enrique Chagoya*, Elvis Meets the Virgin of Guadalupe.* PLATE 47. The work of Enrique Chagoya is profoundly political. Fusing images from the pre-Hispanic past, Western religious tradition, and American popular culture, the artist describes the results as "a nonlinear narrative with many possible interpretations." His images provide both comedy and biting commentary. In *Elvis Meets the Virgin of Guadalupe*, Chagoya juxtaposes two cultural icons, one Mexican and the other North American, thereby exhibiting his penchant for pitting north against south and secular against sacred. His comparison of the Virgin of Guadalupe with Elvis reminds us of both the massive popularity of these figures and the fact that they are treated similarly within popular culture. Both are the subjects of adoration, sightings, and pilgrimages by the faithful. Their images are widely distributed on such objects as belt buckles, postage stamps, and coffee mugs. The Virgin, how-ever, is presented as larger than Elvis. As he has in other pieces, Chagoya is using a hierarchical visual system within the composition to suggest relative power and importance. Elvis's gaze is up toward the Virgin, perhaps suggesting that even "The King," an icon of North American cultural power, is small in comparison to the role played by the Virgin in the lives of people south of the U.S.-Mexico border.

**Santiago Pérez*, First Aztec On the Moon.* PLATE 48. Santiago Pérez is well known for juxta-posing unlikely imagery, and he excels with that technique in *First Aztec on the Moon*. Against a black horizon worthy of a moonscape, we view an incongruous, mostly bare-skinned Aztec warrior sporting a loincloth and a kneepad resembling equip-ment that pre-Hispanic Amerindian competitors used in their sacred ball games. While the warrior does not wear a spacesuit, he does have a space hel-

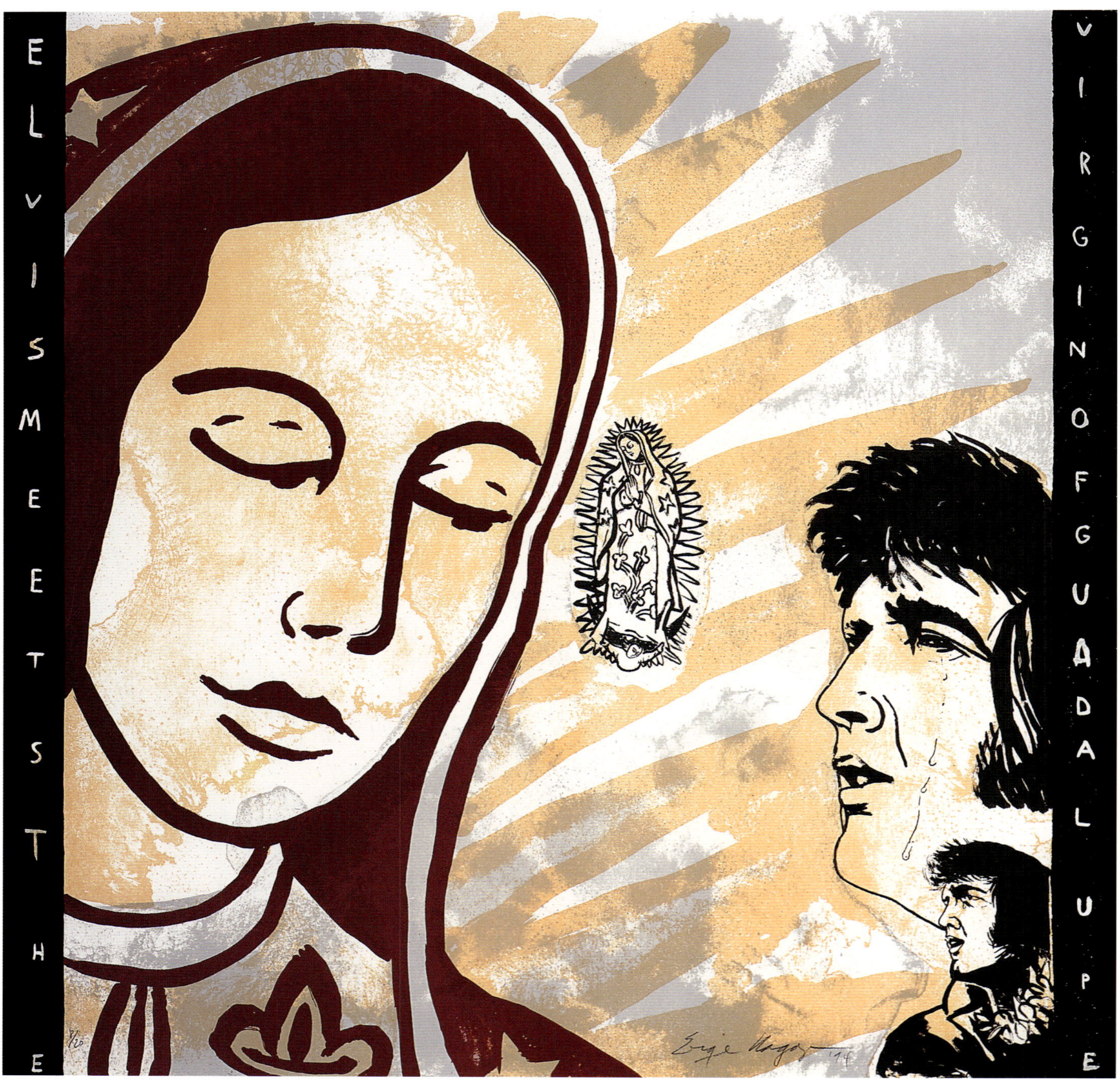

47 Enrique Chagoya, *Elvis Meets the Virgin of Guadalupe*, 1994, lithograph, 32" x 32"

met of sorts, although it mostly resembles a gas mask. His amazing lunar rover at the same time resembles an Amerindian wooden cart. It bears elements from both postmodern and premodern cultures as well as of apparent invention in other periods, particularly the nineteenth century. For example, on the one hand we view an umbrella-like lunar communications device, a headlamp affixed to a miner's cap from which a pathetically dim beam is emitted to light the astronaut's way, and a mechan- ical contraption that protrudes like a red tongue from the mouth of the feathered serpent. On the other hand we see a *calavera* (skull) at the nose of the cart, adornment in the form of Aztec hide-and-feather shields, and a larger-than-life, bright red, living human heart close to the tail of the vehicle, encased in liquid with wires emanating from the ventricles and going to the feathered serpent. The dominant image in the composition is the giant head of the plumed serpent with both its quetzal feather headcrest and its serpent's teeth prominent. The plumed serpent in the Aztec religion stands for the great god Quetzalcoatl, often associated with civilization and learning, including the introduction of science and the calendar. This arresting and somewhat oracular composition, masterfully melding icons from completely different cultures and time periods, lends itself to multiple interpretations, many of which might center around the contributions of various civilizations to the current achievements of humankind and the diversity of cultures that have formed us and which we all carry with us in our voyages, including extraterrestrial ones.

Mary Antonia Wood, *Mudra I.* PLATE 49. Throughout her work Mary Antonia Wood uses juxtaposition—of old and new materials, of images from the past and present and from different cultures—to synthesize an understanding of the connections between them all. In *Mudra I*, Wood uses

48 Santiago Pérez, *First Aztec on the Moon*, 2002, acrylic on canvas, 48" x 48"

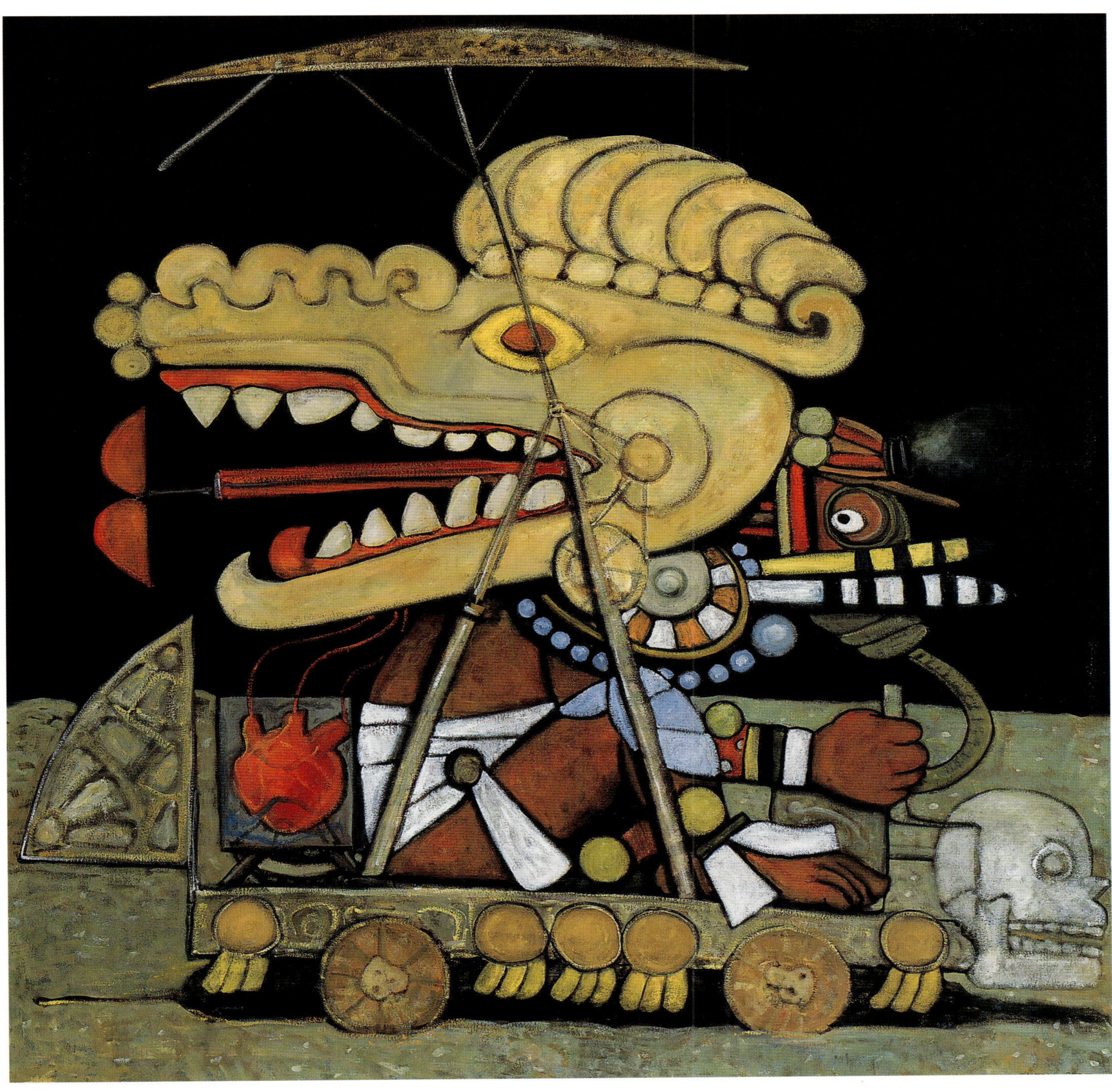

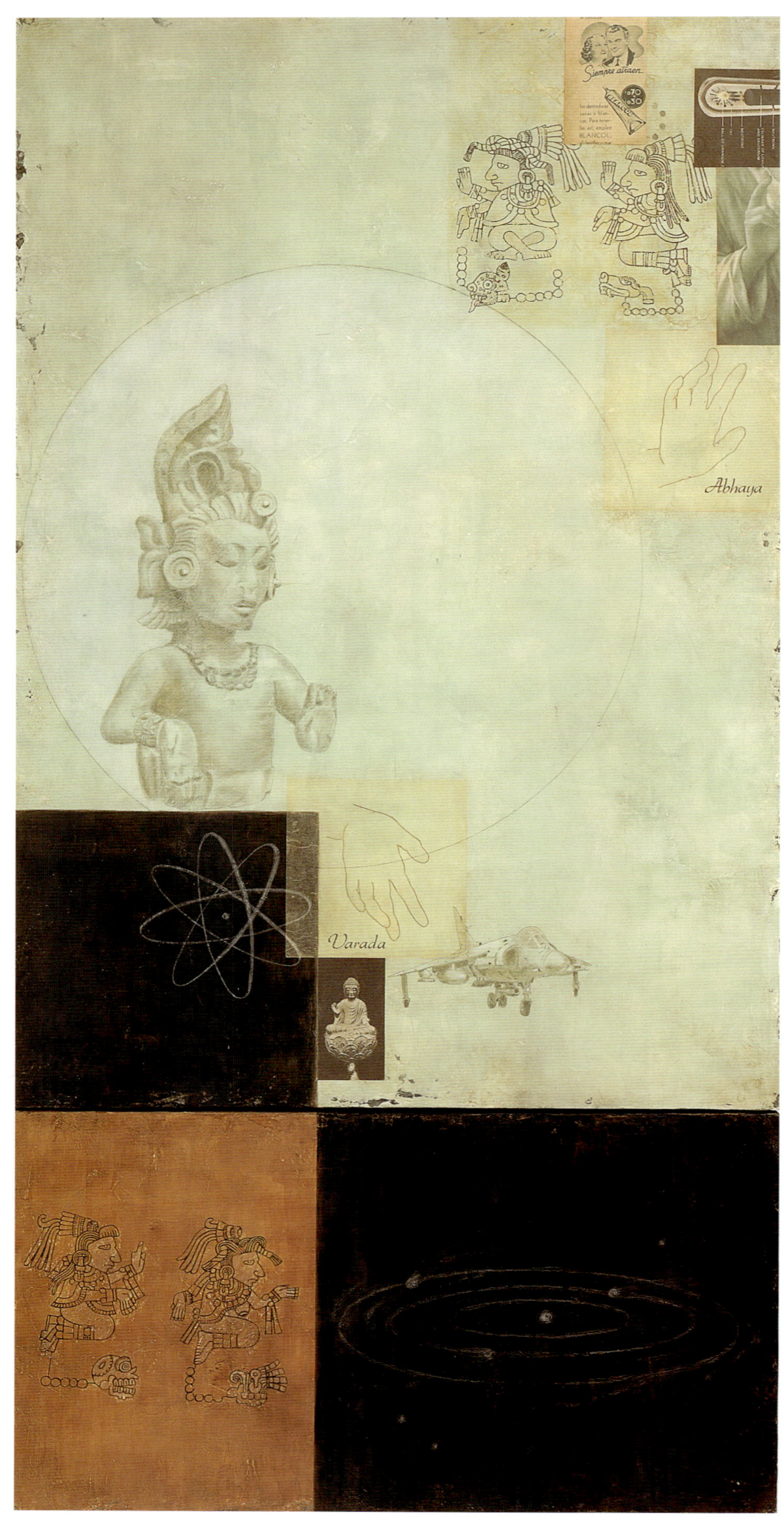

49 Mary Antonia Wood, *Mudra I*, 2003, drawing, collage, image transfers, and Venetian plaster on panels, 60" x 30" x 3". Collection of the artist.

Right: 50 Maya González, *Death Enthroned*, 2002, acrylic on archival paper, 40" x 26"

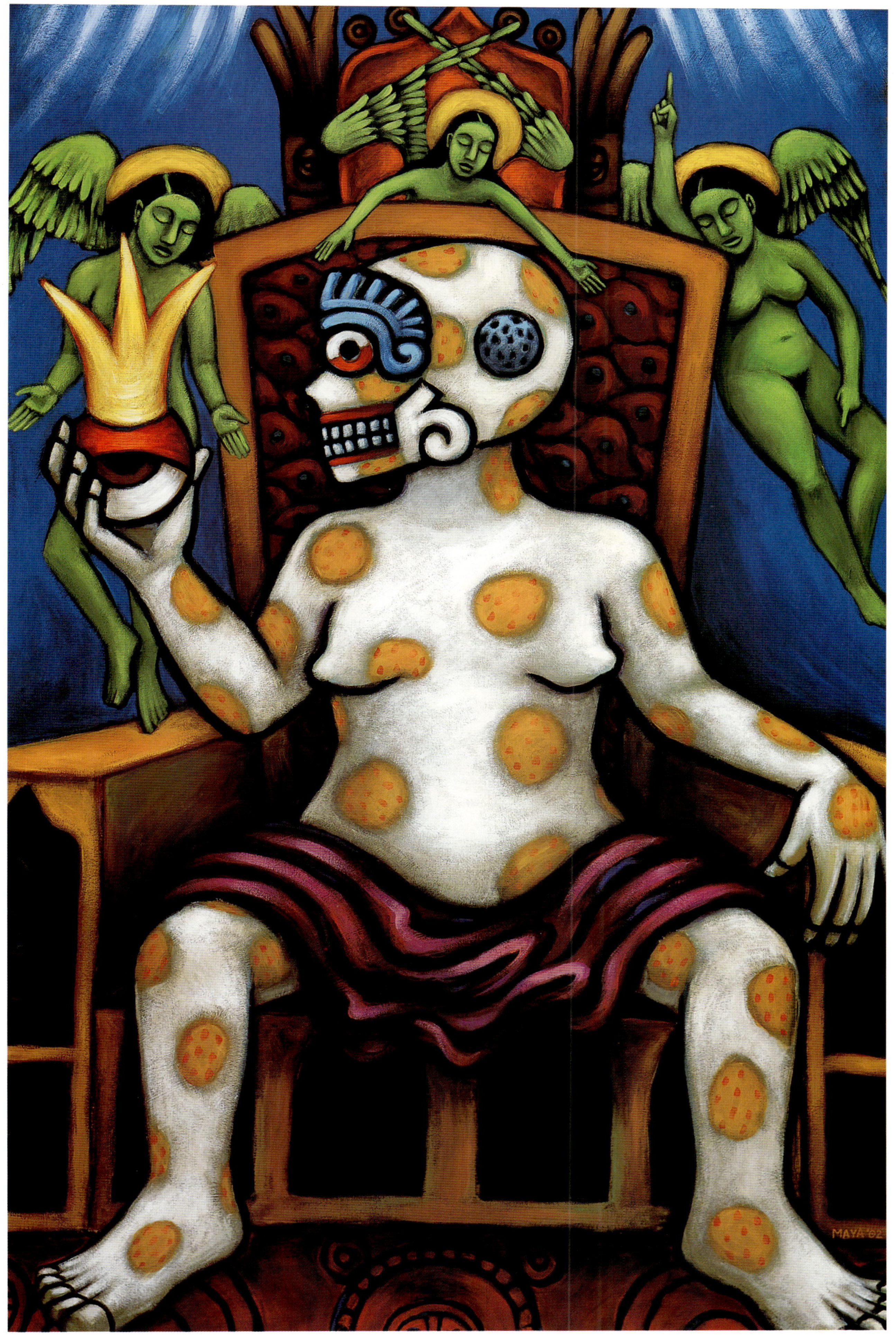

Venetian plaster, wood, graphite drawing, and collage as materials with which to explore parallels between East Indian, pre-Hispanic, and contemporary Western mythology, spirituality, and thought. The piece features a drawing at the center left of a Mayan corn god. The figure appears to be from an East Indian culture. Its left hand is held in the position, or mudra, symbolizing protection. The right hand presents the mudra indicating a blessing. These hand gestures are seen again below in the black-and-white image of the Buddha sitting on a lotus, with hands forming the same gestures in reverse. The black outlined figures at the top right and bottom left of the piece are taken from the pre-Hispanic Codex Nuttall, of Mixtec origin. Their hands are held in the same positions. The single hand at the top right is taken from a larger image of Christ, with the right hand in a gesture of blessing. From our own time, Wood includes a drawing of the atom's structure juxtaposed with a similar diagram of our solar system and a drawing of a fighter plane. By presenting all these seemingly different images together, Wood comments on the ongoing cycles of life and death, war and peace, knowledge and its loss, past and present, throughout many cultures.

Maya González, *Death Enthroned*. PLATE 50. Identifying herself as mestiza—European and Amerindian—González has developed her own iconography bridging the religious traditions of both parts of her heritage and using it to explore her life. In this work, the artist, inspired by European and pre-Hispanic American art, combines elements of Christian and Aztec iconographies to create a meditation on death and possibly—although ambiguously—resurrection. In a composition reminiscent of Renaissance religious painting, the central figure reminds us of the Madonna, who would traditionally be seated displaying the Christ child on her knee. This female figure is also inspired by pre-Hispanic codices. The female, with a calavera face representing death, wears a white skin or suit covered with a lemon-colored pox. Instead of holding the Christ child, a symbol of the promise of everlasting life, Death holds a large crowned eyeball. The eye represents the Aztec Eye of God, an image that some believe was derived from the frightful appearance of the solar eclipse. This eye is repeated upside down in the face of the Death figure. Green female angels surround the top of the throne. The angel on the far right, unique in that she is not only green but also

naked and full-bodied (qualities not typical of European religious painting), at the same time has the feathers and halo that are traditional. Significantly, her right arm and index finger are pointed up, and her left arm and finger are sinisterly pointed down. The angel contributes an important signifier in the composition, pointing to the enigma of death and the fate of humanity upon death.

Carlos Santistevan, *Red and Gold Lowrider*. PLATE 51. Carlos Santistevan employs a *rasquache* sensibility in this piece that transforms a woman's discarded red high-heeled shoe into a fire-engine-red "Chevrolet" lowrider. This is one representative example of a series of lowrider shoes that the artist has executed. At one time connoting vulgarity and tastelessness, the meaning of *rasquache* has been turned on its head and revalidated by the Chicano movement (the term "Chicano" itself at one time was used negatively to denote someone gullible and simplistic) into an irreverent, spontaneous, ironic examination of social, political, or racial injustices or issues of inequality. Often using discarded items and applying his soldering and painting skills to them to create unique artistic assemblages, Santistevan masterfully turns this worn shoe into a shiny hot rod with gold hood and roll bars. Red spike heels are often associated with hotfooting and cruising the night, and here one has been analogically converted into the poor woman or man's hot rod. To many Chicanos/as, lowriders are an intense source of pride, and they enjoy displaying their vehicles during informally designated "cruising" times or during community and social events. This work glosses and at the same time both comically parodies and exalts the cult of the lowrider in the Chicano barrios.

Elizabeth Pérez, *Blue Venus*. PLATE 52. In *Blue Venus* we witness the result of the artist's careful and considered mixing of traditional European Renaissance imagery and thought with Chicano icons and color, resulting in a truly new image, an exciting syncretism for our millennium that parallels the *mestizaje* that resulted from the intermixture of races and cultures following the European arrival in the Americas. Pérez is highly familiar with European painters and painting styles, having spent considerable time studying artworks at the Louvre museum when she lived in Paris for two years. The female figure in this piece, with the position of her arms and her flowing hair, is based on Botticelli's highly familiar *The Birth* *of Venus*, and the banner at the top of the composition, "Ars Longa, Vita Brevis" (Art is long, life is short), comes from Hippocrates. Pérez gives the image a Chicana interpretation by adding the Virgin of Guadalupe's aura of sun rays and a sacred heart in the form of a tattoo. The colors, too, are the opposite of what Botticelli chose for his Venus and are much closer to the colors one sees in Mexican folk art.

Venus holds paintbrushes that have been used recently; in fact, they are tipped with the colors making up this serigraph. Perhaps Pérez is identifying both Venus and the Virgin with the forces of creativity. Or perhaps this is a self-portrait, with Pérez as the mythical, almost holy artist, a combination of her European education and her Chicana heritage, making images we have never seen before.

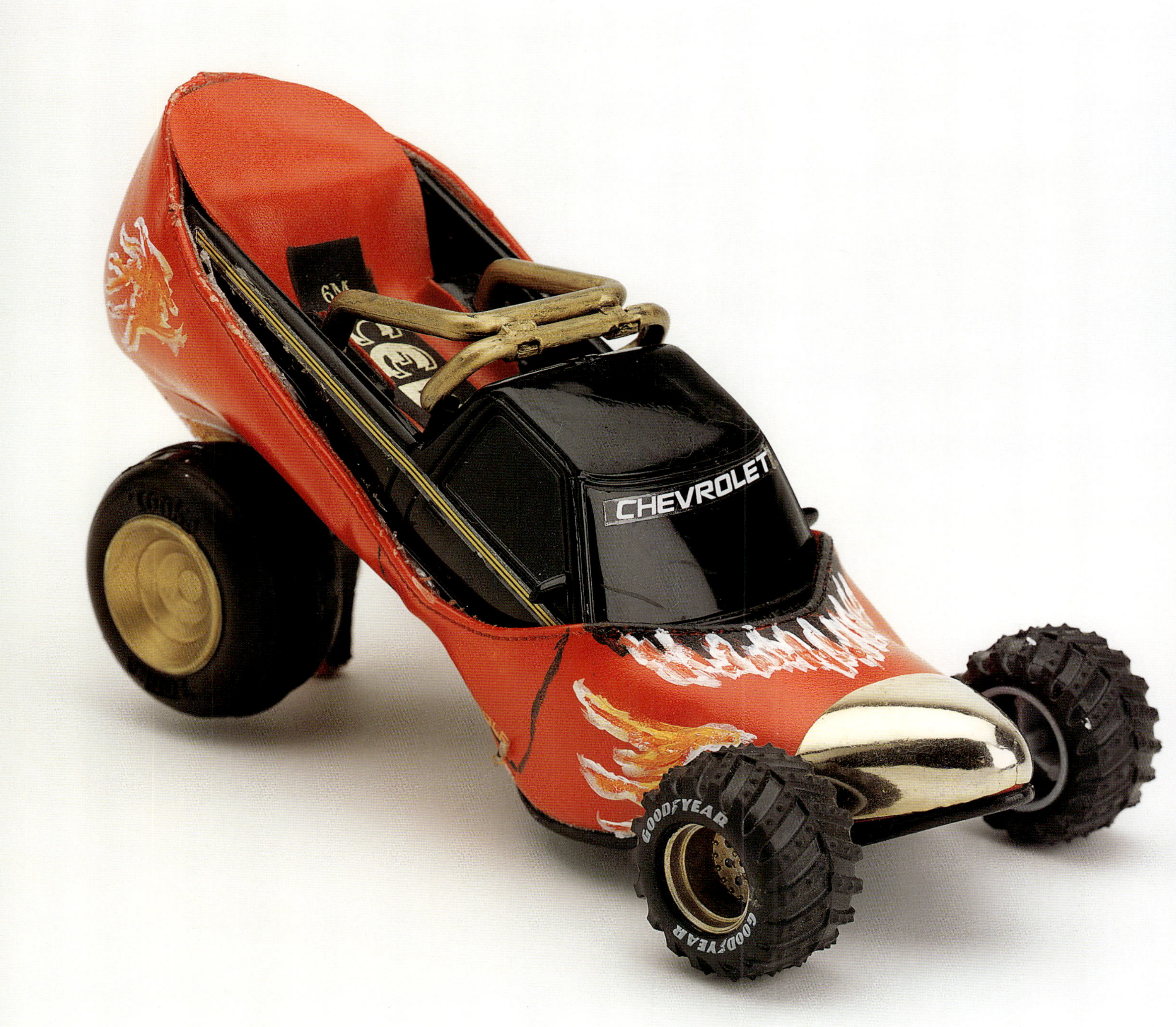

51 Carlos Santistevan, *Red and Gold Lowrider*, 2001, mixed media shoe, 10" x 4" x 11"

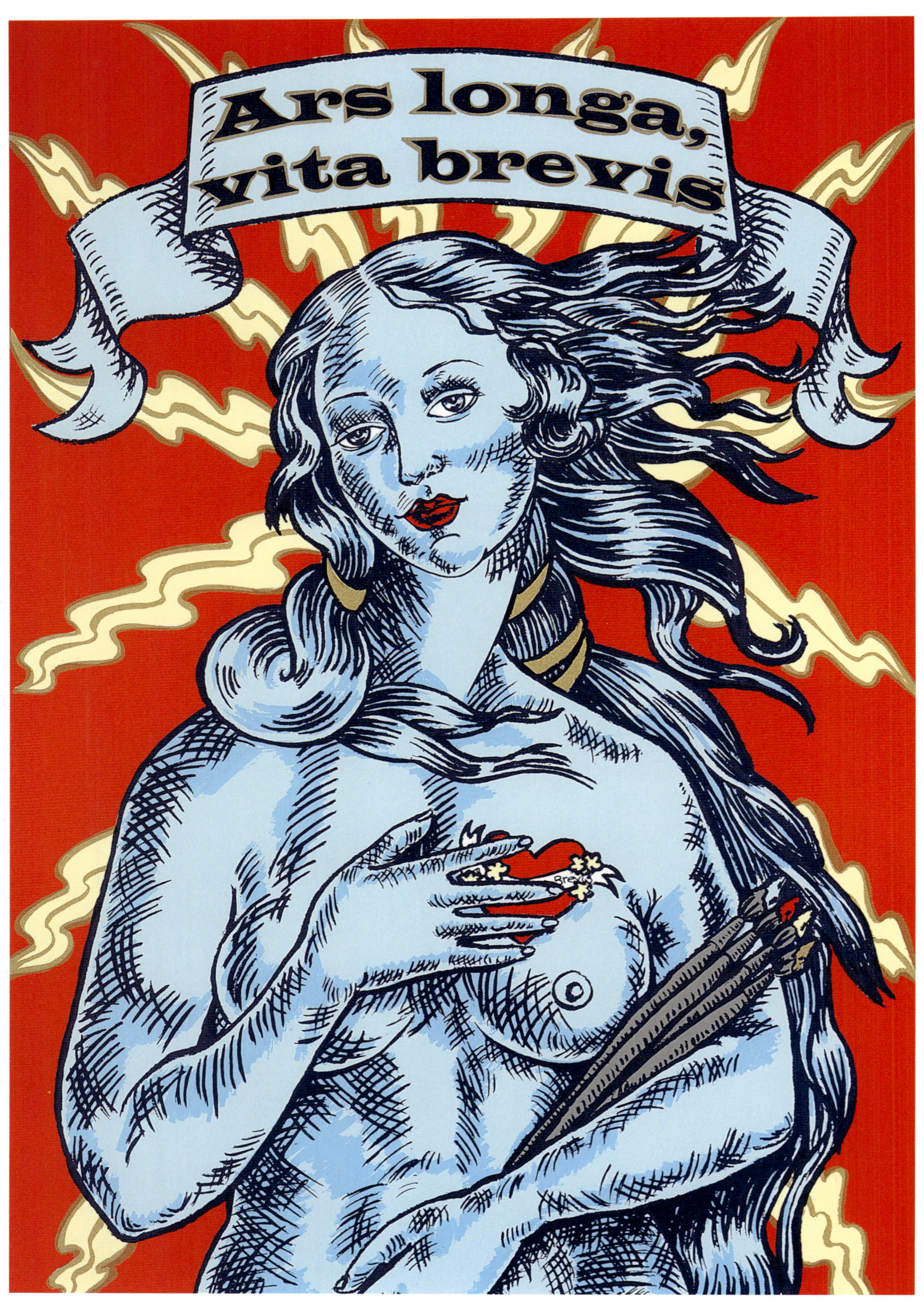

52 Elizabeth Pérez, *Blue Venus*, 2001, serigraph, 30" x 22"

Espiritualidad

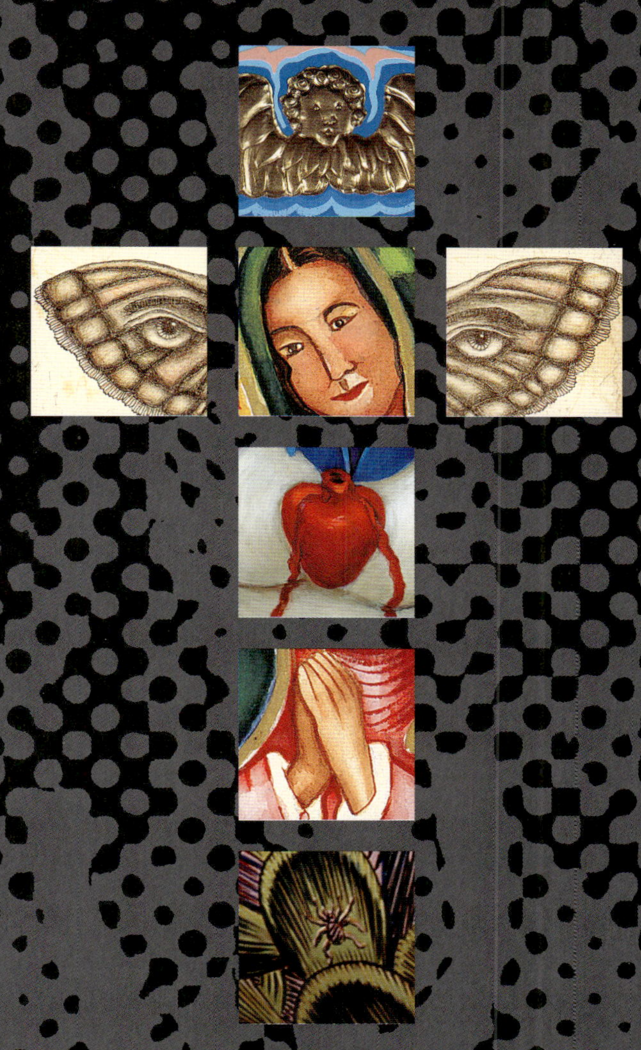

Spirituality

This theme draws attention to a deeply felt component of Chicano culture, which to a certain extent is an embattled culture that has turned to spirituality in order to maintain its value system, especially since the Treaty of Guadalupe Hidalgo (1848) between Mexico and the United States. While the treaty formalized the annexation of about 40 percent of Mexico and in effect legally recognized the newly created Mexican American citizenry of the United States and its rights to the Catholic religion and Spanish language, it is a treaty that has primarily been breached, and as a result, Chicano culture has needed to resist the periodic incursions of Anglo culture. This section has been divided into two themes. "Representación religiosa" depicts an imagery taken from Hispanic and Roman Catholic traditions and conventions but that more often than not produces an iconography notable for its singularity. Many of the pieces in this theme are sui generis in the sense that they depart from the traditional icons of the original homeland of Mexico (or even Spain) in artistically important ways. In fact, in some of the pieces in this theme there is an ironic or even iconoclastic quality. And in still others there is a significant departure from traditional norms of Hispanic society, a postmodern spirituality. "Espíritu humano" contains works of Chicana/o spirituality that are centered primarily on human subjects, rather than overt religious iconography, what in Spanish has often been known as the *morada interior*, the internal dwelling or home, especially in the work of Santa Teresa de Ávila. Within this theme we find works that attempt to evoke the inner nature of humanity, the world of the dreamer, the human identity that turns in upon itself and creates its double, or the spirit that resists the ravages of diseases such as AIDS even as the body fails.

REPRESENTACIÓN RELIGIOSA

Virginia Agüero, *Santa Teresita.* PLATE 53. Agüero is a descendent of the illustrious Peralta family of New Mexico, and this work follows and also expands on the traditions of New Mexican santos (images of saints) art. The two traditional forms are *retablos* and *bultos. Retablos* are images of saints painted on small flat boards of wood or sheets of tin; *bultos* are the carved images of the holy persons. This work is a traditional *retablo* in construction and an example of its most common form: a portable three-part altarpiece (triptych) enclosed in a box that opens up to reveal a complete scene. It also departs from the traditional New Mexican *retablo*, which utilized handmade paint derived from natural colors ground from clay and various plants and thickened with the addition of eggs. This work utilizes a combination of oil and acrylic paints. Wispy cherubs on each wing of the triptych escort *Santa Teresita* in this *retablo* honoring the French-born nineteenth-century Saint Thérèse. Agüero portrays her subject not only as graceful, serene, and loving, but also as friendly and approachable through the representation of familiar elements such as the cross, the white roses in her arms, and the comforting red drapes that frame her. At the same time, those familiar elements have symbolic significance. Entering the Carmel convent at age fifteen, Thérèse explored her faith as an expression of childhood innocence, and she always placed the needs of others before her own. Before succumbing to tuberculosis at twenty-four, she expressed her knowledge and understanding of her Savior in a series of memoirs. Saint Thérèse promoted redemption through "the little way of spiritual childhood," emphasizing a lifetime of small deeds. In *Santa Teresita*, the subject's gentle smile speaks of her joy and devotion; she grasps the crucifix and a bundle of roses, symbols of her passion. Her plain, comforting habit cloaks her in humility. Regal crimson drapes framing the saint evoke images of the blood of Christ. Simple mountains and clouds create a subtle landscape for the accompanying angels, adding motion to the piece. Lines are basic and the style is childlike, a further expression of the artist's understanding of the young saint. In fact, the *retablo* contains few acute angles: lines are gentle, curving, and smooth. As Thérèse let her love for God and humanity "fall [like] a shower of roses," so too does Agüero's appreciation for her subject and her calling.

Marion C. Martínez, *Madre querida* (Beloved mother) and ***Sagrado Corazón*** (Sacred Heart). PLATES 54 and 55. With her "mixed tech media" sculptures, Marion Martínez presents to the viewer a contrast between the traditional and contemporary worlds, the sacred and the secular. She constructs her sculpture by recombining cast-off computer parts and repurposing them into religious icons. Her process is to disassemble obsolete computers, cut the circuit boards and other parts into new shapes, solder them together, and laminate the surfaces to give them a smooth finish. Living in rural northern New Mexico, she has learned to take things that are no longer useful and fashion them into something different that again has purpose.

Madre querida, an image of the Virgin of Guadalupe, is a hanging sculpture made of several types of parts. The Virgin and her robes are made from circuit boards of various colors. Her belt is fashioned from woven cable wire, and her sun-ray aura is made from printer daisy wheels. The entire construction is centered on a computer hard drive,

giving the effect of a halo around the Holy Mother. Creating a devotional icon from the detritus of modern American culture reminds one of the reported Virgin sightings on the surface of a tortilla, the trunk of a tree, and the other places she has been recognized. For the faithful, the signs of God are found in everything he has created.

Similarly, Martínez constructed the wall hanging *Sagrado Corazón* from circuit boards, a bar code, copper, and fence wire. This combination of materi-

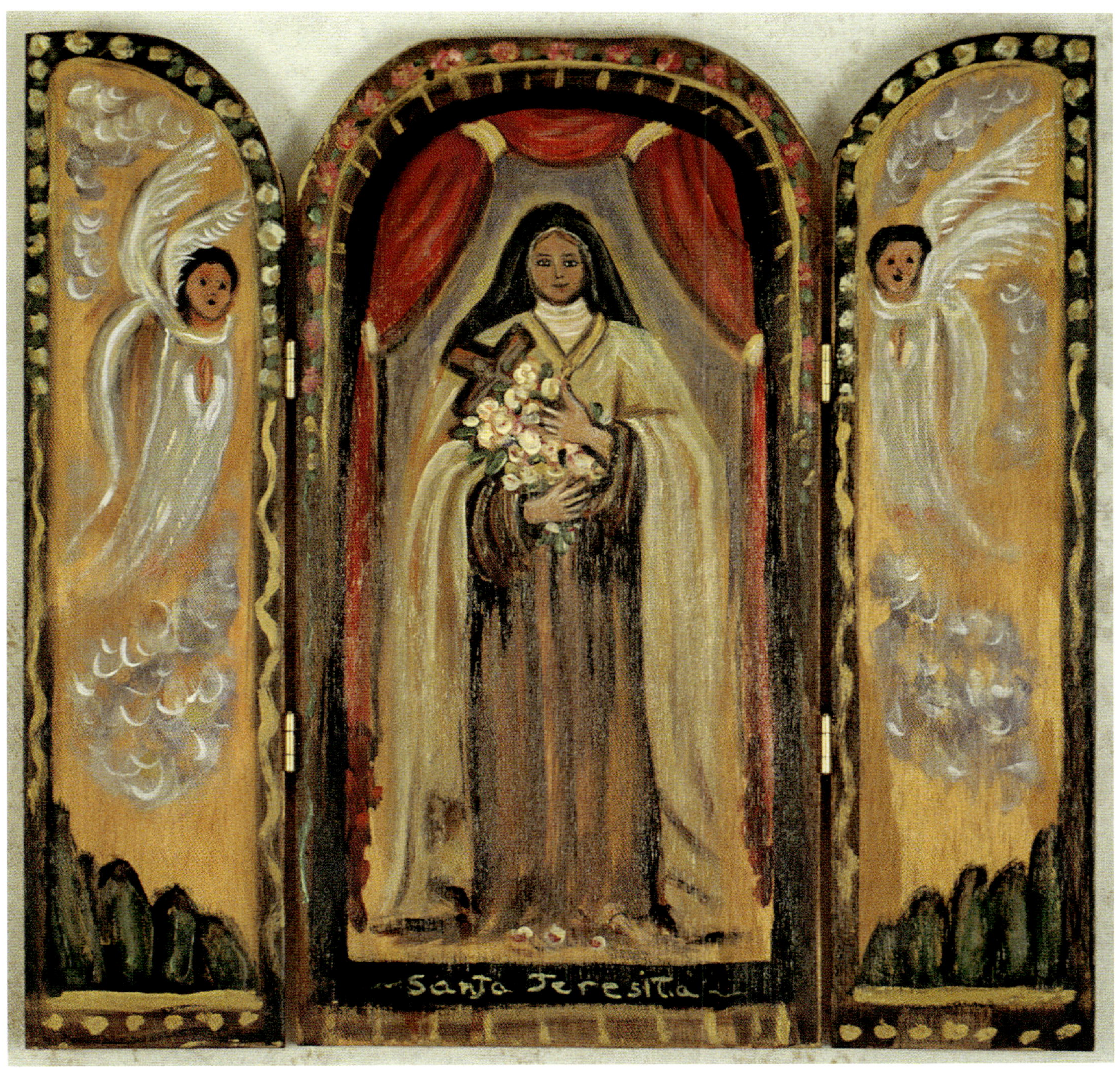

53 Virginia Agüero, *Santa Teresita*, 2001, oil and acrylic on wood, 18" x 18". Collection of the artist.

73

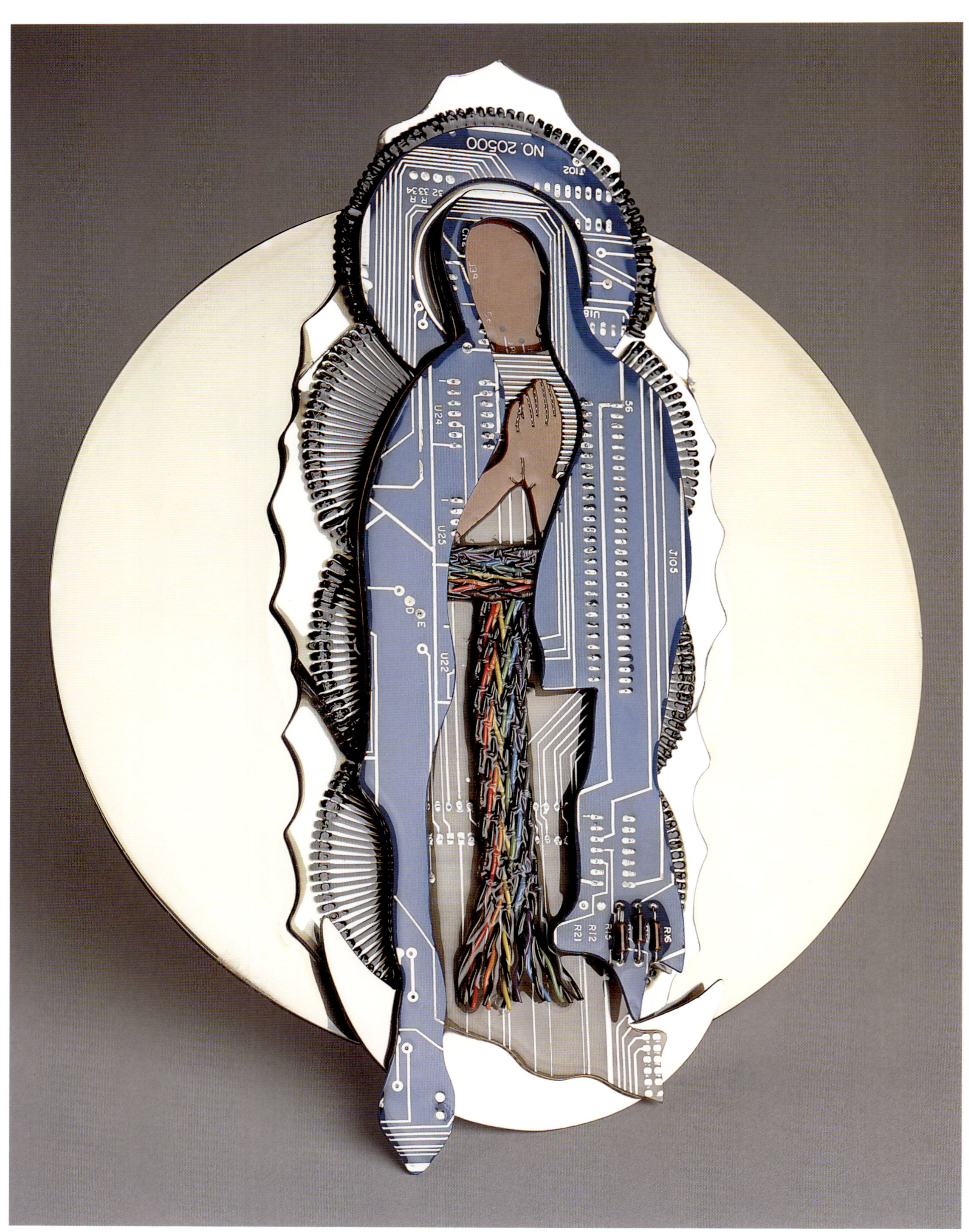

54 Marion C. Martínez, *Madre querida* (Beloved mother), 2002, circuit board, computer disc from drive, CD, daisy print wheels, woven cable wire, 10" x 8" x 0.5"

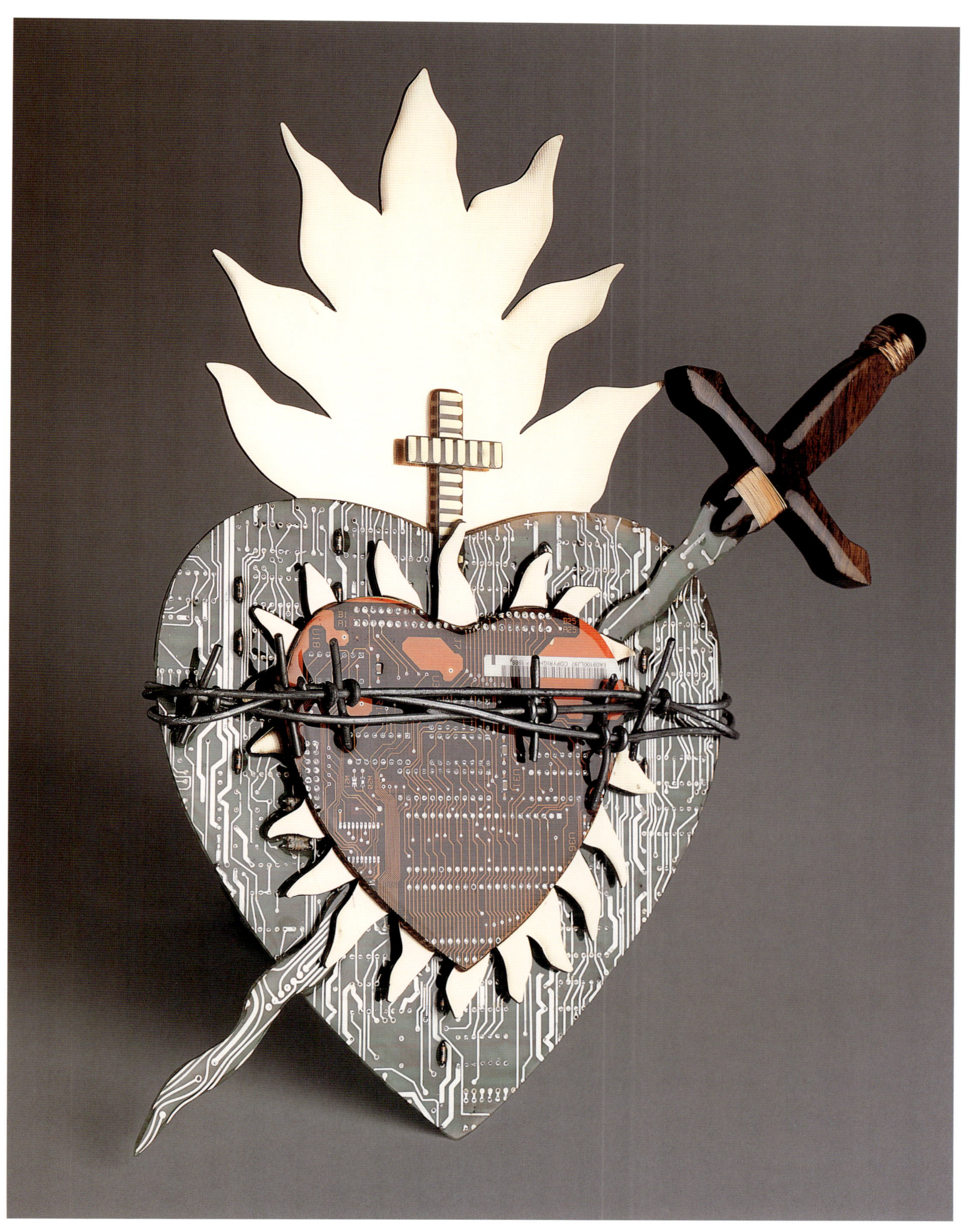

55 Marion C. Martínez, *Sagrado Corazón* (Sacred Heart), 2002, circuit boards, fence wire, bar code, and copper, 14" x 12.5" x .75"

als links the suffering heart of Jesus to both contemporary technology and the ranching lifestyle of New Mexico. A symbol seen in many cultures and contexts, the heart represents love, courage, and the connection between the mind and body. Martínez brings this ancient symbol, and especially its meaning as a Catholic icon, into our own time. She both makes the symbol relevant to young people who may feel alienated from the sacred heart and the materials relevant to older people who may be unfamiliar with the circuit boards from which it is constructed. In another artist's hands, this combination of materials and subject matter might be presented with an ironic or post-modern tone. But Martínez is deeply religious, and these symbols of her Hispanic and Catholic heritage are close to her heart. She creates them to show that the traditions of her family and the symbols to which they directed their devotion are neither obsolete nor useless. Her choice of materials highlights the fact that these symbols are entirely relevant to the life we lead in the twenty-first century.

Daniel Martín Díaz, *Magicus*. PLATE 1. Daniel Martín Díaz's work appears to have come to us from an earlier millennium. A devout Catholic and self-taught artist, he studies and is enthralled by the religious imagery, alchemical symbols, color palettes, and combinations of image and text used in European and Latin American paintings of past centuries. The images he creates use similar elements to make a statement about the mysteries of faith. In the lithograph *Magicus* (Latin for "magical"), Díaz limits his palette to tones of sepia, black, and muted red, and he has used the printing process to give the paper the look of ancient parchment. Díaz depicts the Virgin Mary with the body of a butterfly and the tail of a scorpion. Her face, rather than radiating peace, reminds us of her suffering. The Virgin's butterfly body is marked with alchemical symbols. Her wings are covered with human eyes that could be interpreted as either all-seeing or evil. All of the text on the piece is in Latin, the traditional language of the Catholic Church. At the top of the composition is a banner with the inscription *Spiritus Sanctus* (Holy Spirit), in the lower right center the word *Mors* (Death), and at the bottom the Ave Maria (Hail Mary) prayer, well known to all Catholics: "Hail Mary, full of grace, the Lord is with you. Blessed are you among women and blessed is the fruit of your womb. Holy Mary, mother of God,

Magicus, see page i

pray for us sinners now and at the hour of our death. Amen." This combination of elements is surreal and ambiguous. We are presented with the powerful symbol of the mother of God as a chimera, a mythological female monster of divine origin. This Virgin-monster is capable of providing safety and posing danger, of life-giving love and deadly sting. Díaz has said that his parents, who came from Mexico, had traditional beliefs that seemed to him to have no logical explanation. He uses the unanswered questions from his past, those things that are mysterious and unknowable, in his work today.

Meggan De Anza, *En brazos de una madre/In the Arms of a Mother*. PLATE 56. In this neotraditional *retablo*, created with an acrylic painting mounted on wood rather than in the traditional manner with natural pigments over an undercoating of gesso (in New Mexico, gypsum bound together with glue), the artist's use of soft pastel shades suggests the comfort a mother brings to her innocent young. De Anza intentionally omits identifying features in the images, conveying a sense that the figures could represent anyone, and inviting the viewer to interpret the piece in a highly personal way. Three figures are in the foreground of the painting: a woman and two smaller forms that are children. The color array in the work emphasizes both blue and pink, thereby encompassing both genders. All three are dressed in ecclesiastical garb. The woman wears a blue mantle, signifying her purity and alluding to a similarity to the Madonna. She holds one child and gently guides the other, keeping both close to her, suggesting protection. By using curved lines and few angles, the artist creates a sense of tenderness and compassion, of being held in an embrace. Behind the figures is the outline of a darker blue church with light coming from the inside through the windows, implying that warmth and welcome await those who enter. Numerous crosses mark the overall work above the church, at the base of the composition, on the garments worn by the mother and the child in the foreground, and around one of the series of frames. The cross represents the open arms of the church, an invitation to acceptance and love. Outside the scene, the carefully constructed frame appears to be in the shape of a church itself, replete with a guardian angel. Taken as a whole, the piece conveys a tribute to mothers, who hold the sacred job of guiding innocent hearts and minds, especially the Mother Church.

Right: 56 Meggan De Anza, *En brazos de una madre/In the Arms of a Mother*, 1993, mixed media 23" x 16"

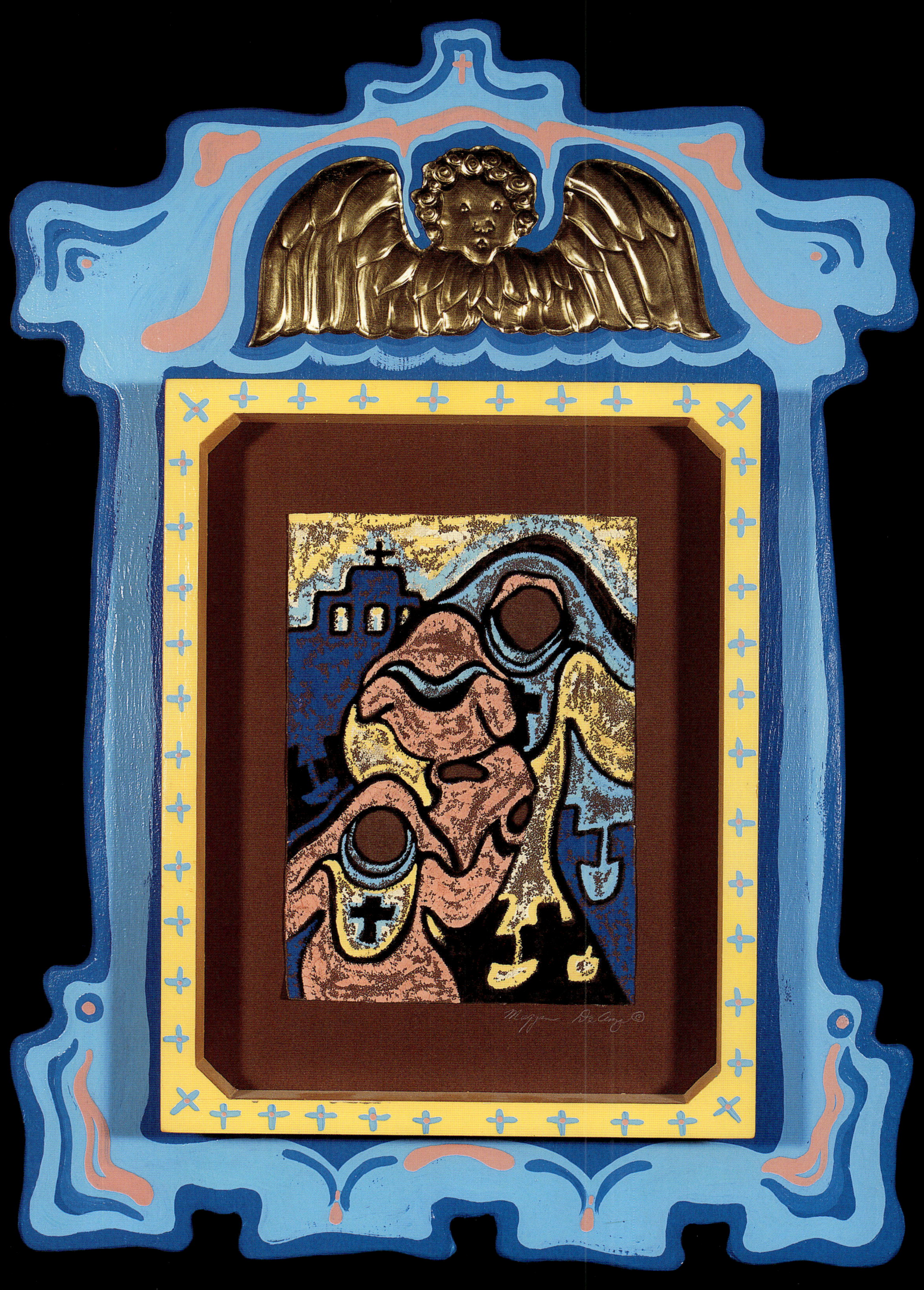

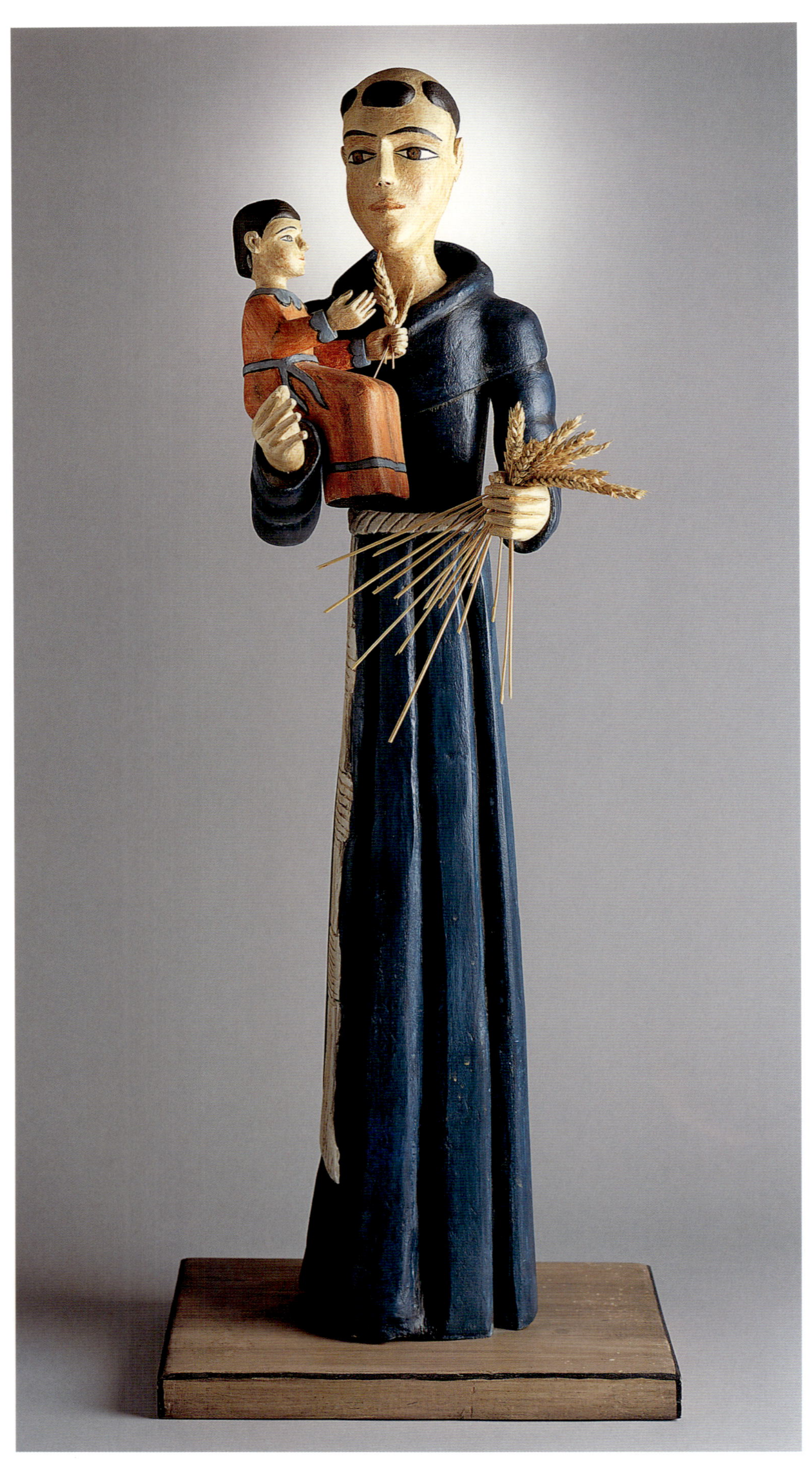

57 Félix López, *San Antonio*, 1985, aspen, pine, homemade gesso, mineral pigments, piñón sap varnish, beeswax, 32.5" x 11.5" x 9"

Félix López, *San Antonio*. PLATE 57. López, originally a language teacher in northern New Mexico, became a *santero* (an artist who makes santos) partly to address his grief after his father, a carpenter, died. Since 1991 he has occupied himself full-time as an artist and has attained recognition as one of the finest *santeros* of New Mexico. The importance of family and tradition are at the heart of López's art. He creates his santos in the traditional manner and has passed on the art to his son, Joseph, and his daughter, Krissa Maria, who are already well known for their work.

On the occasion of the 750th anniversary of his death in 1981, the remains of Saint Anthony of Padua (1195-1231) were officially examined by the Catholic Church, which found that his vocal cords were intact (recognizable), and as a result, the saint, one of the Church's most revered figures, recognized for his evangelizing success, became the object of renewed international attention. López's 1985 *San Antonio*, done not long after the official examination of 1981, depicts the saint in the traditional way, in his Franciscan robe, tonsured in the Franciscan manner, and holding the baby Jesus. The work itself has been created according to the traditional method, constructed from aspen and pine to which gesso has been applied in order to bind the wood and provide a suitable surface for the application of the paint, then painted with mineral pigments, and finally varnished with *piñón* sap.

Susan Elizalde-Holder, *Structure*. PLATE 58. uman faces meld and converge to form the shape of a cross in this thought-provoking clay and acrylic piece. There are a number of points of esthetic tension in this work. One of them is the issue of whether the faces are merging to form the cross (implying death and the promise of resurrection) or emerging from the cross (implying a form of birth). Another issue is the merger of pre-Hispanic imagery with Western Christian iconography. Many of the faces are not clear enough to determine their ethnicity, but one or two are clearly of Mesoamerican vintage, particularly the one that displays the classic Mayan nose and profile. From this intermixture of the pre-Hispanic—including imagery associated with Mayan religious iconography—with the Christian cross, we are confronted with a number of philosophical issues such as the level of power and influence or the subordination and superordination of each cultural sphere, as well as the moral value of the cross for Amerindia. The cross represents compassion, but

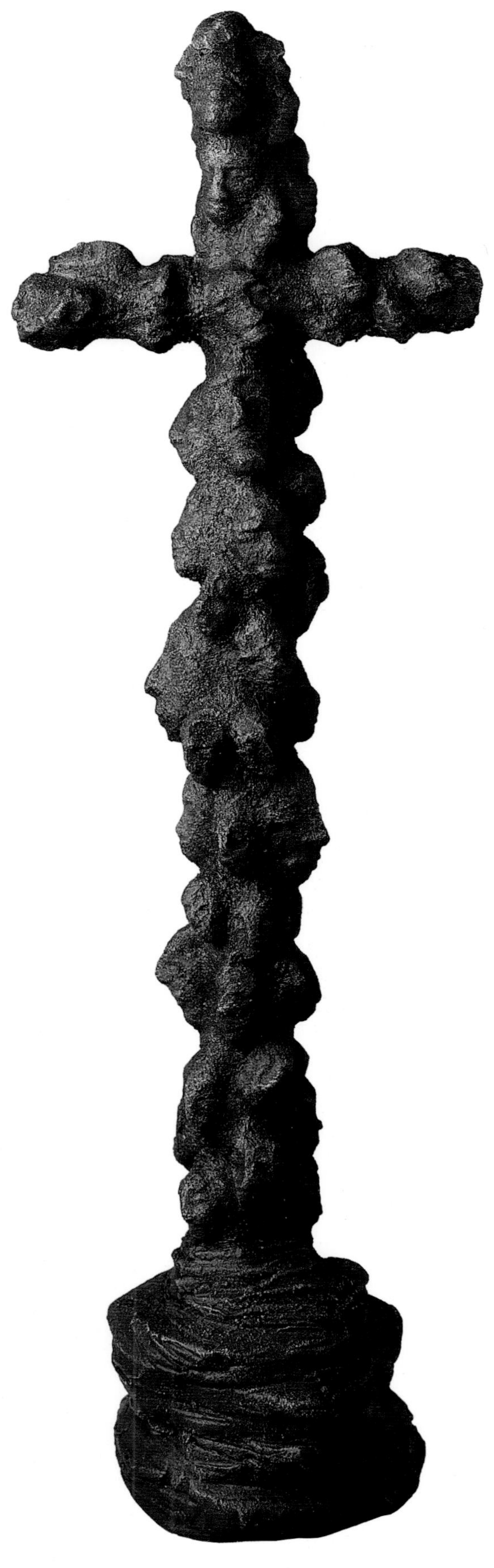

58 Susan Elizalde-Holder, *Structure*, 1998, clay and acrylic, 27" x 8" x 6"

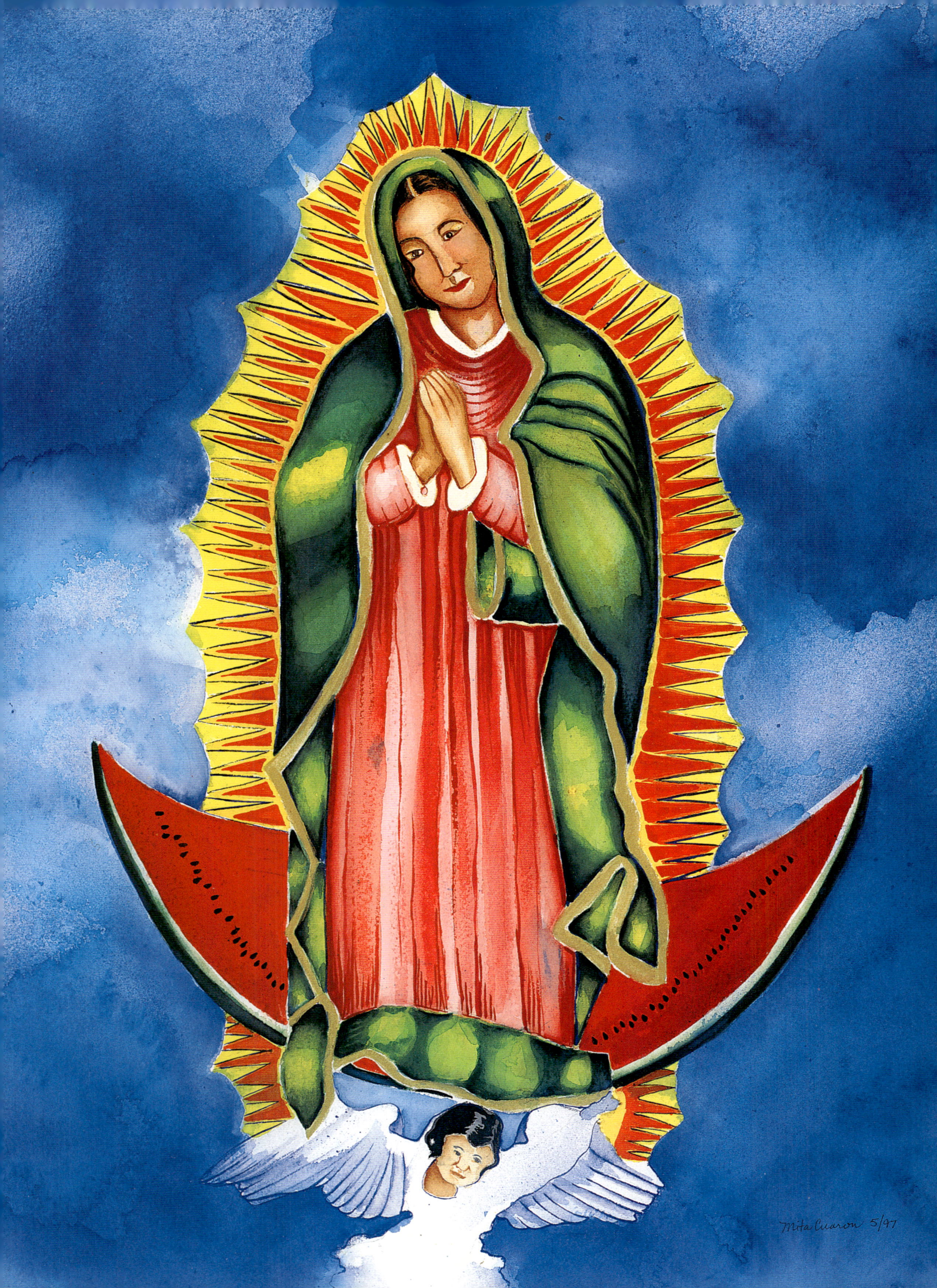

Mita Cuaron 5/97

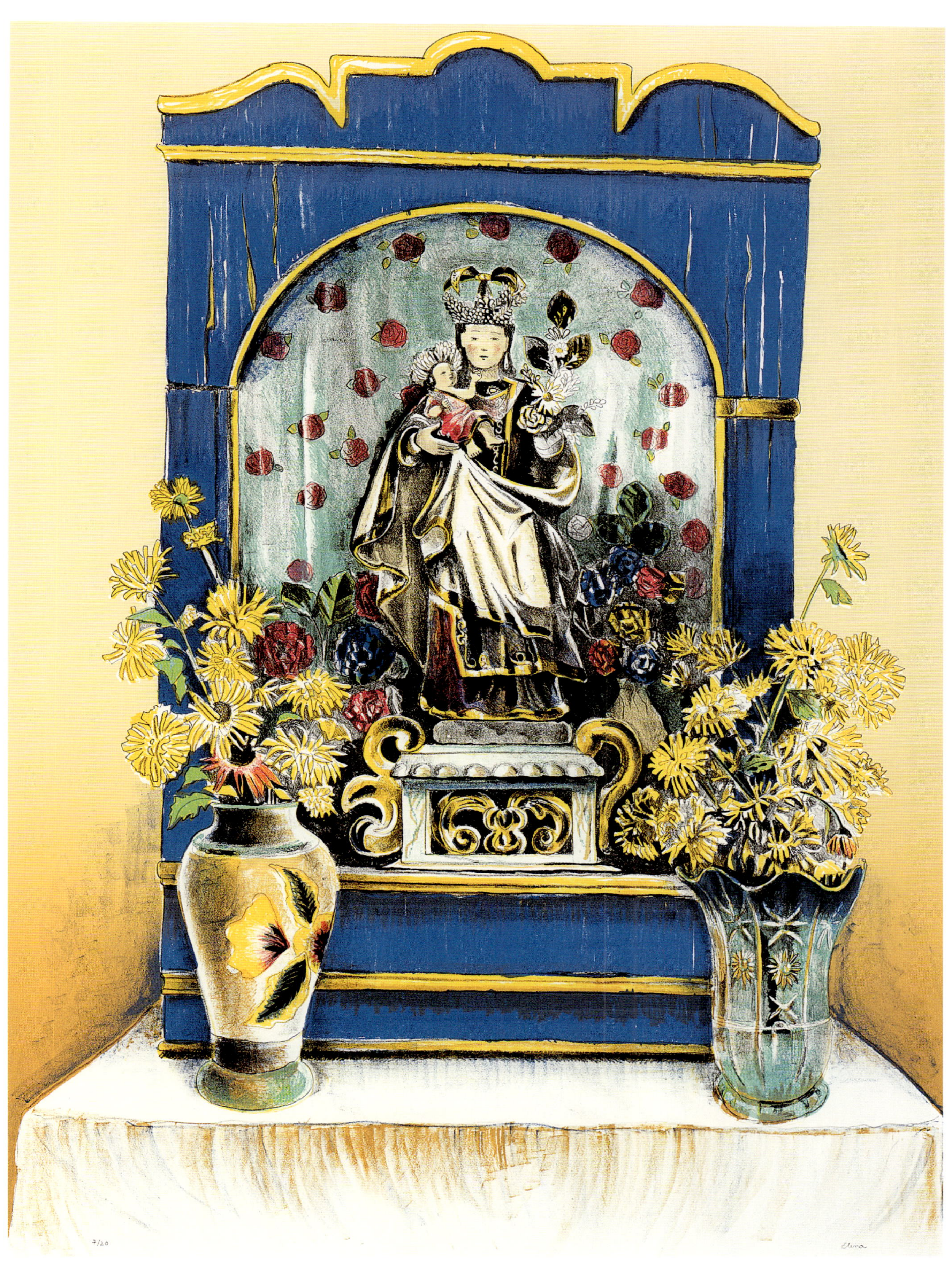

Left: 59 Margarita "Mita" Cuarón, *La Virgen de Sandía*
(The Watermelon Virgin), 1997, watercolor, 26" x 20"

60 Elena Climent, *Virgin in Blue Box*, 2001, lithograph, 30" x 22"

for Amerindians it also represents forced conversion from their religion and effacement of their culture and ethnicities. An additional esthetic tension relates to the platform and the cross. Are the cross and the human components that make it up emerging from the platform, that is, rising? Or is the cross descending and melting into its pedestal? The relationship is deliberately and poignantly ambiguous. This piece may suggest that faith provides the structure and discipline people need to have peace of mind in an otherwise frightening world while also signifying that the humanity behind tradition and symbols is the framework on which institutions are built. A more skeptical interpretation of the piece is as a comment on the power religion can have on its followers, causing them to be blind to the world outside their faith. Elizalde-Holder's intention is to allow the viewer to interpret the work in an intensely personal way, inspiring us to wonder if, instead of looking for the answers, we should be exploring the many questions.

Margarita "Mita" Cuarón, *La Virgen de Sandía* (*sandía* is watermelon). PLATE 59. This image of the Virgin of Guadalupe is representative of Cuarón's work, which often has conjoined the Virgin with fruits or vegetables in order to heighten her connections to the community and her condition as a woman with a woman's life cycle and her social and communal domain, without detracting from her venerability. A notable aspect of this work is that the Virgin does not rest on the customary crescent moon. In Christian symbolism the moon represents Mary because she, like the moon, does not generate any light on her own, but instead reflects the light of the sun, of Christ. In Aztec spirituality the moon is the lesser light that shines at night, giving protection to those who move about in the danger and secrecy of darkness. Here the Virgin rests on a succulent wedge of watermelon that itself has the same general shape as the customary moon icon but whose connotations emphasize fertility and an ordinary human status more than the traditional moon does. These qualities are further elaborated in the vestments that the Virgin is wearing. Instead of the traditional blue robe studded with stars, here, analogous to the watermelon (which replaces the moon), green and red are emphasized, respectively, in the Virgin's surrounding robe and her gown. The gown further indicates womanhood by the white, furry collar and matching trim on its sleeves. Finally, the form of her face and the part down the middle of her hair all inject an element of contemporaneity into the traditional image.

Elena Climent, *Virgin in Blue Box.* PLATE 60. Climent's works, often depicting beauty in everyday or worn items, are tributes to her homeland of Mexico and its industrious, creative peoples. In this lithograph, the artist recreates a household altarpiece, familiar, comforting, and conducive to worship. Against a blue-and-gold-framed background, the Madonna and baby Jesus rest on a pedestal. The Virgin's crown appears to be gold and is adorned with white leaves, and she wears a regal robe. In her left hand she holds a bouquet of white flowers, and in her right arm she cradles her son, who appears to wear a crown made of petals of pure white flowers where later, in adulthood, he will wear the crown of thorns. Red roses painted on the background shower the holy pair. In the foreground, two vases filled with yellow chrysanthemums have been placed slightly in front of and to either side of the *retablo*. One vase is cut glass, the other decorated ceramic, but both feature flowers as part of the decoration on the vases themselves. In mid-ground appears another vase on the right, and there is probably one on the left as well, although the view is obstructed. It is noteworthy that the placement of flowers in these latter two vases merges with the images of the roses that are part of the *retablo* itself, producing a harmonious ensemble that also plays with perspective so that the various layers (from back to front, the painted background, the tier featuring the Virgin and Child flanked by simple vases, the two more elaborate vases filled with flowers, and the end of the table) flow into each other. The *retablo*'s frame appears to be cracked and the paint has chipped, leading the viewer to suspect that it has weathered much, but has nonetheless been cherished. With warm yellows and a deep blue, Climent creates an atmosphere of comfort and home. Although the items in the piece show signs of wear and age, they are soothing, as would be appropriate for a home altarpiece, a familiar and comforting place of immediate worship that has been in use over the long term, perhaps over generations.

Ana Laura De La Garza, *La vida* (Life). PLATE 61. This unusual crucifixion scene takes us to a new dimension. Set high and in the middle of a cross by two paint-smudged arms and hands is an almost naked infant whose morphology is similar to what is identified in countless paintings of the Christ child (usually with the Madonna, never mounted on a cross) but whose position, with outstretched arms and twisted feet crossed one over

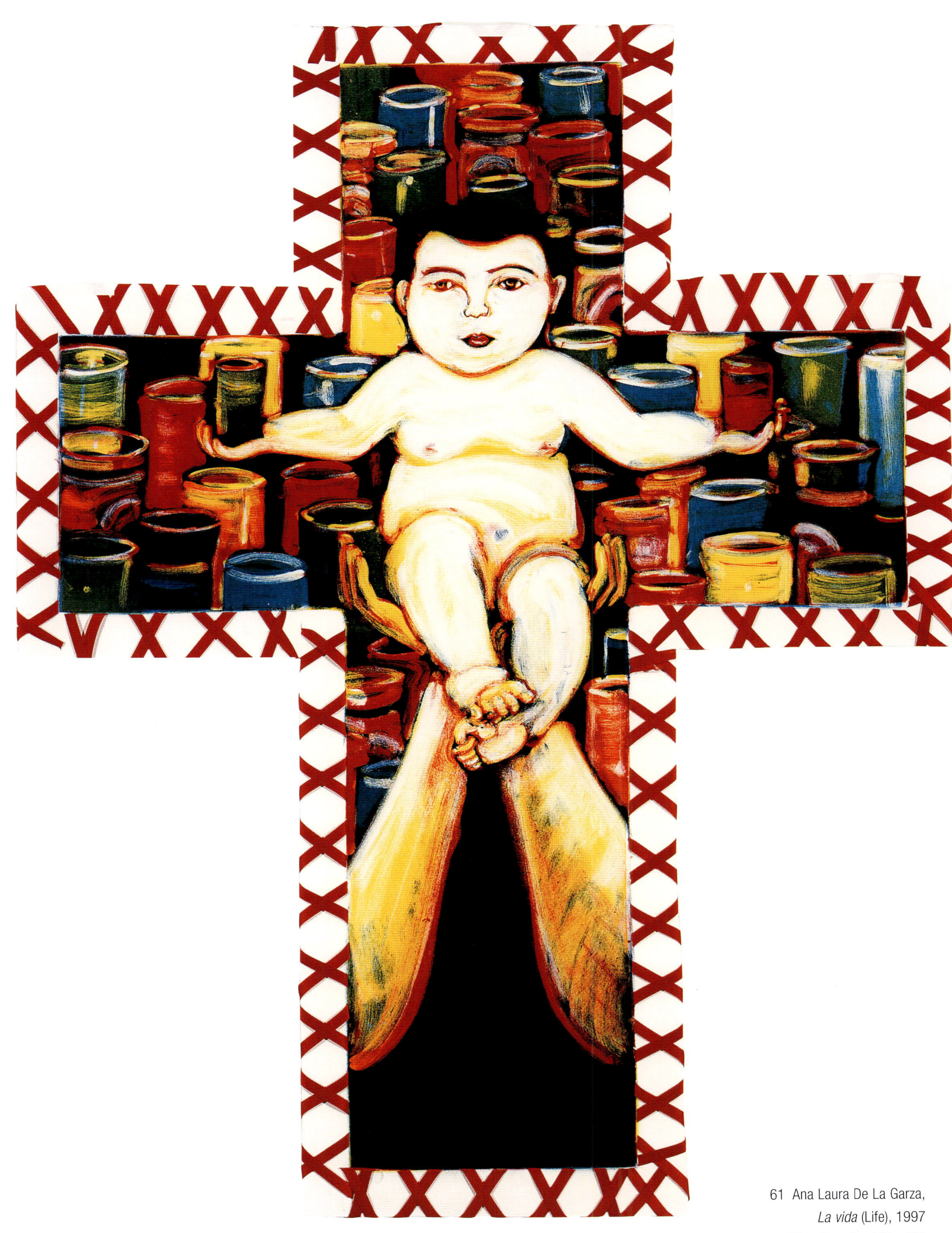

61 Ana Laura De La Garza,
La vida (Life), 1997
Mixed media, 42" x 33"

the other, evokes the crucifixion of Christ. The cross itself is highly idiosyncratic. Bounded by red ribbons, the top portion is filled with multicolored jars of paint (that also resemble votive candles), and each outstretched hand of the child, an icon of newborn life, bears a jar of paint, one dark-colored and the other red. The symbolic implication seems to be that, both analogical to and counterposed to the vision of Christ who died on the cross for the redemption of humankind, we are confronted here with a new icon, a new object of veneration in the form of a paint-bearing infant. Art holds the promise of redeeming us. Also implied are not only the redemptive power of art, but also the necessity of it in order to illuminate to ourselves who we are, what we stand for, and what we believe in. This painterly homage to the powers of art also calls attention in its iconography to the countless crucifixion scenes produced by artists on behalf of the faith and of the visual story of Christianity. The image, at once novel and provocative because of its originality, also carries with it a certain comforting theme, emphasizing redemptive powers and the promise of the creative spirit, of the replenishing and renewing impetus of artistic imagination.

ESPÍRITU HUMANO

Teddy Sandoval, *Angel Baby*. PLATE 62. Completing this work only days before he died of complications from AIDS, artist Teddy Sandoval represents himself as a pugilist, ready to trade blows with his antagonist. Because Sandoval was no boxer in reality, the image is metaphorical in nature and represents the artist's struggle against his implacable illness while also celebrating his spirit and the spirit of humankind generally to not give in to despair. The work makes use of a spare number of images, each of them poignantly symbolic. The intact, unblemished body, exposed from the waist up, is at the point of transformation or metamorphosis. The curtain is held back by a plumed serpent with a cross attached to the end of its rattle so that the artist can make his final curtain call. He is ready to fly up to a Christian heaven but also to one mediated by the god symbolized by the feathered serpent, Quetzalcoatl, the bearded god of the Toltecs, Aztecs, and Mayas (for the latter with the name Kukulkan) who was banished from the Amerindian world but who vowed to return from his exile. The feathers of the boxer's wings evoke the Christian angel, but even more so,

the red-and-green quetzal that makes up part of the composite god Quetzalcoatl. Hope is foregrounded in this work in the form of the word on the banner that crosses the heart tattooed on his arm. With a twinge of humor, the word "Everlast" is found on the boxer's gloves and trunks, mimicking the customary product advertisements that are often placed on a boxer's clothing. It is that "everlast" hope that transcends mere mortality and aspires to the heavens.

Nivia González, *Angelita* (Little Angel). PLATE 63. Nivia González is a celebrated artist whose honors and awards include "Outstanding Achievement in the Arts," awarded by the Mexican-American Women's National Association, and *Hispanic* magazine's "Woman of the Year." Her artwork has appeared on a number of book covers including, notably, the highly recognized *The House on Mango Street* by Sandra Cisneros. The victim of a near-fatal accident several years ago, Nivia González refused to be deterred by her medical condition, and recently she has been able to return to artistic creation. *Angelita* is a highly characteristic work. González almost always depicts women, represented variously as ethereal beings, maternal figures, or simple peasants. Most often, as in the case of *Angelita*, the artist's figures are shown with eyes downcast, which she says "represents their introspective and centered state of mind." This work is also characteristic in its drawing and compositional style, which draws upon typical features of Chicano/Mexicano folk forms of composition, even as it takes this style to a higher level of sophistication. While González usually works with colors that are also characteristic of Chicano folk art, *Angelita* is an unusually shimmering piece, with something of a Christmas ornament quality. Her work can be both compared and contrasted with that of César Martínez. It is similar in that her subject is foregrounded against a solid background color; however, the choice of colors—bright gold as the background and a rich-toned brown emphasized in the skin—leads to a far different, festive result when compared to Martínez's introspective and emotionally expressionistic *Sandra Cisneros*. Additionally, González emphasizes finely drawn decorative patterns in both the angel's feathers and gown, endowing the work with a baroque and folkish quality. On the other hand, the drawing of the angel's face and body, reflecting a geometric and even architectural procedure, drains the work of many human characteristics, substituting in their stead the intimation of a generic or archetypal being.

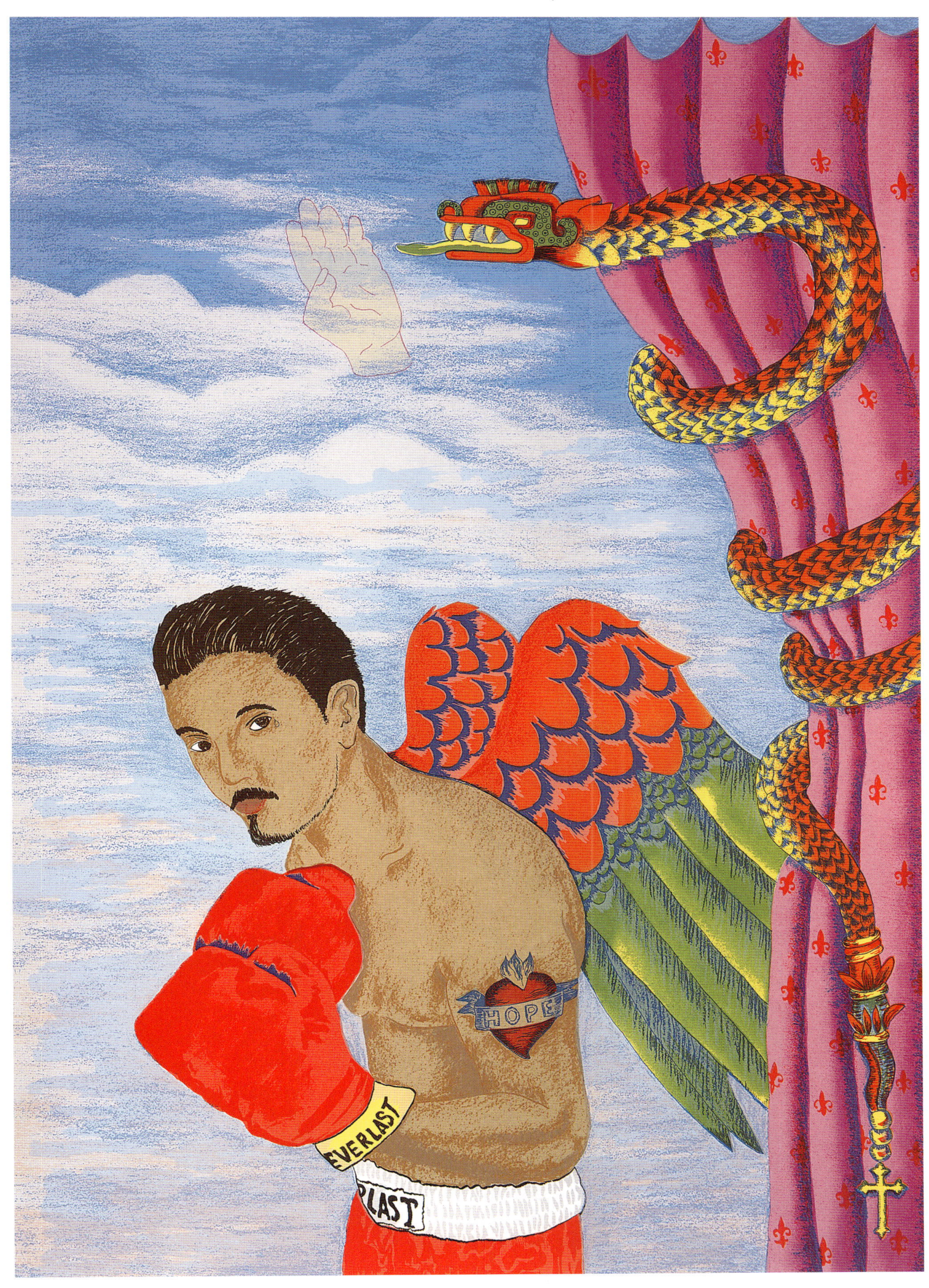

62 Teddy Sandoval, *Angel Baby*, 1995, serigraph, 38" x 26"

Pattsi Valdez, *The Dreamer*. PLATE 64. This romantic, wistful, and magical portrait of a young woman on a moonlit night has elements of what Cuban writer Alejo Carpentier called *lo real maravilloso* (the marvelous real), the analog of which in English is termed magic realism (originally coined in 1925 by German art critic Franz Roh). What is typically *real maravilloso* in the piece is that while the work is realistic in one sense, it well embodies Carpentier's view that *lo real maravilloso* arises from an unexpected alteration of reality, from a privileged revelation of reality "that is perceived with particular intensity by virtue of an exaltation of the spirit that leads it to a kind of extreme state." We are favored in this exterior portrait with an artistic passport into the interior, bittersweet dreams or yearnings of a young woman on a magical and meaningful night. She is solitary and poised within extremes: her right hand limply holds a flowing handkerchief. Her expression implies sadness, probably tears in the context of love lost. Her right hand holds a gorgeous red rose which, oversized and in full bloom, appears to hang like a pendant from the strand of pearls around her neck. The handkerchief bodes the memory of past love's trials, and the rose, the augury of future love's promise. The young woman is dressed in an alluring blue party dress, wearing dangling earrings, and swathed in moonlight and starlight, the strands of her hair radiating outward and bathed in a luminous halo around her head. This is an emphatically secular image with its promise of romance and love, yet there is an underlying hint of a portrait of the Virgin in the halo and in the starry night that surrounds her, similar to the star-studded cape of Guadalupe. Also, the two icons, the romantic woman and Guadalupe, are emphatically *morena*. The dark skin of the dreamer and her flouncy lace ruffles contrast harmoniously with the body of her blue polka-dotted dress, which in turn complements the blue heavens that are decorated by an ordered pattern of stars.

Yreina D. Cervántez, *Disfrutamos la fruta de nuevo* (We're enjoying the fruit once again). PLATE 65. Overtly similar in its use of the mirror to Larry Yáñez's *Camana My House* and implicitly similar to Cristina Cárdenas's *La niña de los espejos*, this work of art is a self-portrait of the artist that is once removed since the artist is looking at herself in the mirror. At one level, the work mimics the artist's method of doing a self-portrait, the need to paint from a reflected image (or possibly a photograph) in order to capture the level of detail that marks this work. Philosophically, the exercise of detachment and refraction involved in a work of art in which the subject and the artist are the same and the work reflects literally the act of reflection raises complex issues about the nature of reality and how it is distinguished from the self's interpretation of it. As in other works by Cervántez, this piece combines self-portraiture with imagery of cultural identity, which is seen by virtue of the form of the skeleton that we glimpse part of, the Amerindian designs that provide the background of the portrait in the mirror, the flowery neck of the very Mexican dress worn by the artist that frames the lower portion of the portrait within the mirror, and even the lemon. Executed with careful attention to detail and a festive, bright color scheme characteristic of Mexican folk art, the work also draws attention to aspects of Mexican/Chicano identity through the personal features of the subject, including the long, straight, flowing black hair, the shape of the nose, and the color and shape of the eyes. This is a figure that Chicanos can identify with readily and, by implication, an artist whose fidelity, simplicity, and lack of pretense we can trust.

Maya González, *The Love That Stains*. PLATE 66. In this provocative work, two female figures, one slightly behind the other, dominate the composition while a hummingbird hovers on the right side, near the figures' ears. The women have identical physical features, but it is their differences that intrigue the viewer. The dominant figure is radiant and filled with life. Her tawny skin glows, and her eyes shine as she glances at the hummingbird to her left. She is wearing several layers of dress that appear to simplify as they progress outward, finally resulting in a plain white sleeveless frock. A pierced heart rests at the woman's breast, spilling its life-giving force on her attire and staining each layer as it flows. Her ears are adorned with turquoise; her hair has a band of roses. The woman's companion wears an undecorated slip or sleeveless dress and other than the roses in her hair has no ornamentation. The muted colors González used to create this figure suggest other-worldliness, that the woman is a spirit or specter. She holds her counterpart in a gentle embrace, and her countenance is calm and at peace. Despite the flowing blood, neither figure appears concerned.

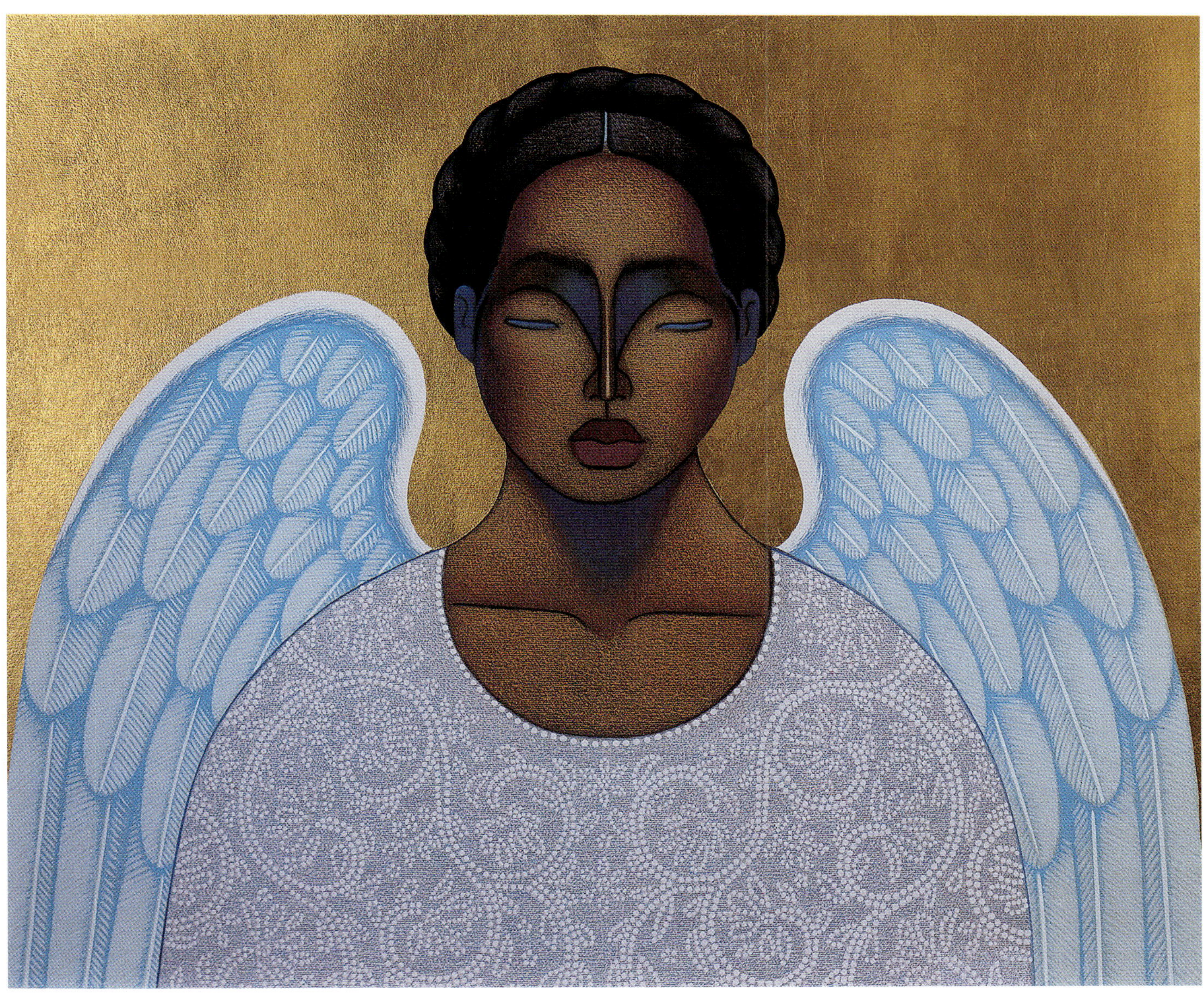

63 Nivia González, *Angelita* (Little Angel), 1995, lithograph, 22" x 25.5"

The symbolism in this piece is striking. Xochiquetzal, goddess of love, flowers, vegetation, and fire to peoples of ancient Mexico, was sometimes depicted as a hummingbird. This goddess was said to protect artists, handicraft-workers, painters, prostitutes, and housekeepers. In explaining the painting, González said she had a vision that a hummingbird pierced her heart, filling her with love that could not be contained. The many dresses worn by the dominant figure hint that the woman is attempting to hide her true identity, but each effort brings her closer to her truth and reveals her inner strength, her connection with the spiritual world and with her heritage. The spilling blood represents love and truth, staining all that it touches, changing it forever.

Paul Botello, *Inner Nature*. PLATE 67. Paul Botello is a painter of both public and private works. His public works are murals, monumental pieces in Los Angeles and other cities in the United States and Europe, that speak to their communities. His private works are paintings on canvas or paper that express more personal concerns. *Inner Nature* bridges these two categories because the serigraph is a version of the central portion of a mural titled *Inner Resources* that he created on a basketball gym wall in Los Angeles City Terrace Park. The 36-by-82-foot mural, begun in 1994 and completed in 2000, resulted from Botello's interviews with neighbors about their hopes for the revitalized park, and neighborhood teenagers assisted him with the paint-

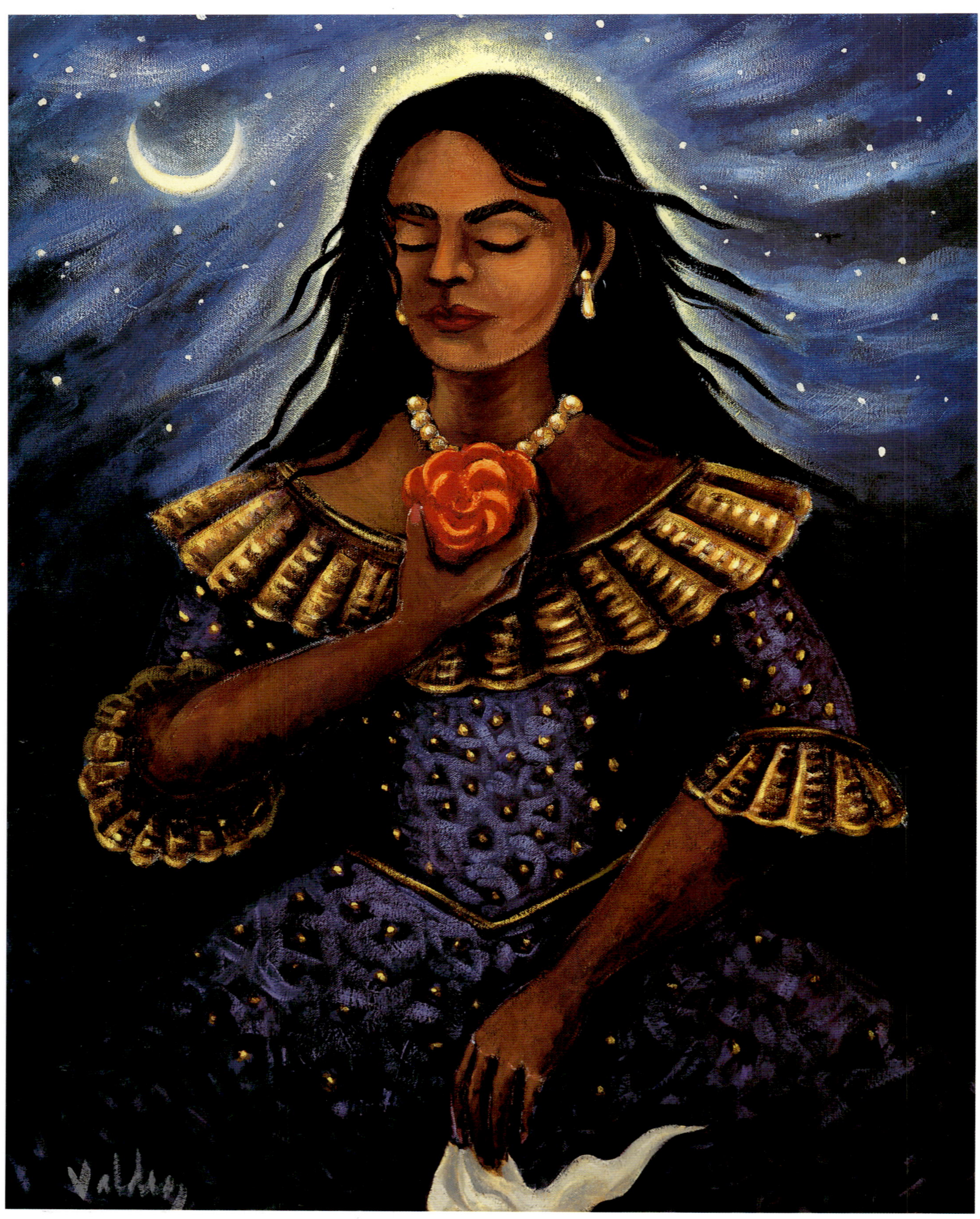

64 Pattsi Valdez, *The Dreamer*, 2002, acrylic on canvas, 30" x 24"

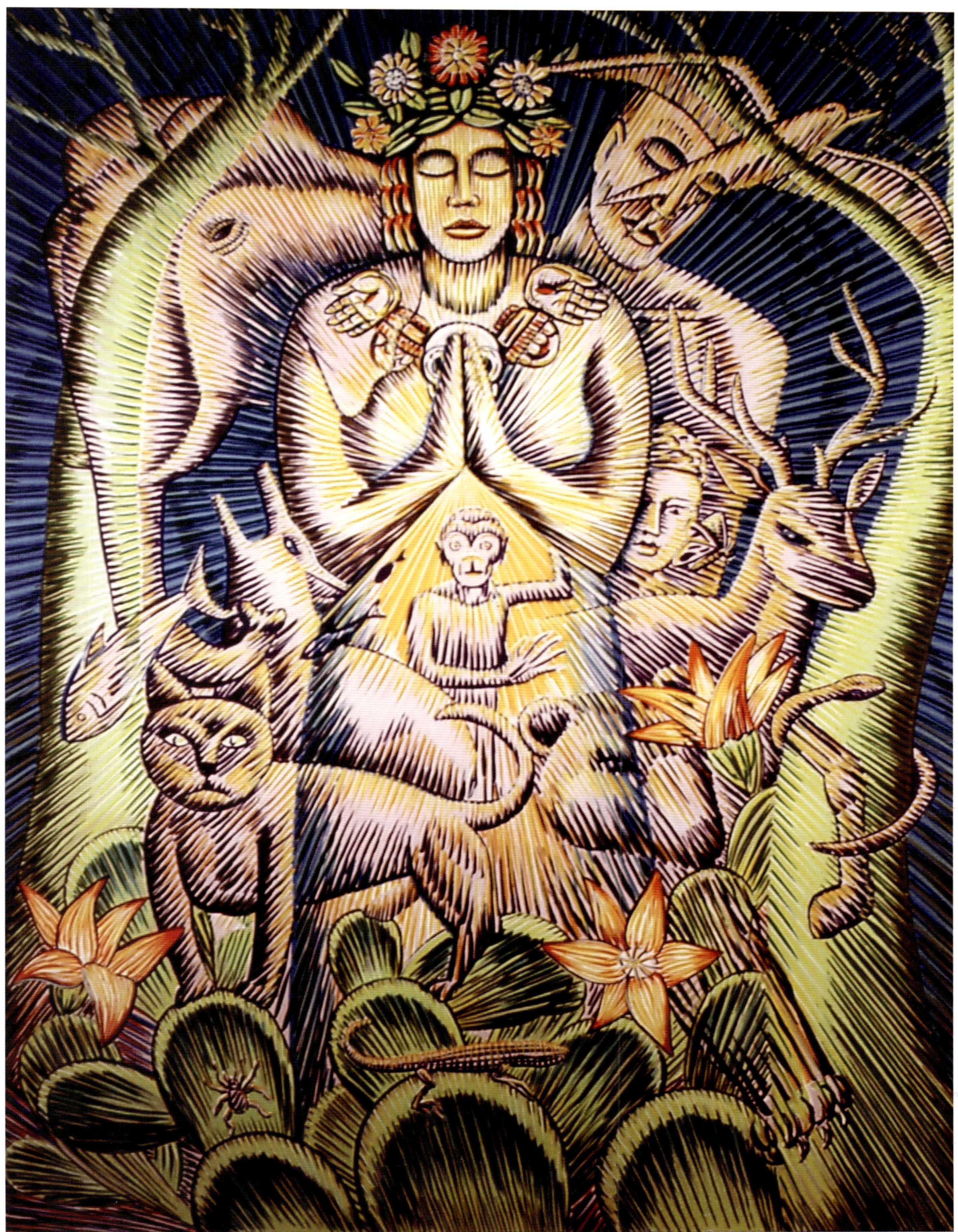

67 Paul Botello, *Inner Nature*, 1999, serigraph, 38" x 30"

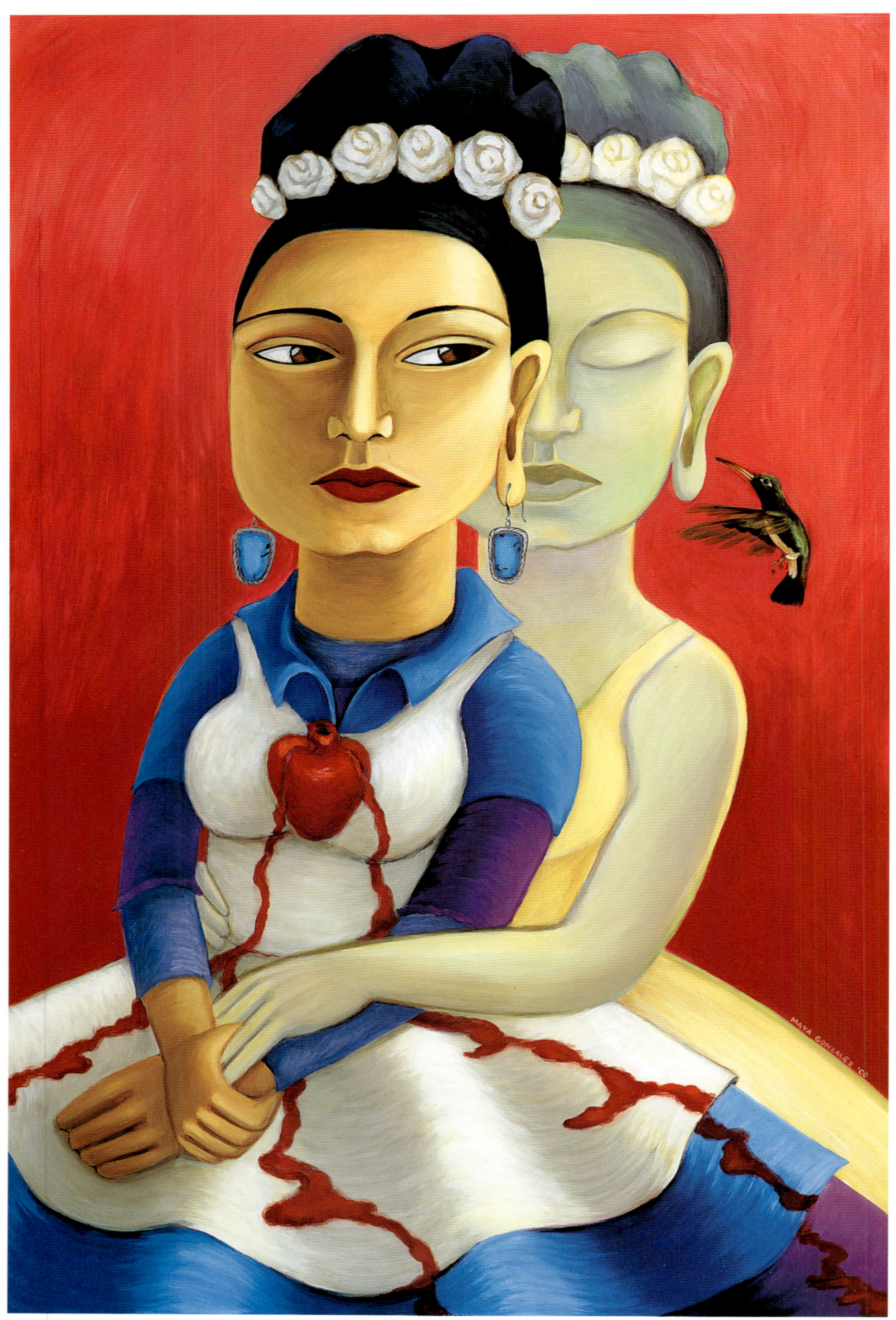

66 Maya González, *The Love That Stains*, 2000, acrylic on Masonite, 36" x 24"

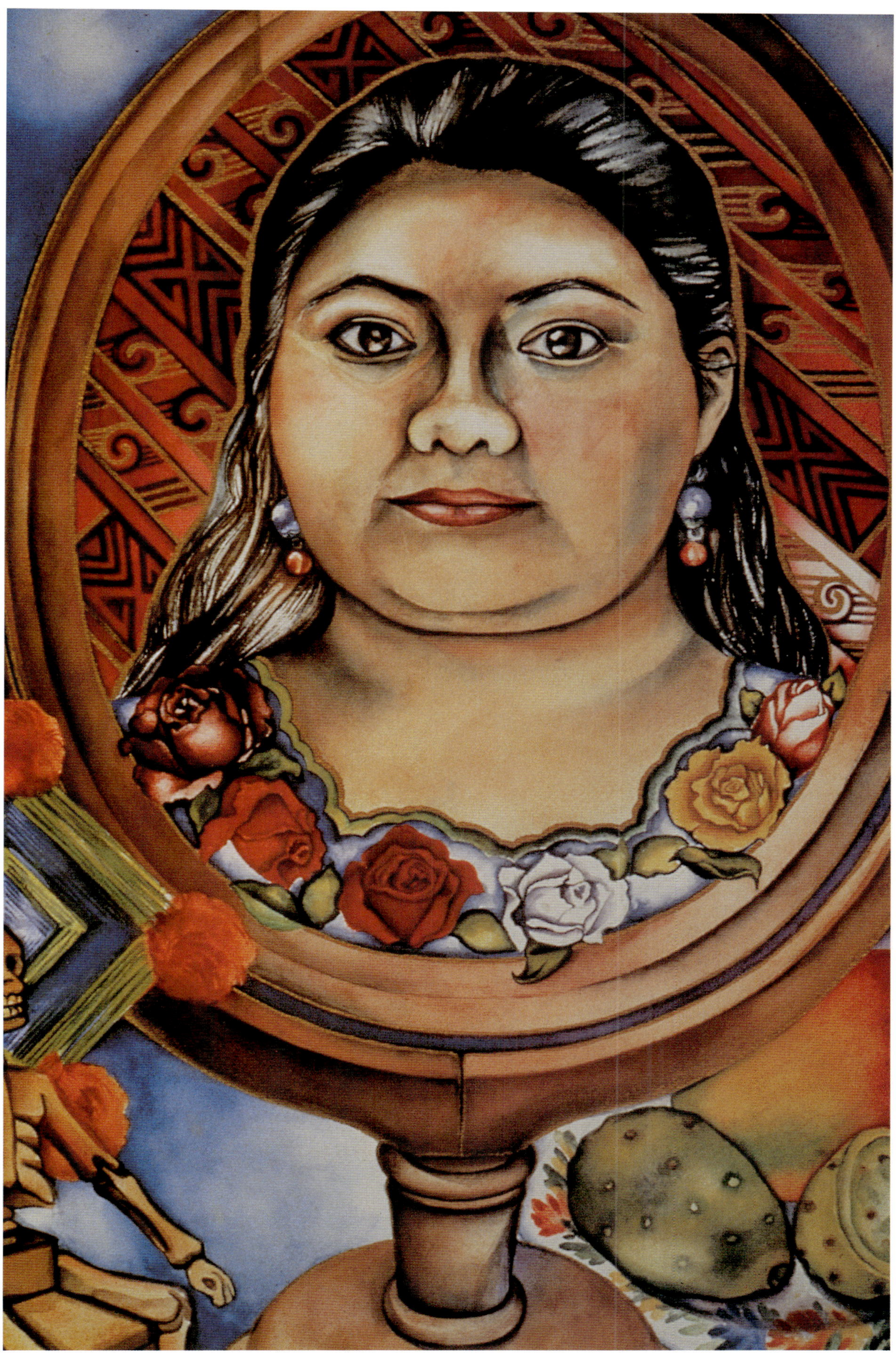

65 Yreina D. Cervántez, *Disfrutamos la fruta de nuevo* (We're enjoying the fruit once again), 1993, watercolor, 12" x 8"

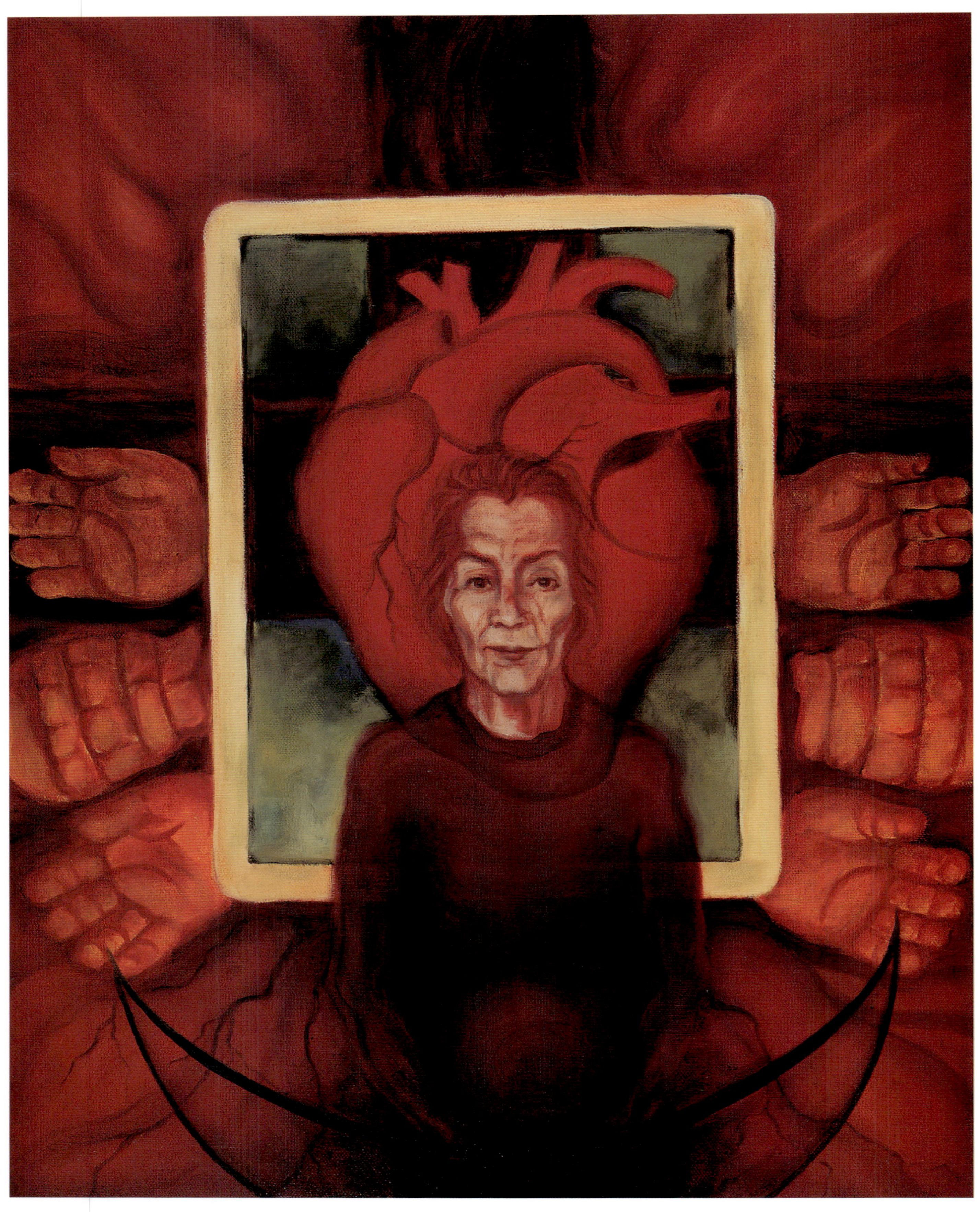

68 Alma Gómez, *El Sagrado Corazón* (The Sacred Heart), 2000, acrylic on canvas, 24" x 18"

ing. The central figure in the serigraph is a woman wearing a flowered headdress, her eyes and hands in an attitude of prayer. She wears a necklace with various icons, including hands with shapes in the palms that suggest either eyes or stigmata. A child peeks out from behind her, and a man is behind them both, giving support and protection. Trees on either side of the composition gently bend toward the center to embrace the family. A warm, golden light emanates from the woman's center, and animals, plants, and insects from around the globe seem to grow from her body. Everything in the composition works to place the woman in the center as the source of life and power. The complex linear structure of the light rays creates an aura similar to the common representation of the Virgin of Guadalupe, another powerful image of a woman representing peace, love, and the unity of all life forms.

Alma Gómez, *El Sagrado Corazón* (The Sacred Heart). PLATE 68. In this captivating work in which deep red predominates, Alma Gómez pays tribute to her dear friend Socorro, a *curandera* (healer) and storyteller who has enthralled the artist with stories of healing, devotion, and life in Mexico. The older woman's countenance suggests a calm, dignified woman who moves through life with humor despite the sorrows she has endured. Behind her is a *Lotería* card, symbolizing the subject's ties to Mexican culture. The image on the card is of a heart, representing not only the subject's capacity to love but also her devotion to the Catholic Church and her heritage by means of imagery associated with Coatlicue, the Mesoamerican goddess of the earth. The card floats atop a background of hearts and hands, further references to the goddess, while a crescent moon, a symbol often connoting the beloved Guadalupe, cradles Socorro. Also in the background of this multilayered composition isa cross, underscoring the subject's complete commitment and dedication to her religious beliefs. Together the images represent the complexity of her culture. "The depiction of all these elements in a single painting parallels the Chicano/a experience of self-reincarnation informed by multiple worldviews," the artist writes. The deep reds and glowing gold and green give the piece depth and intensify the signification of devotion.

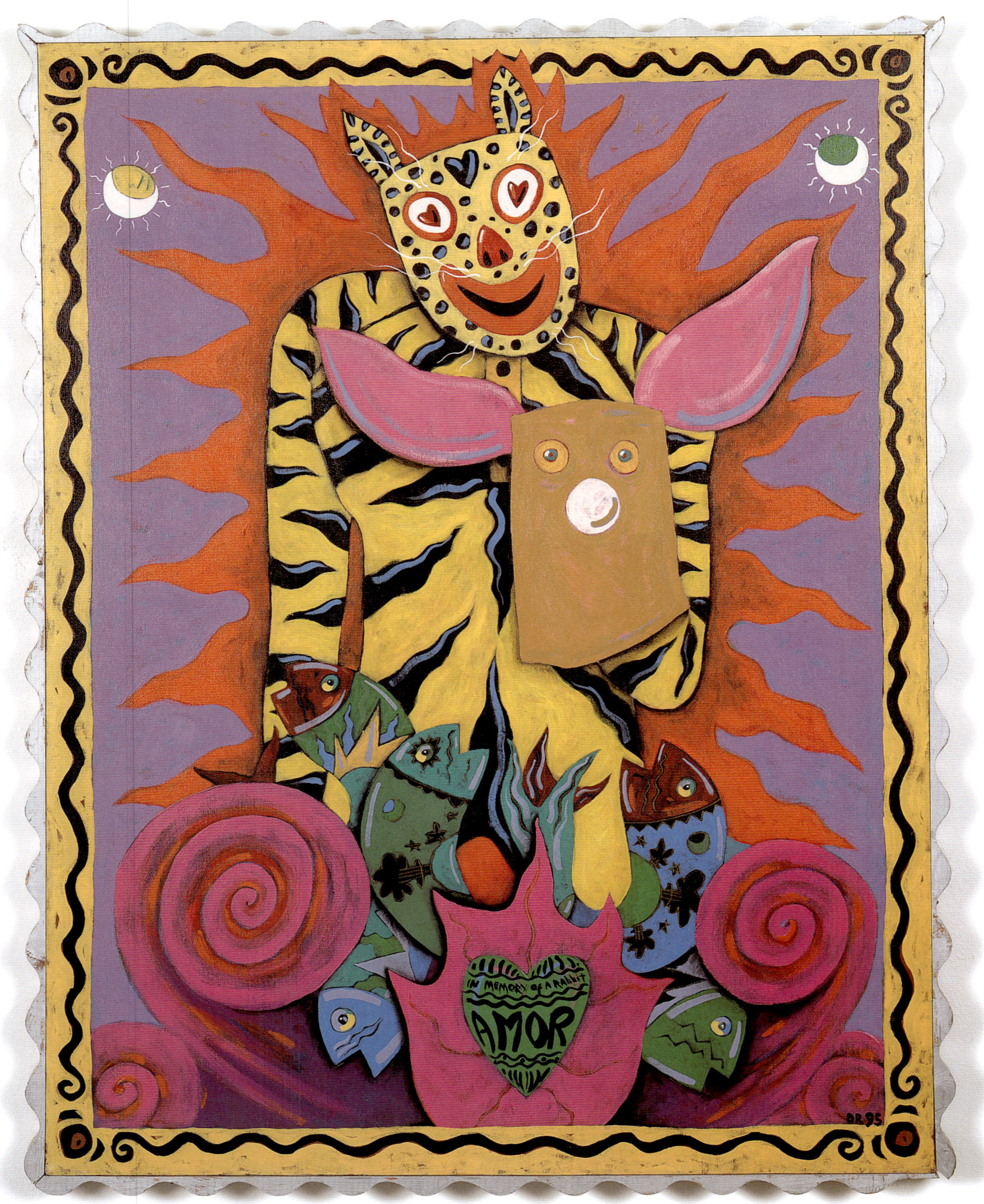

69 David Rosales, *In Memory of a Rabbit*, 1996, acrylic on canvas, 50" x 37.5"

Profundamente sentido, ampliamente reconocido

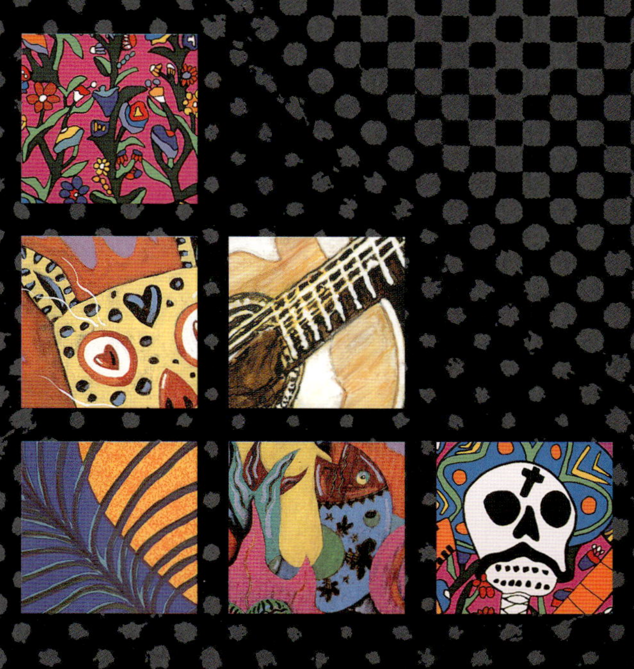

Deeply Felt, Widely Known

his section is divided into two themes dedicated to, on the one hand, certain feelings, intuitions, artistic creations, and events that individuate us all, Chicana/o and other populations alike, and on the other hand those phenomena that are integral components of shared experience and of the social fabric. Thus, in the theme "Profundamente personal" (Profoundly personal), we are exposed to self-identification through self-portrait and to grief, fantasy, reminiscence, religious apprehension, abandonment (even at the altar), and perhaps nightmare. "Compartido por todos" (Shared by all) takes us to the domain of social validation and social identity through shared activities and experiences. In this theme the viewer is exposed to music (including mariachi and *norteño* music), Mexican cinema, and pastimes that are characteristically Chicano/Latino such as the heroic social-justice component of public wrestling (in the figure of *Santo* and other wrestling heroes) or the *Lotería*/bingo-type game that, while it owes something to Tarot cards, is uniquely Hispanic.

PROFUNDAMENTE PERSONAL

David Rosales, *In Memory of a Rabbit.* PLATE 69.

David Rosales lives, teaches, and practices his art in San Bernardino, California, 100 miles east of Los Angeles. He both paints and works in digital technologies, using Internet-based media to explore Chicano culture as it has developed in California's Inland Empire. *In Memory of a Rabbit* is part of a series called Love Tiger that he worked on from 1994 to 1997, inspired by a folk-art tiger costume he purchased on a trip to Mexico. The costume represented for Rosales both the hiding of one's identity and the acting out of an alternative one, analogous to what we all do in our everyday lives as we mark ourselves as belonging or not belonging to a particular group. At the same time that he was producing this series, Rosales worked as an artist in residence at the Patton State Hospital for the criminally insane in San Bernardino. One project was for each inmate to create a paper-bag puppet and narrate a story about it. One inmate's story was about an abandoned and unloved rabbit that died in captivity. Realizing that the inmate was speaking about himself, Rosales was moved to feature the paper-bag rabbit puppet in one of his Love Tiger pieces. In this painting, the tiger appears friendly with a big orange smile

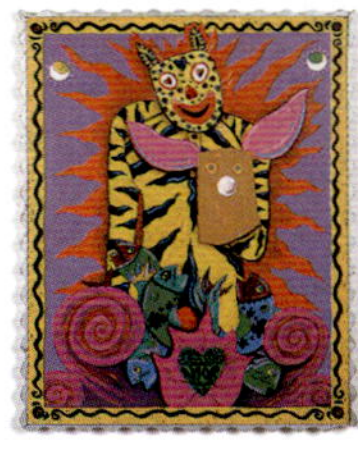

In Memory of a Rabbit, see page 94

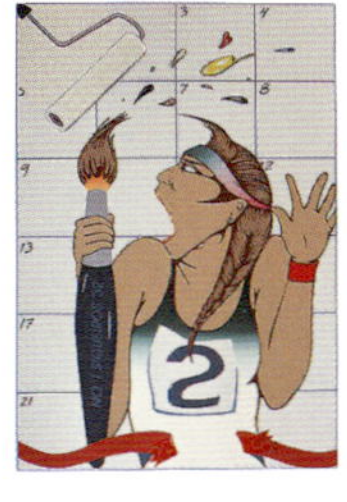

Self-Portrait, see page xiv

and heart-shaped eyes. Fish dance at his feet and the colors are playful and childlike. There is danger, however, and we remember that tigers are carnivores with sharp teeth. The puppet functions as a less important figure in the composition than the tiger, but it also carries the meaning of a mask behind which one can hide. The orange sun-ray pattern surrounding the tiger is reminiscent of the aura around the Virgin of Guadalupe as she is usually depicted. The geometric patterns continue to the edge of the canvas and beyond. Rosales himself constructed the wave-design, silver-painted wooden frame, which complements and combines well with the wavy black line around the edge of the painting.

Barbara Carrasco, *Self-Portrait.* PLATE 6.

Barbara Carrasco created this seventeen-color serigraph in response to the experience of being censored in 1982 as she created a mural entitled *L.A. History: A Mexican Perspective.* The mural was to be ready for the Olympics held in Los Angeles in 1984, but it was judged too controversial by the Los Angeles Community Redevelopment Agency that sponsored it and was never installed. For many years, most of Carrasco's artistic production centered on political statements in support of her struggles on behalf of the mural project and before that by means of her banner paintings for the United Farmworkers. In contrast, *Self-Portrait* was created at Self-Help Graphics in 1985 as an intensely personal statement. As the focus of the piece, the female figure gasps with horror as white paint is rolled onto a grid that has been prepared for painting a mural. It appears it will roll over her as well. The figure is dressed as a runner and is carrying an oversized paintbrush that doubles as an Olympic torch and is also reminiscent of the Statue of Liberty's. On the handle of the paintbrush/torch are the words "No. 1 Siqueiros '32," a reference to the mural *Tropical America* painted by David Alfaro Siqueiros in Los Angeles in 1932. Also judged too controversial for its subject matter and its dedication to the Mexican American community, Siqueiros's mural was whitewashed. Carrasco's mural was the second to be censored, exactly fifty years after the first, hence the number 2 on her runner's jersey. Despite the successful censorship of her mural, Carrasco depicts herself crossing the finish line, carrying the torch of freedom and shining light on the darkness of those who would stifle artistic expression.

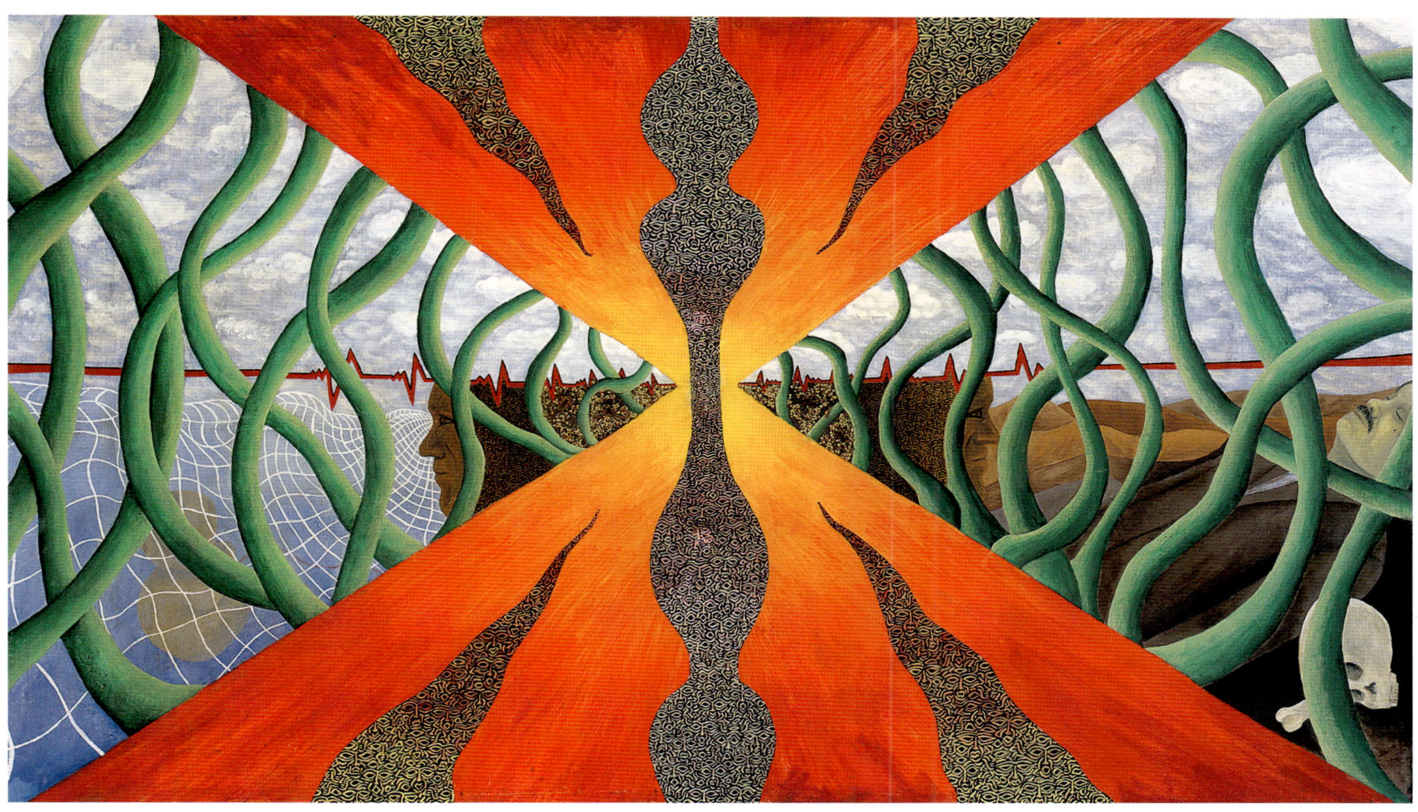

70 David Anthony García, *Requiem*, 2002, mixed media, 42" x 72" x 5.25"

David Anthony García, *Requiem*. PLATE 70. This multimedia, multidimensional, expressionistic piece shocks us with its high color and design contrasts. Bright vertical pointed oranges draw us into the focal point of this large-scale work, which engages our attention and calls for serious thought or meditation, somewhat like an Eastern mandala. Because the canvas itself has been overstretched, the resulting work displays an uneven surface that dips in the four cardinal directions and then rises to a peak at the center. The dead center point protrudes outward like a promontory. Reinforcing the pointed orange vectors are dark brown and earthen-colored flamelike designs that upon closer inspection are revealed to be hundreds of faces or totemic masks in various states of emotion, perhaps representing souls trapped in purgatory. To the right of center is a representation of the individual's physical life. A face looks out on earth and sky. A man in repose on a hilly landscape, his face ashen, indicates the end of his physical journey. A skull rests below him, symbolizing the return of the body to the earth. The left side of the work also shows a face looking in the opposite direction at a web or net above which is a cloud-filled sky. A faint shadow of a baby floats beneath the web. Bisecting the piece is a cardiogram that is flat on either side of the work, with increasing impulses closer to the center. Thick green vines intertwine on both sides of the orange, suggesting that the spiritual and physical worlds are connected, despite a temporary separation. Finally, at the outer bounds of the central area the canvas has been built up with the addition of bodies of actual fossilized scorpions and seeds. The overall theme of this work, emphasized by its title, *Requiem,* is obviously a ceremony of recognition of the life of one individual. This one individual's requiem attains symphonic proportions: it is played out on a grand scale by the artful deployment of line, color, patterns (including patterns of faces), and the addition of organic materials and an icon of medical technology.

Dolores Guerrero, *Jugo de naranja* (Orange juice). PLATE 71. In this striking serigraph, Guerrero uses bright red and orange offset by dark blue and intense green to grab the viewer's attention and impart a message of passion and rage. A red, snarling wolf is set in front of what appears at first glance to be an orange moon. Upon further examination, we can see that the sphere is actually a giant orange, evidenced by the navel at the top of the image. The orange and the palm leaf behind the wolf imply that the picture refers to California and the fruit industry. Its title, *Jugo de naranja,* further supports the interpretation. The dark sky gives a sense of foreboding, and the snarling wolf suggests danger, that a predator threatens the farmworkers who pick the fruit. It could also represent a deep, seething anger at a system that has long profited by subjugating workers. The plight of migrant farmworkers has long been an issue in Chicana/o art; indeed, the Chicano art movement arose from the farmworker struggle for civil rights as activists worked to convince their communities to rise up against the injustices they had been forced to endure. The understated title of the work prompts us to think twice about an industry most U.S. citizens support regularly with little thought about the methods it employs to put that juice on our breakfast tables. Guerrero has long been active in the Chicano art and feminist movements.

Connie Arismendi, *Vigil.* PLATE 72. Connie Arismendi uses simple objects and conceptual design elements to elicit strong emotional reactions from her viewers. In *Vigil* she conveys burden, struggle, and regret, as well as strength, endurance, hope, and the aspiration for transcendence and afterlife, through patches of lead, softly and effectively illuminated by lamplight. By assembling this patchwork of lead and binding it together through the use of hundreds of nails, Arismendi creates an indestructible quilt in this installation piece, alluding to the physical and emotional labor, as well as the intense dedication involved in watching over a suffering loved one. Patience, concentration, and perhaps even tradition are also represented by the work. The piece is stark, save for the small, delicate glass oil lamp that emits a soft glow. The effect of the spreading and diffused light from the lamp

71 Dolores Guerrero, *Jugo de naranja* (Orange juice), 1994, serigraph, 26" x 38"

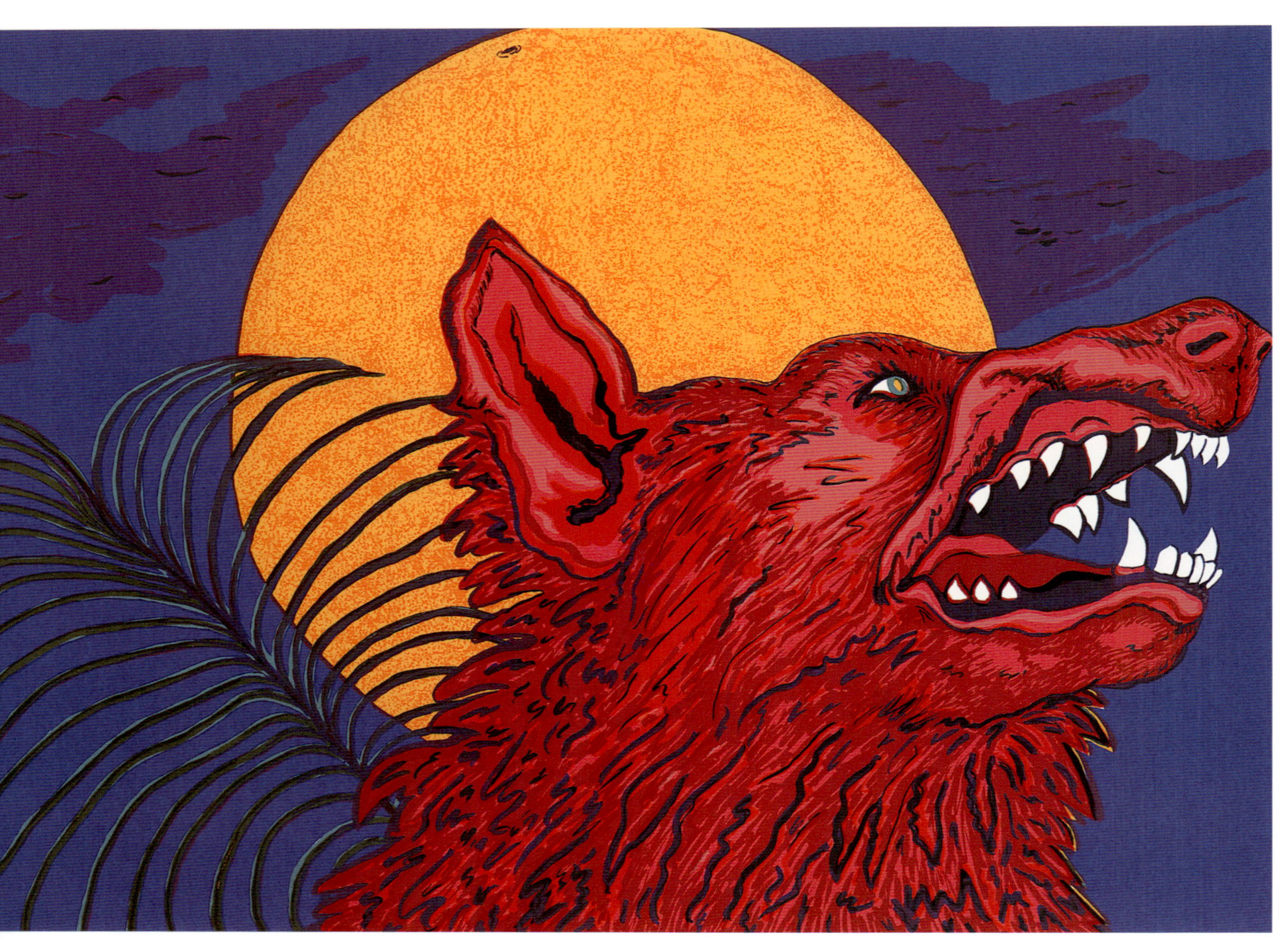

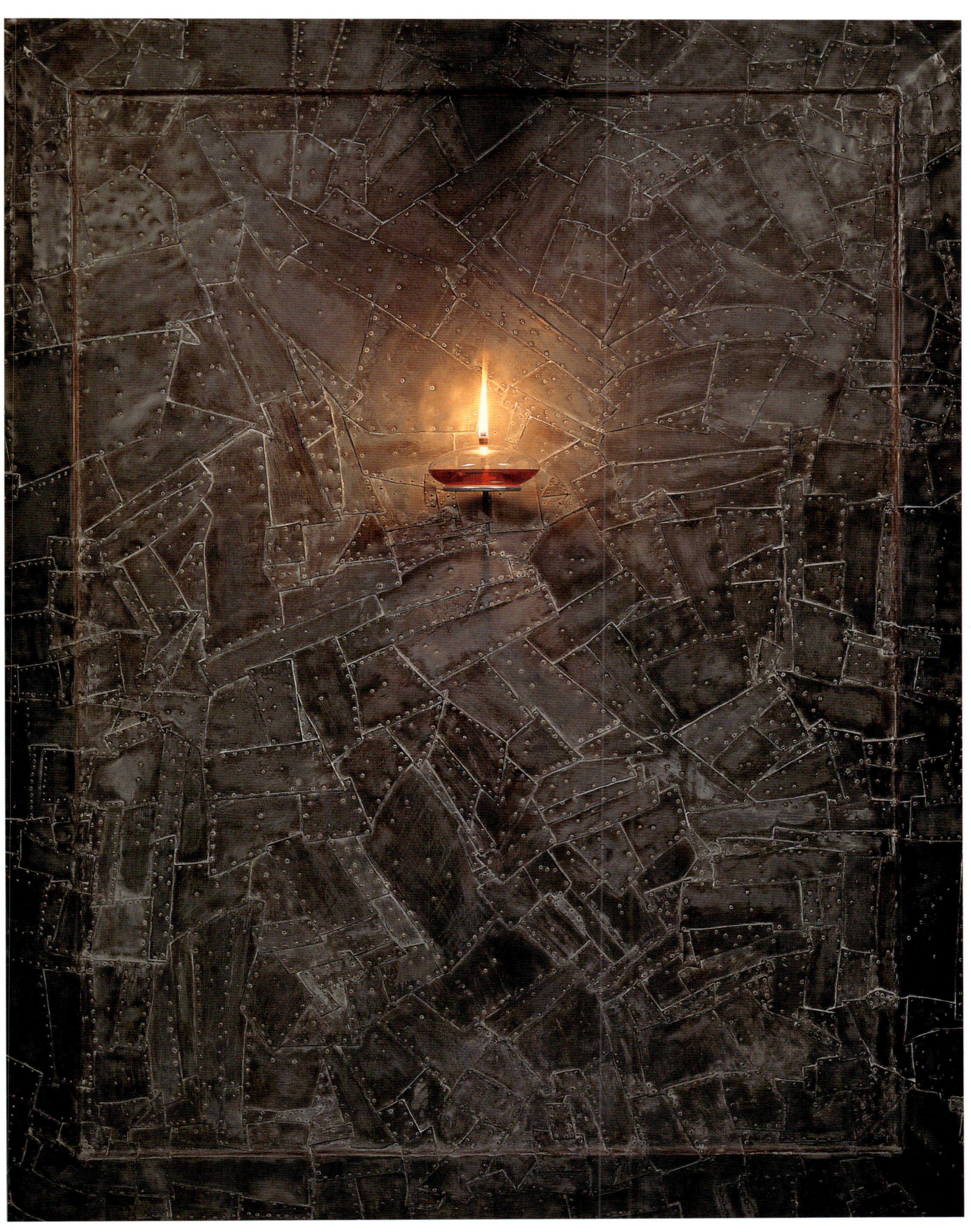

72 Connie Arismendi, *Vigil*, 1993, lead on wood, nails, oil lamp, 57" x 45". Collection of the artist.

against the lead patchwork surface is superbly haunting. This interaction between soft, muted light and dense, mildly variegated lead conveys a panoply and polyphony of emotions: sadness and mourning, hope and the aspiration for transcendence—perhaps life after death—and above all, the light but utterly transforming touch of the human spirit and human cognition on malleable lumps of the dense material world. Intellectually, the lamp symbolizes hope, spiritual enlightenment, and life itself. Inspired by the Prayer of St. Augustine ("Watch O Lord with those that wait and watch while others sleep"), the piece is a testament to the resilience of the human spirit in times of extreme hardship.

Aydee López Martínez, *Out there, someday, maybe I'll have it all together.* PLATE 73. The focus of this work is a woman's body that has been deconstructed and reconfigured into something akin to a flower arrangement. The torso represents the vase; veins and arteries, the foliage; the skeleton functions as the stems; and her head, heart, brain, arms, and legs signify flowers. Her face is olive toned, curiously contrasting with the rich terracotta brown of the rest of her body. Her arms and legs are reminiscent of fetishes. Her eyes are cast downward, her expression sorrowful. López Martínez is known for her highly personal and emotional work that often presents women or girls in various states of angst. This piece appears to represent intense personal dissatisfaction. Although the body is depicted as an object people usually find beautiful (flowers in a vase), the woman's facial expression suggests that she is burdened. The inconsistent skin color of her face could be interpreted in different ways. The green might suggest illness of some sort, perhaps a result of feeling disconnected, of not fitting in or understanding her place in the world, or of not recognizing the beauty she represents, despite its difference from society's generally accepted definition of attractiveness. It could be that she is ailing because she has yet to figure out how she fits together personally and how to overcome a sense of alienation and isolation. The subject's eye and lip makeup alludes to an attempt to mask her true identity, resulting in a sense of confusion and objectification.

Ana Laura De La Garza, *Young Bride.* PLATE 74. Portraits of brides are a common theme for Ana Laura de la Garza. The artist's interpretations are of strong, beautiful women but executed in a manner to refute the stereotypical, romanticized images of brides that are found everywhere in commodity-centered U.S. culture (magazines for example) and in idealized wedding photographs. The artist does not neglect, but she does reinterpret, typical associations with brides and weddings, including lace, red roses, veils, and creamy white icing. The brides in her paintings, wide-mouthed and rouged, are far removed from the picture-perfect, idealized portraits of brides. The features of these women, particularly their enormous rouged lips, are highly exaggerated, a visual tactic employed by the artist to emphasize the façades and masks that women sometimes wear. For the artist, lips are the most sexual aspect of a female; hence her focus on them. The artist has stated, "My brides are memories and my interpretations of beauty—strong, beautiful women with a masculine side. They are not grotesque." *Young Bride* is typical in many ways; she wears an appealing and feminine white wedding gown, complete with a white bridal veil and a bouquet of luscious red roses, which she gently touches with her delicate white fingers. In counterpoint, the roses proliferate to excess elsewhere: she carries a crown of them on her head and they form an oversweet frame within the work, implying that the image of the bride is a formal memento to be treasured. Additionally, opposed to the plethora of roses are the thick, rounded, enlarged lips of the bride, which themselves assume the shape of a rose, but with an opposite emotional charge. The dysphemistic lips refute the rosy artifices, just as the decidedly unpretty bride's face indicates a real person going to the altar.

Laura Molina, *La novia (Waiting for My Love . . .).* (In this context, *novia* means bride.) PLATE 75. Laura Molina said in a statement about her artwork, "I feel the need to assert my identity in the most militant way possible because otherwise as an American I am invisible. An educated, native-born, English-speaking seventh generation Mexican American feminist, there is almost no reflection of me in the movies or television, which is almost as bad as being stereotyped." In furtherance of this identity appraisal, Molina often features her own image and obsessions in her paintings. She has painted works depicting herself and a lover who jilted her, a nude self-portrait after she suffered a miscarriage, and a view of herself outside Walt Disney headquarters to commemorate her discrimina-

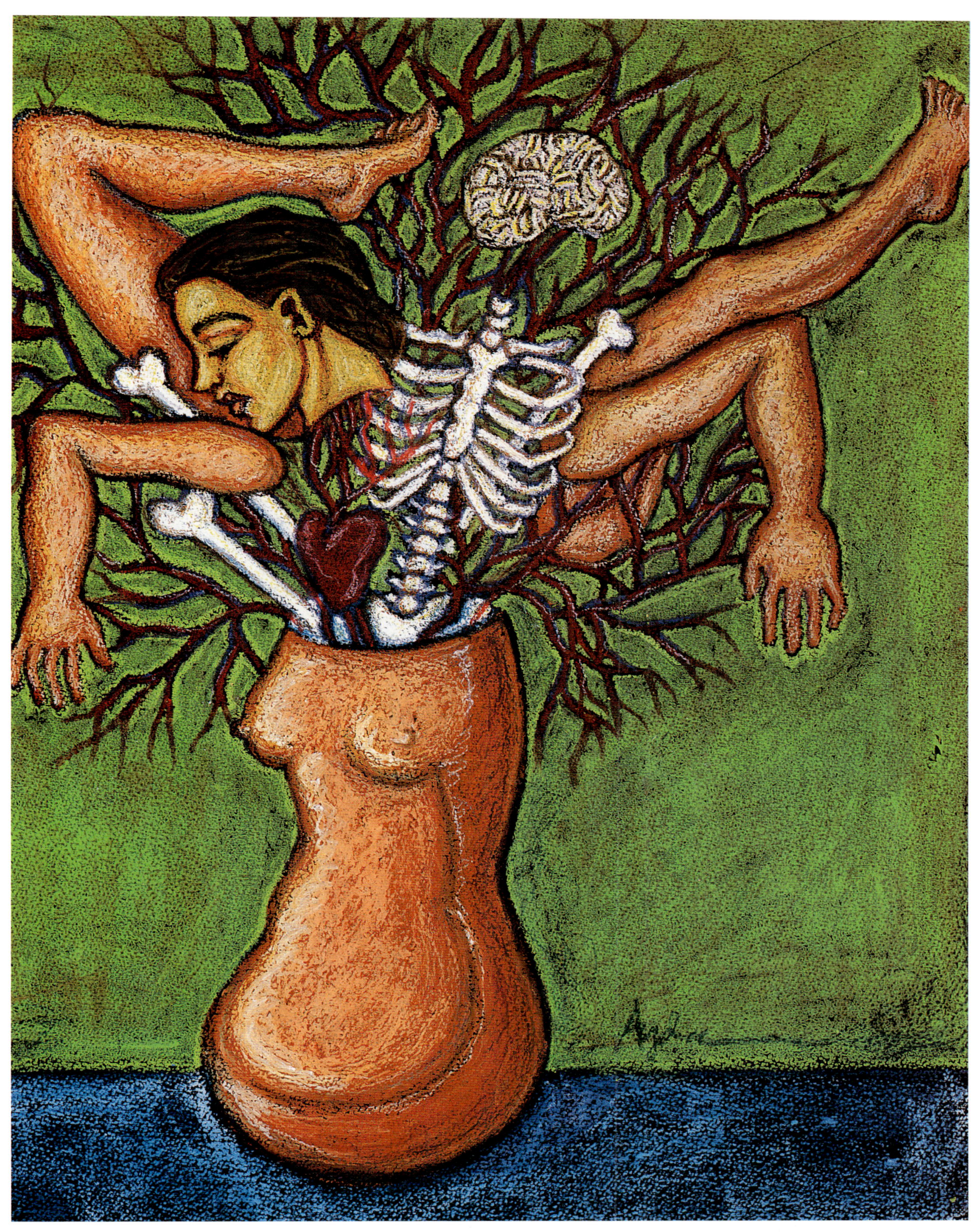

73 Aydee López Martínez, *Out there, someday, maybe I'll have it all together*, 2002, oil pastel on paper, 22.5" x 17"

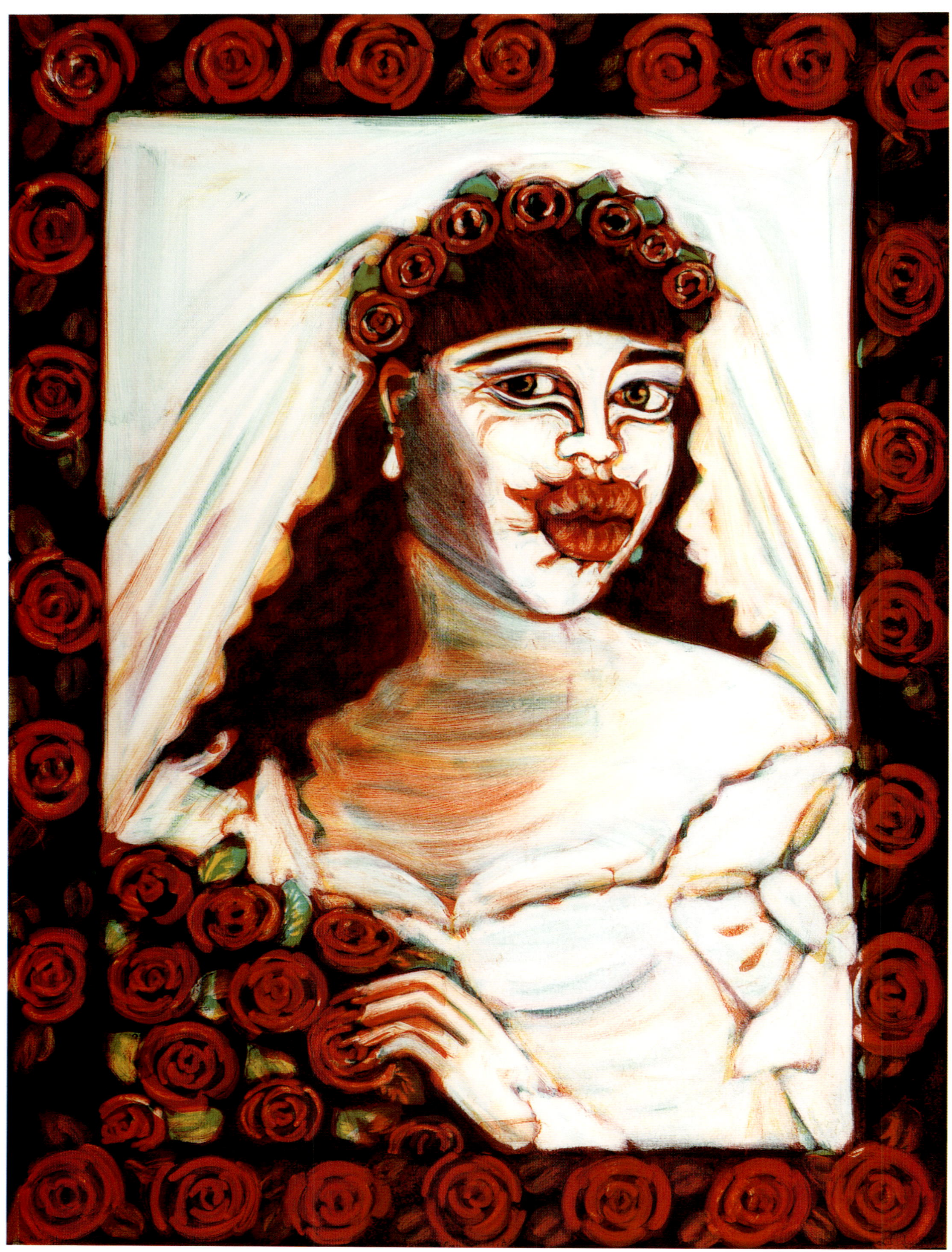

74 Ana Laura De La Garza, *Young Bride*, 1994, monoprint, 30" x 22"

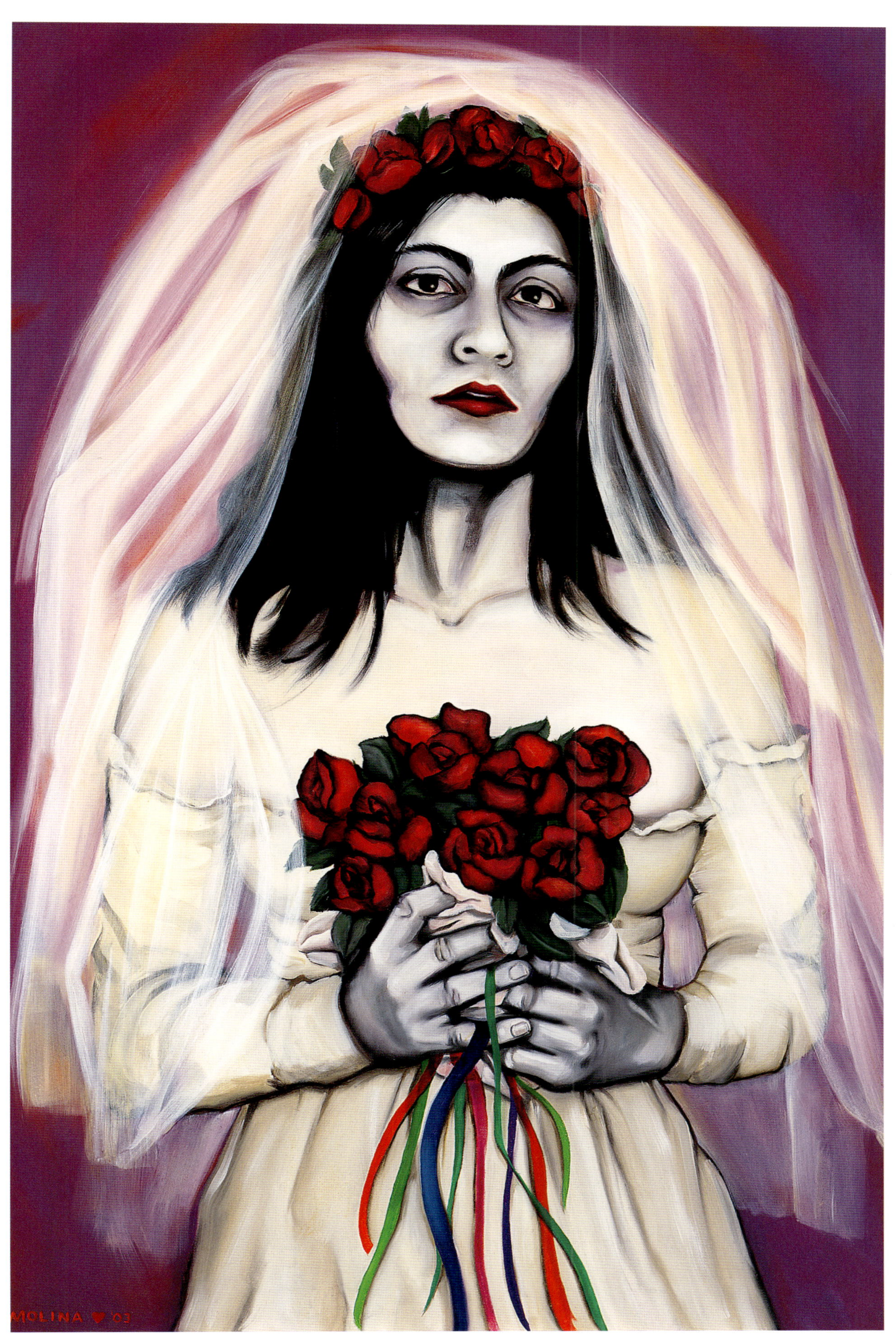

75 Laura Molina, *La novia* (*Waiting for My Love . . .*), 2003, acrylic on canvas, 40" x 22"

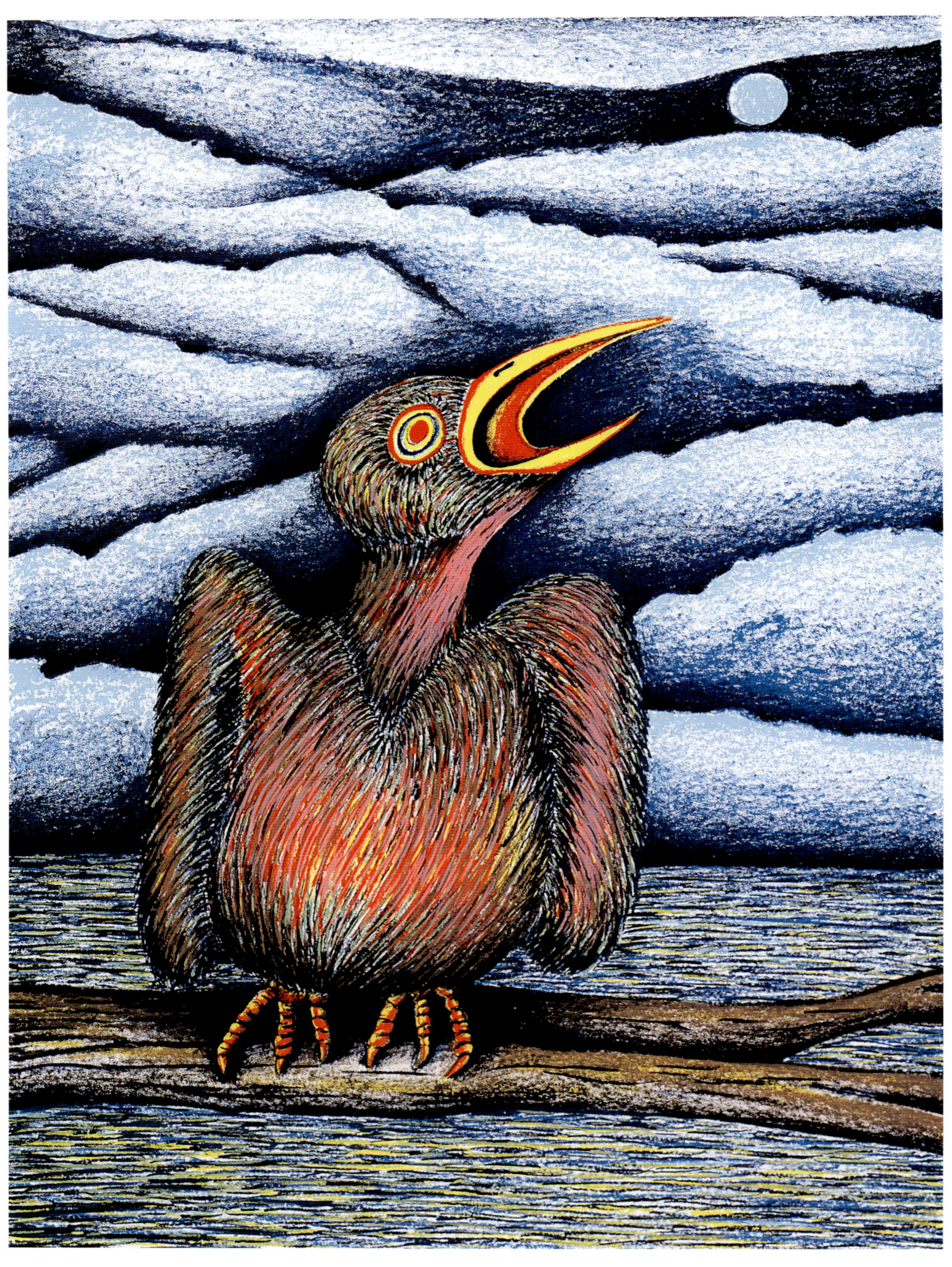

76 Carlos G. Gómez, *Llanto* (Crying, wailing), 2000, serigraph, 30" x 22"

tion lawsuit against the corporation. Molina's work is both very personal and very political. In *La novia (Waiting for My Love . . .)* she depicts herself as a bride, wearing a low-cut white dress and voluminous veil, holding a bouquet of crimson roses, looking directly at the viewer. The composition and title lead us to expect a traditional wedding portrait, but the effect is jarring because unlike the bride we want to see, happy on her wedding day, Molina represents herself as a dead woman in a bridal gown. Her face and hands have the pallor of a corpse, accentuated by the deep red of her lipstick, the flowers she holds, and those in her hair. Molina's bride has failed to meet the expectation that a successful Chicana will find the perfect man and make a home for him. This bride seems to think that time has passed her by and that it may be a long time before her wedding day.

Carlos Gómez, *Llanto* (Crying, wailing). PLATE 76. The Spanish word *llanto* has different meanings, depending on the context. Here there appear to be two meanings: one, the common one of crying or wailing, the second, the evocation of the gypsy *llanto,* a type of song, sometimes part of flamenco, that is associated with deep anguish. The great Spanish poet from Andalucía in southern Spain, Federico García Lorca, composed *llantos.* Carlos Gómez, who lives on the United States-Mexico border, has indicated that he has used the image of the wailing bird to represent abandoned street children who populate the border towns. *Llanto* is a representative work of Gómez's in that it combines a recognizable figure with formal design elements to create a work with symbolic or allegorical purposes. The young bird on a branch is wailing, seemingly alone and abandoned, much like an animal baying at the moon. Except for a few realistic elements such as the branch and the moon, the composition depicts a figure that is clearly a bird, but one that is stylistically drawn with formal elements such as the multicolored circular eyes, the feet with their pattern of horizontal lines, the elliptical geometry of its pronounced beak, and, above all, the multilinear, multishaded pattern of its body. These patterns in turn combine contrastively in both color and composition with the patterned design of the clouds, somewhat like fluffy spearheads, and with the horizontally patterned composition that backgrounds the tree branch and the lower part of the bird's body, which may evoke the border river, the Rio Grande. There is a strong expressionist—even surrealist—element in this work as well. For example, the bird's wings appear like shoulders and arms, and the plaintive beak foregrounds and dominates the composition as in a dream that calls for interpretation. The title also, to the degree that it indicates a song of anguish, similarly calls for decipherment.

COMPARTIDO POR TODOS

Artemio Rodríguez, *The King of Things/El rey de las cosas*. PLATE 77. This work in the form of a handmade picture book for children and narrated (in writing) by a six-year-old affiliates the Mexican *Lotería* game with childhood. Much (although not all) of an ancient connection of the *Lotería* cards to Tarot cards has been eliminated, and instead the work celebrates the reinterpretation and incorporation into a young boy's world of images usually seen only in *Lotería*. A traditional philosophic phrase (coined before sensitivity to gender balance) is that "Man is the measure of all things." In this work, the celebratory variant is that the child is the measurer of all things, and he is crowned for his successes. He also, by dint of his imagination, is the possessor of all things that he has measured, in that categorically triumphant manner of the six-year-old child learning to equate pictures with words and read them in connected passages. In most of the cards, the viewer finds that the young boy, applying the human ability to fantasize, visualize, and project into all sorts of circumstances, has placed himself in the scene. He sits next to the owl; astride the horse; inside the conductor's station of the train; is delivered by the *garza* (heron); rides the rooster, the frog, and the lion; and in the next-to-last *Lotería* card has progressed to the center of it all. It is he, modeling the crown that sits on his head in kingly fashion. The colors are bright and vivacious, the images benign. Even *El diablo* (the devil) seems rather approachable and certainly youthful. The verity that humankind measures all things, including other humans, is evoked in a jocular and fun-loving manner.

Luis Valderas, *El Rocket*. PLATE 78. Similar in one respect to his fellow San Antonio artist Xavier Garza, Valderas has updated the set of *Lotería* cards in this work by adding a new image to its repertoire, which normally dates from a pre-industrial age.

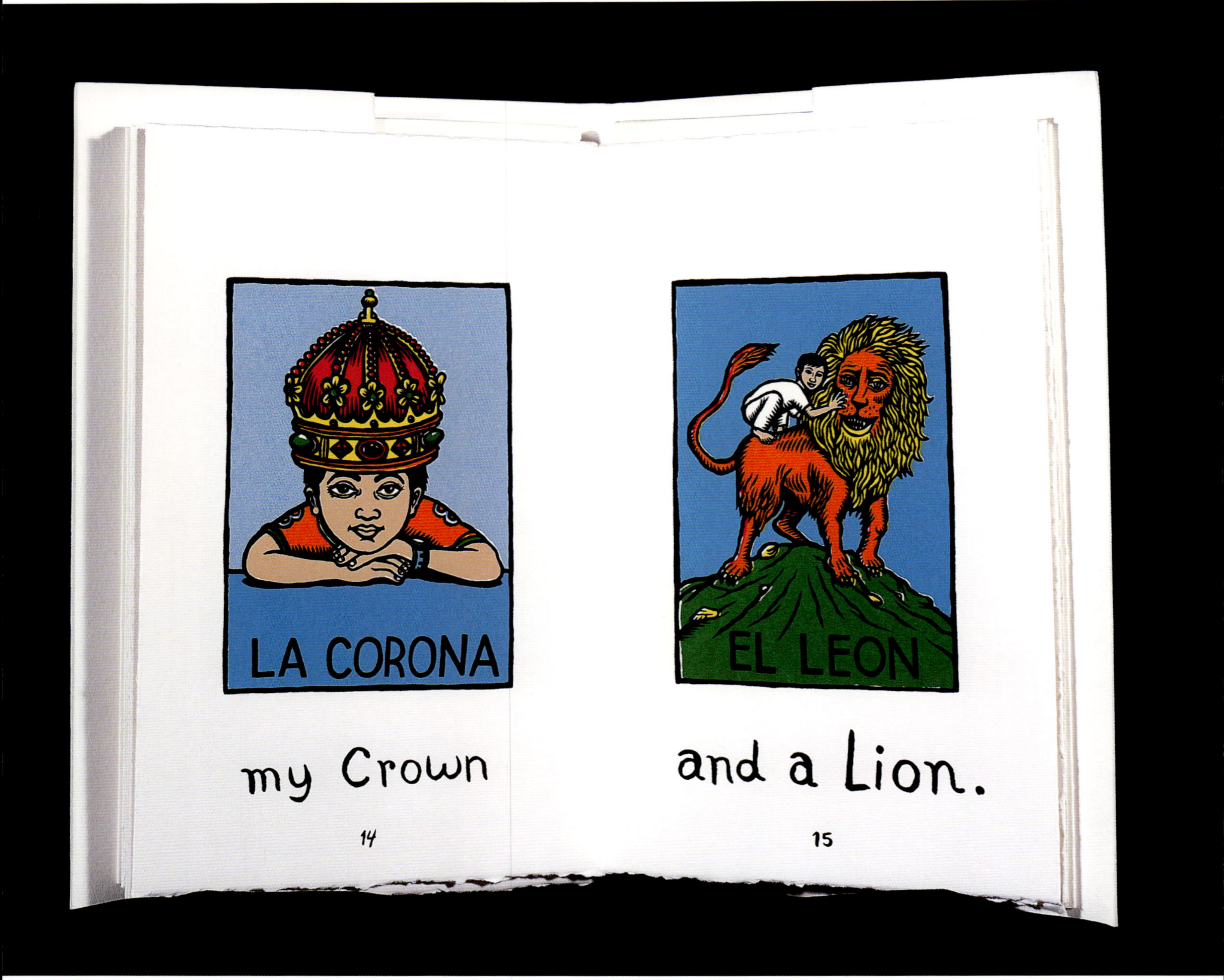

77 Artemio Rodríguez, *The King of Things/El rey de las cosas*, 2001
Handmade book, serigraphs, 10.75" x 7" x 1"

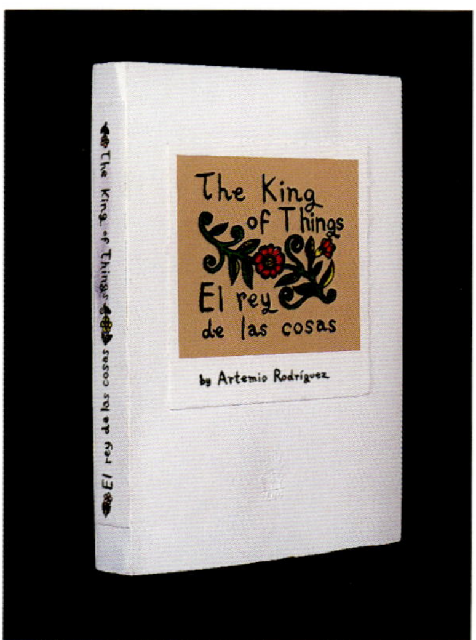

Right: 78 Luis Valderas, *El Rocket*, 2001
Mixed media, 27" x 19" x 7.5"

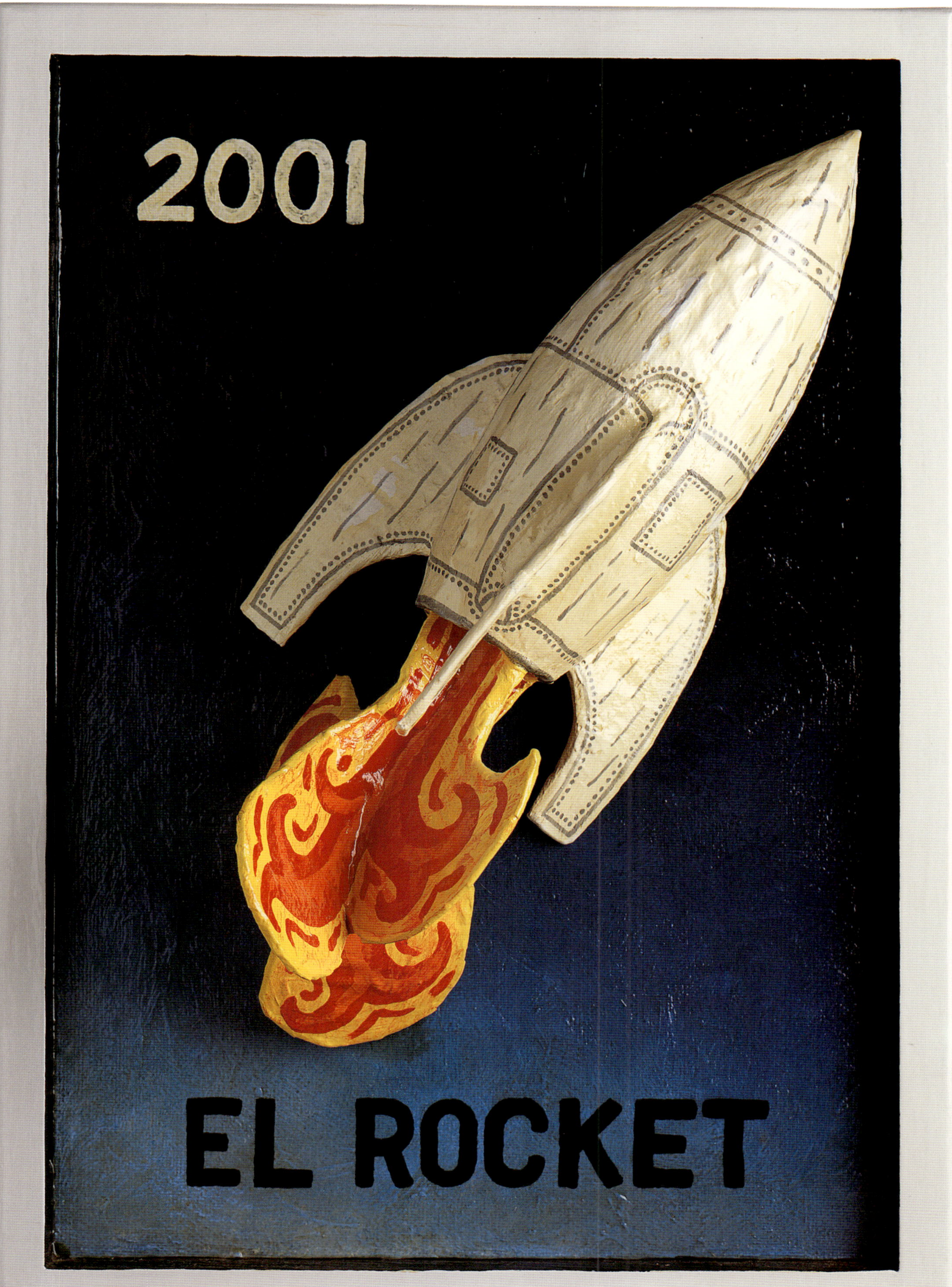

2001
EL ROCKET

Thus, the rocket finds its way into the canon that normally boasts such images as *El diablo* (the devil), *La muerte* (death), or *El corazón* (the heart). However, the fact that this work at the same time commemorates the twentieth anniversary of the first space shuttle to orbit the earth, Columbia (1981), which was the shuttle destroyed in a tragic accident in 2003, is in keeping with the portentous cast of the original *Lotería* game. This work is innovative in another way. Using the vertical format and aspect ratio of the *Lotería* card, it expands its dimensionality so that the rocket, fashioned in sculptural relief, totally surpasses its roots as a card for a board game. Mounted on a wooden frame against a blue painted background that, like space itself, gradually becomes almost black at its uppermost stratum, the spaceship has been sculpted with papier mâché so that it stands in full relief. The configuration of the ship still retains its juvenile quality. Fine details and fidelity to contemporary design have not been emphasized here; in their stead we have a rocket suitable for a juvenile player of the *Lotería* game with exciting red-and-yellow flames and its three fins prominently arrayed.

Eduardo Oropeza, *Héchale*. PLATE 79. (The spelling of the title reflects the artist's misunderstanding of the derivation of the expression *Échale*, which means "Go for it!" or "Pour it on!"; he assumed it was related to *hecho*, "made" or "done" and added a silent *h* where there should not be one.) Firmly rooted in Mexican/Chicano popular art and boasting the liveliest possible color scheme, this work takes the sting out of the Día de los Muertos skeletons that we find in other works, such as those of the original model for most of them, José Guadalupe Posada, or George Yepes's *La serenata*. Here, against a bright background of live flora set on a platform of hot pink, the most colorful band conceivable (similar to mariachis but without the diversity of instruments because they all play stringed instruments) plays in solidarity with itself and with the viewer. The communion and camaraderie of Chicano culture that crosses even the great divide of death is the theme of this work. Surely the group must be playing a piece heroically and *molto allegro* in tempo. Each member has a brightly decorated party hat that is similar in form to a pirate or military cap. Each of them sports a masculine mustache and has received Christian authorization for his existence with a cross on his forehead. Their backbones look like a popular

springlike toy (the Slinky), and the typical *calavera* (skull) grimace or grin is nowhere to be seen. The dead are living together with each other, and they brighten our senses and imaginations as well.

George Yepes, *La serenata* (The serenade). PLATE 80. George Yepes has a reputation as an enfant terrible of Chicano art. The artist's Web site describes him as "formed by a hard street life of poverty, gang life, and womanizing." Married a number of times (and still counting), making a virtue and a bit of a legend out of his birth in Tijuana, his childhood formation within the gangs of East Los Angeles, and his self-education as an artist, Yepes at the same time has had commissions of high importance including *The Promise*, a huge vaulted ceiling mural at the State Archive Museum in Sacramento (a fitting commission given his penchant for the Renaissance masters: his Web site quotes an article that says he is a painter who could have challenged the old greats in the salon or "kicked their asses" in a back alley). Hugely dedicated to his art, he often spends all night painting. He is also well known as a promoter of education for youth. From his commissions of public art and the sale of his work to notables including actor Cheech Marín and director Robert Rodríguez, he has had the resources to set up and fund an Academia de Arte Yepes in both Los Angeles and Chicago that helps youngsters learn to paint.

La serenata is not an entirely characteristic work inasmuch as many of his paintings and murals are either grand in scale in the manner of Tintoretto, Titian, or Velásquez, or they are portraits of women, often dressed (sometimes scantily) in period clothes. Nevertheless, this work is singular for a number of reasons. It is notable for the level of detail in the clothes and hat of the serenading mariachi. Just as it is for Alfredo Arreguín and the recently deceased Eduardo Oropeza, decoration and pattern are an integral, not incidental part of Yepes's baroque artistic project. The work is also wonderfully ambiguous and enigmatic in that the lone mariachi serenader not only exists in a physical twilight world, emerging from shadows, but also resides in an enigmatic state between life and death. Clearly he is a "living" skeleton of the sort we might associate with Oropeza or the nineteenth- to early twentieth-century grand master José Guadalupe Posada. However, in sharp contrast to both of those artists, there is an intense personality in this human figure, which still has its

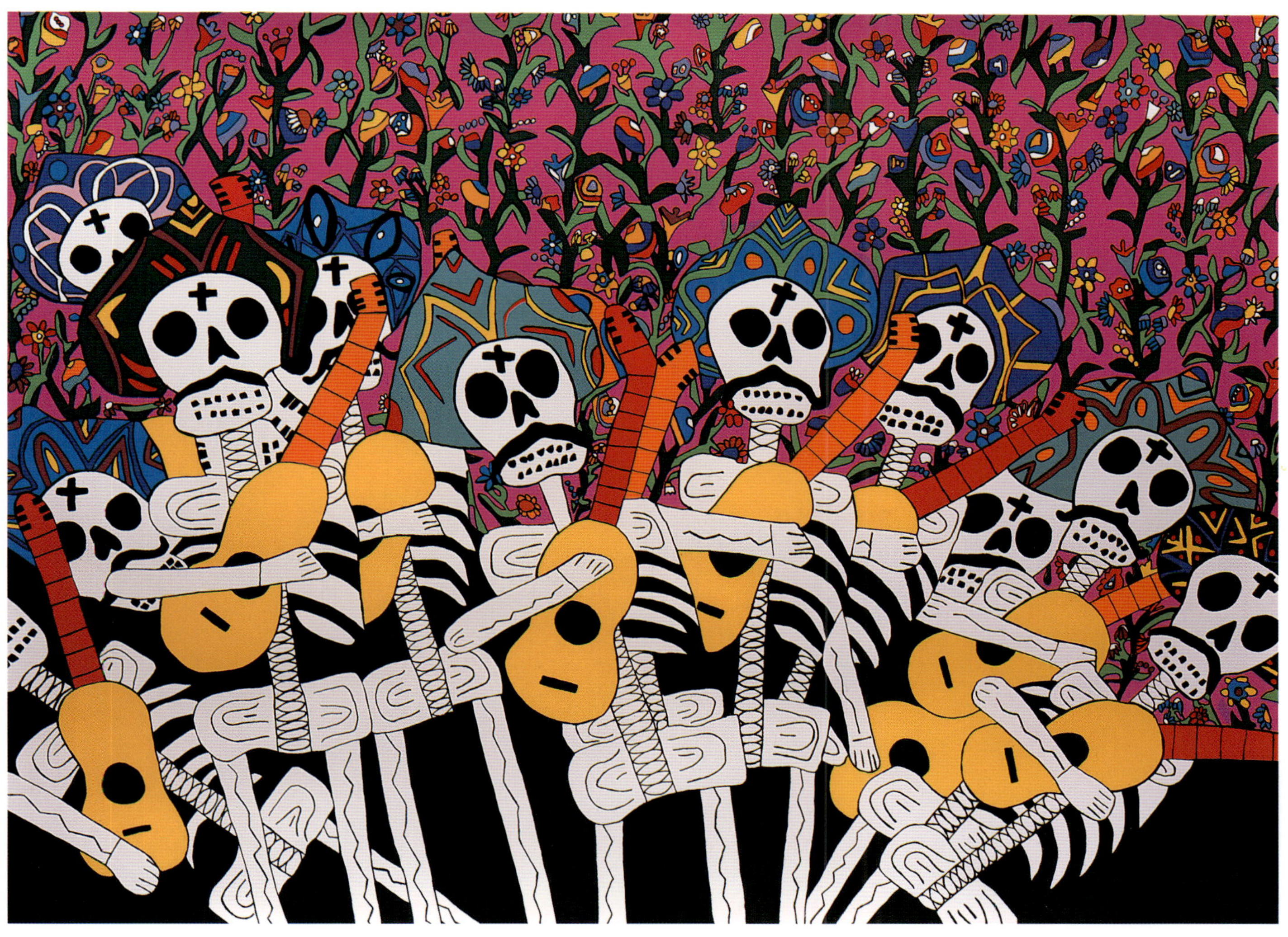

79 Eduardo Oropeza, *Héchale* (Go for it! Pour it on!), 1984, serigraph, 35.5" x 48"

eyes, albeit deep in open sockets, and exudes an expressionistic quality of emotion and sensitivity that we would associate more with the portrait of Sandra Cisneros by César Martínez, also in this exhibition. The serenader is a *calavera* (skull) with real ears, a pinched, semilive and semiskeletal mouth, and hands and fingers that clearly are white bone yet have the delicacy and expressivity of the renowned gypsy guitarist Manitas de Plata. This is a skeleton who remains an impassioned man as well, intent on his mission of romancing his love interest. He looks up toward an unseen woman, goddess or Madonna, his head crooked in a totally human, love-struck pose, rather like Dante seeking Beatrice or Troilus, Cressida.

Ester Hernández, *Con cariño, Lydia Mendoza* (With affection, Lydia Mendoza). PLATE 81. Lydia Mendoza (born 1916 in Houston, where as of 2001 she was living in retirement) was known as *la alon-*

dra de la frontera (the lark of the border) and was the queen of Tejano music. Her work conveyed the strong feelings of the workers and common people of the border: longing, desire, sadness, and exultation. She came from a musical family, La Familia Mendoza, and was particularly popular as a young woman in the 1940s and 1950s, although her song "Mal Hombre," which she first recorded at the age of eighteen, was a huge hit. In this work, the artist has presented her at the top of her form: a mature, seasoned, experienced, and recognized master of her musical style with many years ahead of her in the limelight. She is dressed in a becoming, extravagant dress that, featuring the Mexican national colors and elaborate but recognizably Mexican stitchwork, endows her with characteristics worthy of an emissary for her nation. This sense of her being a national representative is reinforced by the purple background on which appears the outline of the Mexican eagle, the emblem of the nation.

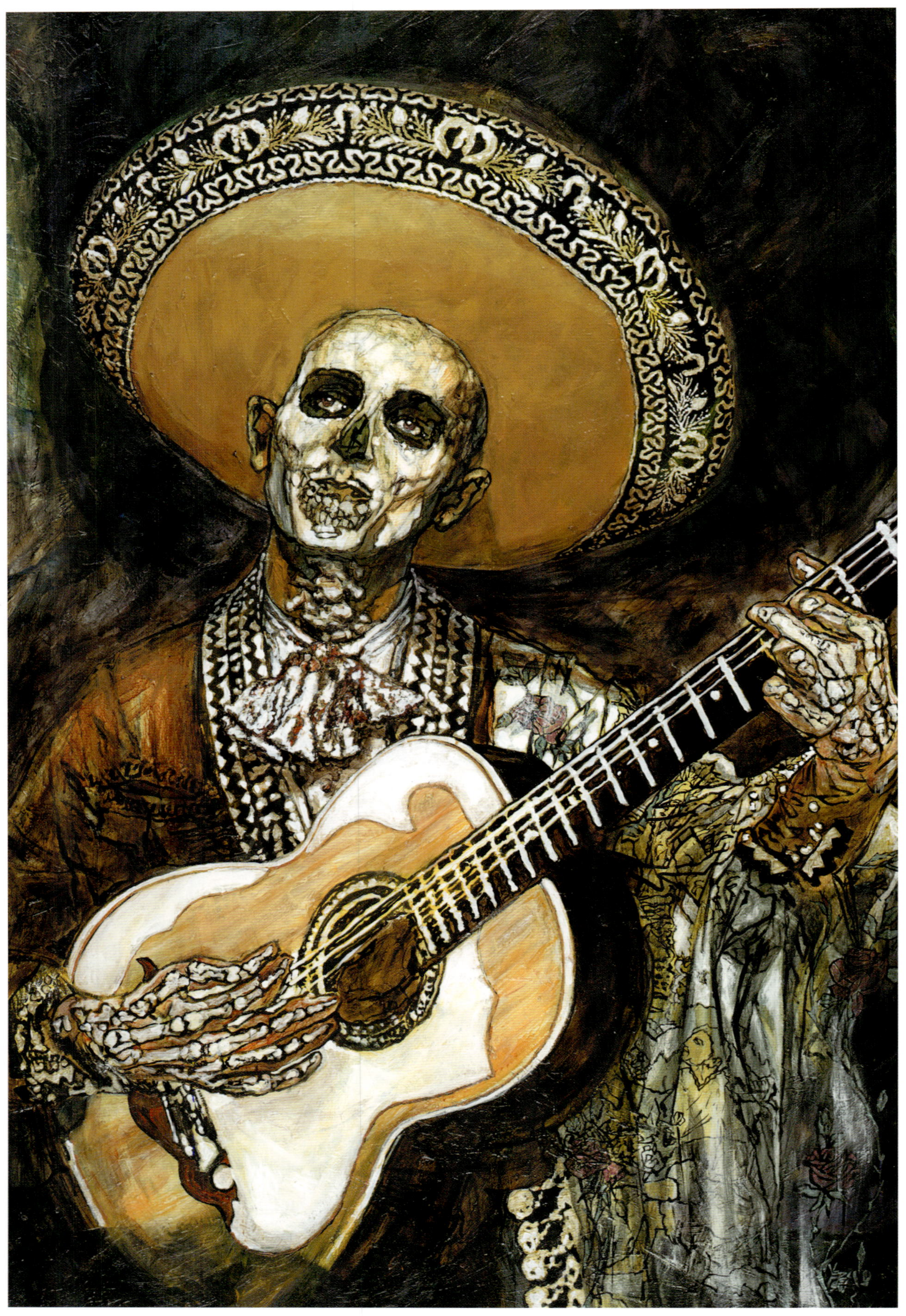

80 George Yepes, *La serenata* (The serenade), 2001, hand-painted print, 40" x 30"

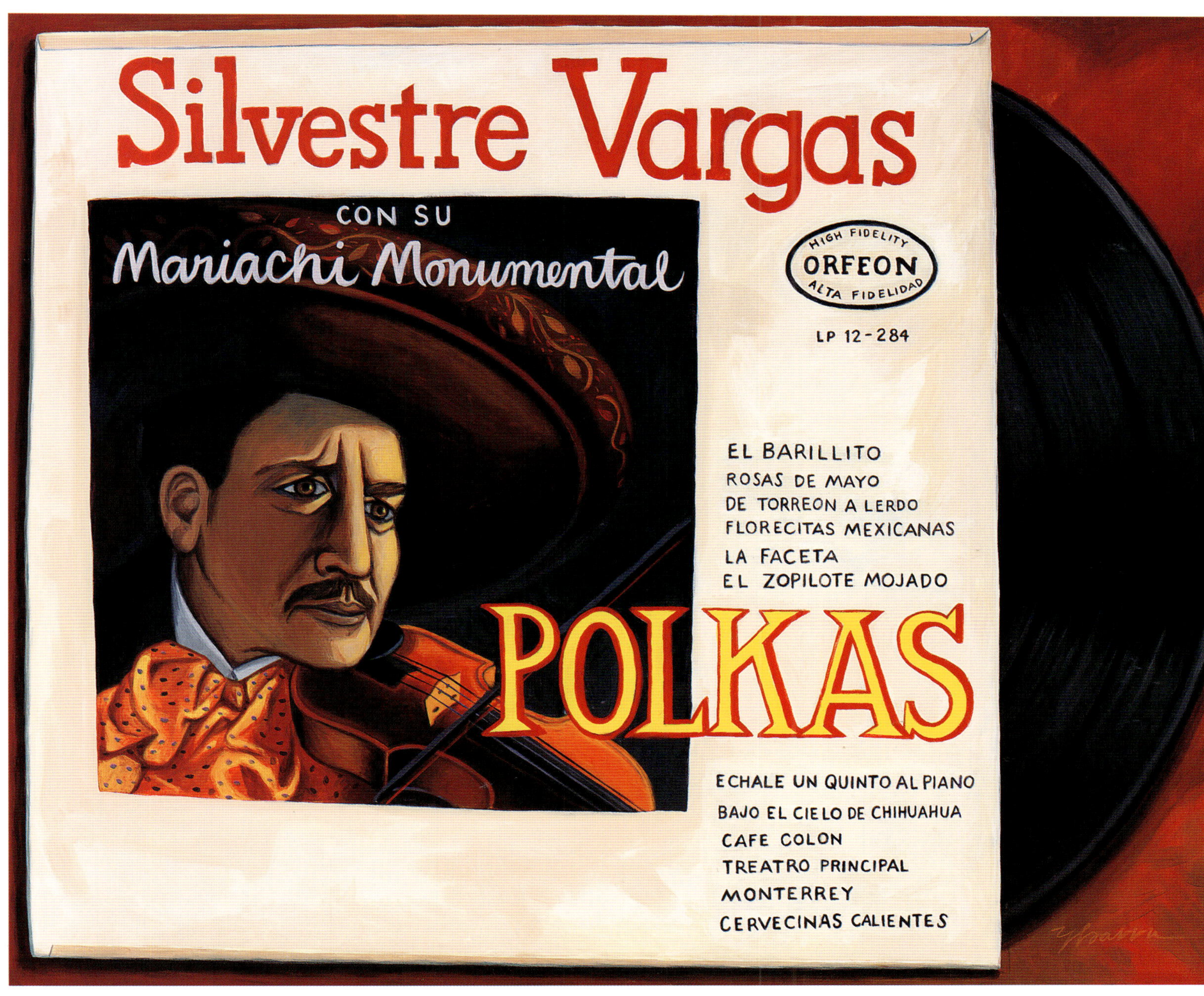

83 Frank Ybarra, *Mariachi LP*, 2003, acrylic on canvas, 48" x 60"

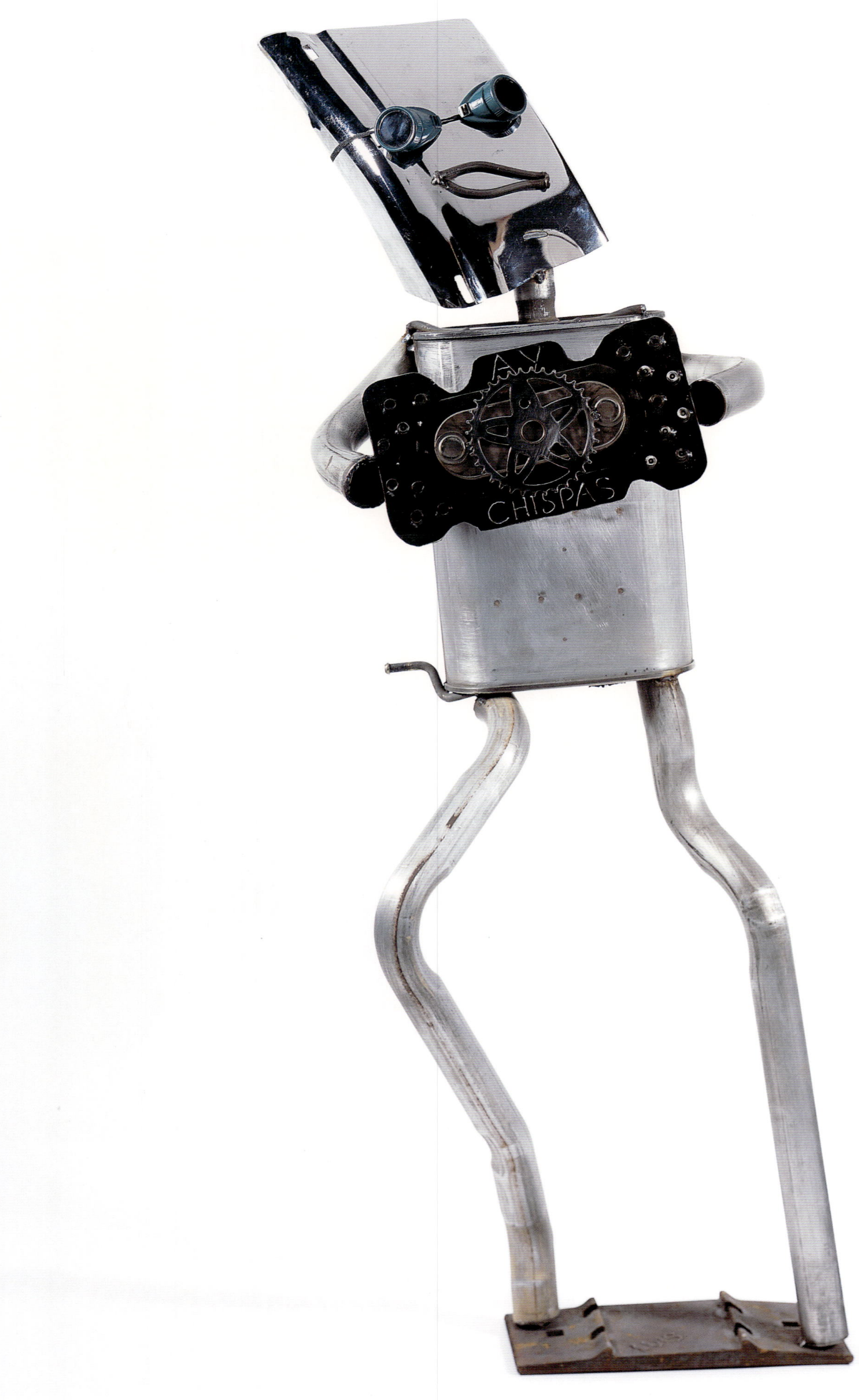

82 Luis Guerrero, *El Chuy*, 2003, mixed media sculpture, 66" x 26" x 16"

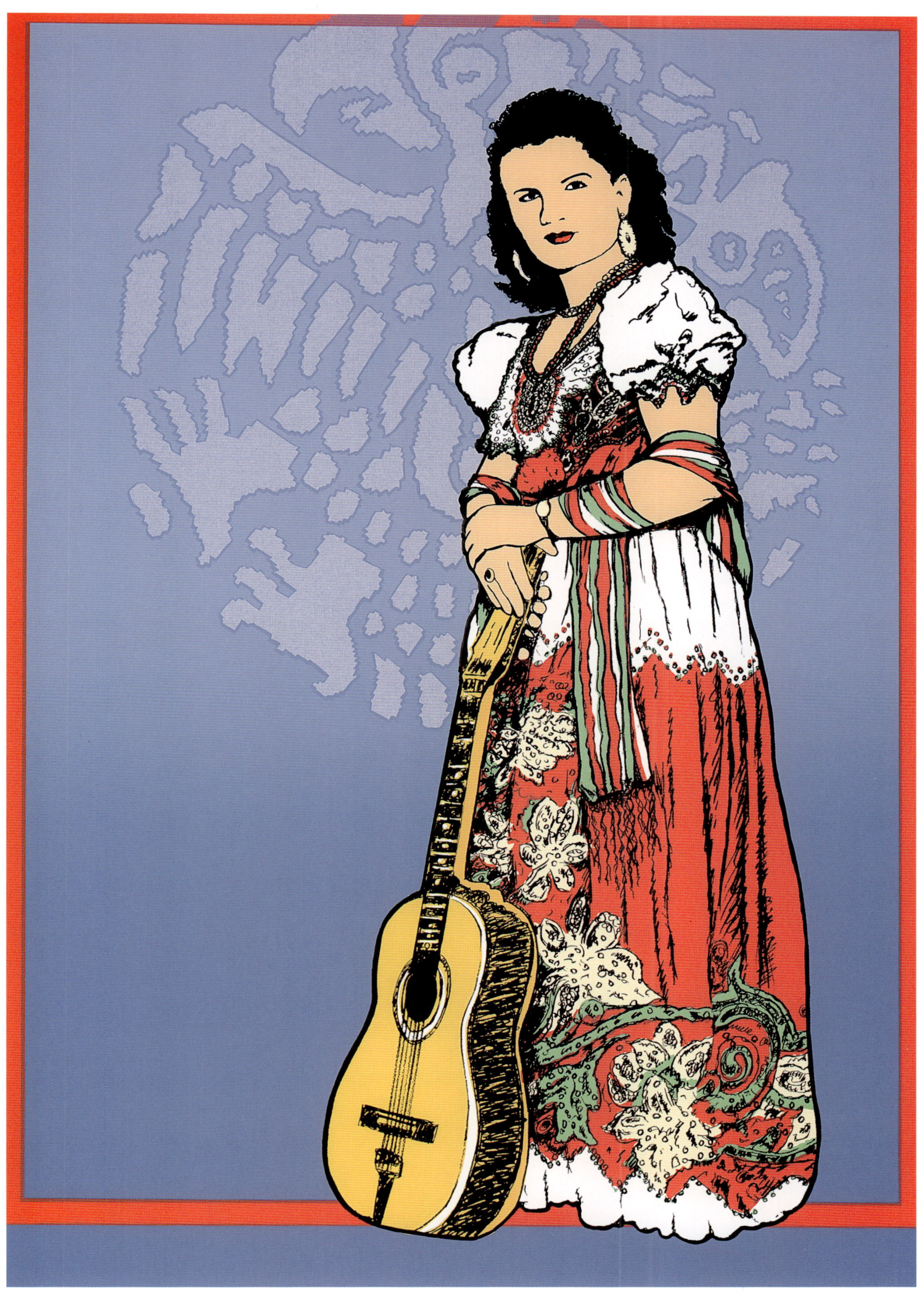

81 Ester Hernández, *Con cariño, Lydia Mendoza* (With affection . . .), 1998, serigraph, 30" x 22"

Luis Guerrero, *El Chuy* (Chuy is an affectionate nickname for Jesús). PLATE 82. This sculpture is a striking example of the art style known as *rasquache* (with alternate spellings including *rasquachi*) in Chicano culture and art. Making a virtue out of necessity as it were, Chicano popular artists ingeniously take found or discarded objects from their neighborhoods and fashion them into icons that are symbolic of their culture and lifestyles. In this work, parts of a muffler—as well as other objects whose former lives were within an industrial context such as gears, a crank, and goggles—have been soldered together to create one of the endearing cultural symbols of south Texas, the accordion player (see the commentary on *Sonido del barrio* for further discussion of this bicultural figure). There is no attempt to hide the origin of the found pieces— quite to the contrary. Their natural qualities are used to full comic advantage to delight the viewer, whose close rapport with the piece, its *rasquache* construc-tion, and the cultural dimension that it cultivates are fully counted on by the artist. For example, the exhaust pipes, unpainted and unadorned, form the spindly legs and arms of our accordionist.

Frank Ybarra, *Mariachi LP.* PLATE 83. The technology of long-playing vinyl records (LPs), their casing in a large-size record jacket, and their enduring influence on Chicano/Latino culture comprise the vehicle for Ybarra's work. Now out of date by virtue of cassettes followed by compact discs and other digital electronic devices for recording and distribution, the LP and its distinctive jacket, which made an excellent medium for commercial art, are retained in memory, sentiment, and nostalgia. As in Andy Warhol's depictions of Marilyn Monroe or cans of Campbell's soup, Ybarra re-creates and sets within the fine arts the design, craft, and emotional resonance of the commercial artisanship of an earlier period. Moreover, he uses a Mexican icon, the

84 Miguel Ángel Reyes, *Época de oro* (Golden age), 2002, serigraph, 20" x 26"

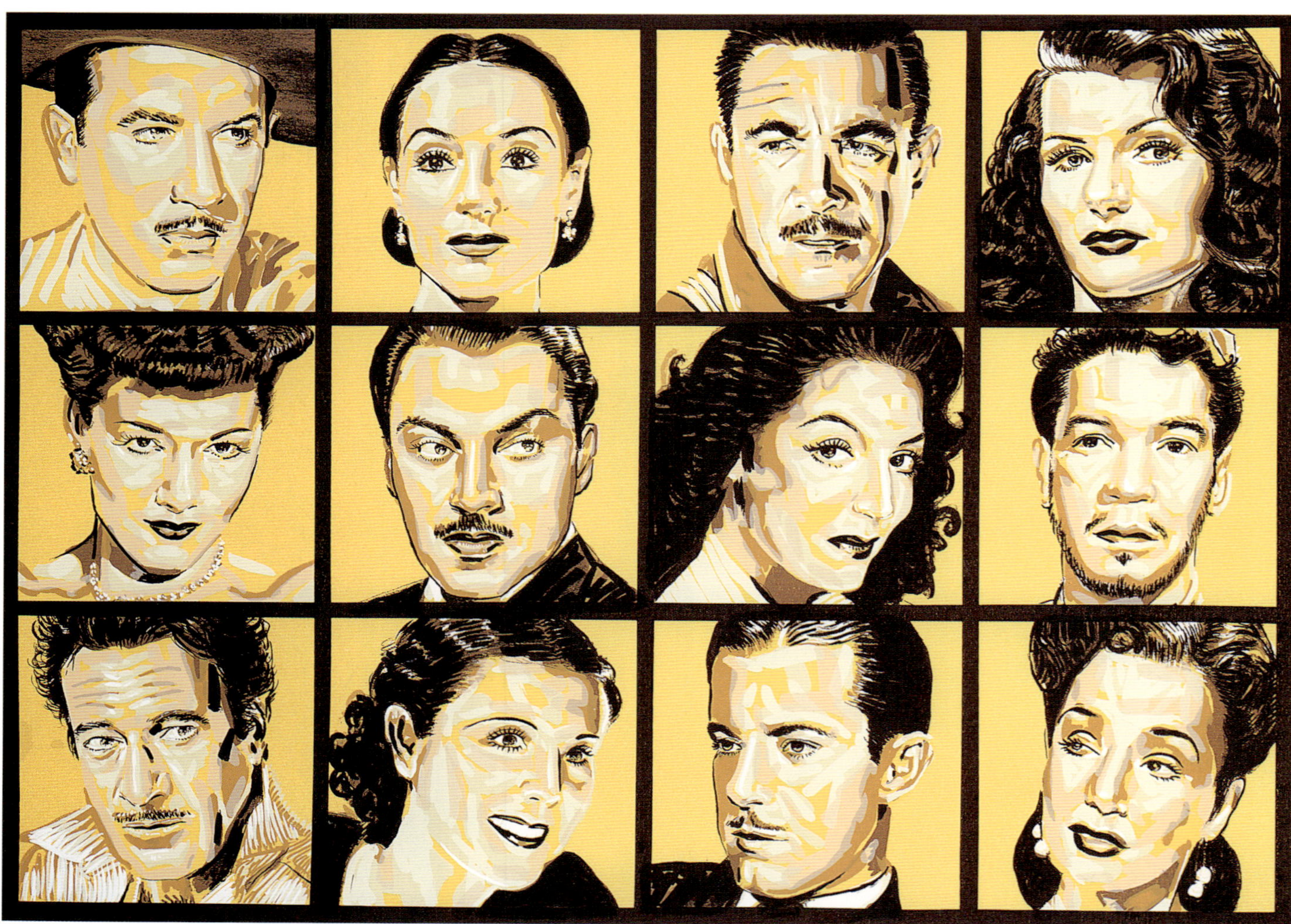

renowned mariachi Silvestre Vargas, and depicts a record cover that treats polka music in the *norteño* (Mexican-U.S. borderlands) style. Often utilizing icons of the "suburban ethnic" lifestyle, as he has referred to it, in this case Ybarra also bridges the gap between his life as a commercial artist and as a cultivator of the beaux arts, unearthing in the same composition the qualities of commercial art that redound on the psyche and re-creating them on canvas. Type styles—their contrastive fonts, colors, and designs—are highly important in this work. Similarly, the titles of the songs themselves (which have not been copied from a record jacket; in fact, the first one reminds us of the tricks that memory plays inasmuch as it is misspelled) evoke the bicultural reality of the border and of *norteño* citizens of either Mexico or the United States. As in *Sonido del barrio*, the musical topic is polkas; whereas the outsider would hardly associate these with Mexican or Chicano culture, the bicultural insider knows better and understands the reference appreciatively.

Miguel Ángel Reyes, *Época de oro* (Golden age). PLATE 84. During World War II, the Mexican film industry received an enormous economic boost that catapulted it into preeminence for some fifteen to twenty years. This premier period, popularly known as *La época de oro*, was partly the result of the disfavor in which the Argentine film industry found itself with the allies, particularly the United States, which embargoed the shipping of U.S. raw film stock to that Axis-sympathizing country. In contrast, the United States built its war ally Mexico a state-of-the-art sound studio called Churubusco, which to this day continues to have the same connotation as Hollywood in the United States, or Bollywood (outside of Bombay) in another third-world film-producing nation, India. Reyes highlights, fittingly, using an abundance of bright gold, twelve filmic gods and goddesses who were the instrumental actors of that period, including such larger-than-life figures as Pedro Armendáriz, Dolores del Río, María Félix, Pedro Infante, Libertad Lamarque (who came to Mexico from Argentina), and Mario Moreno "Cantinflas." Using new technology for the time, and filling the needs of a worldwide Spanish-speaking market that craved films during a period of grave dangers and a dearth of movies from the traditional film-producing countries, Mexico re-created itself in many ways. It was during these years, for example, that "typical" dances and *mariachi* and *ranchera* music were elaborated from their local folk origins and turned into international hits known around the world such as the Mexican Hat Dance or the song "Cucurrucucu paloma." The now elderly Mexican public who lived through this period of wonderfully entertaining films and the equally wondrous and disconcerting loves, trials, and misfortunes of the actors will resonate to this work, which imitates a movie lobby card.

Xavier Garza, *El Santo* (The Saint). PLATE 85. El Santo was an actual wrestler whose masked professional persona so captured the popular Mexican imagination that he became a hero, the analog of Superman or Batman in the United States. Mexican films were eventually produced that had him combating the forces of evil ranging at the beginning of the cycle from the merely mortal, as in *Santo contra el Rey del Crimen* (Santo vs. the king of crime) or *Santo contra el Estrangulador* (Santo vs. the strangler), to, as the popularity of these films grew exponentially, the supernatural, as in *Santo contra los zombies* (Santo vs. the zombies), *Santo contra las mujeres vampiro* (Santo vs. the vampire women), and *Santo el enmascarado de plata vs. la invasión de los marcianos* (Silver-Masked Santo vs. the Martian invaders). El Santo in Garza's work has attained the iconic status of a *Lotería* card, the equivalent of attaining such fame as to have entered a pantheon for which there is no precedent, since these cards retain a traditional status that does not genuinely allow for revision based on contemporary phenomena. El Santo is depicted in this work as the most important *Lotería* card of all, No. 1. Against a vivid red background, emphasizing excitement, danger, and solidarity with the working classes and their children, the masked wrestler in a white cape, knee pads, and athletic boots is crouched, catlike and poised to spring into action to combat any maleficent individual or force that might come his way.

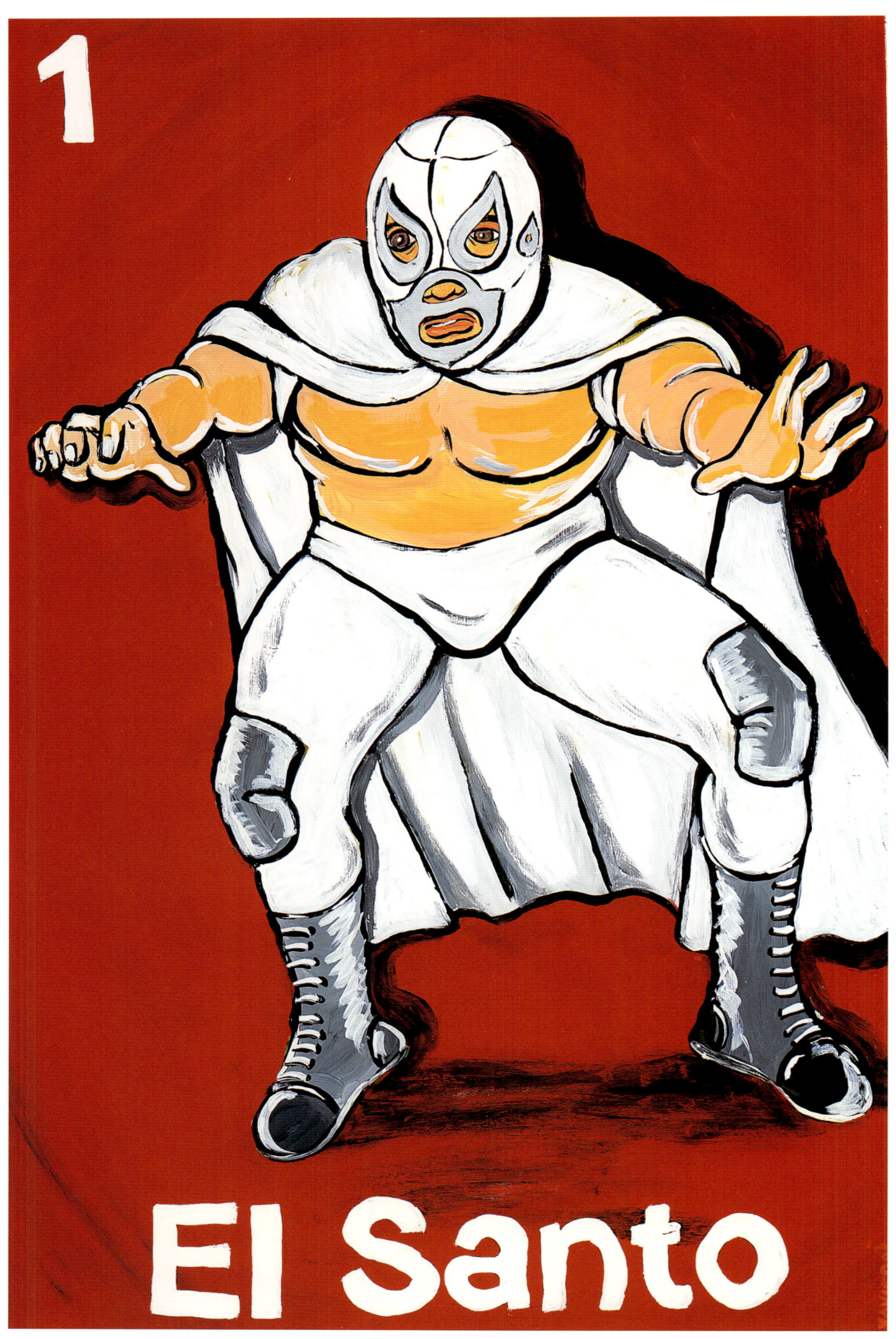

85 Xavier Garza, *El Santo* (The Saint), 2003, acrylic on Masonite, 28.25" x 19.25"

Temas culturales

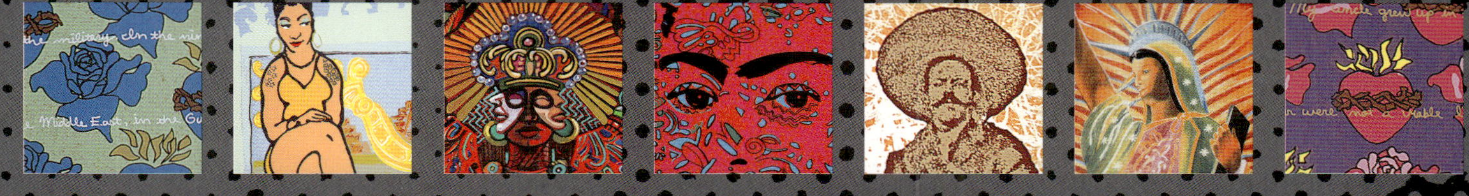

Cultural Icons

ultural Icons/Temas culturales is divided into three themes. "Héroes" evokes many of the Chicana/o community's role models or individuals of renown, including the Mexican revolutionary and bête noire of Americans (because of his transgressions on the border) Francisco "Pancho" Villa; the extraordinary engraver and producer of works on paper José Guadalupe Posada; Frida Kahlo, the renowned Mexican surrealist painter who has become a symbol of and for the women's movement in the Latino/a world; contemporary Chicana writer Sandra Cisneros; Mexican American farmworker, union organizer, and notable militant (but nonviolent) civil rights activist César Chávez; and legendary figures such as the Cisco Kid of fiction and film fame and Muffler Man, a caped Chicano everyman hero. "¡Venceremos!" (We shall overcome) reproduces a slogan from Chicana/o civil rights and social justice militancy in order to depict such cultural icons as *Zapatista* guerrillas of the Ejército Zapatista de Liberación Nacional (the Zapatista National Liberation Army); Ricardo Flores Magón, a foremost intellectual of the Mexican Revolution of 1910, who died or was killed in the federal prison at Leavenworth; a syncretic Virgin of Guadalupe/ Statue of Liberty and a Statue of Liberty/pre-Hispanic woman; a lone Chicana struggling against conglomerated corporations; and another Latina who has arrogated the identity of the conventional *bandolero.* "Nuestros símbolos" develops a variety of notable icons from such sources as the pre-Hispanic world, traditional folklore, and the Southwestern environment itself with its notable flora and fauna. Here we find various well-recognized icons, including the legendary *La Llorona* who searches for her lost children; the famous lovers who were transformed into the adjacent volcanoes Popocatepetl and Ixtaccihuatl; Quetzalcoatl, the god in the form of a plumed serpent; and the "angel" in Mexico City who represents a figure of liberty and was constructed on the centenary of the Mexican Revolution of 1810.

Héroes

Sam Zaragosa Coronado, *Pancho Villa and the Cisco Kid.* PLATE 86. Sam Coronado was primarily a painter until 1990 when he participated in one of the Self-Help Graphics print ateliers in Los Angeles. He fell in love with the process of serigraphy and has devoted himself since then to printmaking. Coronado's Serie Project in Austin, Texas, modeled on the Self-Help Graphics program, celebrated its first decade of existence in July 2003. Coronado has made it possible for a wide array of Latino and other artists to experience the silkscreen process, the results of which are seen in this exhibit and book (see, for example, work by Candace Briceño, Benito Huerta, Daniel Maldonado, and David Moreno). He provides a supportive environment for artists who participate in the Serie Project, allowing them to pursue their individual creative visions. In his own printmaking, Coronado often uses the juxtaposition of images from diverse sources to create meaning. In *Pancho Villa and The Cisco Kid* he combines and layers cross-cultural meanings of real and fictional characters from history and popular culture. We see at the left of the composition a famous image of Pancho Villa, hero of the Mexican Revolution of 1910, astride his horse. Standing next to him, we see a child dressed as the Cisco Kid, on horseback, an image taken from a photograph of Coronado's childhood neighbor. As poor Chicano children, it was their dream to have horses like the Cisco Kid's. In the Hollywood and television narrative, "Pancho" is the Mexican sidekick to the suave Spanish Cisco. In Coronado's version, the Cisco Kid is a boy, less important and less competent than the great Pancho. The patterned background creates an iris shape around the two figures, giving the composition the atmosphere of a dim memory or a silent film.

Alfredo Arreguín, *Frida's Messengers.* PLATE 88. Utilizing his signature pattern-recognition technique, the artist creates a portrait of Frida Kahlo, the celebrated Jewish Mexican artist of the first half of the twentieth century, that is embedded within and emerges from a complex design formed by varied and subtle patterns created partially through a highly strategic color scheme that uses to great advantage both warm shades of red, brown, and pink, and the contrasting colors turquoise and black. Arreguín shares with Kahlo a dedication to the depiction of animals within a composition that is notable for its design elements, and perhaps she cleared the path for him to develop his highly original style. In this homage to Frida, she is surrounded by, immersed within, and emerges semidistinctly from a milieu of highly patterned plants and animals. Her prominent eyes and characteristic eyebrows, nose, and mouth are the most distinct elements of

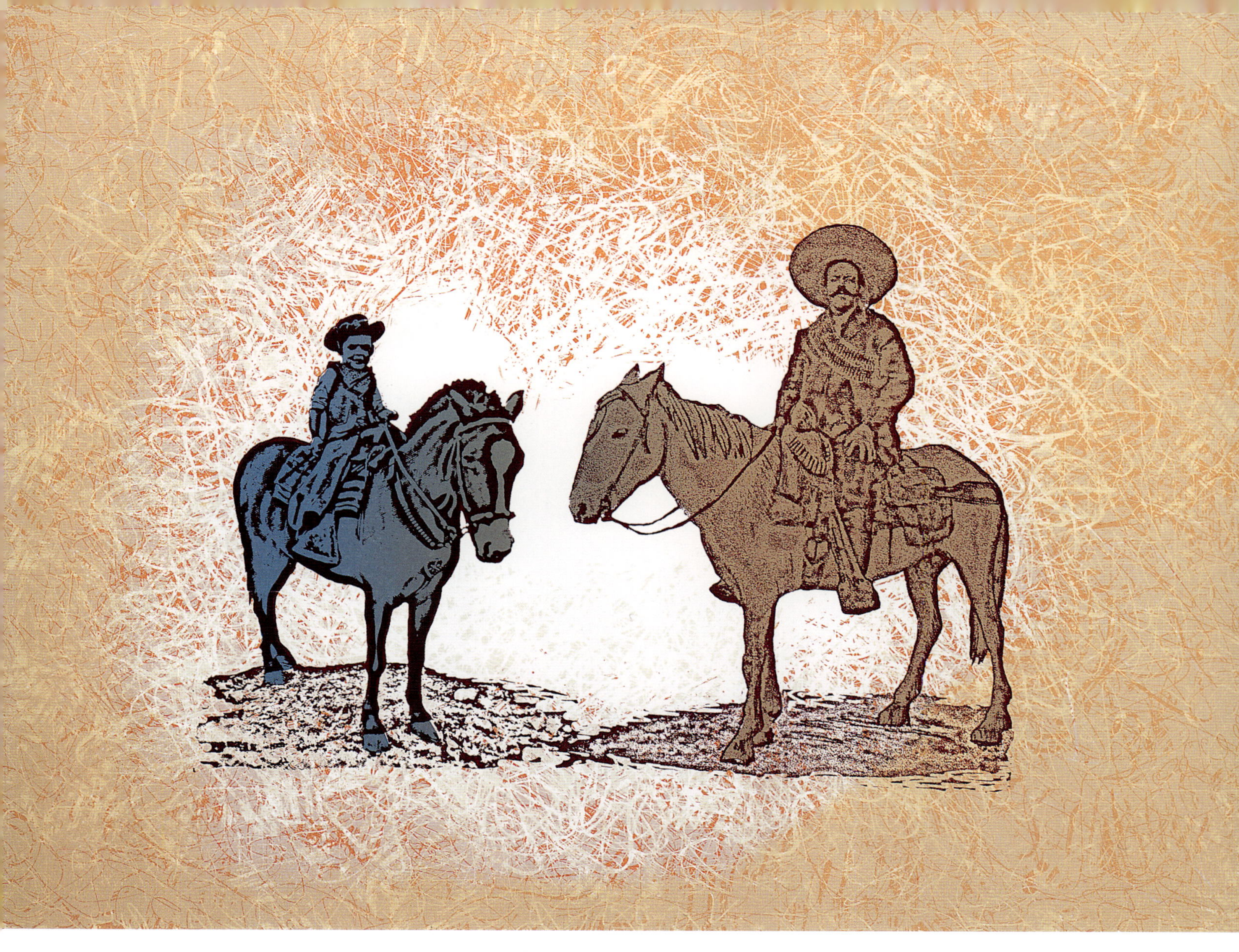

86 Sam Zaragosa Coronado, *Pancho Villa and the Cisco Kid*, 1999, serigraph, 22" x 30"

her portrait; other features are immersed in the overall pattern that at once seems ancient and partaking of psychoactive contemporaneity. Birds function as messengers to Frida, as they do in another work by Arreguín, *Zapata's Messengers*. The message itself is oracular and not readily interpretable, but part of it relates to the intimate, connecting spiritual web between plants, animals, humankind, and the esthetic patterns that their interaction creates.

César A. Martínez, *Sandra Cisneros.* PLATE 87. Martínez often has painted portraits of *vatos* and *cholas*, savvy navigators of the Mexican American urban barrios whose dress and demeanor reflect a hip lifestyle. This portrait is typical of the artist's general formal style in that he places the figure, who is painted head-on so that she or he is face to face with the viewer, against a color-field background that complements but does not distract from the portrayal.

Another characteristic feature of this artist's work in general is his ability to capture the emotional depth of the subject within the work of art. Attention in Martínez's works is concentrated on the expression of the face, almost as a vehicle for penetrating into the *fuero interior,* the inner identity, although some elements of dress figure in his work as well, especially when they establish the figure's status as a barrio habitué. On the other hand, *Sandra Cisneros* is a highly exceptional piece inasmuch as, far from depicting an unrecognized *vato* or *chola*, it is a portrait of a leading and internationally known Chicana fiction writer and intellectual. The work was done in 1980 during a period when the artist had a personal relationship with her, and the qualities of intelligence and creativity that he captures in his subject, particularly through the painting of the eyes and the lips that carry just a hint of irony in them, make this one of his most memorable portraits.

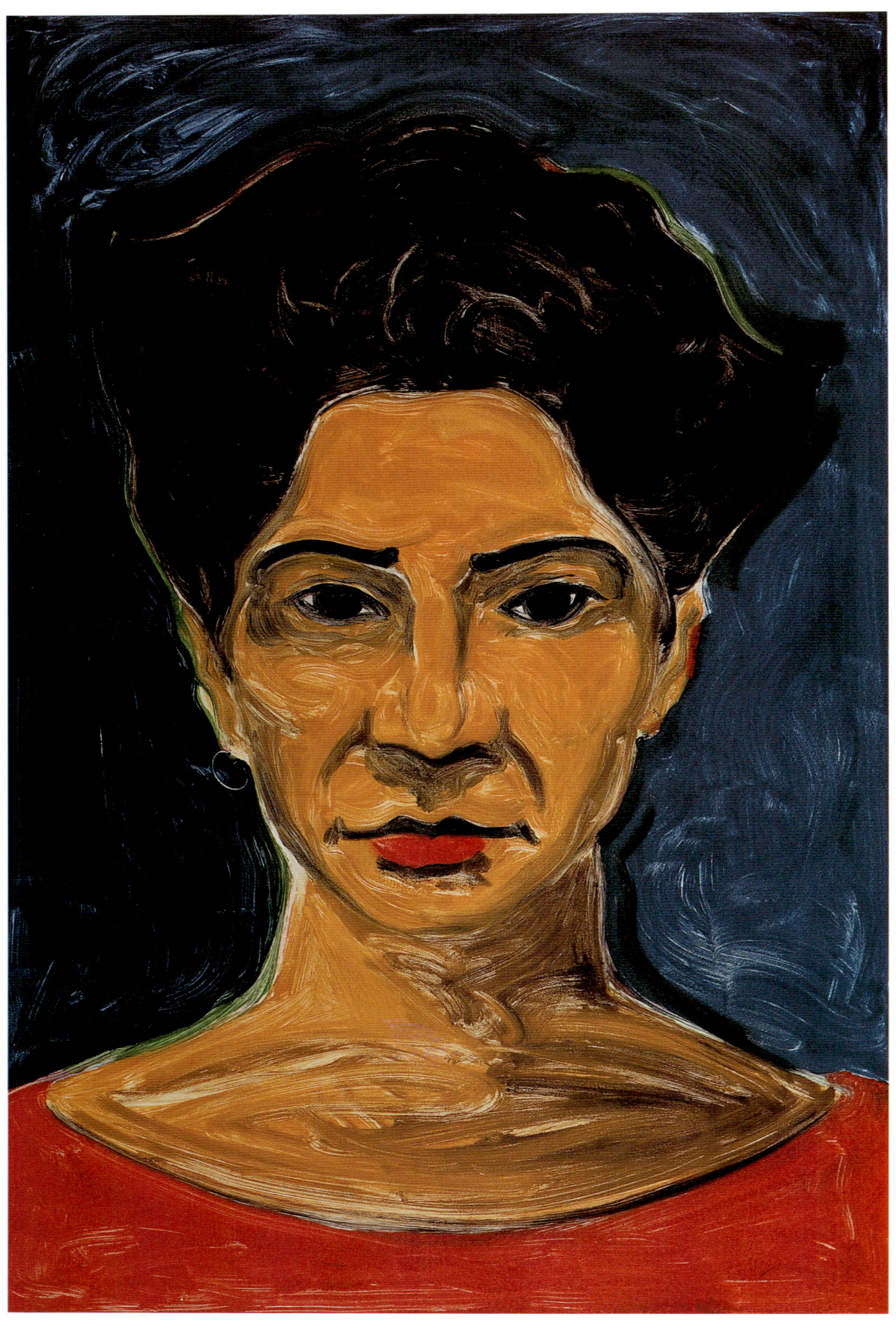

87 César A. Martínez, *Sandra Cisneros*, 1980, monoprint, 26.75" x 19"

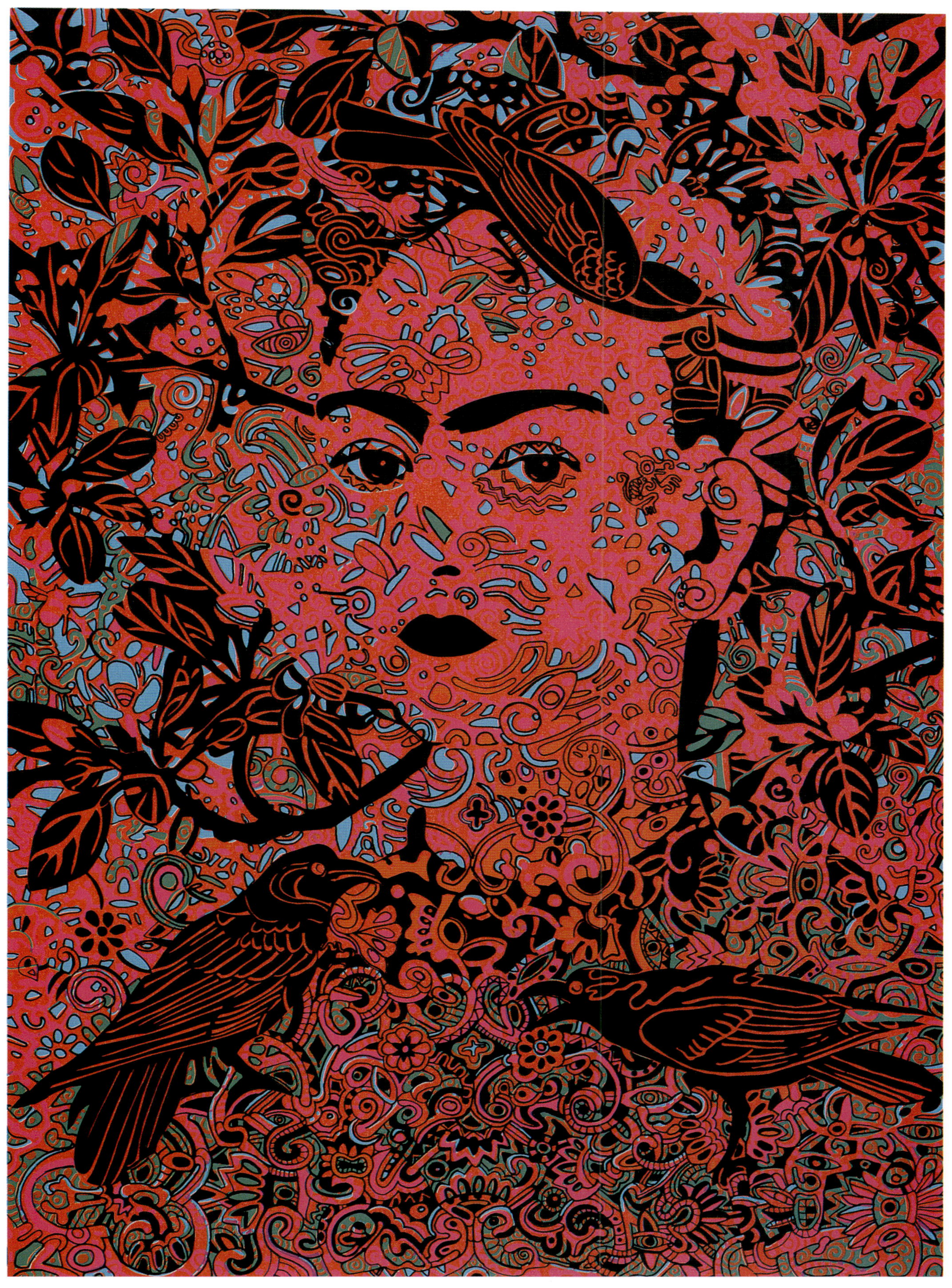

88 Alfredo Arreguín, *Frida's Messengers*, 1992, serigraph, 42" x 30"

Ester Hernández, *Homenaje a César Chávez* (Homage to César Chávez). PLATE 89. Composed in 1993, the year of his death and ten years before the creation of the actual postage stamp honoring him, this work both presages and triumphantly militates for a national recognition of the fallen farmworker organizer and foremost hero of the Chicano community. Celebrating a Chicano hero as also an American hero, the work utilizes the national colors of red, white, and blue and the profile of an American eagle that has been transformed to evoke at the same time the characteristic United Farmworkers' eagle, the most significant emblem of Chávez and the farmworkers. The UFW logo was originally created in 1962 as both an eagle, a binational symbol since it figures prominently in the history and symbology of both the United States and Mexico, and as an evocation of an inverted Aztec step pyramid. To the left are the vital statistics of the national hero and to the right his characteristic message of hope and attainment, "Sí se puede" (Yes you can!). The

likeness of Chávez himself exudes authority and satisfaction. Silver and pepper-haired, with only a hint of the life of fasting that was a significant factor in his demise, César Chávez has been depicted in this work as a hero, role model, father figure, and encouraging mentor for all time and all people.

Luis Guerrero, *Super Muffler Man.* PLATE 90. Part of the sculptor's Muffler Man series together with the accordionist *El Chuy*, who is also featured in this exhibit, this caped figure evokes a legendary folk hero who intervenes on behalf of the powerless and needy, combats evil where he finds it, and rights wrongs. In the place where Superman would have the emblazoned S, this caped hero boasts an M. Of course, there is a powerful artistic tension established between the hero and the materials from which that hero is constructed. Displaying his customary exquisite *rasquache* ingenuity and sensibility, Guerrero ingeniously creates the eyes of his caped hero by affixing gear sprockets to his metal head,

89 Ester Hernández, *Homenaje a César Chávez* (Homage to César Chávez), 1993, serigraph, 22" x 30"

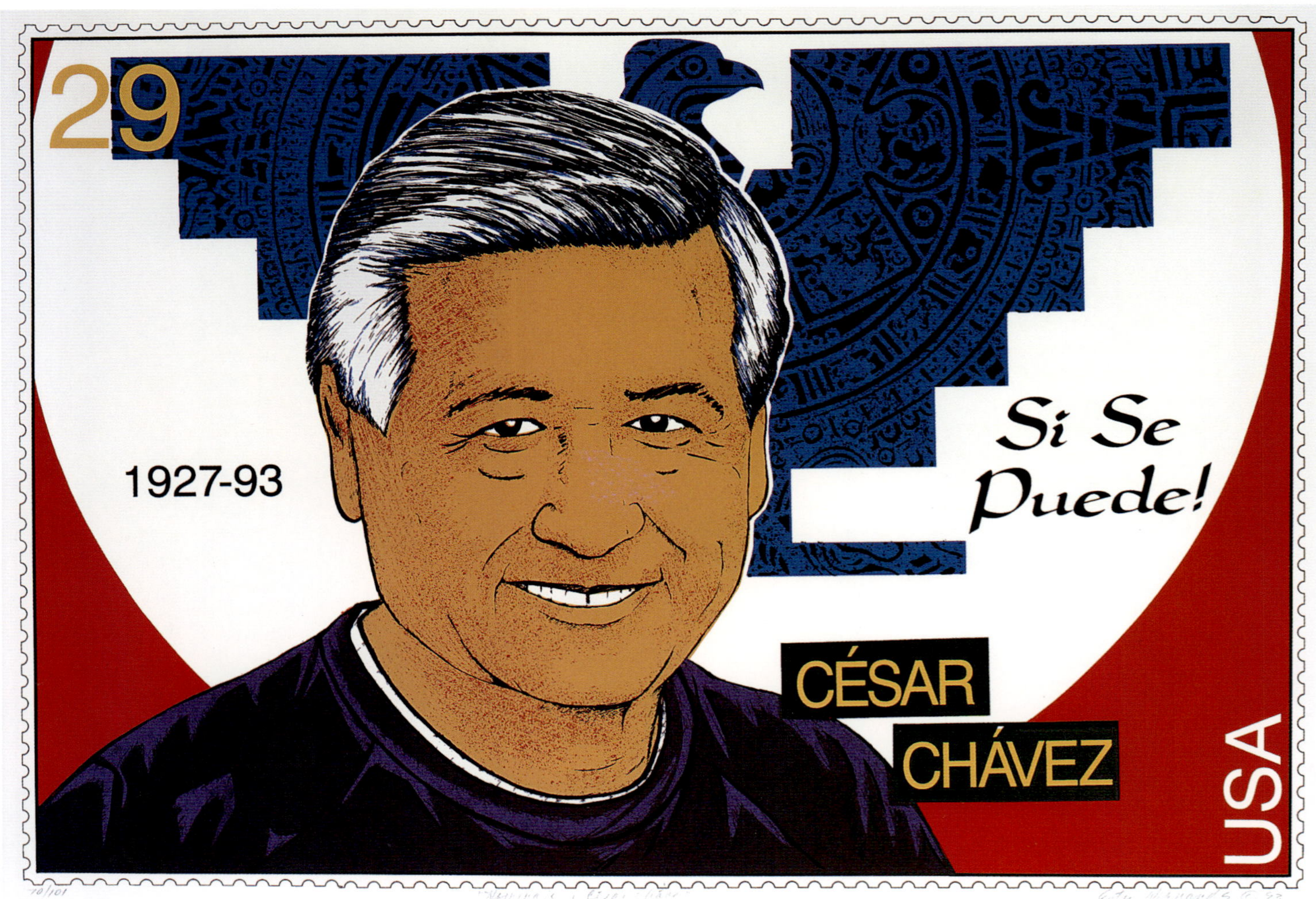

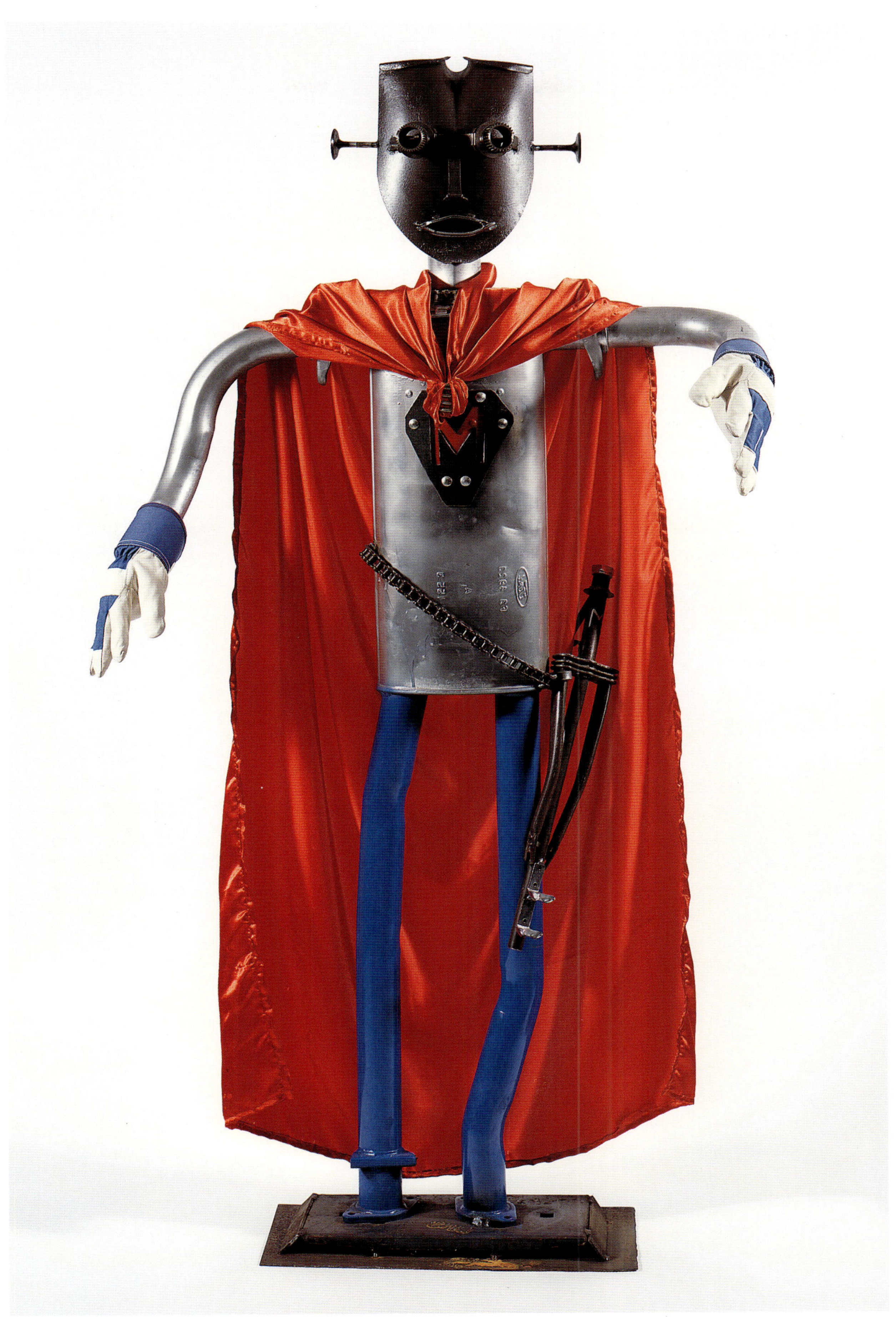

90 Luis Guerrero, *Super Muffler Man*, 2003, mixed media sculpture, 69" x 35" x 20"

and the weapon ensemble around his waist includes what appears to be a bicycle chain. As for the torso, only the best part will suffice: an original, numbered Ford muffler. Keeping such authentic industrial provenances in his sculpture only enhances its resonance. For example, the best-known collection of cartoons by Mexico's most renowned caricaturist, Abel Quezada, is entitled *El mejor de todos los mundos imposibles* (The best of all impossible worlds). One of the noteworthy cartoons in the collection has a Mexican fantasizing about how wonderful it would be if his country were the premier industrial nation of the world. Then car advertisements would state, "There's a Martínez in your future," instead of "There's a Ford in your future!"

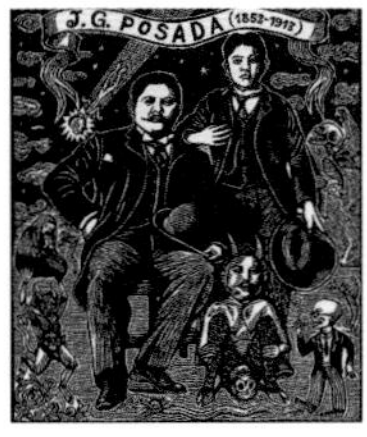

Posada y su hijo,
see page vii

Artemio Rodríguez, *Posada y su hijo* (Posada and his son). PLATE 3. José Guadalupe Posada has been recognized as Mexico's most important and influential popular artist of the late nineteenth and early twentieth centuries. Producing a prodigious number of prints—etchings, zincographs, and the like—from his Mexico City printshop, he was the illustrator of all of the events of historical and cultural significance of his time, as well as a masterful re-creator of Mexican popular culture and its imagery. He is especially well known as the force behind the transposition from popular culture to the beaux arts of the *Día de los Muertos* (Day of the Dead) celebrations with their attendant iconography of skeletons engaged in animated activity (dancing, drinking, warring, romancing, and so on). Equally significant, he was the primary figure that both the post-Mexican Revolution group Taller de Gráfica Popular in Mexico and the Chicano printmaking community recognize in their efforts to bring art with accompanying social and political messages to the Mexican people, who are often illiterate. Artemio Rodríguez, master etcher in residence at the renowned East Los Angeles community arts organization Self-Help Graphics, has created an *homenaje* (homage) etching to Posada and his son on the ninetieth anniversary of the father's death. Presumably taken from a vintage photograph, the etching re-creates, under a celebratory banner indicating the senior Posada's birth and death statistics, a realistic likeness of the two as if they were posing in their Sunday best for the camera. Surrounding them is an arresting miniature display of some of the Posada iconography that includes both the *calavera* (skull) theme and social and political satire.

Libertad,
see page 182

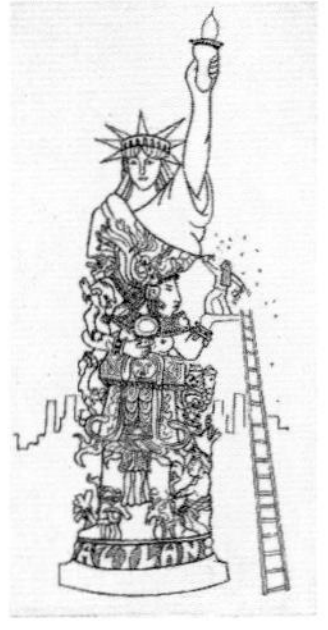

¡Venceremos!

Laura Molina, *One Little Indian Versus the Corporate Trolls.* PLATE 91. Laura Molina proclaims herself to be "the angriest woman in the world," and points out that as a Chicana living in American culture she has suffered enough insults and indignities to warrant her feelings of rage. For Molina, expressions of rage function as a way of standing up for herself and others who have been taken advantage of by an unfair system, whether the system is patriarchy in one's personal life or capitalism in corporate life. Molina has worked extensively as a scenic artist in film, television, music videos, and theme parks, and her images are shaped by these experiences in the entertainment industry. At one point in her career, she worked for the Walt Disney Company as an artist, but her employment relationship ended with her suing the company for discrimination. This is the root of her painting *One Little Indian Versus the Corporate Trolls*. Molina represents herself standing outside the Disney Company's corporate headquarters in Burbank, California, wearing a feather earring that marks her as the one little Indian of the title. The headquarters building is designed with Snow White's seven dwarfs functioning as pillars holding up the façade of the company that was "all started by a mouse." In Molina's narrative, this supposedly happy place resembles a prison complete with chain-link fence with razor wire on the top and a guard station. One wonders if this security is to keep people in or out. Molina is entangled in barbed wire, and she displays her "Laura" name badge impaled in her palm. Blood drips from her hand, the stigmata of those who have been crucified by the trolls. The artist represents herself as outside the corporate enclosure, bleeding but unbroken. It appears that the angriest woman in the world has been victorious against corporate injustice.

Ester Hernández, *Libertad* (Liberty). PLATE 121. In this etching, a graphic form used often for political purposes by the nineteenth- and early twentieth-century master José Guadalupe Posada, Hernández creates an ingenious work reminiscent of a satirical political cartoon that refashions the Statue of Liberty more to her liking. Liberty carries the torch of freedom in her right hand; the artist's *Libertad* is a left-handed vision that retains

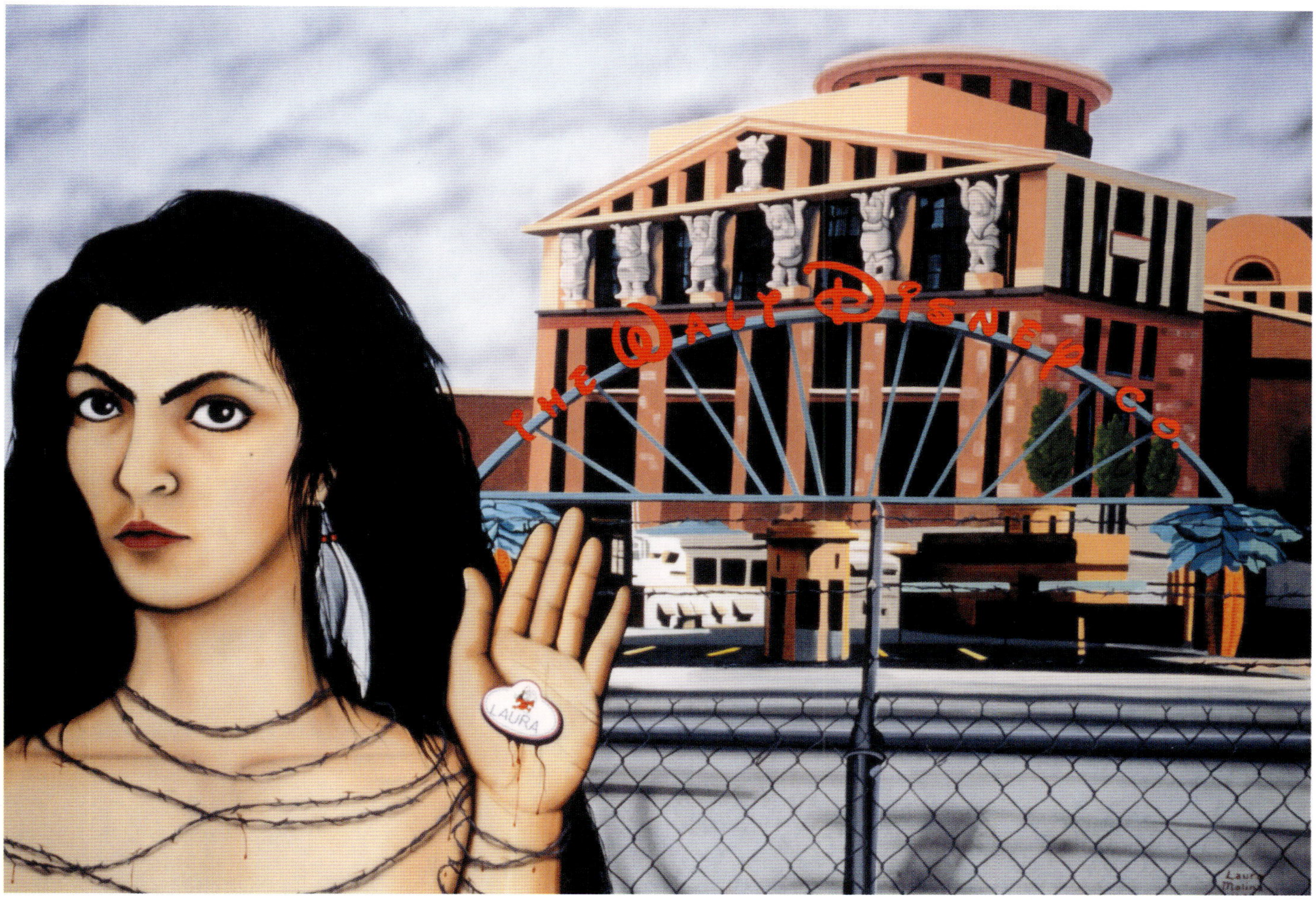

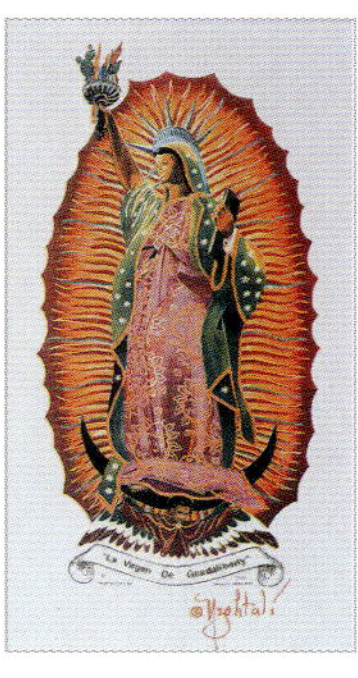

91 Laura Molina, *One Little Indian Versus the Corporate Trolls*, 1994, acrylic on canvas, 47" x 50"

the higher elements of the original, including the torch of freedom and the starred crown, but has a young Latina with long, flowing dark hair busily refashioning the original. She stands atop a platform that is also the outstretched hand of a pre-Hispanic glyph, one of a number that cover the statue from the upper middle portion down to the base, at which is emblazoned the word "Aztlán," referring to the Aztec peoples' place of origin. Many Chicanas/os use the term Aztlán to refer to the portion of Mexico that was taken over by the United States after the Mexican-American War of 1846, an area that includes California, Arizona, Texas, and New Mexico and that they regard as their mythopoetic and political homeland within a multicultural United States that not only respects but encourages diversity. The artist seems to be communicating the message that U.S. notions of liberty should include and embrace Aztlán and all of the unique Mexican/Chicano cultural elements that go with it.

Nephtalí de León, *La Virgen de Guadaliberty.* PLATE 113. In this serigraph, Nephtalí de León endows the Virgin of Guadalupe with certain symbols proper to the Statue of Liberty, thus uniting two of the most recognizable female figures in the Americas. Although the Virgin of Guadalupe is a Catholic symbol of faith, many of her attributes, and indeed the place in which she is said to have first appeared, are associated with the Aztec goddess Tonantzin, or Mother Earth. To many Americans of European heritage, the Statue of Liberty represents international friendship, freedom, and democracy. Coupled with Emma Lazarus's "The New Colossus" ("Give me your tired, your poor, your huddled masses yearning to breathe free . . ."), the statue represents the ideals of a newly formed republic. By combining the two symbols, de León makes a powerful comment on issues Chicanas/os have grappled with for decades: displacement and oppression. The specific attributes of the statue that de León applies to Guadalupe are the tablet, the torch, and the crown. While the crown

La Virgen de Guadaliberty, see page 170

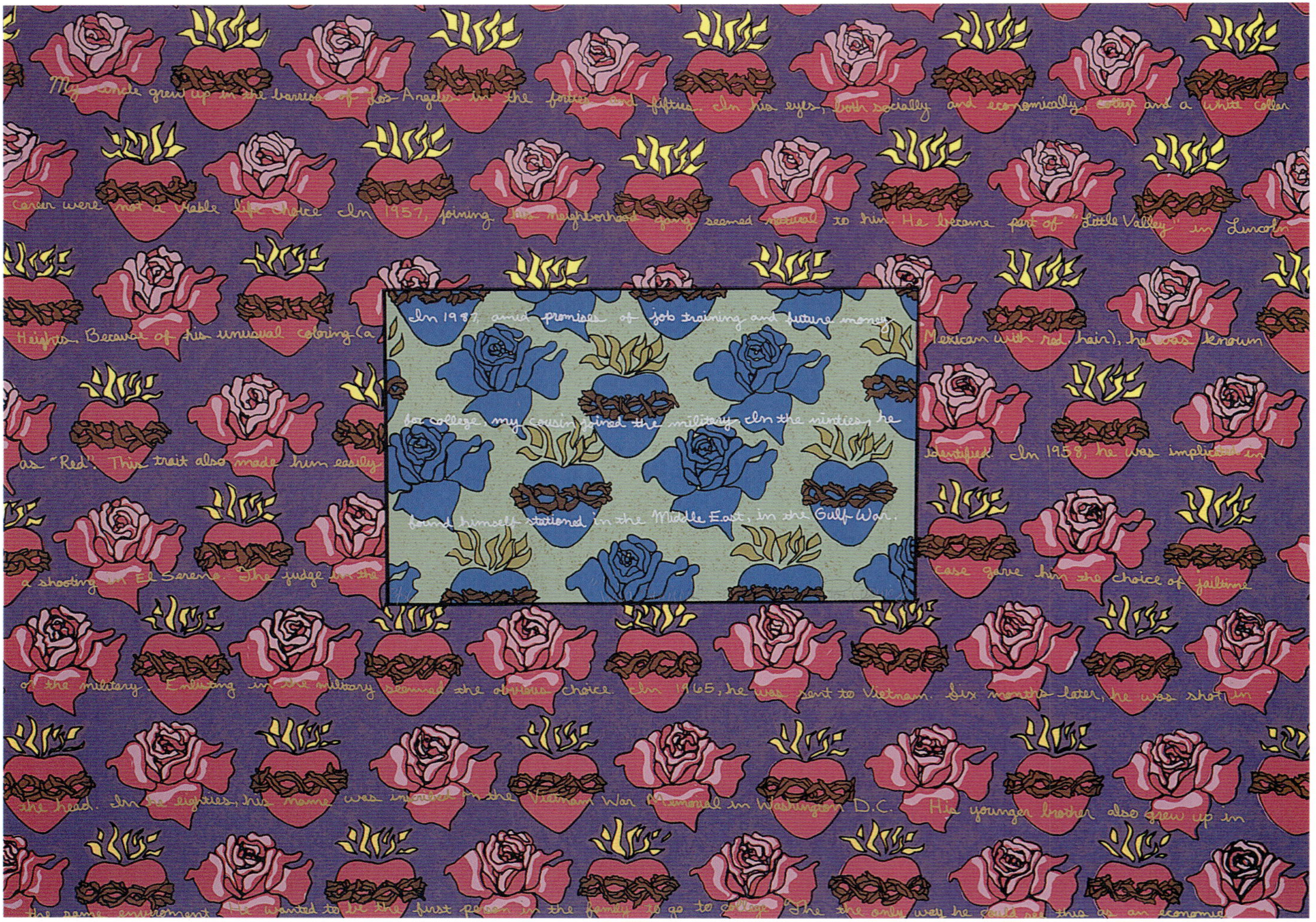

92 Pat Gómez, *War Stories*, 1991, serigraph, 25" x 35"

appears much the same as the statue's original, the torch has been modified to include cacti, and the tablet appears to be a prayer book or hymnal. The artist appears to be implying that the promise of the Statue of Liberty—that America is the home of the free for all peoples—has not been fully realized and that the symbol attains more impact for Chicanas/os when it is combined with certain socially recognized attributes of the Virgin of Guadalupe, including love, acceptance, faith, and kindness.

Pat Gómez, *War Stories*. PLATE 92. This artist's works draw upon past and present events, and this one depicts a personal family tragedy that transpired when the artist's uncle, implicated in a shooting, was given by the judge the choice of either enlisting in the military or serving time in jail. Choosing the former, the uncle was sent to Vietnam, where he was subsequently killed in action. The work itself embeds a biting textual message and a bittersweet iconic one as well, deceptively delivered

in a decorative pattern that creates a sense of safety for the viewer who is drawn into the narrative message. Through interpretation of the text we discover that the outer design of red roses and red hearts has no Valentine message, but instead a scathing one, further reinforced by the central rectangle which, implying death, repeats the pattern of roses and hearts in cold stone blue. Through this strategic alternation of design patterns into which is woven a text, the artist has created a written and visual narrative that expresses family, loss, false hope, and broken promises. Gómez's *War Stories*, Briceño's *Las rosas de mi güelita*, and Oropeza's *Héchale* all use to strategic advantage a flower design pattern, but each for contrasting purposes and with different results. Briceño's pattern is a remembrance of love between a grandmother and her granddaughter, while Gómez's preserves a more bittersweet memory and delivers a poignant message packaged in decoration. Oropeza's pattern establishes a foundation for the celebration of the joyful, active, creative dead.

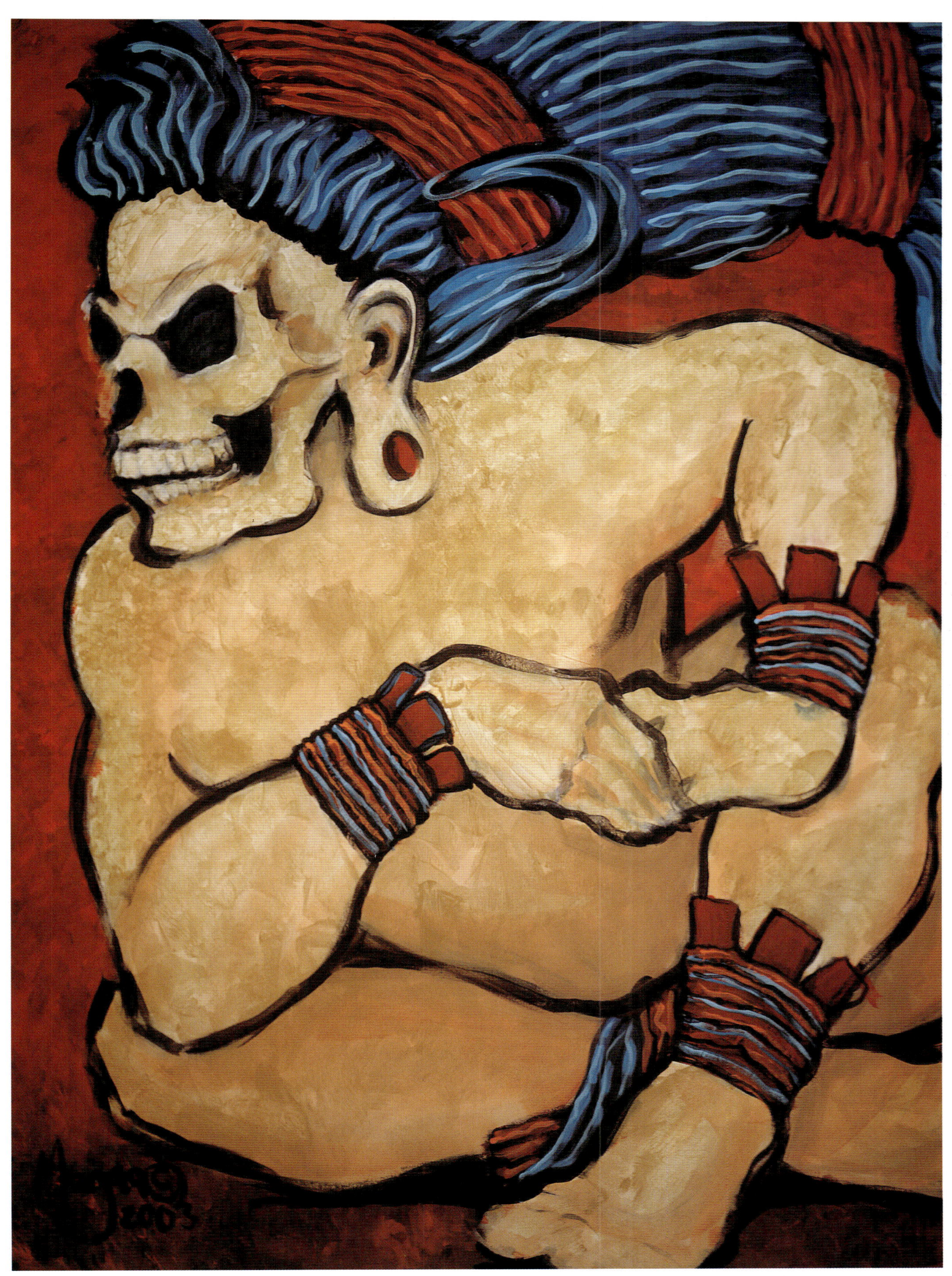

93 Magda Bowen, *Warrior*, 2003, acrylic on canvas, 40" x 30". Collection of the artist.

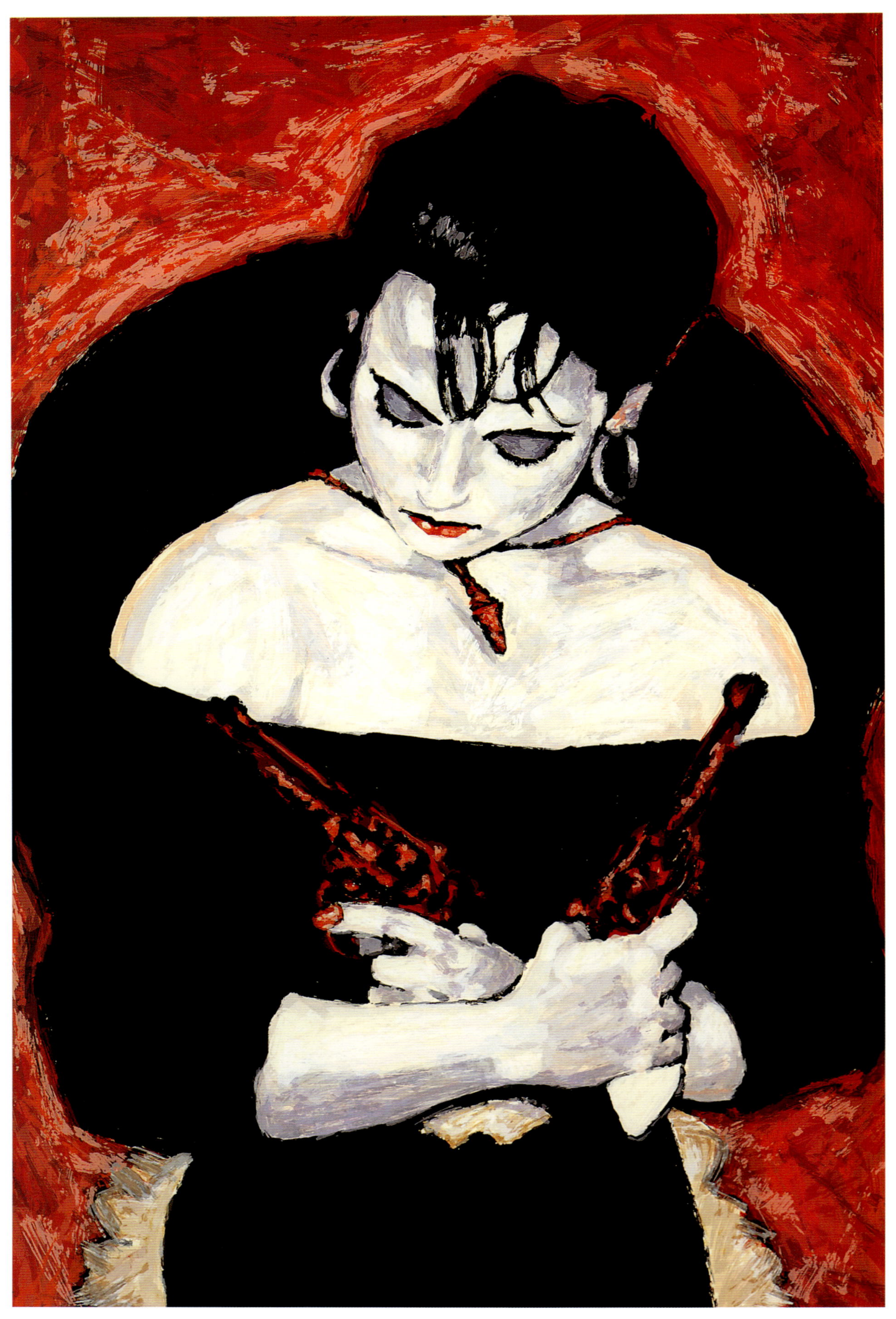

94 George Yepes, *Adelita*, 1991, serigraph, 38" x 25"

Magda Bowen, *Warrior.* PLATE 93. This piece emphasizes ambiguity and blurs distinctions along many lines. The scantily dressed figure seems to have a coat of skin, although this is not certain due to its petrified or hidelike quality. Interpreting the figure is made more difficult upon examining the head—especially the eye sockets and nasal cavity—which seems to be a *calavera* (skull) not covered by skin, although the color and shading of the head are not distinguishable from those of the torso. The gender of the figure is also unclear. The earlobe ornament or plug would seem to indicate a female, but not necessarily in the representation of pre-Hispanic peoples where these are frequently seen on men. The long, flowing hair might indicate the female gender (as well as a living entity), but again it is hardly definitive. Finally, it is uncertain what culture or time period this figure inhabits, although it is fairly conclusive that it is Amerindian. In presenting such an ambiguous figure neither definitively alive nor dead, male nor female, and so on, Bowen raises ongoing issues about the identity of *mestizo* (mixed heritage) or autochthonous peoples that have persisted for centuries.

George Yepes, *Adelita.* PLATE 94. The colors red and black have often been used to emphasize contrast and opposition, often within a political or cultural context. In the nineteenth century, for example, the French novelist Stendhal (Henri-Marie Beyle, 1783-1842) wrote a famous novel about a womanizing social arriviste, *The Red and the Black*, in which those colors alternately referred to the red uniforms of Napoleon's army and the black robes of priests, to the colors on a roulette wheel, and to the colors of blood and mourning. In *Adelita* this color scheme is used effectively for several purposes. *Adelita* evokes perhaps the most famous song of the Mexican Revolution of 1910, a time during which records and histories have documented that a small but significant number of women participated as active revolutionaries and even *cacicas,* military heads, rather than in mere support roles. *Adelita* suggests that period subtly, although the overt reference is more to popular culture, such as the films of Robert Rodríguez. (Interestingly, *Adelita* was executed before Rodríguez's first film, but subsequently works by Yepes have been commissioned by the director to illustrate his Westerns.) Severe opposition is both established and synthesized in the figure of the emphatically dangerous and beautiful woman. She is to be both feared and desired inasmuch as she carries not one but two pearl-handled *pistolas,* each emanating a red aura, even as she is carefully made up and elegantly dressed as a party *vaquera* (cowhand) in a black gown and festive sombrero, with her shoulders bare and her head turned down in what normally would be interpreted as a demure or submissive pose. *Adelita* evokes the contemporary femme fatale, who, as in James Bond films or their Hispanic counterparts set in the Wild West, can bring you down either in the traditional way, through her feminine wiles, or in the postmodern fashion, by dint of her expert use of weapons.

Sam Zaragosa Coronado, *Guerrillera II.* PLATE 95. As with *Pancho Villa and The Cisco Kid* (see the "Héroes" section), in *Guerrillera II* Sam Coronado juxtaposes unexpected elements to make his artistic statement. This serigraph, one of a series of seven variations on this theme, features a row of seven images of the same size lined up across the page on a background of burlap, contained on the top and bottom by rows of barbed wire. Five of the images are of identical rifle bullets. Two items in the row are different: an extended tube of red lipstick is in the second position from the left and a very young indigenous woman carrying a rifle is placed upside down in the center position. This simple grouping of items untaps a flood of associations for the viewer. While it is not overtly presented as the subject matter of this serigraph, one is reminded of the contemporary revolutionary Zapatista movement of the Maya people in Chiapas, Mexico. We see the resemblance between the bullet and the lipstick, both products of the capitalist culture that oppresses the Maya and other indigenous peoples around the globe. We become aware of how unlikely it is that lipstick, a luxury taken for granted in the United States, could ever become a part of this young woman's world, while it appears that she is very familiar with the bullet. The image of the contemporary young woman with a gun also reminds us of the female fighters of the Mexican Revolution of 1910, bringing into focus the fact that current struggles are not the first time that the downtrodden have risen up against their oppressors, or the first time that women have participated in armed struggle. The woman's placement upside down suggests her role in opposition to the other images, bullets and lipstick, presented in this piece.

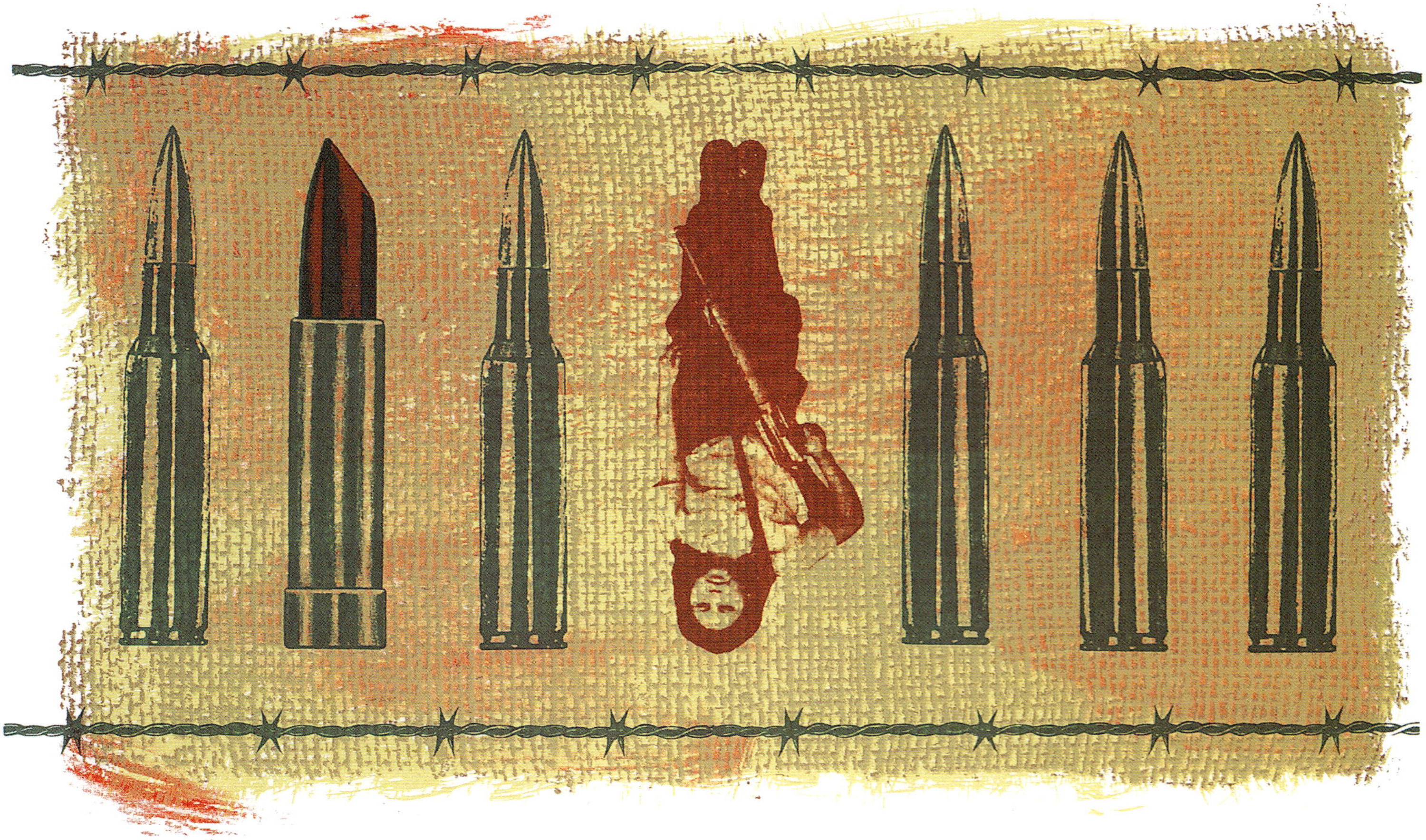

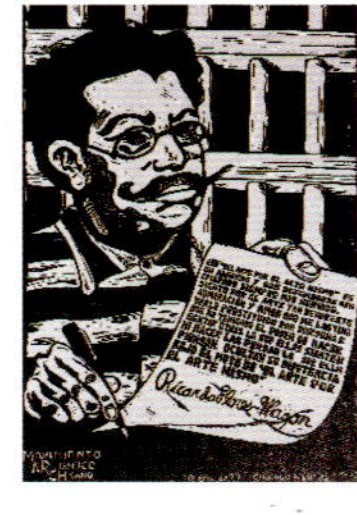

Ricardo Flores Magón, see page viii

95 Sam Zaragosa Coronado, *Guerrillera II*, 2001, serigraph, 9.5" x 15"

Carlos Cortez, *Ricardo Flores Magón.* PLATE 4. The artist depicts the exiled Mexican political thinker and activist Ricardo Flores Magón wearing the prison uniform that would become his funeral shroud. Flores Magón fled Mexico in 1910 to publish the newspaper *Regeneración,* an intellectual forebear and impetus for the Mexican Revolution. He eventually died under suspicious circumstances in Leavenworth Prison after being convicted of sedition by the U.S. government in collusion with Mexican authorities. In this linocut, the image of Flores Magón presents a manifesto for inspection by the viewer. The medium and the message are in perfect harmony here: the work uses only black and white, lending itself to the production of a linocut that is inexpensive to duplicate and distribute. Esthetically, black and white are contrastively combined to great advantage. This is vividly apparent in Flores Magón's striped prison suit; the interlacing of the white bars and the black spaces between them; the black mustache, eyeglasses, and hair set against the background of the white face; the black pen held in the white hand; and the manifesto that appears in black against a sheet of white paper. The contrasts of black and white reinforce the manifesto itself, which is neither subtle nor nuanced but rather expresses direct antagonism toward the notion of "art for art's sake," leaving no doubt of the paper's importance in the composition. Created in 1977 at the time of the flowering of the Movimiento Artístico Chicano (MARCH), a group of muralists seeking social and political justice through their art, Cortez is saying that the need to create responsible art, to fight against oppression through the expression of art, is as necessary now as it was in 1910.

Nuestros símbolos

Joe López, *The Spirit of Machismo.* PLATE 96. "Macho" and "machismo" are two words and their underlying concepts that have become grossly entangled in cross-cultural confusion. For Anglos they have come to refer to a cult or set of behaviors characterized by outsized and untoward masculinity. Sometimes the words are rendered in English in ways that violate the grammar of Spanish, as in "mucho macho." The word "machismo" is not used often in Spanish, and "macho," which is

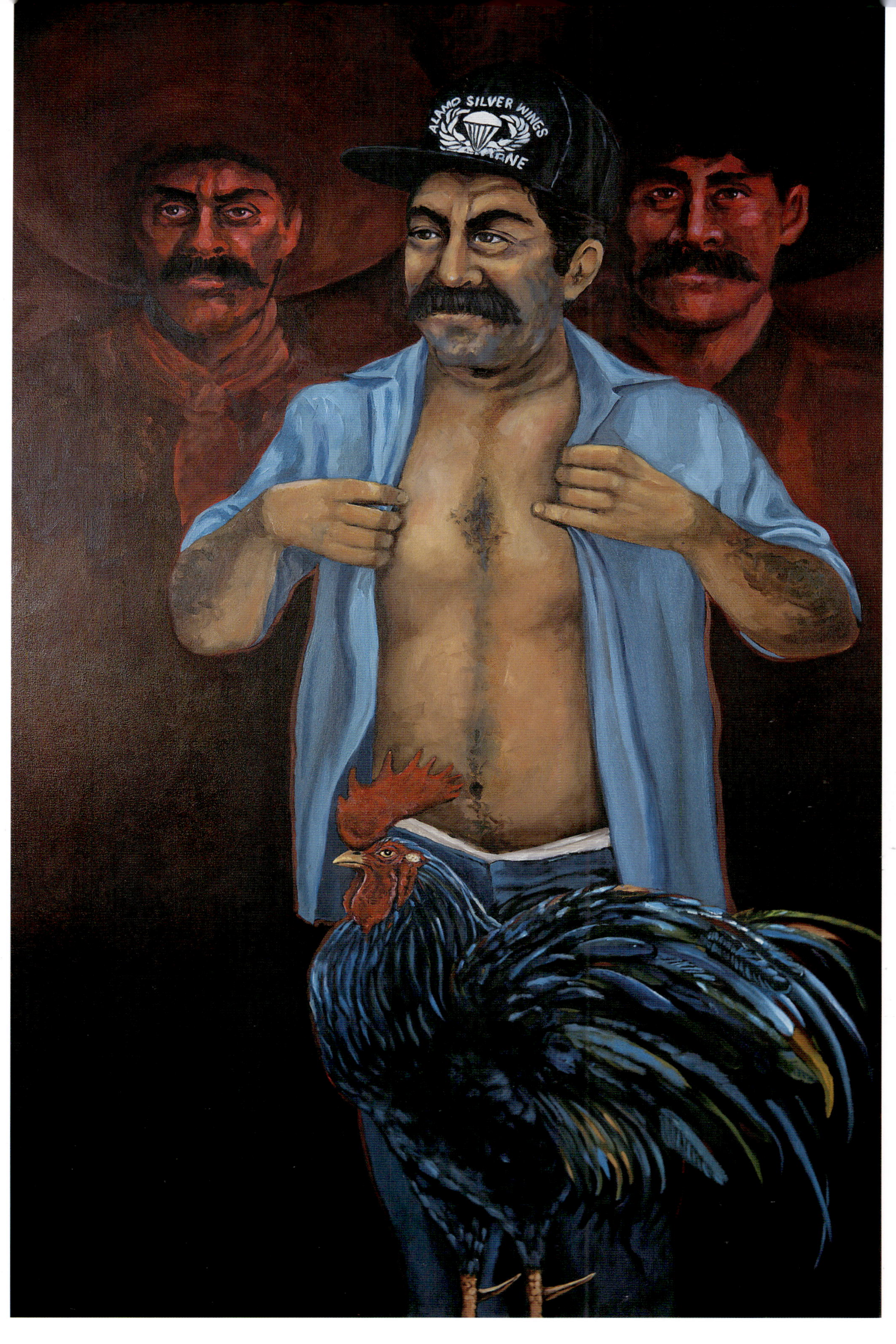

96 Joe L. López, *The Spirit of Machismo*, 2003, oil on canvas, 60" x 36". Collection of the artist.

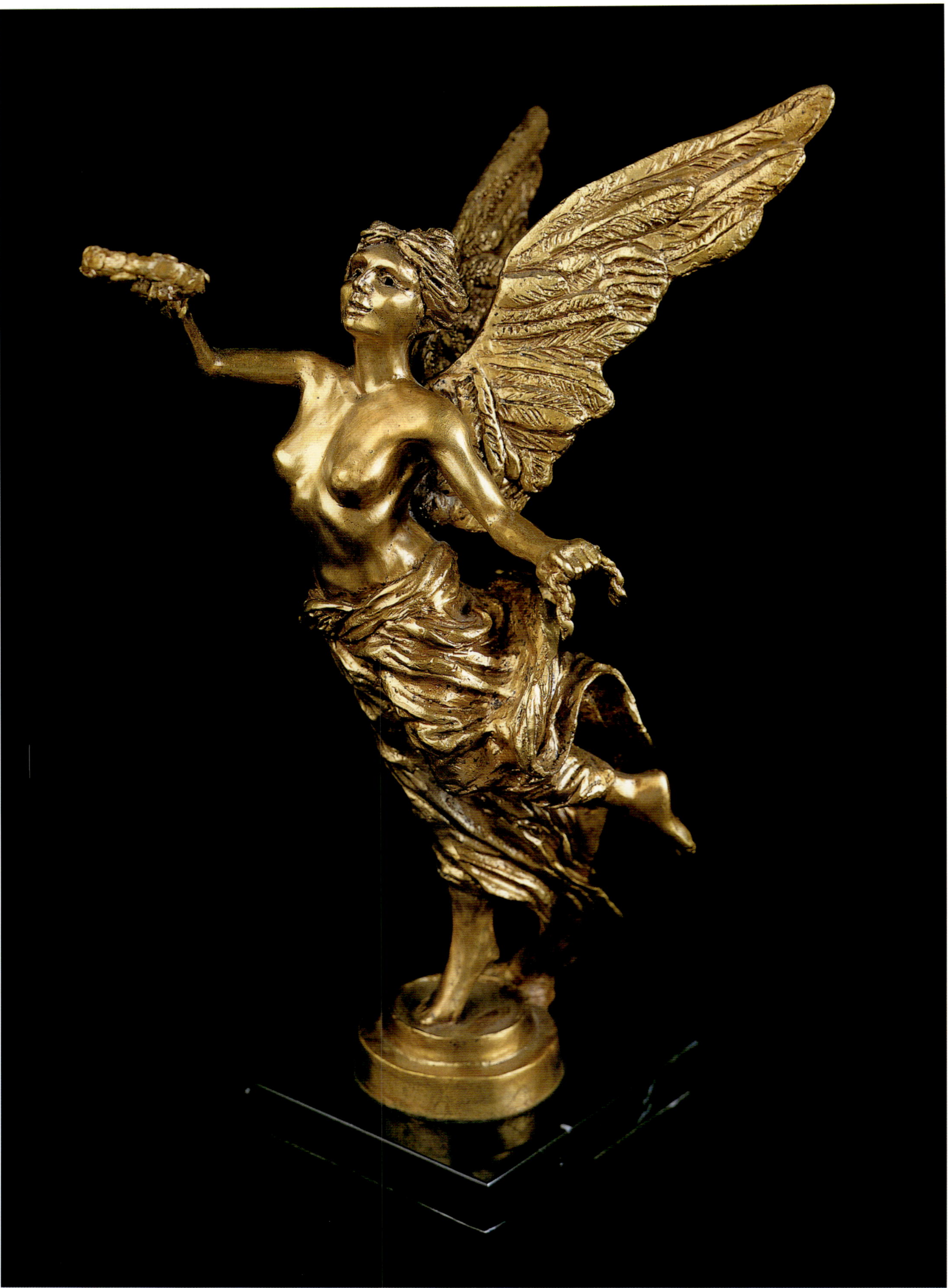

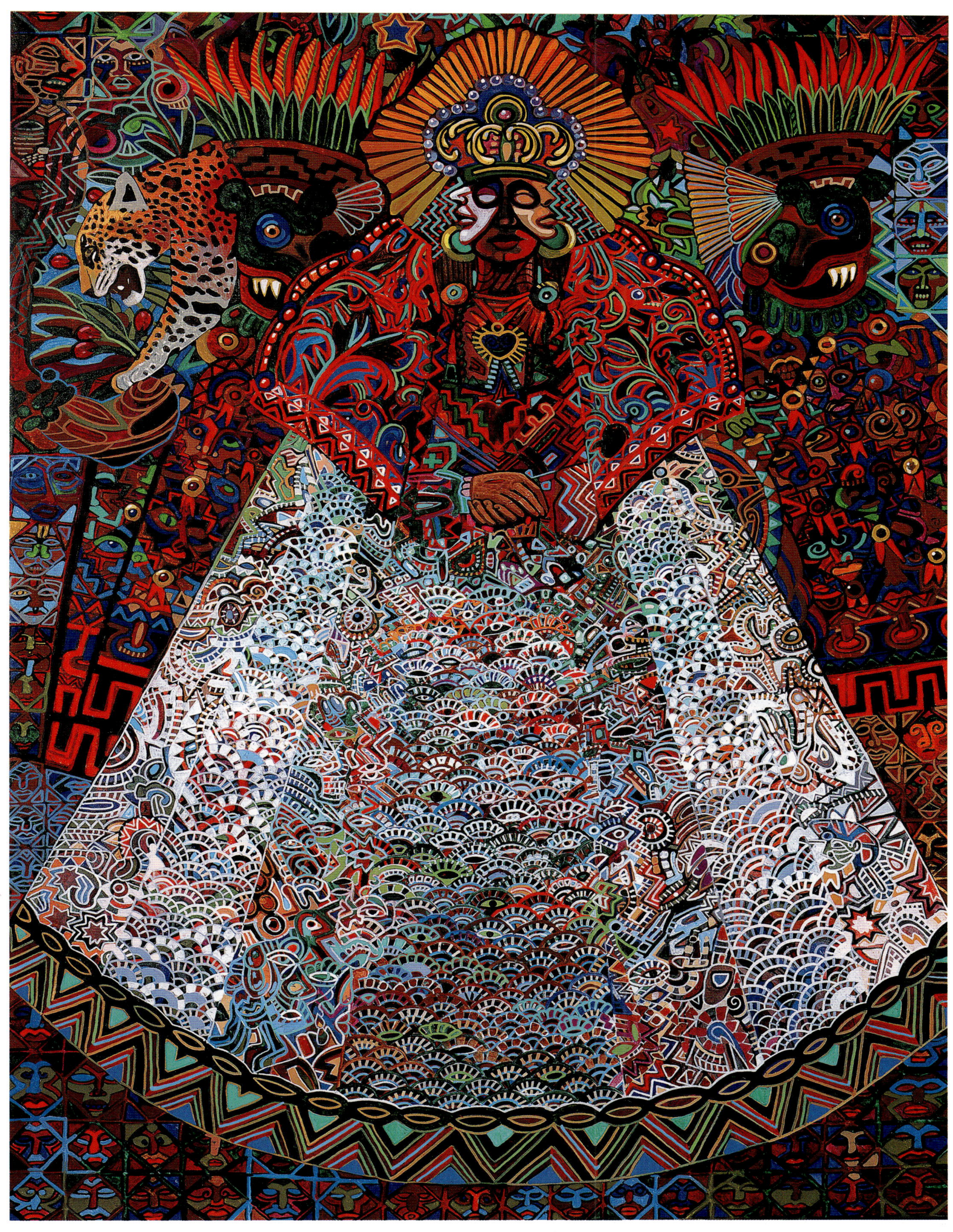

Left: 97 Riley Roca, *El ángel de Chilangolandia*, 2000, Bronze, 15.5" x 9" x 11"

98 Alfredo Arreguín, *La Malinche*, 1993, oil on canvas, 48" x 36"
Collection of the Artist.

frequently used, usually has a different context. It is simply male, the gender counterpart of *hembra*, female. When "machismo" is used in Spanish, it is less often given its American connotation and more often refers to behavior that is customary or suitable for a *macho*. A *macho* in Hispanic culture is required to live up to his obligations, to be *a la altura de las circunstancias* or "to rise to the occasion." In Joe López's work we have a representation that is in keeping with Hispanic interpretations of machismo. First of all, in Latino culture, "macho" and "machismo" primarily relate to behavior among males. This is the case in this work, in which females are not overtly referenced but rather implied by the sexual or romantic attraction suggested by the presence of the rooster and the bare chest, although both icons are primarily male-to-male. What is present is a working man without pretensions who has done his duty, as can be seen by the presence of his cap, as a parachutist for the "Alamo Silver Wings" unit (the use of "Alamo" to indicate the patriotic behavior of a Chicano has a hugely ironic connotation). He is an incarnation of a long line of males whose spirits are present in the background and who have similarly done their manly duties. This is a line of males who are not particularly educated, sophisticated, or refined, but who have served when called upon and have lived up to their responsibilities. In the foreground is one of López's favorite icons, the rooster. In Spanish there is a phrase, "*buen gallo*," that is used to connote machos who have fulfilled their obligations within the concords of society, the social contract. These are *buen gallos*, roosters who have performed in accordance with their expected roles.

Riley Roca, *El ángel de Chilangolandia.* PLATE 97. (A *chilango* is a resident of Mexico City; *landia* is the equivalent of the English "land.") Riley Roca is the obverse of a Mexican American. She is a Mexican citizen of American heritage, fully bilingual and bicultural. A sculptor, she has specialized in well-known Mexican icons, including the Virgin of Guadalupe and *La Catrina*, the famous skeleton of a woman created by José Guadalupe Posada and made internationally famous by muralist Diego Rivera as a central figure in his *Sunday in the Alameda.* This piece, based on the monumental statue popularly known as *el ángel* in Mexico City, to which Roca has wryly added the moniker Chilangolandia, is, together with the Monument to the Revolution, the most important architectural symbol of the Mexican Revolution of 1910. Both the original and Roca's household-size bronze sculpture are the representation of a huge, triumphant golden angel, bare-breasted, somewhat emulative of work by the French revolutionary artists (for example, Eugene Delacroix's *Liberty Leading the People*), that rests on a high pedestal in one of the most prominent places in Mexico City. Commissioned to commemorate the Mexican War of Independence of 1810, it was officially christened by Porfirio Díaz in 1910 only weeks before the outbreak of the Mexican Revolution that would sweep him out of power in 1911. Roca's interpretation brings this huge monument to a personal level, endowing a symbol as important to Mexicans as the Statue of Liberty is to the United States with its triumphant, radiant aura and the highly positive historical associations for which it is known.

Alfredo Arreguín, *La Malinche.* PLATE 98. Making full use of the pattern-recognition style of which Arreguín is one of the founders and most successful cultivators, the artist creates an arresting, complex, and superbly rich portrait of *La Malinche*, who at the same time, syncretically, assumes aspects of the Mexican national symbol, the Virgin of Guadalupe. *La Malinche* has had a varied and checkered status in Mexico and perhaps even more so in Mexican American culture. The work depicts an actual adolescent girl who was the captive of a tribe in what is now the state of Tabasco, Mexico, and who was given along with nineteen other slave girls to Hernán Cortés and his men upon their arrival in Mexico. She later became an invaluable resource as a translator and interpreter of indigenous culture to the Hispanics. She also became Cortés's mistress and bore him a son, Martín Cortés, before he discarded her and awarded her to one of his lieutenants. Traditionally, in Mexican culture she has been a symbol of the creation of *mestizaje* (the racial mixing of Hispanics and Amerindians) but viewed with a negative cast because of her status as a submissive female and proxy for the indigenous culture defeated by the Spaniards, who imposed themselves by force. However, the feminist dimension of the Chicano movement completely vindicated La Malinche (often called Malintzin by feminists, who use her original name) as a very canny young woman who succeeded in creating out of her condition of captivity and

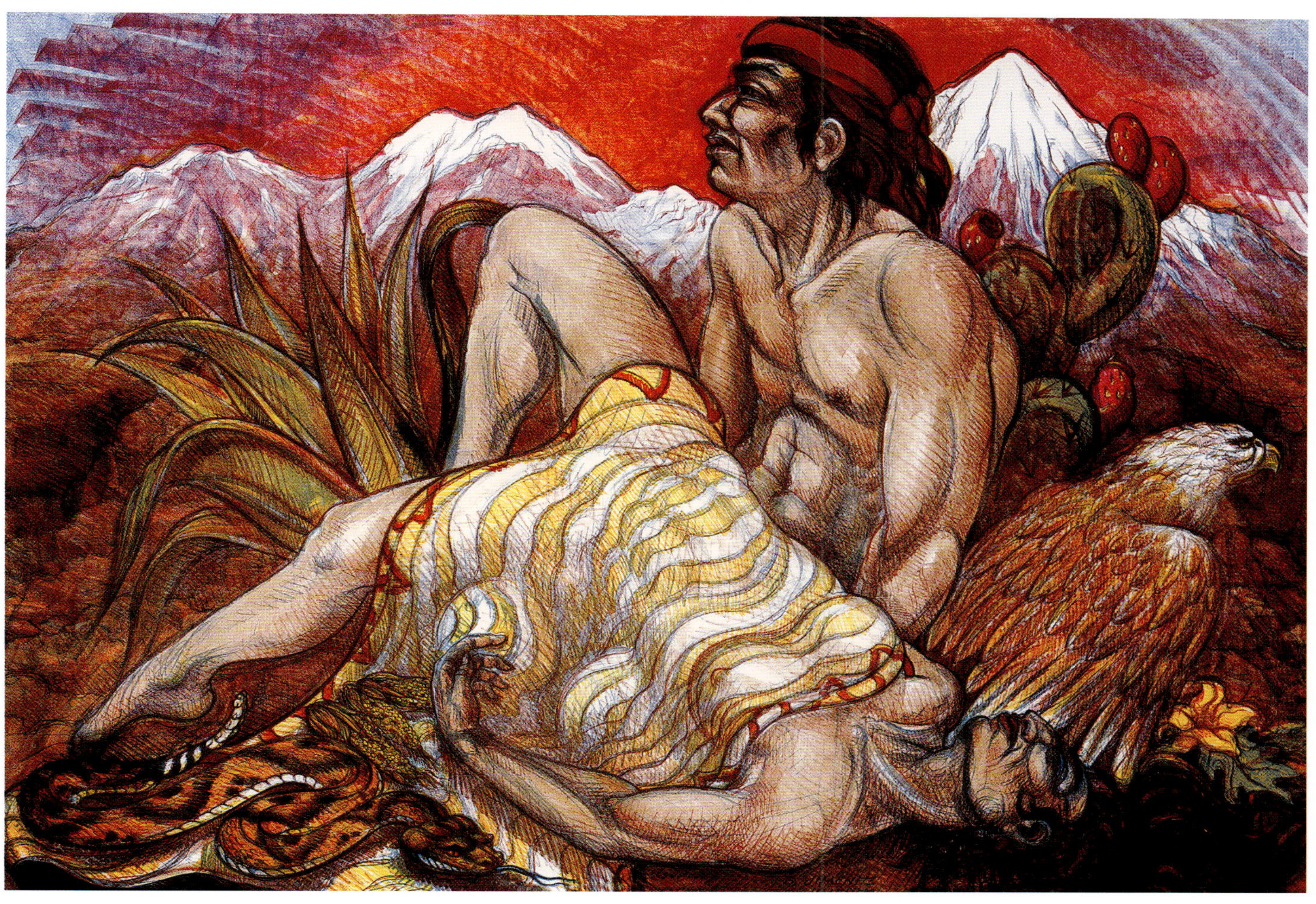

99 Luis Jiménez, *Southwest Pietà*, 1983, lithograph, 30" x 44"

enslavement a position of enormous influence and significance. The artist takes the concept of La Malinche as the mother of the *mestizo* people to a new, powerful dimension, creating a portrait of her flanked by Amerindian icons and totems of all kinds, both large ones and others embedded in the rich patterns that populate this work. Simultaneously, she assumes the aspect of the Virgin of Guadalupe, who, as the *virgen morena* (dark-skinned Virgin), also bridges the gap between Hispanic and Amerindian culture, but who in the traditional Mexican interpretation is the polar opposite of La Malinche. The former was the symbol of Mexico's freedom from Spain, the latter of its conquest and submission. The placement and combination of component icons, including the radiating designs that emanate from La Malinche; the flanking Aztec deities in full-feather headdresses, the crown that we associate with Christian iconography; the face on which is superimposed two Janus-like masks; the radiating heart that occupies a signal position in both Christian and Aztec religions; the folded hands typical of religious iconography; and the elaborate white vestments that at the same time are richly occupied by pre-Hispanic motifs, all make for a composition of enduring richness and transcendent complexity.

Luis Jiménez, *Southwest Pietà*. PLATE 99. A famous subject of Mexican folklore, and above all, a theme of countless Mexican and Mexican American calendars and other works of commercial art is that of the Aztec lovers who were converted into the towering, majestic, and phallically symbolic volcano Popocatepetl and the undulating volcano Ixtaccihuatl, which is reminiscent of a recumbent woman. This is a theme that has been treated by Jiménez several times, both in sculpture and two-dimensional art. This work uses the traditional iconography of the Aztec prince who has returned from war only to find his beloved dead, she having terminated her life in despair because of a malicious

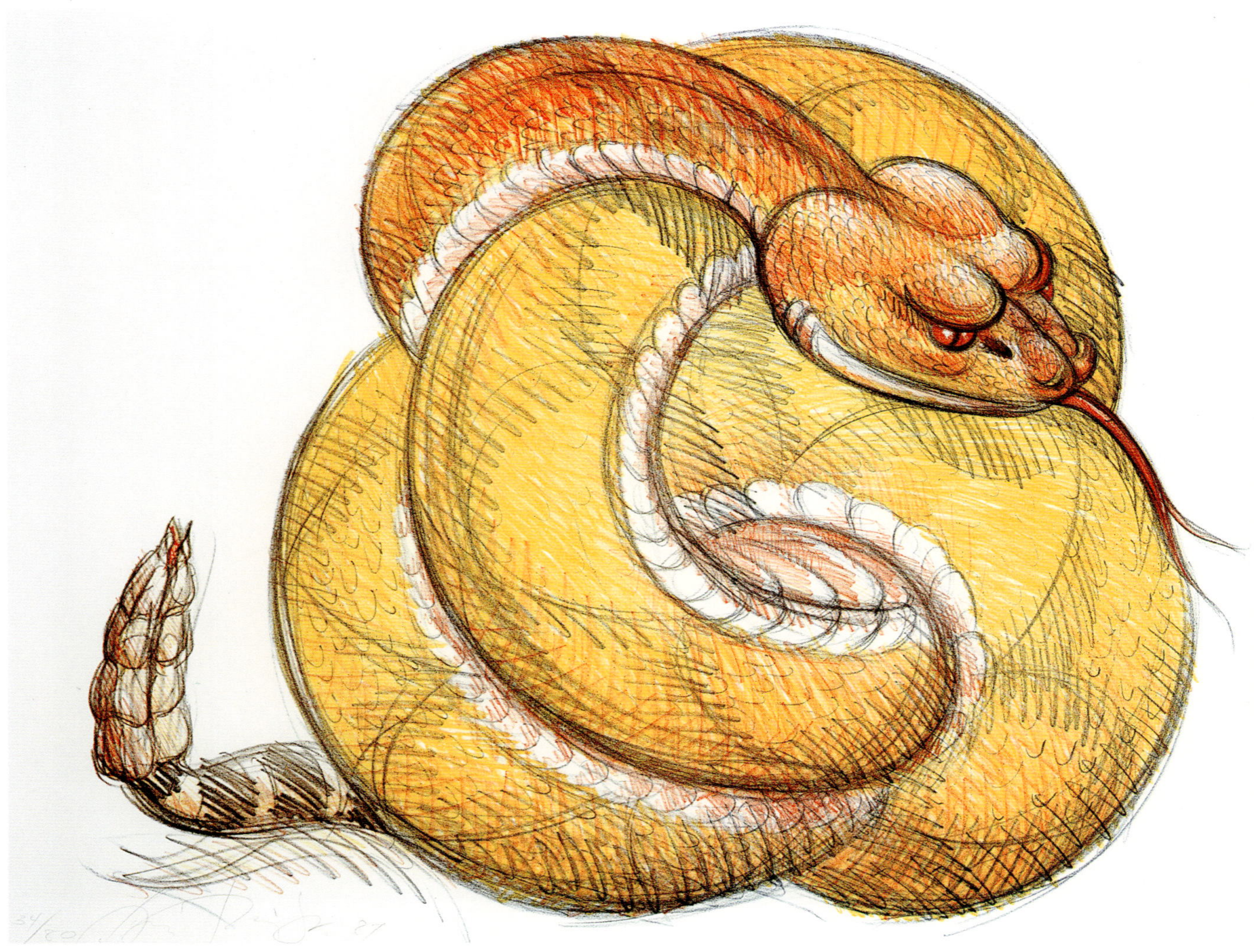

100 Luis Jiménez, *Ball Rattlesnake*, 1987, lithograph, 25" x 34"

lie uttered to her by a rival suitor, that the prince had died in battle. All of the elements of the imagery of the myth are present. The prince is before his maiden, and in the background are the two "lover" volcanoes, usually abbreviated as "Popo" and "Ixta," into which the compassionate Aztec god, moved by the depth of their love and the fidelity of the prince to his beloved, transformed the human lovers. At the same time, the artist introduces highly novel elements, such as the positioning of the lovers in a fashion that evokes the famous Pietàs with the Virgin Mary and the crucified Christ, so that both the autochthonous Mexican and the Christian European iconographies cross over and nourish each other. Another such element is the introduction of the Mexican eagle into the work, perched at attention; it is the symbol of the nation, the icon on the Mexican flag, and at the same time, an important symbol of the Aztecs, who are alleged to have founded their capital city of Tenochtitlan (later renamed Mexico City) on a site

marked by an eagle. The introduction of a nationalistic element into the folk symbolism of Popo and Ixta is highly significant for a Mexican American work, inasmuch as it establishes for the Chicano a heritage identity that crosses borders and goes back in time to the creation of the Mexican nation as well as much further back in time to the founding of the Aztec culture and its constituent myths.

Luis Jiménez, *Ball Rattlesnake*. PLATE 100. The rattlesnake is of considerable symbolic importance to the triculture of the southwestern United States. To the mainstream U.S. population it is a univalent symbol of menace and possible death. At the other extreme, while of course acknowledging its deadliness—in fact, because of its deadliness—the Amerindian cultures have a bivalent relationship with the reptile, admiring and prizing its rattle, its skin, its endurance in the desert, and its proven abilities to protect itself. In this work, the artist removes all extraneous terrain, details, and environmental context to concentrate on the rattlesnake solely by itself. However, the work is anything but a naturalistic depiction of the animal. The snake is depicted in vivid, uncharacteristic gold, its body wrapped up to such an extreme that it resembles, as the artist presents it, a ball. Above all, its head is depicted anthropomorphically with the facial characteristics of determined, even enraged aggression. This rattler assumes the quality of a cartoon with each of its prominent characteristics caricaturized: the long forked tongue, the erect rattle, the aggressive posture and demeanor of the head, and the body seemingly irrevocably tied up into itself. Humans are not overtly present in the composition, but in fact the achievement of the artist lies partly in the esthetic result that the emotions that we project onto the animal become the primary topic of the work.

Benito Huerta, *Hands of Fate.* PLATE 101. With results somewhat in contrast to Jiménez's *Ball Rattlesnake*, this work emphasizes a linguistic double meaning. *Hands of Fate* actually depicts an

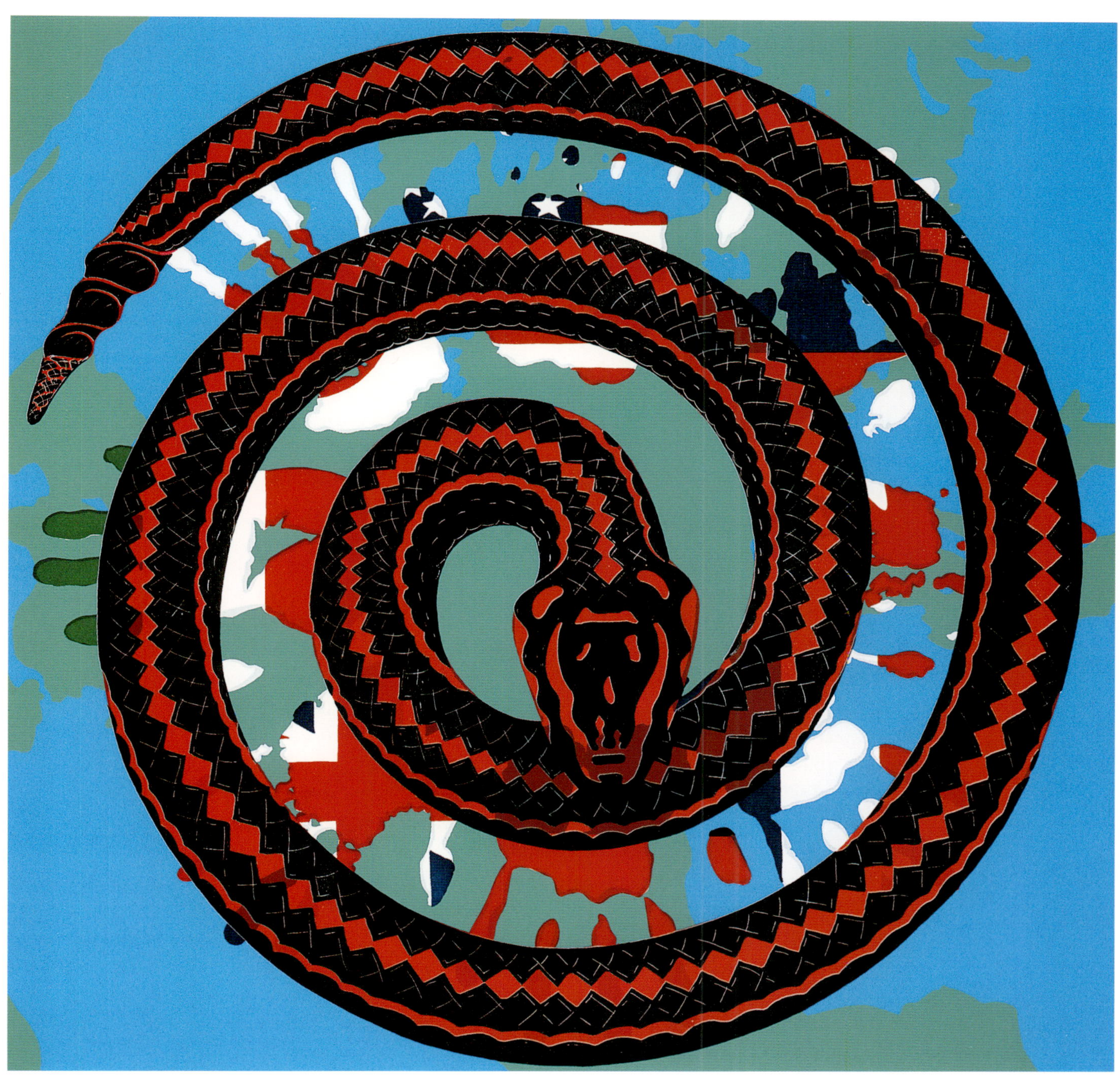

101 Benito Huerta, *Hands of Fate*, 1998, serigraph, 30" x 22"

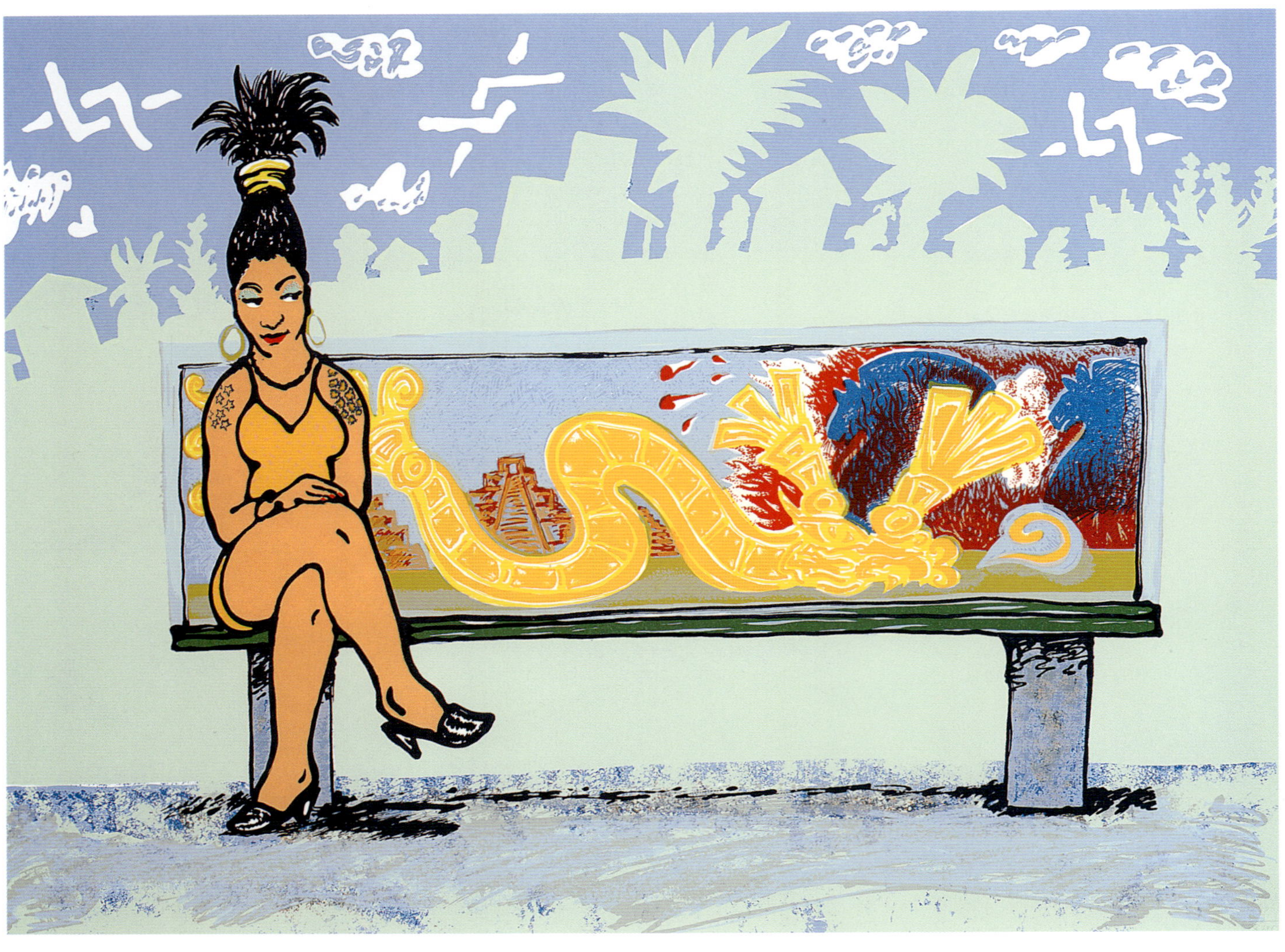

102 Leo Limón, *Morena y Quetzalcoatl*, 2001, serigraph, 20" x 26"

array of eight flat hands that, displaying a shred of a star here and there as well as red and white swaths, has been designed to represent the American flag. Superimposed on the hands lies a similarly flat, coiled rattlesnake, noticeably bereft of detail. This stylized figure, with the highly geometric, regular circles of its body, does not evoke fear or any other deep emotion in us. Instead, it seems to pose a riddle or an enigma that the title of the work is hinting at. Part of the work seems to refer subtly to the motto "Don't Tread on Me" that appeared on early U.S. flags, especially in the year 1775 (one of these also included "Give Me Liberty or Give Me Death"). The rattlesnake was a favorite symbol of the colonies in their approaching war for independence from Great Britain, a creature unique to the land and deadly if stepped upon. The symbolism of the flat hands in Huerta's work made out of seeming pieces of a flag points to a certain crisis that the United States is undergoing in its national identity. The sense of the enigmatic, including the linguistically enigmatic, is heightened not only by the very sparse detail and the focus on just a few elements—flag hands and geometric snake mostly—but also by the use of strong colors with little diversity of hue.

Leo Limón, *Morena y Quetzalcoatl*. PLATE 102. (A *morena* is a dark-skinned woman; the word carries a connotation of affection. Quetzalcoatl is one of the major gods of Toltec culture who was subsequently incorporated into Aztec culture. It is symbolized by a plumed serpent.) Backgrounded by a wall with rudimentary images in colors that seem to indicate fading, the *morena* sits on one side of a bench, perhaps waiting for a bus. She is alone, but at her side on the back of the bench is a painting in brighter colors featuring a long, undulating image of the plumed serpent, the icon of Quetzalcoatl. The background images on the wall appear to be an old mural that has been covered with some graffiti in the top area, which was dominated by sky in the original. A pre-Hispanic temple and a snow-covered volcano can be glimpsed in the background of the bench painting. The two popular paintings, one in fresh, vivid colors, and the muted one behind it seem to indicate a cultural and historical cycle of duration and constant replenishment that is, of course, further reinforced by the faded images of a southwestern urban environment in the background and the plumed serpent and temple in the foreground. Additionally, the Quetzalcoatl image is linked to the *morena* in that the woman's long hair, fastened and then radiating in all directions from the top of her head like the fronds of a plant or an array of quetzal feathers, is strikingly similar to the gathered spray of quetzal feathers that protrudes from the sinuous body of the snake. The works of street art and the woman who faces out at the viewer seem, on the one hand, to have nothing to do with each other, but their conjoining by the artist, who arrays them so that the viewer can see the different images with minimal obscurity and who creates the analogies between the plumed serpent and the woman's hair, speak to symbolic connections that emerge adroitly from the work.

Tlisza Jaurique, *Ancestral Roots*. PLATE 103. Innumerable tiny pieces of glitter, painstakingly applied over an acrylic-on-foam-board surface, comprise this work drawn directly from imagery

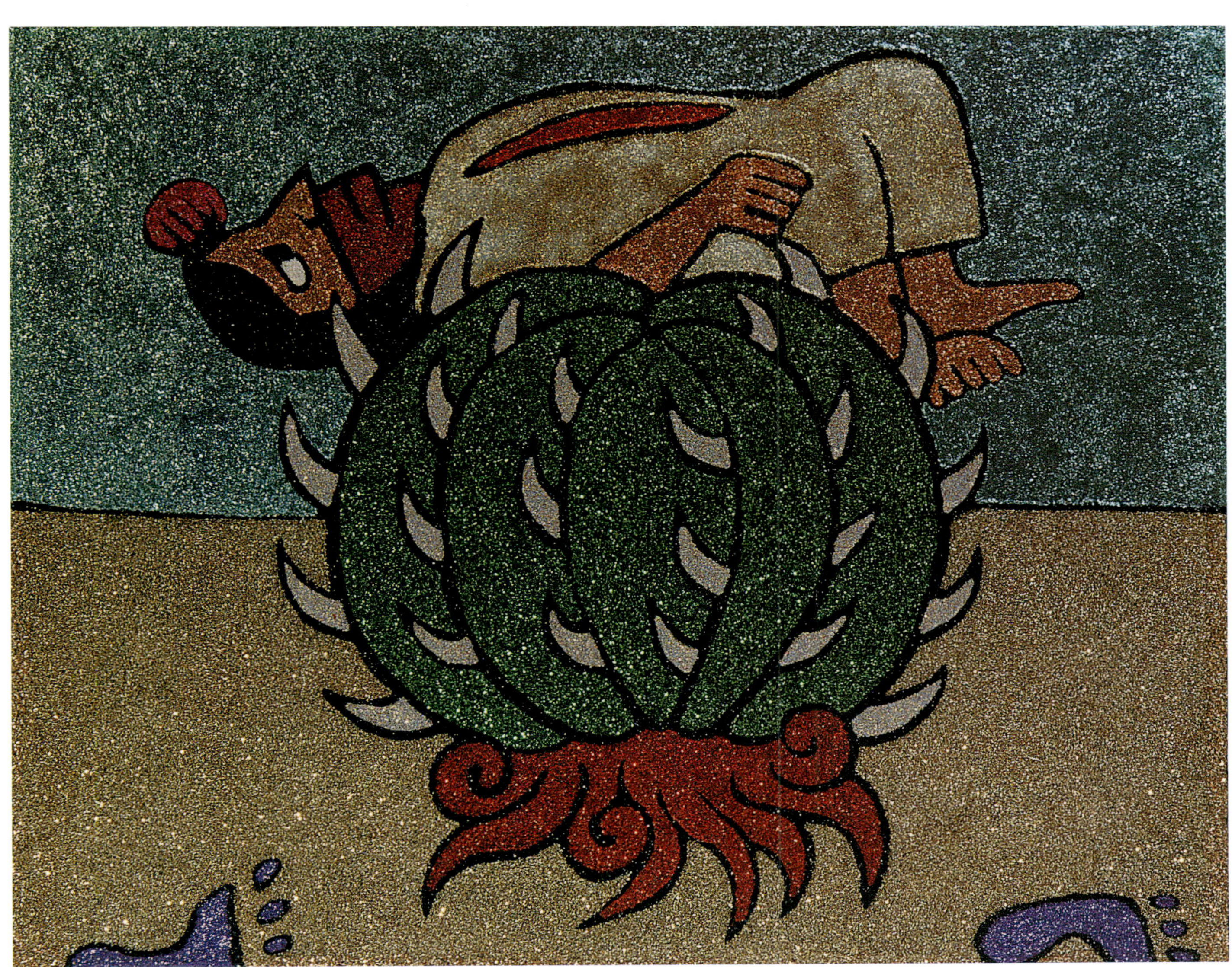

103 Tlisza Jaurique, *Ancestral Roots*, 1996, glitter on board, 34" x 42"

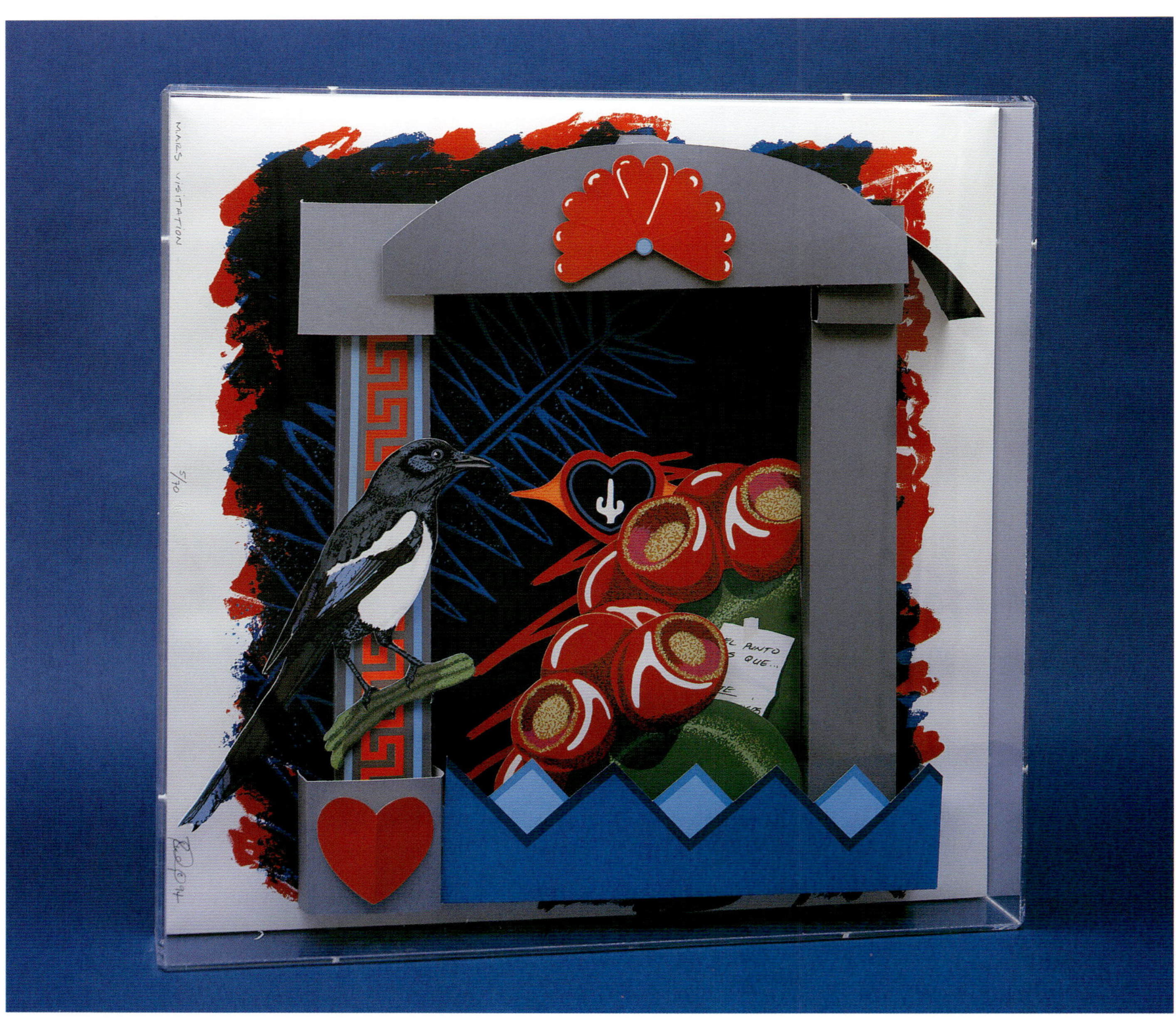

104 Rudy M. Fernández, Jr., *MARS Visitation*, 1994, mixed media, 26" x 26" x 4"

seen in ancient Mesoamerican codices and wall paintings. Tlisza Jaurique uses the glitter to recapture the brilliance of now faded symbols of her heritage, as well as to reflect the viewer. "The imagery is physically composed of thousands of individual pieces, and only in unity are these images formed," she explains. She equates that philosophy with cultural preservation: "Only in unity are a culture's symbols narrated and preserved by individuals." *Ancestral Roots* depicts a man in the moments before death, left to ponder the state of his being, the path he has taken to get there, and the possibilities of what comes next. Impaled on a cactus, his heart ripped from his chest and balanced on his

forehead, he appears to be calmly but sorrowfully reflecting the true nature of his heart. The cactus on which he rests is lush and full of life, defying its sun-baked, arid surroundings. While its plumpness suggests abundant water within, its large spines have kept the thirsty at bay. The mixed-media work implies the cycles inherent in what might seem to be dichotomous elements: life and death, bounty and drought, earth and sky, past and future.

Rudy M. Fernández, Jr., *MARS Visitation*.
Plate 104. Fernández has expressed the view that his art is both therapy and communication and that his imagery and use of symbols stem from lifelong

experiences and personal associations rather than from icons consensually associated with his cultural heritage. This mixed-media shadow box with its own case crafted by the artist is representative of Fernández's work. The three-dimensional format displays the influence of Mexican and New Mexican *retablos* (see the entry on Virginia Agüero) and *nichos* (niches or recesses with images of saints) but converts them into a contemporary genre that makes public his personal world. The shadow box functions as a stagelike setting for this visitation that takes on the quality of a surreal, personal drama. Commissioned as a fundraiser for the Phoenix, Arizona, art organization MARS (Movimiento Artístico del Río Salado), the work includes numerous symbols that the artist has used frequently: the saguaro cactus in the middle of a multilayered heart that is dark at the core and red on the exterior; other red hearts, one set in the center of a characteristic design that may be interpreted as a fan made of red chiles; and the luscious red cactus flower (a favorite symbol of the Southwest thematically opposed to the thorny prickly-pear cactus from which it blooms). On the left appears a traditional meander design that has been used not only in Amerindia but also in Europe (the original word comes from the Greek river the Meander). Then of course there is the bird, perhaps a blue jay, that bears witness. The artist's system of symbols prevents literal readings of his thoughts and experiences. The message highlights that reality. "El punto es que . . ." means "the point is that . . ." The viewer is invited to fill in the blank!

Zarco Guerrero, *Con Sapos, Nagual Mask* (With toads . . .). PLATE 105. Zarco Guerrero has made a career out of pairing unlikely elements, creating works that are at once amusing yet profound. The artist brings to his work a global understanding realized through extensive travel and study while remaining loyal to his Chicano artistic traditions. In his masks he employs irreverent humor while promoting social change through the use of traditional colors found in Mexican art as well as by juxtaposing images of ancient spirituality with contemporary entertainment and devising effective wordplays. The title of this piece plays on a common graffiti tag, "Con Safos" or "C/S," which barrio graffiti artists

use to warn others not to change the message or art they applied. *Con Sapos* literally translates as "with toads," and indeed, a toad, a symbol of fertility and rain, emerges from the mouth of this mask. A *nagual* is a guardian spirit in animal form. The colors used (a lime green base with blue, yellow, and turquoise designs) for this sculpture are drawn from the papier-mâché traditions of Oaxaca, Mexico. The design surrounding the eyes and spreading over the forehead is reminiscent of the masks Mexican wrestlers wear. Horns jut from either side of the forehead against a sheepskin backing. Guerrero explains that his intention is to remind his audience "of our origins and kinship to the beast" and that humankind must be aware of and take responsibility for the destruction we wreak on the environment and its creatures.

Xavier Garza, *La Llorona* (The weeping woman). PLATE 123. *La Llorona* carries with it pedagogical as well as folkloric, legendary, and esthetic components, specifically posing in the work and also answering the question: "La Llorona. Who is she?" Packaged in a self-contained box that recalls the *nichos* (niches, recesses) of Mexican colonial art in which resided a venerated saint, the object of interest is the well-known figure of La Llorona, the Latino equivalent of the boogey man of Anglo culture. This is a folktale that has roots in pre-Hispanic culture and subsequently was associated with La Malinche, Hernán Cortés's mistress and aide. However, the version here dates from nineteenth-century Romanticism. As the folktale goes, La Llorona either lost or killed her children, depending on the version, and as a consequence she wanders wailing through the night in search of them. She is a figure that is often used to admonish or discipline naughty children who are warned to behave lest they be taken by her. This folk *nicho*, instead of containing the symbols of a reigning saint such as San Antonio (see Félix López's work in this exhibition), San Miguel Arcángel, or San Isidro Labrador, is adorned by baby shoes, glossing the tale of the lost children. The box itself, studded with glass beads and decorated in a juvenile style, has been crafted in a fashion that invites children to learn more about La Llorona in a nonthreatening way, and thus it even includes an explanatory text within it.

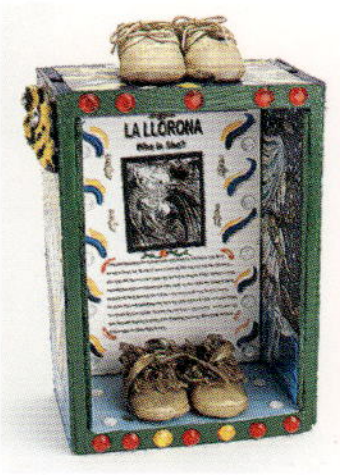

La Llorona,
see page 193

Overleaf: 105 Zarco Guerrero, *Con Sapos, Nagual Mask* (With toads . . .), 1994, mixed media mask, 19" x 14.5" x 9.5"

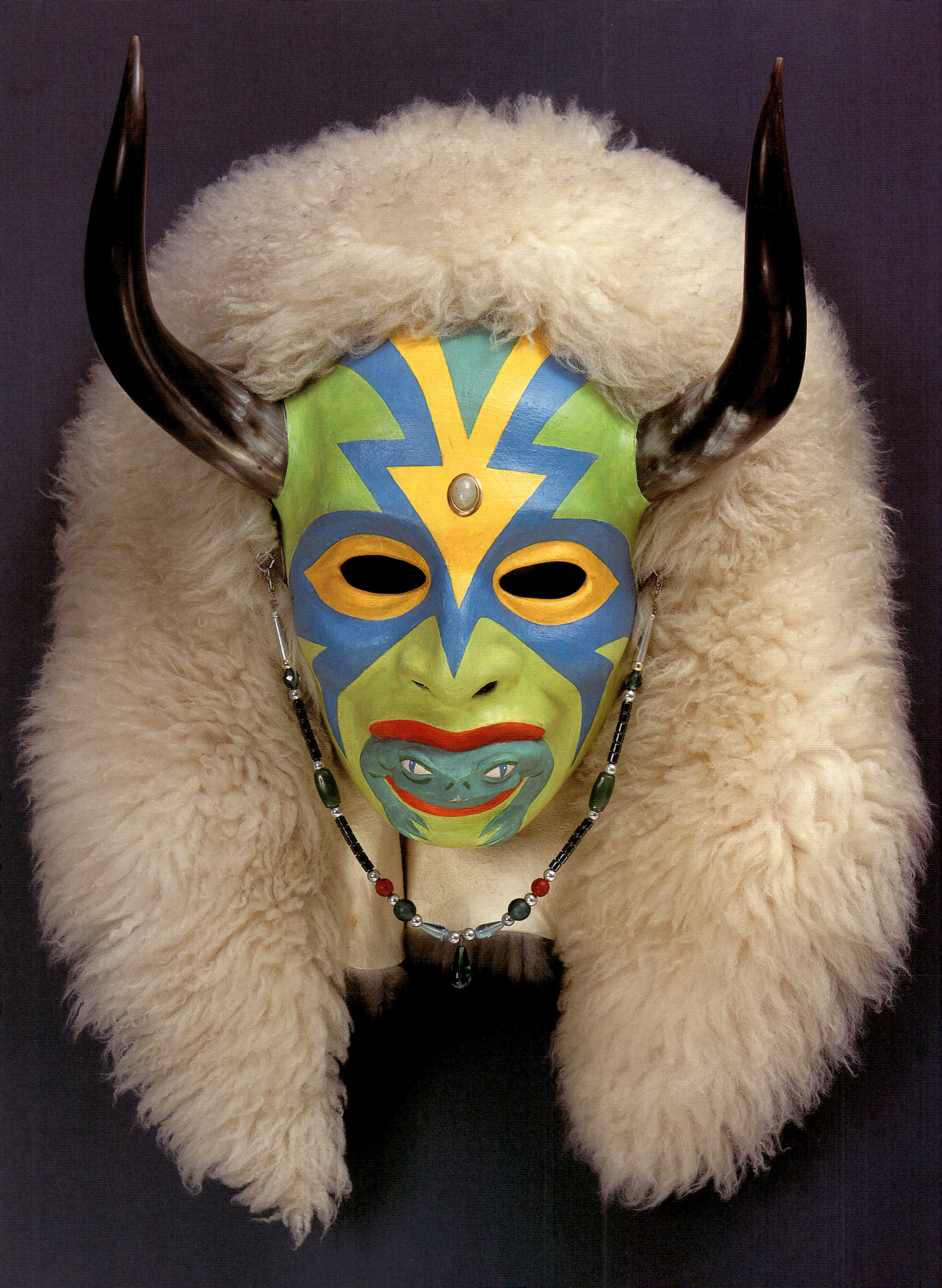

Sobrepasando lo convencional

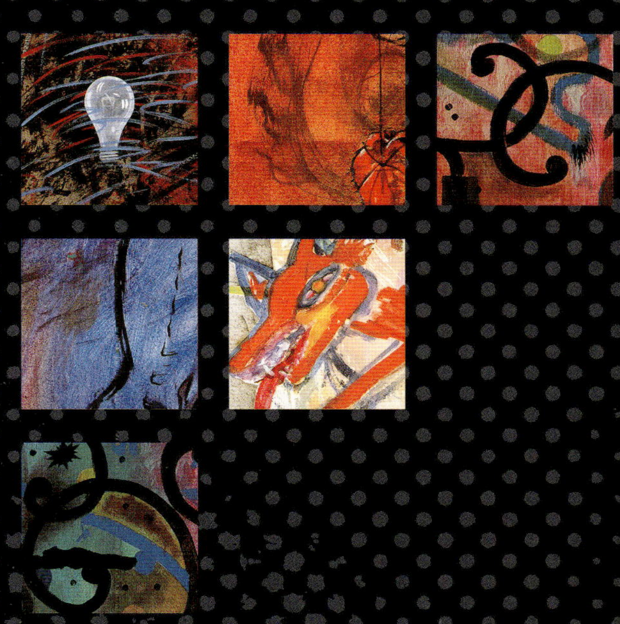

Beyond
Conventional
Themes

"Beyond Conventional Themes/Sobrepasando lo convencional" presents works that expand or transcend the traditionally assumed dimensions, scope, and limitations of Chicano/a art. Contradicting the conventional wisdom that our art is exclusively a folk art rooted in Chicano culture and the figurative evocation of that culture and its value system, we are confronted here with nonfigurative work that is preoccupied with color, composition, line, the interplay of shadow and light, or the foregrounding of substances or spaces. Additionally, those works that are figurative cultivate figures in novel ways, at least for the artistic understanding and conventional appreciation of Chicano art.

Silvia Capistrán explores a panoramic, nuanced, and variegated space in her *Atardecer/Dusk,* which also contains a few textual and imagistic surprises. Margaret García combines abstraction with the representation of powerful canine-lupine energies. Quintín González utilizes his mastery of postmodern digital technology to work with religion, myth, and legend and to project them into a personal, surreal domain. Marcus Zilliox synthesizes line and color and adds a dash of cartoon to create a unique oeuvre that ranges from anime to graffiti. Juan Farias develops the Chicanesque skills that he uniquely acquired as a billboard and sign painter to execute abstractions that use color and line to depict his relationships with the opposite sex on a grand scale. Jerry De La Cruz combines abstraction and surrealism in masterful collages. Mónica Aíssa Martínez creates a polyphonic whimsy of flasks, chalices, flagons, and other modern alchemical vessels—all of which can dance under a tilted roof. Maximiliano Pruneda III works with the ironic portrait form that has been with us at least since Rembrandt and develops that irony through novel interplays of surreal images and reinforcing colors.

Quintín González, *Spectre*. PLATE 2. A central issue in considering Quintín González's work is his appropriation of high technology as a Chicano artist to create images that speak to Chicana/o concerns. Of wide societal interest in recent years has been the "digital divide," the fact that people from minority groups have less access to computer technology than the majority culture. As more people of color have accessed technologies of all types, the question arises as to how technology can be used to improve lives without all ethnic groups being subsumed into a homogenous mass. As an artist belonging to an ethnic group supposedly alienated from technology, González is using digital image manipulation to develop a Chicano voice with just those technological tools purportedly beyond his grasp. González creates haunting, surreal scenes with strong references to traditional images and concepts from religion, myth, and legend. His work explores how devotional images serve to help oppressed peoples survive in racist societies. In *Spectre,* he depicts a female figure in the foreground. She is part human, part monster, her eye sockets empty and her hair taking the shape of feathers. An apparently male figure is in the background, his fleshless body a scaffolding of veins and connective tissue. Both figures wear red, which is startling against the stark black background. González intends for the female to represent a vengeful spirit, a mythic femme fatale figure reminiscent of La Llorona (The weeping woman), and the male is the recipient of her justice.

Silvia Capistrán, *Atardecer/Dusk*. PLATE 106. Capistrán grew up in Los Angeles and traveled extensively in Mexico after finishing her bachelor's degree at California State University, Northridge. At first she painted in a small watercolor format, mixing text and image, then worked in printmaking at Self-Help Graphics, and only recently has begun to work in larger sizes and with increasingly abstract content. In *Atardecer/Dusk* she has created what appears to be a peaceful, infinite orange-red field grounded with contrasting cooler blue-greens in the foreground. Space stretches in all directions like the unbroken vastness of the ocean and sky. As our eye follows the white horizon punctuated by modest verticals suggesting pilings breaking the surface of the water, we discover a tiny, seated nude woman. Her gaze sends us back to three snippets of type that read like clues in a mystery: "NO SECRETS," "STOP LOOKING," and, upside down, "PROTECTED SPECIES." We must look closely to make out the figure of the woman or the obscured text phrases, which makes the command to stop looking an ironic surprise. The woman is small and lonely in the composition and the phrases alienate. This in com-

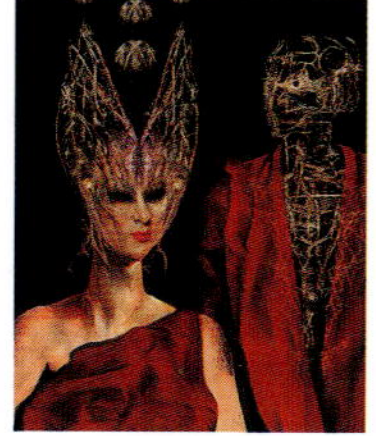

Spectre, see page ii

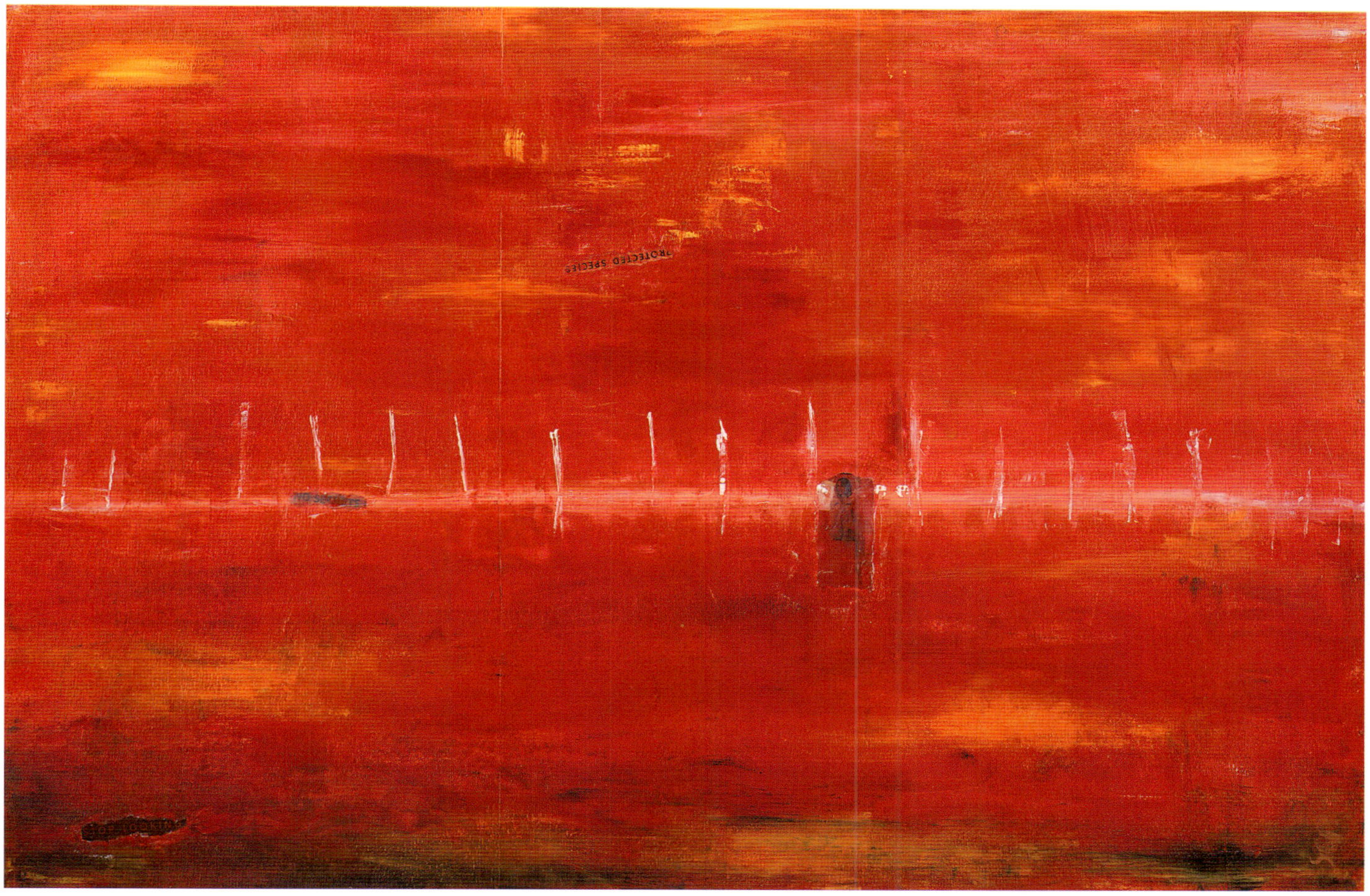

106 Silvia Capistrán, *Atardecer/Dusk*, 1999, acrylic on canvas, 26" x 38"

bination with the infinite space creates a feeling of distance and loneliness in the viewer.

Jerry De La Cruz, *Failing to Communicate.* PLATE 107. An accomplished artist, Jerry De La Cruz has mastered formal and experimental painting techniques, allowing him to express both abstract and surreal images in one context. *Failing to Communicate* is an example of this adroitness. Abstract splays of black, brown, gray, and white dominate the left side of the painting, partially contained there by a diagonal line that almost gives the impression that the canvas was cut. Within the darkest section of this piece is an unlit light bulb. To the right of the line are the head and shoulders of a female. A yellow line bisects her face. The expressive areas of her face have been obscured: Her eyes hide behind mirrored lenses, and her mouth is carefully covered by what appears to be a folded and jaggedly cut piece of white paper. The viewer cannot determine the expression her face would bear without these obstructions, but the skin on her forehead is smooth, and the lines of her

cheeks suggest a smile. We hope to decipher the object of her gaze through her shiny lenses, but they reflect only more abstract brushwork. An image of the artist's hand holding a paintbrush applies a swath of red between himself and the image of the woman, suggesting anger. Perhaps he was jilted, or perhaps this woman seems unreachable to the artist. Streaks of red and blue wash over the bottom portion of the painting, expressing frustration and uncertainty.

Marcus Zilliox, *Wink and Jab Ennui.* PLATE 122. Marcus Zilliox sees his art as neither abstract nor figurative but rather as a synthesis of multiplicities characterized by layers of materials and references. Of Native American and Mexican American descent, his influences come from many cultures and times, from traditional Southwest designs to anime to graffiti. *Wink and Jab Ennui* is a dance of color and swirling line. The background is made up of subtle washes of color, predominantly in the red family, but also blues and yellows. Thick black lines form organic tendrils that repeat across the compo-

Wink and Jab Ennui, see page 192

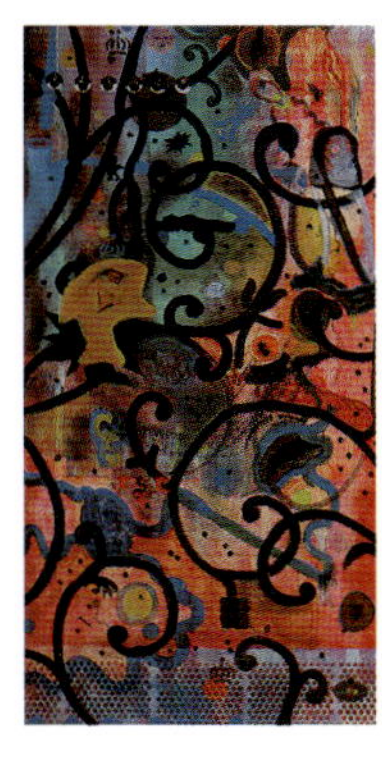

145

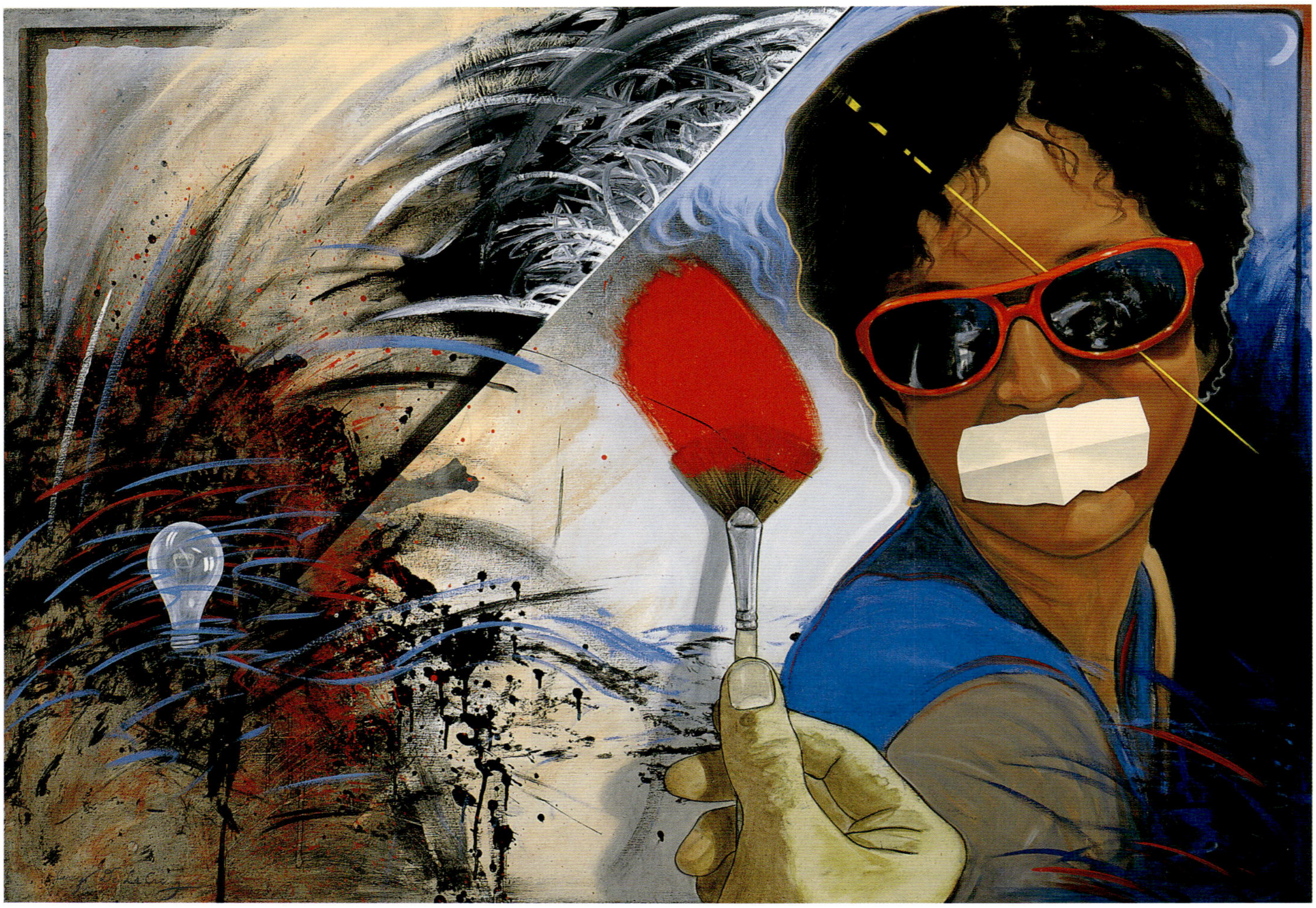

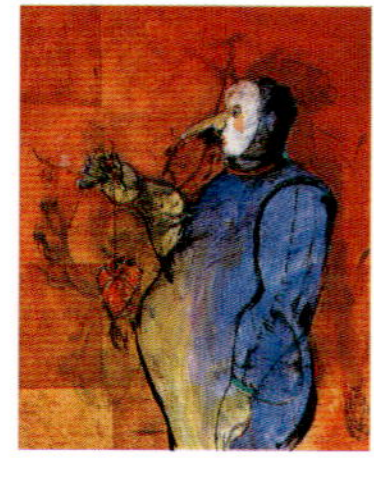

107 Jerry De La Cruz, *Failing to Communicate*, 1993, acrylic on canvas, 42" x 60"

sition. In combination with the tendrils, circles form eyes and begin to suggest fish and other sea creatures. In fact, a focal point of the piece is a small blue cartoon fish in the upper center of the piece, its mouth wide open, and a larger yellow fish to its left that appears prepared to swallow the smaller fish. The painting is vertical in orientation. The pattern of tendrils and a sprinkling of small black dots create a chaotic movement in the piece. The movement contrasts with a horizontal band of light blue at the bottom, covered with a highly organized set of small circles and a line of black-and-white circles at the top.

Recompensa del amor/The Reward of Love, see page 176

Maximiliano Pruneda III, *Recompensa del amor/The Reward of Love.* PLATE 120. Unrequited love! One's heart hanging from a string. Is love its own reward? One of the lines of a famous twentieth-century poem about the laments of love sought but not returned, T. S. Eliot's "The Love Song of J. Alfred Prufrock," reads: "To prepare a face to meet the faces that you meet. . . ." This colorful, expressionistic work by Maximiliano Pruneda III depicts a figure reminiscent of Prufrock in the poem. We view an elderly, portly, introspective, self-deprecating sort of fellow who assumes a face on the order of a clown's mask with rouged lips and an overly long and somewhat more phallic nose than Cyrano de Bergerac's. The mask/face functions both to conceal him and perhaps his secret feelings and to arm him in confrontations with the outside world and perhaps with his love object. The eyes of this figure are tilted upward with an exquisite look of wistfulness, while the phallic nose is pointed down toward the heart that is on a string. The heart is a double-edged symbol in this clown's charade of love in which, as in war, everything is permitted. It is double edged in the sense that it is the symbol of the object of one's love and of one's own yearnings for love. Exteriorized, this icon of the heart plays out on a string, like a yoyo. The portly figure is dressed in a nondescript outfit emphasizing blue with a blaze of greenish-yellow at the midriff, and he stands against a background of variegated, saccharine reds, oranges, and pinks, quite appropriate for the somewhat ridiculous figure that he presents. The combination of colors artfully expresses this human comedy. Clearly the recompenses of love are somewhat spare. Toward the end of his love song, Prufrock turns from his incantation to his lover and ruminates upon himself: "I grow old . . . I grow old . . . / I shall wear the bottoms of my trousers rolled. . . ." This clown might be uttering something along those lines.

Margaret García, *RLD 89*. PLATE 108. This work is a combination of representation and abstraction. A jagged central area is filled with gentle pastels that intensify and darken as they move out from the center. A hard edge demarcates this pastel area from a gray pattern outside. A bright orange wolf-dog with its teeth and tongue exposed, outlined in blue, explodes from the central area, its ferocity mirrored in colored partial handprints and gray exploding marks radiating out from the center. The feeling is of intense movement as the central shape charges outward into the surrounding space, as though the paper had ripped open to release the beast. The dog is painted in a primitive style, and, along with the handprints, the painting as a whole is reminiscent of the rock art seen throughout the Southwest. Known for her paintings of individuals, in this piece García uses the similarly expressive and bold brush strokes, texture, and contrasts of warm and cool colors that

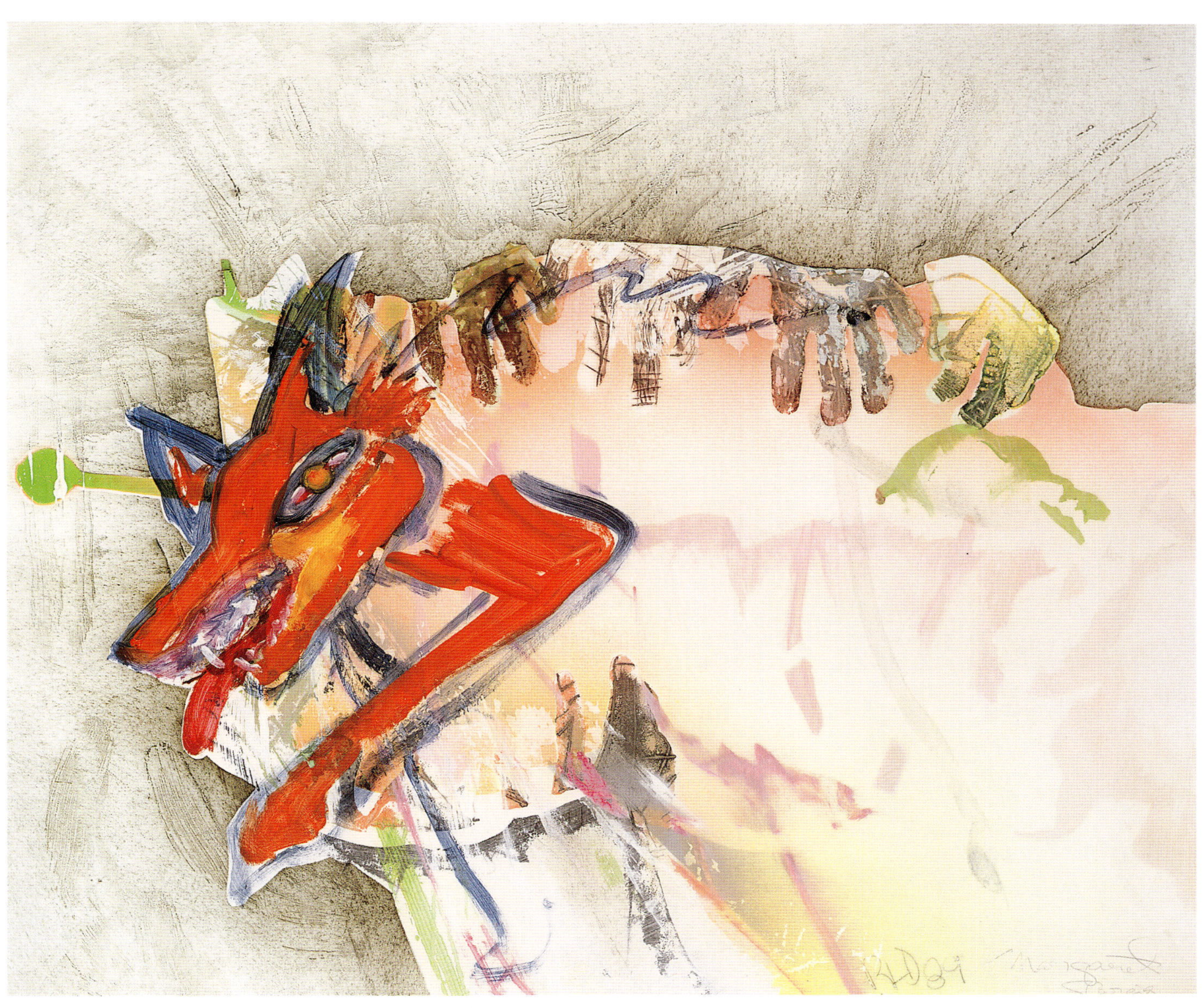

108 Margaret García, *RLD 89*, 1989, monoprint, 27" x 32"

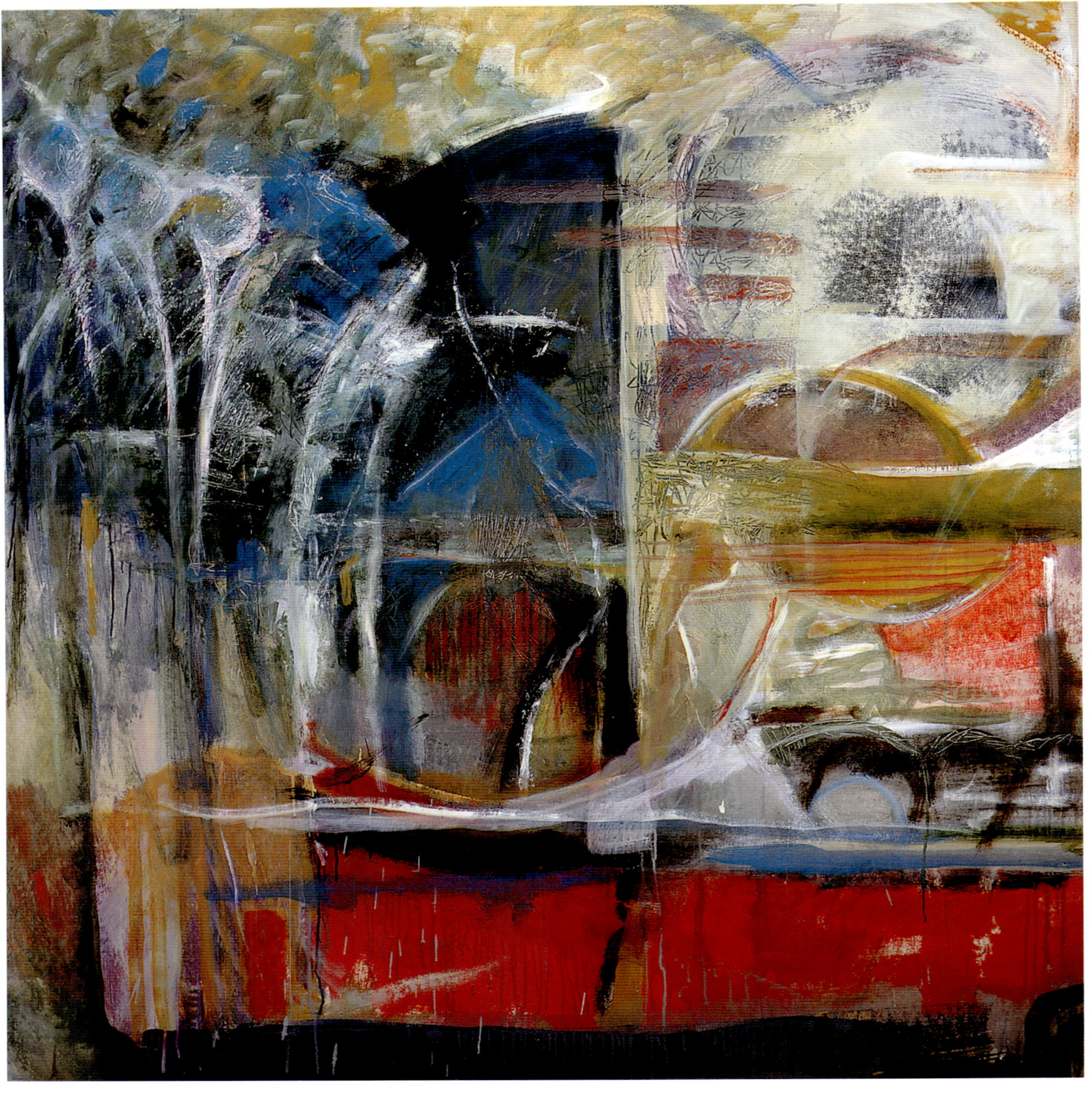

109 Juan Farias, *Nos ponemos como que tenemos calentura, bien sudaditos* (It feels as if we have a fever, very sweaty), 2000, acrylic on canvas, 72" x 72"

are so successful in her portraits. García and her family have roots many generations deep in California. Her recent projects include designing the Universal City Metro station in Los Angeles in a major collaboration with architects and historians. The theme was the Treaty of Cahuenga that ended the Mexican-American War in California. In addition, a group of her portraits was selected for the set design of a television series.

Juan Farias, *Nos ponemos como que tenemos calentura, bien sudaditos* (It feels as if we have a fever, very sweaty). PLATE 109. Juan Farias started his career as a billboard and sign painter, eventually transitioning to fine art and finally evolving to purely abstract painting. His works are characterized by their monumental sizes and extraordinarily rich painterly surfaces. His process is to tack the canvas to his studio floor, then apply color from all sides. When he is satisfied with the results as he views the painting from all directions, it is complete. *Nos ponemos como que tenemos calentura, bien sudaditos* comes from a series of paintings about his relationships with the women in his life. In this painting his colors range from brilliant saturated hues to tints, shades, and subtle mixtures of contrasting warm and cool colors. The wide band of red at the bottom serves as a pedestal upon which everything else rests. The arcs of white paint create the feeling of a passageway into the canvas, and a dark blue rectangle in the center of the composition beckons the viewer into its depths. Controlled movement is created through the interplay of beautifully orchestrated broad strokes, rapid marks, fluid slashes, delicate drips, and intricate scratches. The composition is unified by the rhythmic interplay of horizontals, verticals, circles, and arcs. Farias achieves a sense of depth with overlapping shapes, lines, and forms. This painting engages, works, and rewards the viewer's eye as it experiences the passion and emotion suggested by the title.

Einar and Jamex de la Torre, *Nomás enchúfala* (Just plug it in). PLATE 112. Glass-blowing sculptors Jamex and Einar de la Torre are widely recognized for their works that express "the morbid humor of Mexican folk art" and satirize "the absurd pageantry of Catholicism, and machismo . . . [as well as] the American culture of excess." At first glance, a viewer is drawn to their glasswork for its rich and inviting color; further study of the work reveals acerbic commentary on society. Their creations suggest a contradictory eschewing and embracing of cultural and religious elements. *Nomás enchúfala*, part of his Easy Spirituality series, is described as "a spiritual appliance with easy plug-in convenience," obviously a commentary on a tendency to use religion as a convenience instead of as a deeply held and profoundly sought-

after truth. The piece sports an electrical socket into which a cord has been plugged. The Kewpie doll head at the top of the work, with its spermlike blue-hair covering, its uneven gaze, and its smile, connotes a sexual encounter. The horseshoe design below the Kewpie doll head further references "getting lucky," whereas images inside the horseshoe appear to represent Jesus and his disciples. With the de la Torre's tendency to marry the sacred with the profane, we might surmise that the piece is an effigy of the usually beloved figure of Mary. Whether the church or its consistent congregation is the object of the artist's scorn is left for the viewer to decide.

Mónica Aíssa Martínez, *Chemism.* PLATE 110. Vessels and motion are common elements in Mónica Aíssa Martínez's complex yet whimsical compositions. To the artist, the vessels are metaphors for the human body, and the sense of movement flowing through and eventually emerging represents the life force. These elements are stripped to the core in *Chemism* in a clear celebration of creation and life. The piece conveys sexual attraction as truly chemically induced, bringing to mind the adage "For every action there is a reaction." Here, two round figures top two separate hemispheres, one green, possibly representing earth, the other blue, reminiscent of the sea. The two are connected through wispy and abstract forms. As motion, often depicted as spermatozoa, flows through the figures, it is propelled upward toward two chalices, passing through them and again twisting and snaking beyond. The forces rejoin in an apparent zygote beneath another vessel, this one sprouting a plant within it. The painting's canvas is in the shape of a house; a faux frame surrounds the main images, mimicking wood. Tiny musical scores and creatures decorate this "frame," further suggesting a joy for life and creativity.

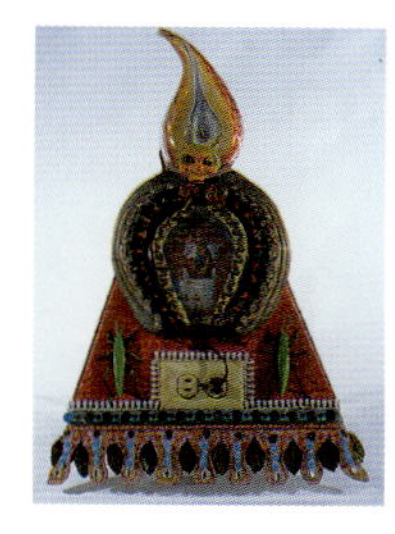

Nomás enchúfala,
see page 154

beyond

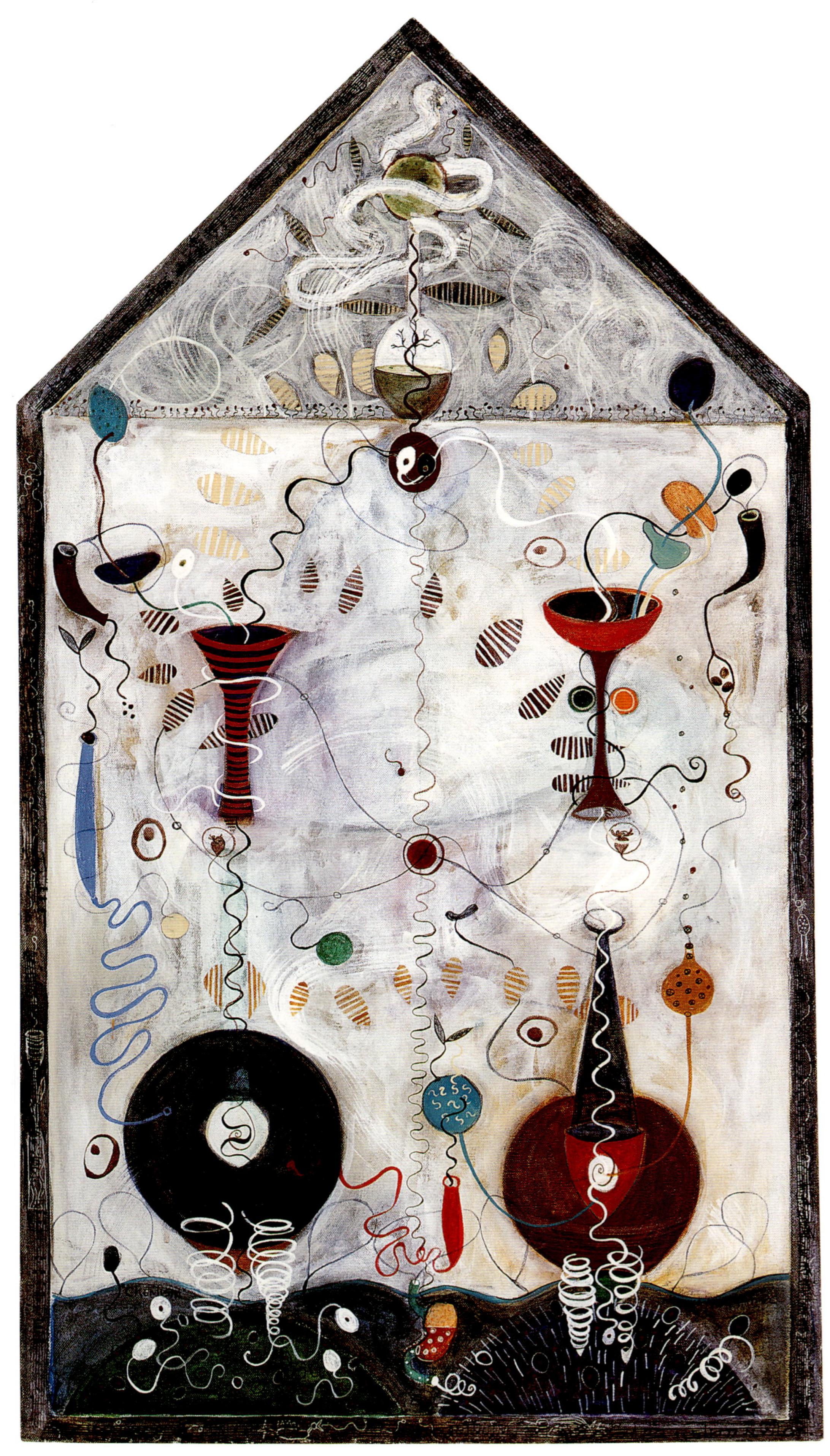

110 Mónica Aíssa Martínez, *Chemism*, 1998-9, collage and egg tempera on canvas, 34" x 18"

The End . . . .

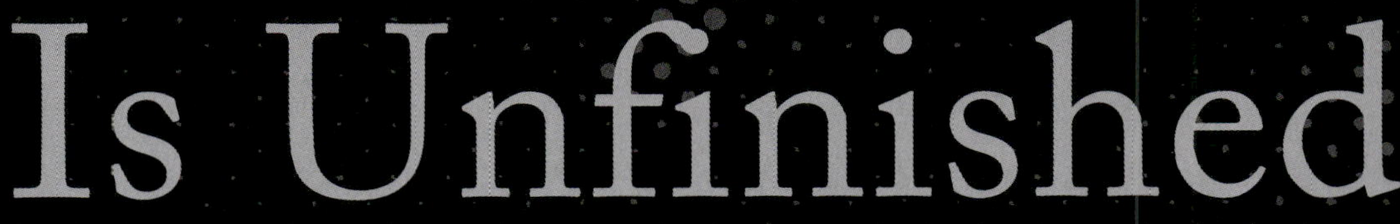

Is Unfinished

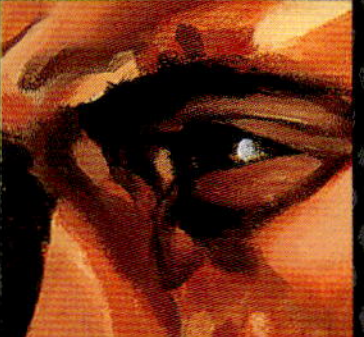

hicano art is a design on a canvas in constant evolution. We close this exhibition on a note of ongoing development with a work by one of our youngest representatives. He has recently finished a beautiful work that we share with you.

Gabriel García, *Broken Sidewalks: The First Defeat.* PLATE 111. This young artist, who was residing in San Antonio at the time he did this work, has executed a portrait that is somewhat reminiscent of the *vatos* (dudes) depicted by his older San Antonio counterpart, the renowned César Martínez. Like Martínez's portraits, this is a close-up of the head, neck, and chest. It also features a mostly solid field background, although there is a thematically important element in this background that is not evident in Martínez's work in the form of light that breaks through the dark brown sky. The interaction between the primarily solid but also clouded and turbulent background and the young man in inner turmoil in the foreground is one of complementarity; in Martínez's portraits the color field contrasts with and sets off the portrayed figure. Also like Martínez, García adroitly paints the face and features so that we have the sense through the portrait of penetrating into the station and character of the young man. Quite in contrast to Martínez's work is the emotional impact of the subject. In Martínez's work the *vatos* look directly at the viewer and are poker-faced, conveying the impression that they are street-savvy individuals who do not reveal their inner turmoil. *Broken Sidewalks* is totally different both in execution and title. Here, rather than looking at a figure that is facing us almost as if he were in a police line-up, we feel a certain privileged, insider's status. As in a poignant moment in a work of fiction or poetry, we catch a glimpse of this character in a revelatory manner. Reinforced by the title, this portrait is an emotionally stirring depiction of a young man who appears to be recovering from an event (obviously a defeat of some kind) and is considering his circumstances and working out cognitively and emotionally his future course of action. His plans, feelings, and development as a young adult, as the work tells us, are unfinished and undergoing transformation and growth.

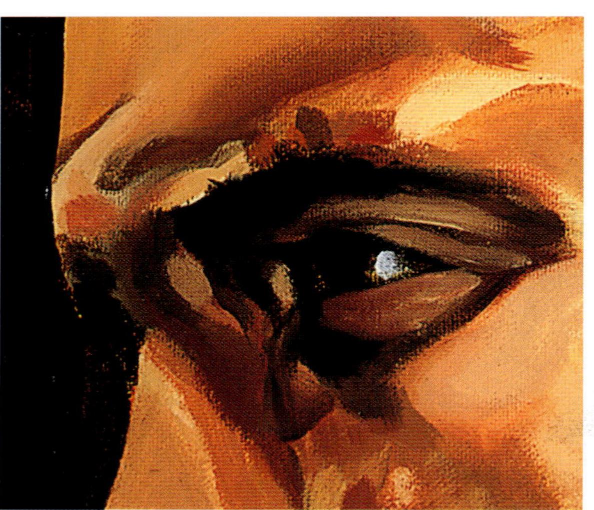

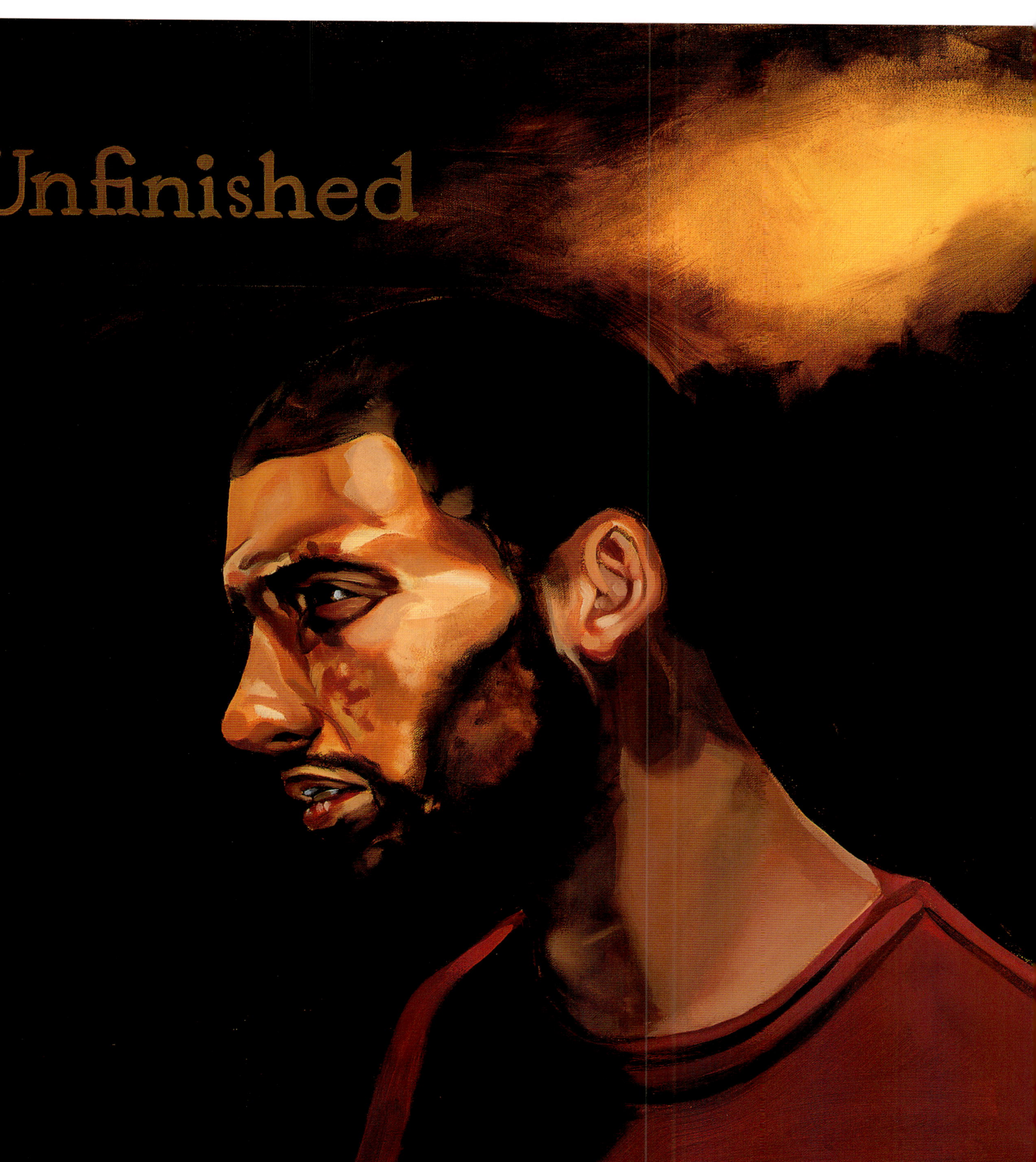

Unfinished

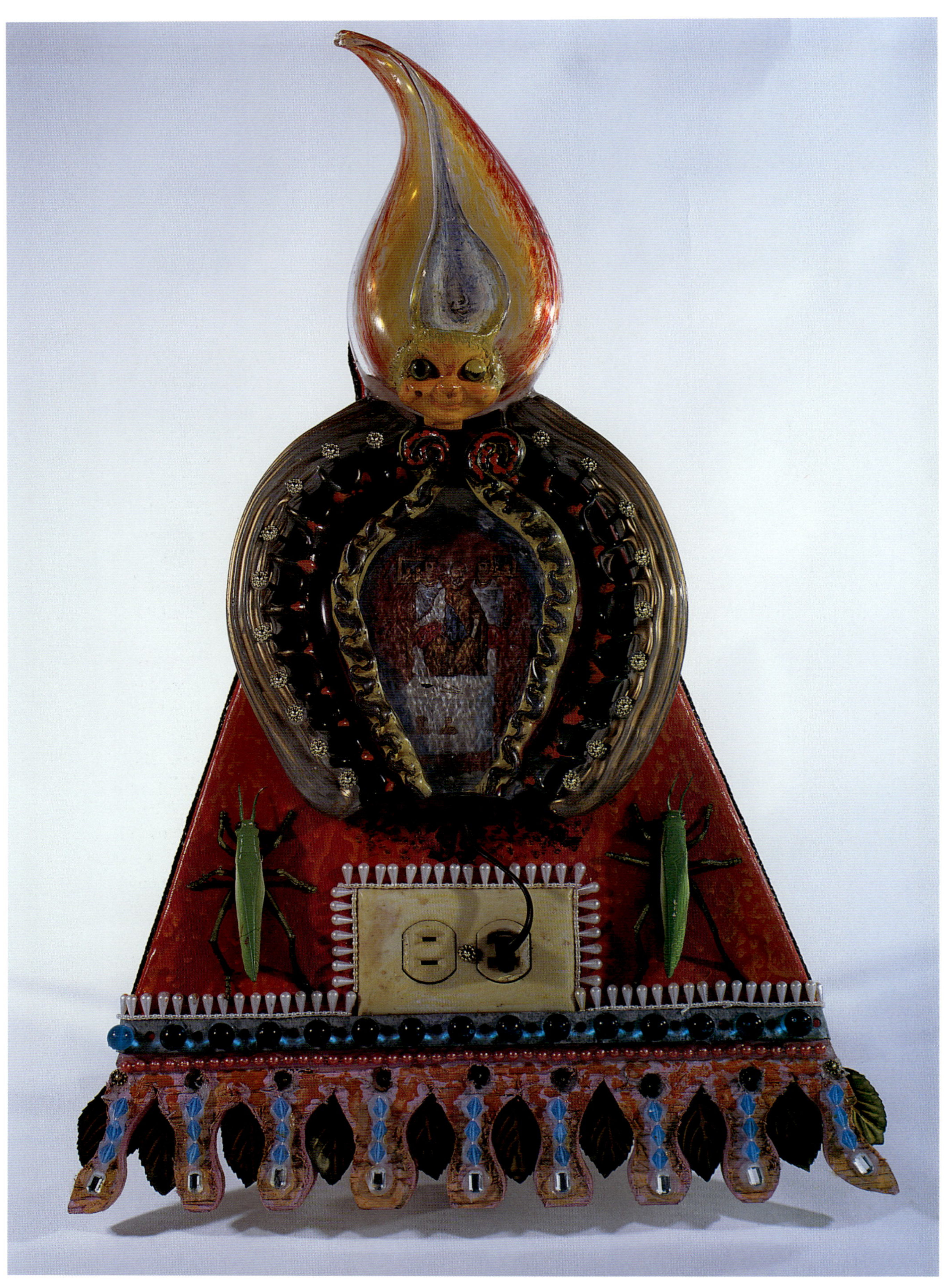

112 Einar and Jamex de la Torre, *Nomás enchúfala* (Just plug it in), 1995, mixed media with blown glass, 26" x 17" x 4"

introduction

LEARNING ABOUT AND THROUGH CHICANA/O ART

The artworks reproduced in *Chicano Art for Our Millennium* and the accompanying text are invaluable resources for educators seeking to introduce Chicana/o art and culture to students in schools and universities, to museum visitors, and to adults who may be unfamiliar with the richness of Chicana/o art. The educators' section of this book provides guidance to assist in planning learning experiences for students. Guidance includes suggestions to help students find meaningful connections to Chicana/o artworks regardless of their cultural background. Additional suggestions include projects that ask students to apply what they learn from their study of Chicana/o art to art from other cultures and also to their own art making. Potential interdisciplinary connections accompany each theme.

A THEMATIC, INQUIRY-BASED APPROACH

Two instructional approaches provide the structure for this educational resource: themes and inquiry.[1] Most students are more willing and able to learn when they can relate new ideas and skills to larger issues they already know and care about. A theme is a general topic that can help students see relationships and make connections. If a theme is to be effective in providing focus for learning, it needs to be developed and clearly articulated. One way to develop a broad cross-cultural theme is to articulate it in two ways: (1) as a general theme in life and (2) as a theme in art. Developing these two versions of one theme can be useful in building connections across cultures, generating ideas for students' own art making, and building connections to other subject areas. A carefully written introduction serves as a short explanation for students and builds connections to their prior knowledge. A good theme introduction also helps educators clarify their focus. An educators' introduction to each of the six themes of *Chicano Art for Our Millennium* includes a theme-in-life statement, a theme-in-art statement, and a student introduction to the theme.

In addition to its thematic approach, this educator resource uses an inquiry approach to help students make meaningful connections to their lives and to the art of others. When students can articulate their own questions, they can begin to take charge of their own understanding. The ability to ask questions is the foundation of inquiry. When students can ask questions, they can begin to make discoveries about themselves and others. Sometimes they discover that people disagree about answers. Sometimes they discover that different people's answers depend on their different viewpoints. Sometimes one question leads to more questions. Sometimes students' curiosity leads them to try new things. In the end, the information students discover and the directions they take often depend on the questions they ask. Looking at art can bring up many questions to explore. Art can lead students to new discoveries about themselves, others, and the world in which they live.

---

[1] For a fuller introduction to thematic, inquiry-based art instruction, see *Stories of Art* by Mary Erickson, published in 2002 by Crizmac Publications in Tucson, Arizona. Crizmac Publications granted permission to include a modified version of the introduction to the theme of spiritual worlds from *Stories of Art*.

The artwork itself

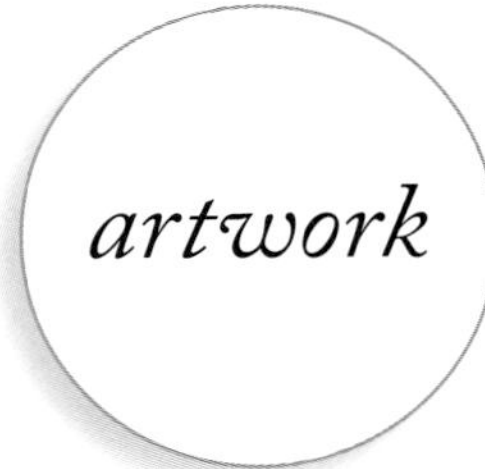

What the artwork means from different points of view

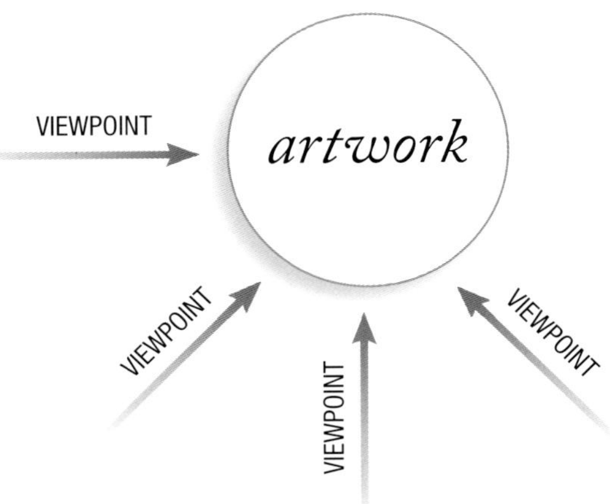

The life and times in which the artist lived and worked

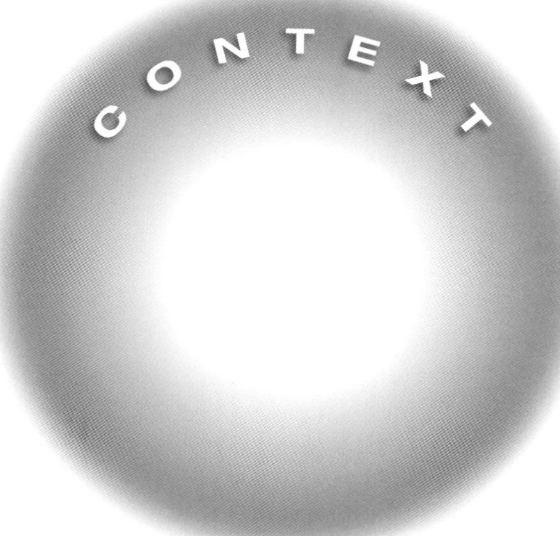

How the artwork is connected to other artworks

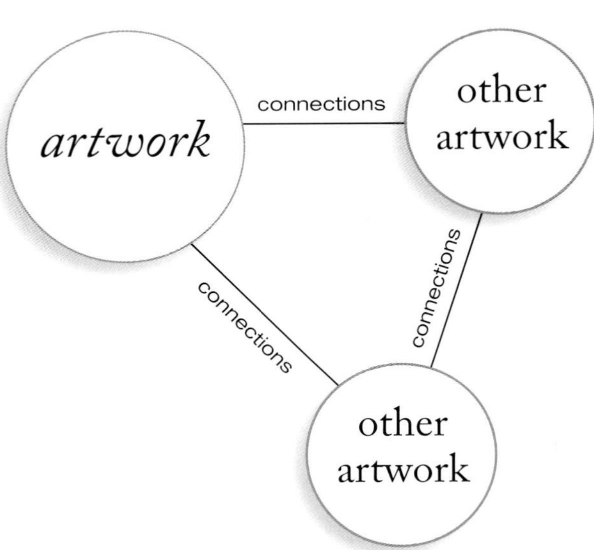

Some questions about art lead to facts; other questions call for conclusions.[2] Factual questions can focus on a particular artwork (What can I find out about the artwork itself?) or on its context (What can I find out about the life and times in which the artist lived and worked?).

[2] When is a fact a conclusion? "Fact" is a word commonly used to name a statement that most reasonable people agree is true once evidence is pointed to. Statements made when evidence is not clear and well-informed people disagree are better thought of as conclusions. The dividing line between facts and conclusions is not always sharp.

However, a lot of what students wonder about artworks is not resolved through discovery of facts, but rather requires that they draw conclusions based on those facts. The more facts students have, the better informed their conclusions are. As students try to make sense of an artwork, they can gain insights from learning how others have viewed it. Students can discover relationships as they compare one artwork with other similar and dissimilar artworks. Questions that call for conclusions can focus on diverse viewpoints for interpretation (What can I find out about what the artwork means to different people?) or on relationships among artworks (What can I find out about connections between this artwork and other artworks?).

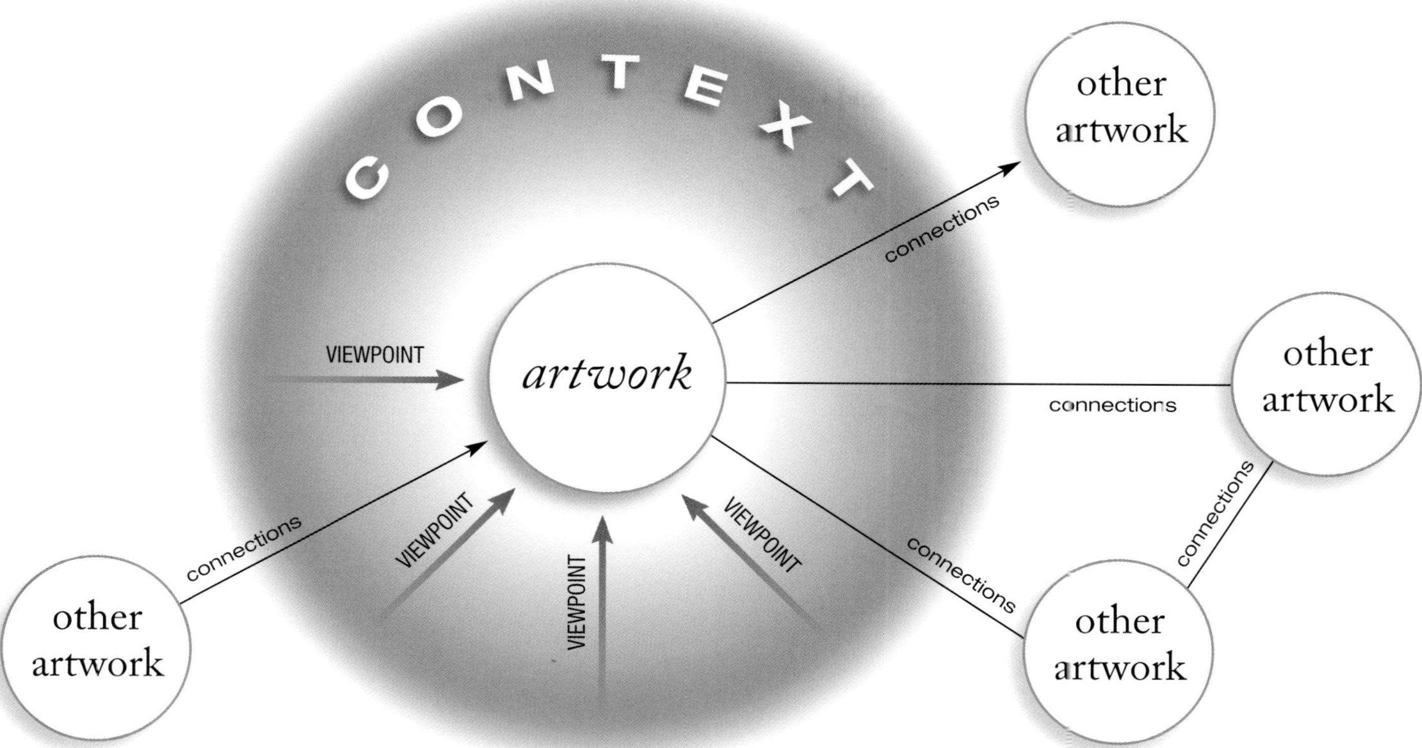

Connections: People use theme, style, and influence (or combinations) to connect artworks.

This resource distributes key questions across the six themes of *Chicano Art for Our Millennium.* Each theme includes specific teacher-directed inquiry activity ideas for each of its key questions. Educators may choose to focus on fewer, more, modified, or different questions in association with each theme. Their curriculum and local resources and needs may lead them to make different decisions about which questions work best with which themes. Factual questions and questions that call for conclusions appear below, together with their location in the educator resource.

Questions About the Artwork

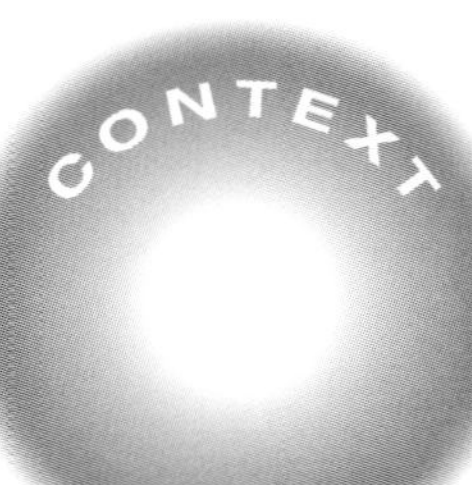

- *Subject matter:* What people, places, or things does the artwork show? (addressed briefly with Theme Six)

- *Technical features:* What tools, materials, and processes did the artist use? (Theme Three)

- *Visual and tactile features:* What visual and tactile features did the artist use? (Theme One, line; Theme Two, color; Theme Three, texture; Theme Four, shape; Theme Five, light and dark; Theme Six, space)

- *Reproduction:* How is the reproduction (printed, digital, or projected image) different from the original artwork? (introduced below)

- *Care:* How is the artwork exhibited and protected from harm? (introduced below)

Contextual Questions

- *Artist's life:* What is the background and life experience of the artist? (Theme Five)

- *Natural and built environments:* What are the natural and built environments like where the artwork was made? (Theme One)

- *Function:* What does the artwork do? (Theme Five)

- *Artworld context:* What art training, traditions, movements, and expectations surround the artist? (Theme Six)

- *Cultural context:* What do people think, believe, or do in the culture in which the artwork was made? (Theme One)

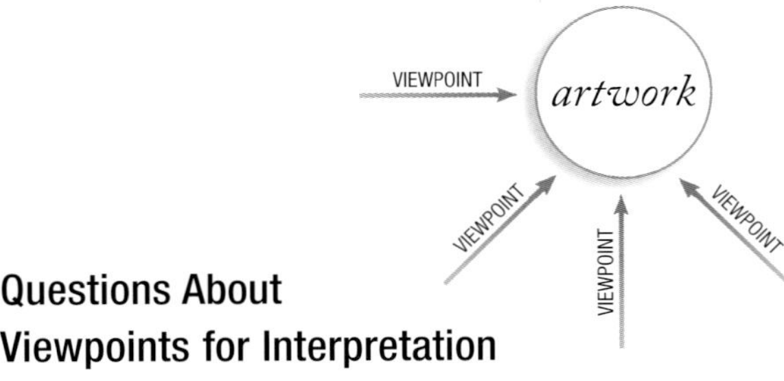

Questions About Viewpoints for Interpretation

- *Artist's intention:* Why did the artist want the artwork to look the way it does? (Theme Four)

- *Art specialists' understanding:* How do specialists in art understand the artwork? (Theme Two)

- *Cultural understanding:* How is the artwork understood within the culture in which it was made? (Theme Four)

- *Personal viewpoints:* How do individuals' personal experiences affect how they understand the artwork? (Theme Two)

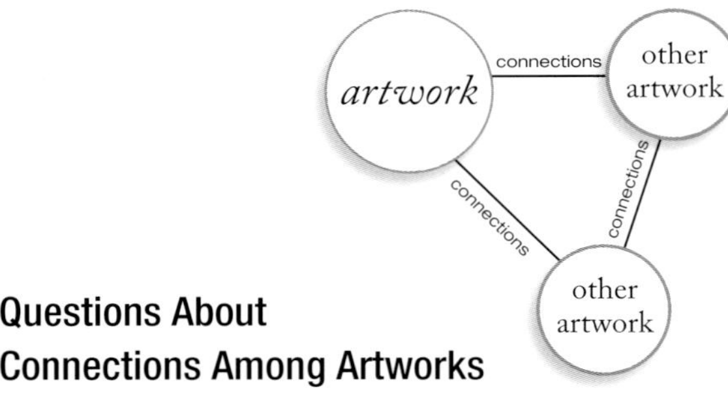

Questions About Connections Among Artworks

- *Style:* How does this artwork look like other artworks? (Theme Six)

- *Art influences:* What other art influenced the artist? (Theme Three)

- *Themes:* What other artworks address the same general topic? (introduced above and in the first section of this book)

Some educators might prefer a student-centered inquiry approach. They might help students to plan the direction of their own inquiry by inviting and assisting students to formulate their own questions, including, for example, factual questions about particular artworks and contexts or interpretive and comparative questions that call for conclusions based on facts. They might select one or two preplanned inquiry discussions provided in this resource to give their students guided inquiry practice and to demonstrate the power of focused inquiry.

TEACHING FOR TRANSFER

Transfer is what happens when learners are able to recall information and use it appropriately in new situations. How to achieve transfer is the subject of many scholarly publications. This resource facilitates transfer of three different kinds of knowledge: content knowledge, procedural knowledge, and dispositional knowledge.

Content knowledge includes basic facts, core concepts, and relationships among concepts. Themes and a structured inquiry process provide the conceptual structure for activities suggested in this educator resource. If the conceptual structure is successful, it provides students with a model they can use to understand new information.

Understanding a process is necessary but not sufficient to achieve procedural transfer. Students must also use that process to perform a new task. This educator resource presents an explicit inquiry process that educators can model through teacher-directed inquiry, that students can practice through guided application activities, and that students can internalize through student-centered inquiry. When students write journal entries, they demonstrate their ability to apply their understanding.

Dispositional knowledge includes attitudes such as willingness, interest, persistence, and a desire to succeed. When learning is meaningful to students, their disposition to transfer that learning increases. That is, they are more inclined to make an effort to use what they learn. This educator resource suggests activities to introduce themes and inquiry questions by building on students' own prior experiences. The suggested studio activities challenge students to use learned concepts, procedures, and strategies to express personal meaning through their art production.

ASSESSMENT AND VISUAL ARTS STANDARDS

Carefully articulated objectives are the key to planning effective assessment. Each theme in this educator resource presents fifteen teacher-directed objectives to guide an array of suggested activities, each of which can lead to multiple good results. Educators who prefer a student-centered approach to inquiry might choose to focus their planning on helping students achieve objectives such as the following:

- Students formulate factual questions about artworks and about the contexts in which artworks are made.

- Students formulate questions that lead to conclusions about meanings of artworks and about relationships among artworks.

- Students identify sources for factual information.

- Students use facts and persuasive argument to support conclusions.

- Students revise their original questions and generate new questions based on the results of their own inquiry.

Teachers of art are responsible for addressing state and national visual art standards. The thematic, inquiry-based approach presented in this educator resource provides guidance in addressing all the national visual arts content standards. Theme Three with its focus on technical features addresses Standard One: Understanding and applying media, techniques, and processes. The key questions about visual or tactile features included with all six themes address the first part of Standard Two (structures). Theme Five addresses the function issue also identified in Standard Two: Using knowledge of structures and functions. The thematic approach used with all six themes—and especially Themes Four and Five—addresses Standard Three: Choosing and evaluating a range of subject matter, symbols, and ideas. Cross-cultural activities suggested for each theme and key cultural questions in Theme One and Theme Four address Standard Four: Understanding the visual arts in relation to history and cultures. Theme Two's emphasis on art specialists' understanding and Theme Six's focus on the art-world context address Standard Five: Reflecting upon and assessing the characteristics and merits of their work and the work of others. Each theme identifies potential interdisciplinary connections to address Standard Six: Making connections between visual arts and other disciplines.

EDUCATORS

The principal audiences for this educator resource are K-12 teachers, university faculty, and art museum educators.

K-12 teachers can use themes to introduce their students to Chicana/o art, made within an important culture in the United States. At the same time, they can use themes and key questions as foundations to help their students explore art from other cultures or as a basis for art making. Teachers of younger learners or novices might choose to focus on one key question or theme at a time. These teachers can use the instructions to guide them in searching for information and structuring how they share the information with their students.

Spanish- and English-language teachers can use images, issues, questions, and discussion suggestions to stimulate writing and oral presentations. History and social science teachers can use the six themes and selected key questions for cross-cultural analysis of both contemporary and historical cultures.

At the university level, this book can serve as a supplementary text or resource in American studies, Chicana/o studies, or contemporary American art history courses. Professors might adapt themes or key questions as potential assignments for research papers or independent study projects or as the basis for student-centered cooperative learning activities.

University teacher educators can use the book as a model that preservice teachers can consult in the designing of their own thematic, inquiry-based curriculum units. Art teacher educators may find the book useful to supplement their understanding of art made by members of the fastest growing cultural group served by public schools in the United States. The broad cross-cultural themes and key questions offer a curriculum approach that preservice teachers can adapt for culturally diverse student populations in schools where they will ultimately teach. In addition, the educator resource provides a model of interdisciplinary planning that places art at the core of learning.

Museum educators on their own or in collaboration with other educators can play a crucial role in helping students understand two important issues in art inquiry: How is a reproduction different from an original, and how is an artwork exhibited and protected from harm? *Chicano Art for Our Millennium* is a rich resource for teaching about and through Chicana/o art, but it does not, in itself, present students with direct experiences with works of art. The reproductions in this book are photographic images printed on paper. Reproductions cannot duplicate the experience of direct interaction with original works of art that is possible through a visit to an art center, museum, gallery, community center, or artist's studio—or working with art objects in the classroom. Reproductions of artworks in printed, projected, or digital form can vary from originals in size, color, luminosity, texture, detail, and emotional impact. Context or setting can also affect viewer response. When educators plan activities that allow students to compare reproductions with original works of art, they help them understand the limitations of reproductions without restricting their access to myriad artworks they could never hope to see in person.

Because artworks are important and valuable, museums and others strive to take good care of them. Art museums in the United States strictly control temperature and humidity in galleries and storage spaces to help preserve art objects they exhibit or collect. Works on paper (drawings, prints, and photographs), textiles, and paintings are generally displayed under lower light conditions to protect them from fading. Many works of art are also protected from potentially damaging human contact by frames or coverings, display cases, or barricades. When art is damaged, museum conservators assess its condition and recommend whether and how to restore it. These measures, along with security precautions, reflect the value museums place on artworks and their commitment to preserving them for generations to come.

USING THIS BOOK

Educators will find different ways to work with the images in this book. If using only one copy, a teacher might gather students in one location to look at reproductions, move throughout the classroom displaying each image, or display a selected artwork for viewing. Some educators will prefer to disassemble a second copy to work with loose reproductions. Teachers with multiple copies can allocate books for small-group work. Educators and older students will need access to appropriate library and Internet sources. Information about Chicana/o artists and their cultural context, as well as specific information on individual artworks, is available in the first section of this book, in *Contemporary Chicana and Chicano Art: Artists, Works, Culture, and Education*, at www.latinoartcommunity.org, and in other print and electronic sources. Artworks mentioned in this educator resource but not reproduced in the book are all readily accessible through an Internet search engine.

Museum educators can use this book for teacher and docent training in conjunction with the exhibition *Chicano Art for Our Millennium*. The thematic, inquiry-based approach offers a model that can be used to study other exhibitions, artists, or artworks as well. Educators in the museum setting are in an excellent position to teach important concepts about reproductions and care of art objects, as mentioned above.

Educators can use the images in this book in other ways as well. For example, they can make other groupings of reproductions that focus on their educational priority. Groupings can be done by artist, region of the United States, genre (such as landscape, portrait, still life) studio process, artist gender, subject matter, style, elements and principles of design, other themes, or other disciplines (such as mathematics, history, or literature).

However it is used, this book invites educators into a world of exciting and important art and suggests many ways to help them introduce that art to others.

Mary Erickson
ARIZONA STATE UNIVERSITY

Pat Villeneuve
FLORIDA STATE UNIVERSITY

REFERENCES

Erickson, Mary. "Images of Me: Why Themes? Why Focus on Inquiry? Why Use the Internet?" *Art Education* 54, no. 1 (2001): 33-40.

———. *Stories of Art*. Tucson, AZ: Crizmac Publications, 2002.

Keller, Gary D., Mary Erickson, Kaytie Johnson, and Joaquín Alvarado. 2002. *Contemporary Chicana and Chicano Art: Artists, Works, Culture, and Education*. Tempe, AZ: Bilingual Press, 2002.

Latina/o Art Community. Ed. Hispanic Research Center, Arizona State University. www.latinoartcommunity.org

theme one:
community values

heme in Life: We all seek support through our connections with others.

Theme in Art: Art can express the strengths and values of a community.

Introduction to the Theme

As children we usually get our first support from members of our families, beginning with parents and often extending to grandparents, aunts and uncles, cousins, and other relatives. Families show children what is important and how to get along with others. As we grow older, our connections to others grow: for example, in our neighborhood, town or city, or within a rural community. We explore the world around us and the people we meet there. People connect with others in many ways—through family and religious celebrations, through sports and play, through school and work, and through many other shared activities. Throughout history all over the world people have made and continue to make art that expresses the values that communities share.

Key Questions

NATURAL AND BUILT ENVIRONMENTS

What are the natural and built environments like where the artwork was made?

CULTURAL CONTEXT

What do people think, believe, or do in the culture in which the artwork was made?

VISUAL FEATURE

How did the artist use line in the artwork?

THEMATIC ACTIVITIES

Introduce students to the Theme Title, the Theme in Life, and the Theme in Art. Post and ask students to read the Introduction to the Theme to help orient them in the general topic they will be studying. Read and explain that they will be using key questions to guide their investigation of the theme of Community Values in Art.

Students' Experience with the Theme

OBJECTIVE

- Students identify values held within their families and community.

Use discussion starters such as the following to help students identify how the theme of Community Values relates to their own lives:

- Name members of your immediate family and tell how you are related to each.

- What do you do together?

- What family values has your family passed down to you?

- When do you see members of your extended family (grandparents, aunts and uncles, cousins, etc.)?

- What do you do when you are together with members of your extended family?

- Name some people who live in your neighborhood.

- Where and when do you see your neighbors?

- What are some things you think your neighbors care about?

- Name some people you see regularly at school or work.

- What do people at work and school care about?

Sometimes artists express family and community values in their art.

Student Discussion of the Theme in Chicana/o Art

OBJECTIVE

- Students interpret artworks as expressions of family and community values.

Display *Un maestro pa'l futuro* by Malaquías Montoya (PLATE 33), *Backyard Pachanga* by Frank Ybarra (PLATE 16), *Cumpleaños de Lala y Tudi* by Carmen Lomas Garza (PLATE 18), and *San Bernardino Art Gallery* by David Rosales (PLATE 34). Lead a group discussion comparing the four artworks or divide the class into groups and assign each group one artwork. Use discussion starters such as the following to help students apply the theme of Community Values to Chicana/o art:

- Describe the activities the artists depict in each of these artworks.

- Where do you think the activities are taking place?

- What do you think the people in the artworks care about?

- What community values are celebrated in these artworks?

ADDITIONAL INQUIRY ACTIVITIES

The Introduction outlines an array of questions from which you might select specific directions to extend students' inquiry. Questions about natural and built environments, about cultural context, and about line are offered here as examples. Your curriculum may lead you to adapt or replace one or more of these questions.

Inquiry into Students' Experience

OBJECTIVES

- Students analyze the natural and built environments in which they live.

- Students analyze culture(s) in their community.

- Students describe different kinds of line.

NATURAL AND BUILT ENVIRONMENTS

- Describe the natural environment where you live. (Landforms, bodies of water, climate, plants, and animals are some features of the natural world.)

- How does your natural environment affect you and your family?

- How are some of your school or work activities affected by your natural environment?

- What have people built in your environment? (Commercial, residential, religious, and government buildings, transportation and irrigation systems, streets, bridges, and granaries are some features people build within the natural environment.)

- How does the built environment affect your family, neighborhood, school, or work?

CULTURAL CONTEXT

- Who are some of the important people in your culture? (Individuals see themselves as part of a larger group or culture. That is, they are familiar with many of the same people and places and share many of the same activities and ideas as others in their culture.)

- To what groups or cultures do you belong (generation, ethnic group, club, religion, organization, school, etc.)?

- Where are some of the places where some people in your culture get together?

- What activities do many people in your culture believe to be fun or important?

LINE

- What lines do you see in your classroom (on posters, clothing, books, furniture, etc.)?

- Describe different kinds of lines you see (straight, curved, tapered, dotted, broad, thin, jagged, etc.).

- Think of an object's edge as its outline. Point to angular and curved outlines in your classroom.

Artists sometimes show the natural and built environment or aspects of their culture in their art. Line is a visual feature artists can use to organize their artworks.

Inquiry into Chicana/o Art

OBJECTIVES

- Students identify in artworks representations of natural and built environments.

- Students identify in artworks representations of people, places, activities, and ideas that are important to a culture.

- Students explain how artists use lines both to represent subject matter and also to organize the artwork visually.

Display *Stilts* by Fidencio Durán (PLATE 24), *Nopalitos frescos* by Carmen Lomas Garza (PLATE 32), *Panchito y Tía Tita* by Antonio Rael (PLATE 19), *Still in Reverence* and *Reyna's Cantina* by Celina Hinojosa (PLATES 27 and 15), and *Sonido del barrio* by José Treviño (PLATE 35). Use discussion starters such as the following to help students apply key questions about Chicana/o art.

NATURAL AND BUILT ENVIRONMENTS

- Did the artist choose to show mostly things from nature or things constructed by people, or both?

- Point to details of the natural or built environment shown in the artwork.

- What are the figures doing in their environment?

- Could they do what they are doing just as well anywhere, or does the environment contribute in some way to what they are doing?

CULTURAL CONTEXT

- Are you familiar with everything shown in these artworks?

- Have you done the same activities, or do you know someone who has?

- Look carefully at *Sonido del barrio* by José Treviño. Have you ever heard a Mexican or Mexican American style accordion player or watched Mexican or Mexican American dancers?

- Look carefully at *Nopalitos frescos* by Carmen Lomas Garza. Have you ever harvested or eaten prickly pear cactus fruit? Have you harvested any crop?

- Look carefully at *Panchito y Tía Tita* by Antonio Rael. Do you have any idea why an artist might show a woman skeleton with her skeleton dog? Do you recognize the figure on the little table on the right side of the couch?

- Are you of Chicana/o or Mexican American background? These cultures often share activities and ideas, but not always. Newer immigrants may be more familiar with Mexican traditions. People who live and work in cities have different experiences from people who live and work in the countryside. Chicana/os or Mexican Americans who live in different parts of the United States (for example, in Los Angeles, the Imperial Valley, south Texas, Phoenix, Santa Fe, Iowa, or New York City) have developed some of their own special activities and ideas. Compare the activities shown in Celina Hinojosa's urban and rural paintings, *Still in Reverence* and *Reyna's Cantina*.

- If your culture helps you understand some of the details in one or more of these artworks, think about volunteering to explain those details to your classmates.

- Whatever your culture, consider talking with any people you know who are Chicana/o or Mexican American (for example, members of your family, friends, or neighbors) to seek more information about details in the artworks.

- Whatever your culture, reading the first part of this book will tell you much about many features of Chicana/o culture.

LINE

- Which artists use definite outlines to define their shapes? (Rael and Lomas Garza)

- Which artist uses long, lanky limbs to give a linear quality to his work? (Durán)

- Which artist subtly implies lines by placing similar elements in rows that suggest lines? (Treviño made a horizon line of trees, a fence, and buildings. He ran a line of footprints right through his image. He defined the dancers in the sky with rows of blue dots or stars.)

- Does the artist use mostly the same kind of line throughout the artwork (thin, thick, tapering, dotted, angular, curved, etc.), or does the artist combine several different kinds of lines?

- Do the lines add variety to the artwork, or do they help unify it? Explain.

- Which artworks have lines (or suggested lines or edges) that help lead your eye around the artwork?

CROSS-CULTURAL ACTIVITIES

The theme of Community Values as well as questions about natural and built environments and about cultural context can guide students' investigation of art made in any culture. You might choose art from cultures identified in your curriculum or from cultures of local interest to replace those suggested here.

OBJECTIVES

- Students investigate and report on natural and built environments where members of a culture live.
- Students investigate and report on factors that characterize a culture.
- Students investigate and report on values shared within a community.

Group students into teams to locate reproductions of artworks from an assigned culture and to investigate that culture guided by key questions. Assign each group to one of the following cultures:

- A Native American culture (for example, Navajo, Hopi, Ojibway, or Lakota)
- Aboriginal Australian culture
- Prehistoric cultures in what is now Europe (for example, Lascaux in France and Altamira in Spain)
- An urban culture (for example New York City, Miami, Chicago, or San Francisco)
- A rural culture (for example, in Appalachia or in the Midwest)

Teams should locate reproductions of artworks made in their assigned culture. Each team should seek as much information as they can about the natural and built environments where people in these cultures live or lived. Ask students to focus specifically on the natural environment (landforms, climate, animal and plant life) and on any natural tools and materials used by artists in that culture. They should also find out all they can about the culture, including such factors as social classes, religions, technological developments, transportation, and work. They should seek information on how art helps people in these cultures to become and stay connected with each other, that is, how art helps maintain community values.

Teams should share their findings, illustrating their presentation with artworks from their assigned culture. They should report on:

1. the natural and built environments
2. the Cultural Context
3. how art helps maintain community values

STUDIO ACTIVITIES

If you choose to extend your instruction to include art making, the theme of Community Values and the key questions you select as your focus can provide the basis for a follow-up studio activity.

OBJECTIVES

- Students make artworks that reflect community values.
- Students seek ideas for their art from their cultural contexts.
- Students make artworks that draw on their own natural and built environments as a source of subject matter.
- Students use line both to define subject matter and to organize their work visually.

Select available media appropriate to the skill levels of your students. Review the theme and key questions to help students transfer what they have learned to their own art making. For example, students might work in teams to investigate assigned features of their natural and built environments and assigned factors about their culture(s) to get ideas for one or a series of murals painted on large sheets of craft paper. Groups could focus on key people, places, activities, and ideas in their community as possible subject matter. Students should make sketches to plan how to organize their mural. They should repeat similar lines and use continuous lines that run through their sketches to help unify their work.

Student Exhibition

Exhibit the Theme Title, Theme in Life, Theme in Art, and Key Questions with samples of student writing and artwork. You are invited to send samples of student work to hrcartprojects@asu.edu for possible publication on the Latino Art Community Web site, www.latinoartcommunity.org.

Interdisciplinary Transfer Potential:

Social studies: social, economic, religious, and governmental systems

History: local tradition and heritage

Geography: landforms, bodies of water, and climate

Biology: native plants and animals

Language arts: interviewing, listening, reading, oral reports

art across cultural borders

heme in Life: We are all members of cultural and other groups.

Theme in Art: Art can help us reflect on our distinct and overlapping identities.

Introduction to the Theme

Over the years people who live together or share experiences come to know some of the same people and places and participate in similar activities. They also sometimes share a common language, religion, political beliefs, or other values. "Culture" is a word used to name the many things people share as they live, work, play, and interact together. The United States is a large, complex culture that is made up of many smaller enduring, evolving, and overlapping cultures. Many Native American cultures have endured as the United States spread across the continent. Some people in the United States maintain cultural traditions brought with them from around the world. Through the years, the border between Mexico and the United States has moved as a result of conquest, colonization, military action, and purchase. One might say that Chicana/o culture began in 1848, date of the Treaty of Guadalupe Hidalgo that ended the U.S.-Mexican War, when the southern border of the United States moved far south into territory that had been Mexico.

As immigrants cross borders to live and work in the United States, they encounter different cultures. Their new lives force them to reflect on challenges to their traditional cultural identities. When cultures meet, all cultures have an opportunity to reflect and grow. Art can help us better understand the diversity of our cultures.

Key Questions

ART SPECIALIST UNDERSTANDING

How do specialists in art understand the artwork?

PERSONAL VIEWPOINTS

How can an individual's personal experience affect how she or he understands the artwork?

VISUAL FEATURE

How did the artist use colors?

THEMATIC ACTIVITIES

Introduce students to the Theme Title, the Theme in Life, and the Theme in Art. Post and ask students to read the Introduction to the Theme to help orient them in the general topic they will be studying. Read and explain that they will be using key questions to guide their investigation of the theme of Art Across Cultural Borders.

Students' Experience with the Theme

OBJECTIVE

- Students identify cultural and interest groups to which they belong.

Use discussion starters such as the following to help students identify how the theme of Art Across Cultural Borders relates to their own lives:

- If you are aware of the cultural background(s) of your family, consider volunteering to tell your classmates about the culture(s) of your ancestors (parents, grandparents, etc.).

- To what other groups do you belong? For example, are you a member of a club, team, religious or political organization, or other interest group, such as computer game players, musicians, car buffs, comic book collectors, dancers, soccer fans, etc.?

- What are some of the things members of your cultural or interest group know a lot about?

- Who are the prominent people, experts, or "stars" in your group?

- Where do people in your group meet to share activities and ideas that are important to your culture or interest?

- List at least two different cultural or interest groups to which you belong (or wish to belong). What concerns or values do both groups share? About what concerns or values might the two groups sometimes disagree? How have you managed to balance these groups within your own life?

Artists who identify with more than one culture sometimes make artworks that express what happens when cultures meet.

Student Discussion of the Theme in Chicana/o Art

OBJECTIVES

- Students interpret artworks as expressions of the interaction of cultures.

Divide your students into six small groups and distribute one of the following reproductions to each group: *California Dreaming* by Jacalyn López García (PLATE 7), *VG Got her Green Card* by Isabel Martínez (PLATE 8), *Mona Maya* by David Moreno (PLATE 39), *Mudra I* by Mary Antonia Wood (PLATE 49), *First Aztec on the Moon* by Santiago Pérez (PLATE 48), and *Bridge Over the Rio Grande* by Luis Valderas (PLATE 43). Ask each group to identify two different cultures or interest groups that are directly or indirectly shown in their artwork. Depending on students' prior knowledge, you may need to provide the following information:

- The ancient Mayans built pyramids and are known today for their fine textiles.

- Images of powerful bulls appear in bullfighting posters in Mexico and Spain.

- Skulls and hearts are commonly represented in Aztec art.

- The Virgin of Guadalupe, patron saint of Mexico, wears a blue cloak and is surrounded by rays of light.

- The *Mona Lisa* is a famous painting by the Italian Renaissance artist Leonardo Da Vinci.

- People who practice various religions, including Buddhism, Christianity, and pre-Conquest Mayan and Mixtec religions, sometimes use symbolic hand gestures.

Ask students to identify the two cultural or interest groups they discovered in their group's artwork and to explain their conclusions.

Display all six artworks listed above along with two thematic titles: "Borders Divide" and "Cultures Overlap." Ask students to vote on which artworks best express which theme. Finally challenge students to support their conclusion for any artworks about which the class vote was split.

ADDITIONAL INQUIRY ACTIVITIES

The Introduction outlines an array of questions from which you might select specific directions to extend students' inquiry. Questions about art specialists' understanding, about personal viewpoints, and about color are offered here as examples. Your curriculum may lead you to adapt or replace one or more of these questions.

Inquiry into Students' Experience

OBJECTIVES

- Students give examples of what specialists may know or be able to do.

- Students give examples of how different people sometimes see the same thing in different ways.

- Students identify warm and cool colors in the world around them.

(ART) SPECIALIST UNDERSTANDING

- What makes someone a specialist?

- Name specialists in your community (for example, an expert in soccer, needlework, carpentry, singing, gardening, writing, etc.). Explain what each specialist knows a lot about or can do very well.

- Tell about a time an expert explained something to you or showed you how to do something.

PERSONAL VIEWPOINTS

- Have you ever been in a situation in which you discovered someone who had a different understanding of that situation than you did? List some occasion when your own viewpoint was different from some someone else's; for example, a parent's, teacher's, your brother's or sister's, or a friend's.

- Speculate about why someone might have a different viewpoint from your own. For example, what previous experience, worries, or goals might affect that person's point of view?

COLOR (WARM AND COOL)

- Are you wearing warm colors today? (Warm colors are those that are associated with warm or hot things like the sun or fire. Yellow, red, pink, and orange are warm colors.)

- Who is wearing cool colors today? (Cool colors are colors that are associated with cool things like water, ice, and grass. Blue, green, and bluish purples are cool colors.)

- Are you wearing a mix of warm and cool colors today?

- Who is wearing neutral colors, such as black, white, or in-between colors?

- Point to the warmest and the coolest colors you can find in your classroom.

Specialists in art sometimes help us understand and appreciate an unfamiliar artwork. They can also help us make better art. At the same time, we each can respond to artworks from our own personal point of view. Color is a visual feature artists can use to make their works more expressive.

Inquiry into Chicana/o Art

OBJECTIVES

- Students analyze artworld specialists' responses to artworks.

- Students analyze points of view that might cause people to understand an artwork in a particular way.

- Students analyze how artists use warm and cool colors in their work.

ART SPECIALIST UNDERSTANDING

Distribute *VG Got Her Green Card* by Isabel Martínez, *Una familia* by Malaquías Montoya (PLATE 44), and *Los de abajo* by Tony Ortega (PLATE 42) to different groups of students. Ask students to examine their artwork carefully. Then ask students to write a sentence that sums up what they think is important to understand about their assigned artwork.

Next provide each group with the statement below (quoted in Keller et. al., *Contemporary Chicana and Chicano Art: Artists, Works, Culture, and Education*, Tempe, AZ: Bilingual Press 2003) written by an art specialist about the group's assigned artwork:

Isabel Martínez: Susan Rinderle wrote in *Latin Style* that the artist's "paintings . . . often echo the color, bold lines, and social conscience of . . . Diego Rivera and José Clemente Orozco. . . Martínez uses the canvas not only as a window, but as a mirror—a forum for honesty and personal testimony" (Vol. II, p. 139).

Malaquías Montoya: Art historian Dr. Ramón Favela says, "With strident forms of great simplicity . . . the messages conveyed by Montoya's posters are exceedingly clear—his images are of a dispossessed humanity restrained and shackled by an incomprehensible and nefarious political condition." Exhibition notes from San Francisco Art Institute solo exhibition, 1997 (Vol. II, p. 155).

Tony Ortega: Carol Dickerson wrote in *Southwest Art*, "Many scenes have the stillness and timelessness of people caught in a moment, as in a photograph. But Ortega's simplifications and color arrangements are so obviously the stuff of art that a more apt analogy is a stained glass window—at the instant it is 'ignited' by the sun" (Vol. II, p. 177).

- Compare your group's statement with that written by the specialist. How is your statement alike and different from the statement of the art specialist?

- What other art does the specialist mention to help viewers see the artwork in a particular way? (the art of Diego Rivera and José Clemente Orozco, posters, photography, and stained glass)

- Has reading the art specialist's statement helped you notice some new aspect of your assigned artwork or understand it differently? Explain.

- Consider locating examples of the art to which your art specialist compared your assigned artwork. See if viewing that other art helps you better appreciate your assigned artwork.

PERSONAL VIEWPOINTS

Explain that anyone can have a personal viewpoint about any artwork. Display *La Virgen de Venice* by Wayne Alaniz Healy (PLATE 5). Ask students to consider how an elderly nun and an inline skater might view the artwork differently. For example, the skater might think the woman is having fun, while the nun might think the Virgin of Guadalupe is not being not shown appropriate reverence.

Next display *The Double Agent Sirvienta: Blow Up the Hard Drive* by Laura Álvarez (PLATE 45) and *Una familia* by Malaquías Montoya. Ask students to propose at least two personal viewpoints on each artwork. Encourage students to consider and respect multiple viewpoints, even if they disagree.

Finally, ask students to think of two different friends or family members and speculate about what their viewpoints might be on one of the three artworks. (Álvarez, Healy, or Montoya)

COLOR (WARM AND COOL)

Display *The Double Agent Sirvienta: Blow Up the Hard Drive* by Laura Álvarez, *La Virgen de Venice* by Wayne Alaniz Healy, and *Una familia* by Malaquías Montoya. Help students analyze the artists' use of warm and cool colors by asking:

- What warm and what cool colors did each artist select?

- Which artist uses a cool foreground color in front of a warm background color?

- Which artist uses a warm foreground color in front of a cool background color?

- Which artist uses almost all warm and cool colors with very little black or white?

- How do each artist's color choices contribute to the overall feeling or mood of the work?

- Which colors suggest danger, drama, excitement, distance, etc?

CROSS-CULTURAL ACTIVITIES

The theme of Art Across Cultural Borders as well as questions about artworld (specialist) understanding and personal viewpoints can guide students' investigation of art made in any culture. You might choose art from cultures identified in your curriculum or from cultures of local interest to replace those suggested here.

OBJECTIVES

- Students investigate art made by artists in the United States whose experience crosses cultures.

- Students investigate and report on how art specialists understand specific artworks.

- Students identify personal viewpoints that different people might bring to the understanding of artworks.

Group students into teams to locate reproductions of artworks from an assigned culture and to investigate that culture guided by each key question. Assign each group to artists from one of the following "bicultures":

- African American (for example, Henry Tanner, Elizabeth Catlett, or Faith Ringgold)

- Asian American (for example, Roger Shimomura or Hung Liu)

- European American (for example, Albert Bierstadt or Rosa Bonheur)

Teams should locate reproductions of artworks made in their assigned culture. Each team should seek as much information as they can about the cultures from which the artists get their art ideas. Ask students to look specifically for any comments they can find made by specialists in art (art historians, other artists, reviewers, art critics, art collectors, etc.) and compare them with more personal viewpoints, including their own.

Teams should share their findings, illustrating their presentation with artworks from their assigned culture. They should report on:

1. the cultures from which the artists draw ideas

2. the viewpoints of art specialists

3. their own or others' personal viewpoints on the artwork

Studio Activities

If you choose to extend your instruction to include art making, the theme of Art Across Cultural Borders and the key questions you select as your focus can provide the basis for follow-up studio activity.

OBJECTIVES

- Students use overlapping cultural or group membership as a source of ideas for their own art making.

- Students look for assistance from art specialists (for example, an art teacher, artist in the family or community, or skilled classmate) to help them make the best artwork they can.

- Students solicit the personal viewpoints of others as they make choices in their art making.

- Students use warm and cool colors to organize their work.

Select available colored media appropriate to the skill levels of your students. Display Rolando Briseño's *Bicultural Tablesetting* (PLATE 38). Ask students to design a table setting that represents a cultural or interest group (their own or someone else's), complete with dishes, flatware, tablecloth, and food. For example, they might design an imaginary table setting for an Inuit or for a child at a theme park. If you are an art teacher, or if an art teacher or another art specialist is available, choose supplies with which you or the art specialist can demonstrate techniques (for example, effective cutting and gluing, use of paint and brushes, or use of colored chalks). Stop the class from time to time to provide an opportunity for students to walk around to view each other's work and offer suggestions. When all table settings are complete, ask small groups to organize all their table settings into one large arrangement. Help students use warm and cool colors as one way to organize similar table settings or to set up contrasts between table settings. You might provide a selection of large pieces of warm or cool colored craft paper on which groups can organize and exhibit their collection of table settings.

Student Exhibition

Exhibit the Theme Title, Theme in Life, Theme in Art, and Key Questions with samples of student writing and artwork. You are invited to send samples of student work to hrcartprojects@asu.edu for possible publication on the Latino Art Community Web site, www.latinoartcommunity.org.

Interdisciplinary Transfer Potential:

Social studies: social, economic, religious, and governmental systems

History: local tradition and heritage

Language arts: point of view, voice, listening, reading, journal writing, interviewing, oral reports

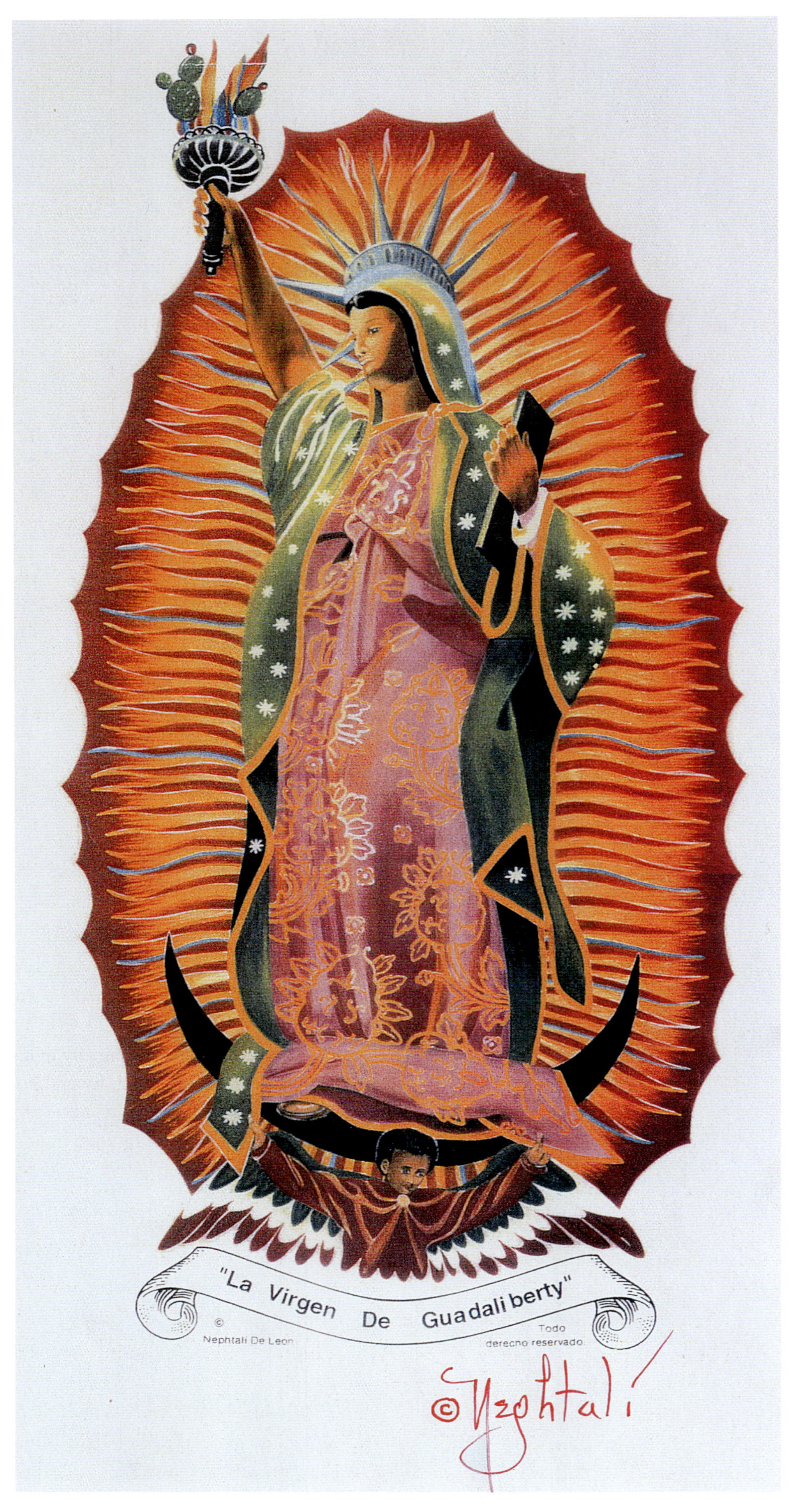

113
Nephtalí De León,
La Virgen de Guadaliberty,
1999, Serigraph,
10.5" x 6"

theme three:
spirituality

Theme in Life: For many people, spirituality is an important part of their lives.

Theme in Art: Art leads many people to great mysteries, powers, and wonders.

Introduction to the Theme

For many people, there are very real worlds that we cannot see or touch. These people believe that there are places beyond the world we know, such as heaven, hell, the land of the dead, or other worlds where god(s), demons, or other beings live. Some people find something very powerful within themselves when they pray, meditate, or sit in silence. For them, their spirit world is deep inside. Religions of the world help their believers understand and get in touch with spiritual mysteries, powers, and wonders. Some people find mystery or deep meaning in the world around them. For example, for some the grace and power of an eagle in flight or the awesome beauty of the Grand Canyon is spiritual. In its many forms, spirituality provides comfort and inspiration to a great many people.

Some religions are concerned that people may worship statues or pictures, treating images as idols; therefore, they prohibit artists from showing living creatures in their art. Other religions make other decisions. Many believers throughout time have made artworks that express their deep spiritual beliefs.

It is important to remember that when we study spiritual art, we learn about what some people believe, or used to believe, not what we should believe.

Key Questions

TECHNICAL FEATURES

What tools, materials, and processes did the artist use?

ART INFLUENCE

What other art influenced the artist?

TACTILE AND VISUAL FEATURE

How did the artist use texture in the artwork?

THEMATIC ACTIVITIES

Introduce students to the Theme Title, the Theme in Life, and the Theme in Art. Post and ask students to read the Introduction to the Theme to help orient them in the general topic they will be studying. Read and explain that they will be using key questions to guide their investigation of the theme of Spirituality in art.

Students' Experience with the Theme

OBJECTIVE

- Students identify religious organizations in their community.

Use discussion starters such as the following to help students identify how the theme of Spirituality relates to their own lives:

- What religious buildings do you know about in your community? (Check the phone book for a more complete list.)
- Consider describing any religious ceremony, such as a wedding, funeral, membership ritual, or healing ceremony, you may have attended.
- Besides through religion, describe other ways you may have heard of that some people find spiritual meaning.

Artists sometimes express spiritual ideas and feelings in their art.

Student Discussion of the Theme in Chicana/o Art

OBJECTIVES

- Students describe the expressive impact of spiritual artworks.

Display *Santa Teresita* by Virginia Agüero (PLATE 53), *Inner Nature* by Paul Botello (PLATE 67), *El Sagrado Corazón* by Alma Gómez (PLATE 68), and *Angelita* by Nivia González (PLATE 63). Lead a group discussion comparing the four artworks or divide the class into groups and assign each group one artwork. Use discussion starters such as the following to help students apply the theme of Spirituality:

- Which artworks show religious subject matter? Point to and name religious references.

- Which artworks suggest an inner spirituality? Explain.

ADDITIONAL INQUIRY ACTIVITIES

The Introduction outlines an array of questions from which you might select specific directions to extend students' inquiry. Questions about technical features, about art influences, and about texture are offered here as examples. Your curriculum may lead you to adapt or replace one or more of these questions.

Inquiry into Students' Experience

OBJECTIVES

- Students identify tools, material, and processes used to make things in the world around them.

- Students explain how the achievements of others have influenced their own decisions.

- Students describe textures in the world around them.

TECHNICAL FEATURES

Assemble a collection of handmade and manufactured objects to display to the class or to distribute among small groups of students.

- List materials from which objects are made (glass, plastic, leather, wood, tin, stone, thread, etc.).

- What tools or equipment do you think were needed to make the objects (for example, knife, needle, saw, drill, hammer, grinder, mold, loom, or chisel)?

- Name a specific or general process used to make the objects, such as assembly, carving, embroidery, construction, molding, etc.

- What tools, materials, and processes have you used: for example, in cooking, sewing, woodwork, computer graphics, gardening, ceramics, paper folding, or painting?

- What have you made through a particular process?

- What tools and materials did you use?

- How did the tools, materials, or process affect the final appearance of your product? What can viewers see in your product that might tell them how it was made?

INFLUENCE

- Think of a person whose work you admire (a singer, religious leader, actor, teacher, politician, athlete, etc.).

- List ways that person might influence you; for example, hard work, dedication, passion, cleverness, skill, style, etc.

- Think of an important decision you made in the past or are thinking about for your future (career choice, schooling, friendship, romance, travel, recreation, etc.). Whom do you know (or know of) who has made a similar decision whom you could talk to or learn more about to help you make your own decision?

TEXTURE

- Touch as many surfaces as you can near you. Describe each, using words such as soft, hard, slick, smooth, bumpy, fuzzy, prickly, ridged, or slimy. These examples of texture that we can feel with our fingers are called *tactile textures*.

- Look for and describe a texture that is really just an illusion—that is, you can't feel any actual texture with your fingers (a slick photograph of a furry pet, simulated wood furniture, or smooth gift-wrapping paper covered with images of wispy clouds). These are examples of *illusions of texture*.

Artists use many tools, materials, and processes to make their art. Most artists are influenced by successful art they have seen and admired. Artists can use both tactile texture and the illusion of texture in their work.

Inquiry into Chicana/o Art

OBJECTIVES

- Students identify evidence of technical processes in artworks.

- Students identify and explain how artists are influenced by the art of others.

- Students analyze how artists use texture in their art.

TECHNICAL FEATURES

Display *La Virgen de Sandía* by Margarita "Mita" Cuarón (PLATE 59), *San Antonio* by Félix López (PLATE 57), and *Madre querida* by Marion C. Martínez (PLATE 54).

- Which artwork was carved from aspen and pine and painted with colors made from natural pigments? (*San Antonio.*) Look carefully at the detail to see carving marks and real wheat included in the sculpture. (PLATE 114.)

- Which artwork was made with transparent watercolor? (*La Virgen de Sandía.*) Point to areas that are darker and lighter (less and more transparent) depending on the amount of water mixed with the paint. (PLATE 115.)

- Which artwork was made by cutting and soldering together computer parts? (*Madre querida.*) Point to pieces of circuit board, tiny woven wires, and a CD-ROM disk. (PLATES 116–7.)

ART INFLUENCE

Display *La Virgen de Sandía* by Margarita "Mita" Cuarón, *La vida* by Ana Laura De La Garza (PLATE 61), *Structure* by Susan Elizalde-Holder (PLATE 58), *San Antonio* by Félix López, and *Madre querida* by Marion C. Martínez.

- Even though the works by Marion Martínez and Margarita "Mita" Cuarón are made from very different materials, why do you think the subject matter is so similar? (They both borrow subject matter from earlier traditional paintings and sculptures of the Virgin of Guadalupe.)

- Martínez used contemporary materials to update her Virgin. What detail did Cuarón change? (A slice of watermelon replaces the traditional moon.)

- Which other of the displayed artworks do you think was influenced by traditional religious sculpture? (Félix López's father was a *santero*,

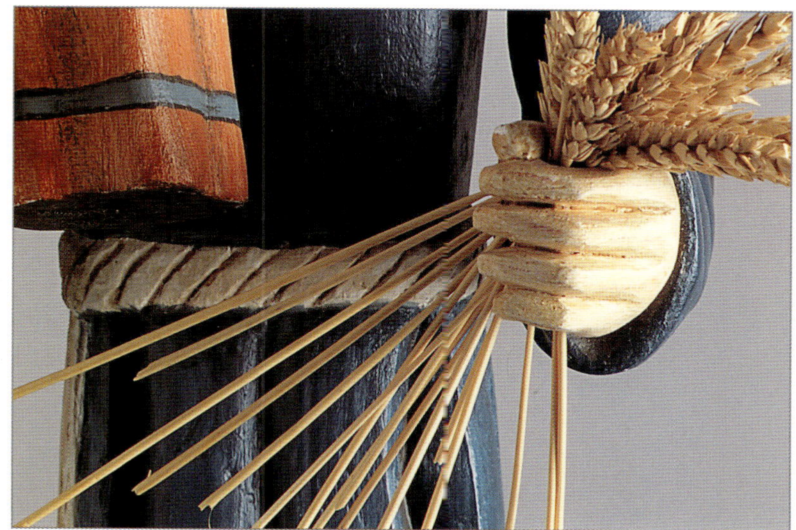

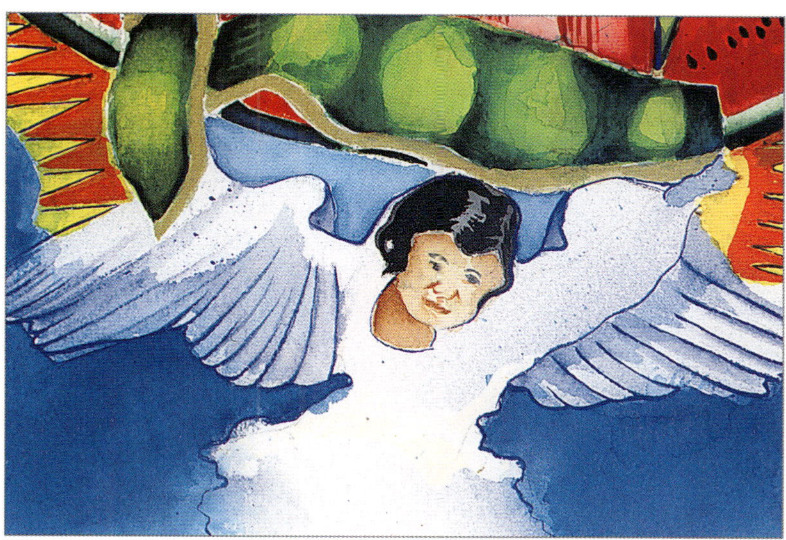

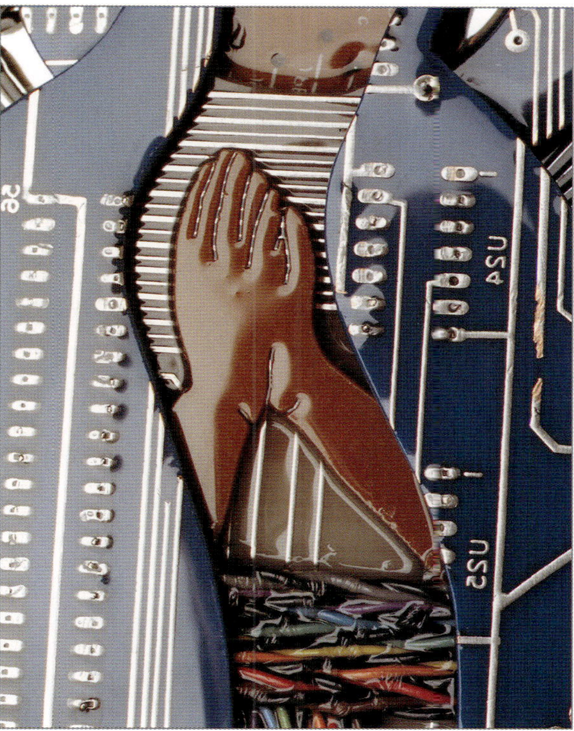

This page:
top, PLATE 114;
middle, PLATE 115;
bottom, PLATE 116.

Next page:
top, PLATE 117;
middle, PLATE 118;
bottom, PLATE 119.

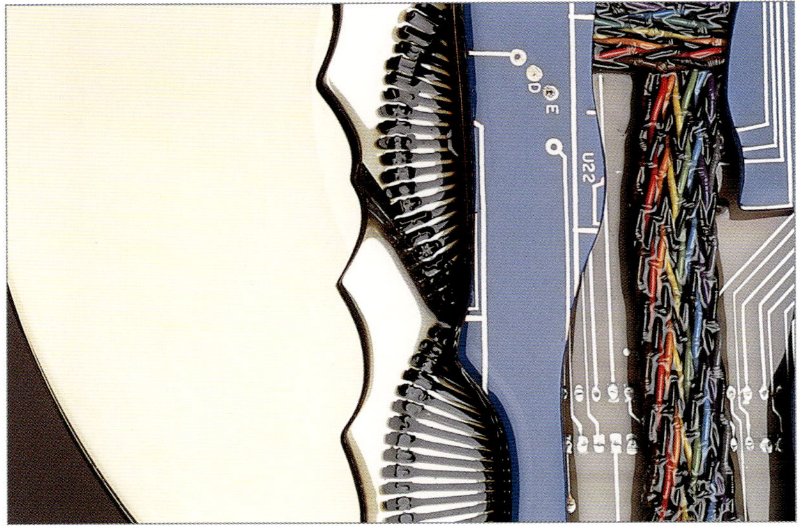

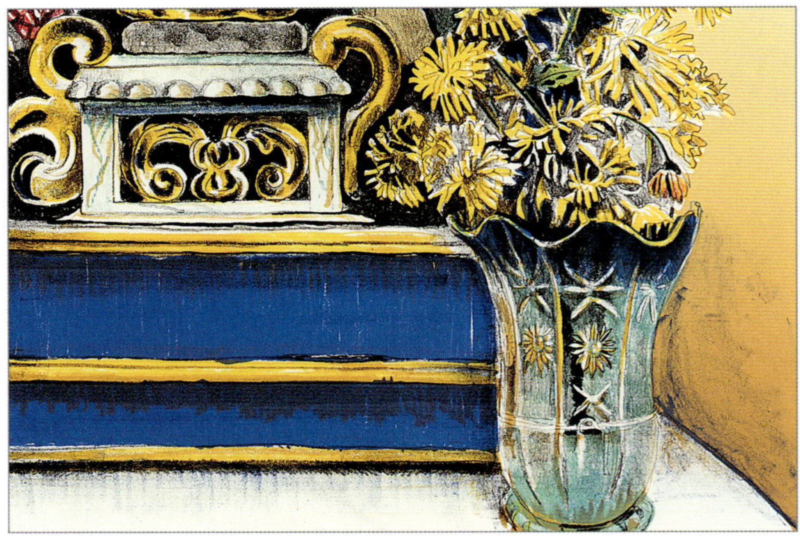

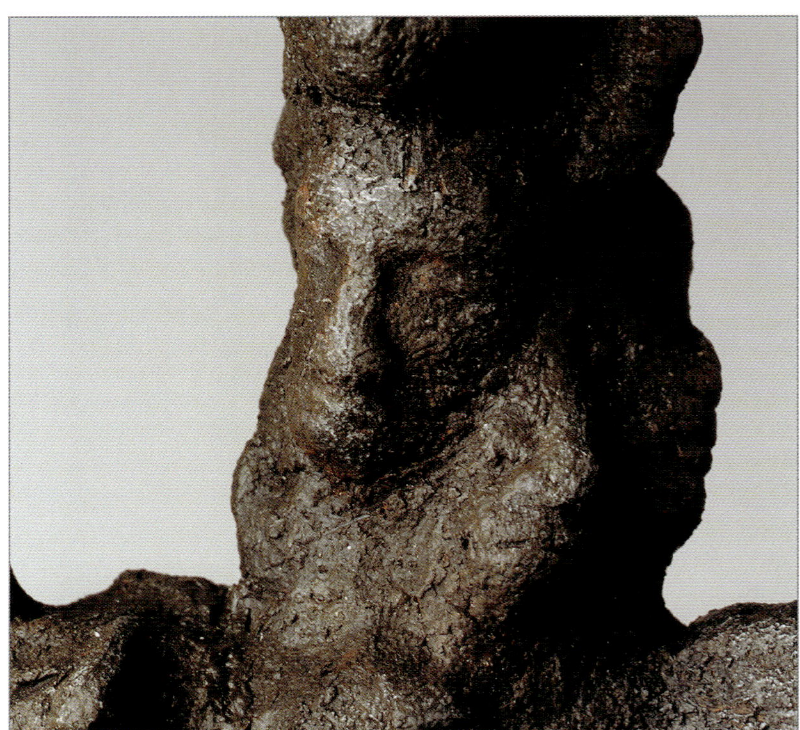

that is, a maker of images of saints. Félix López admires the work of a nineteenth-century *santero* named José Rafael Aragón. López follows the *santero* tradition of collecting wood for his sculptures from forests near his home in Taos, New Mexico, and making his own paints from natural materials, such as indigo, boiled leaves, crushed rocks, and clay.)

- Ana Laura De La Garza was influenced by the successful Chicana artist Carmen Lomas Garza. Several works by Lomas Garza are reproduced in this book. Does De La Garza's work look like paintings by Lomas Garza? Sometimes art influences are not obvious. Ana Laura De La Garza says that she was influenced by Carmen Lomas Garza's use of childhood memories in her art. Perhaps De La Garza's religious childhood upbringing inspired her painting *La vida.* As a child she worked "backstage" on weddings catered by her aunts. Take a look at her *Young Bride* (PLATE 74) to see how she followed Carmen Lomas Garza's influence of drawing on child-hood memories, though in a different style.

Artists can be influenced by art made a very long time ago and far away. Susan Elizalde-Holder was influenced by seeing figures made over 4,000 years ago on the Cycladic Islands (now Greece). What similarities can you find? (anonymous faces, tall, slender forms)

TEXTURE

Display *Virgin in Blue Box* by Elena Climent (PLATE 60), *Structure* by Susan Elizalde-Holder, *San Antonio* by Félix López, and *Madre querida* by Marion C. Martínez.

- Which artwork has smooth surfaces contrasted with woven and intricately ridged surfaces? (*Madre querida*) (PLATES 116–7.)

- Which artwork contrasts the delicate, fragile texture of a dried plant with the slight uneven-ness of carved surfaces? (*San Antonio*)

- Which artwork creates the illusion of the tex-tures of glass, draped fabric, and wood on a flat paper surface that is actually quite smooth? (*Virgin in Blue Box*) (PLATE 118.)

- Which artwork is textured with large conglom-erated bumps (heads) on a base textured with a linear pattern? (*Structure*) (PLATE 119.)

CROSS-CULTURAL ACTIVITIES

The theme of Spirituality as well as questions about technical features and about art influences can guide students' investigations of art made in any culture. You might choose art from cultures identified in your curriculum or from cultures of local interest to replace those suggested here.

OBJECTIVES

- Students investigate and report on spiritual artwork (architecture).

- Students investigate and report on how earlier art has influenced later art within a cultural tradition.

- Students investigate and report on (architectural) tools, materials, and processes.

Group students into teams to investigate religious architecture guided by key questions. Assign each group one of the following types of religious architecture:

- An Islamic mosque
- A Catholic cathedral
- A Shinto temple
- A Hindu temple

Teams should locate reproductions of architecture made for their assigned religion. Each team should seek information on basic beliefs of the assigned religion and about how the buildings they are investigating reinforce beliefs of that religion. They should seek as much information as they can about the tools, materials, and processes used to construct the buildings. They should also locate other religious buildings made in the same or nearby cultures that show the influence of tradition within buildings made for their assigned religion.

Teams should share their findings, illustrating their presentation with buildings made for their assigned religion. They should report on:

1. roles of architecture in reinforcing religious beliefs

2. architectural tools, materials, and processes

3. traditional architectural influences

Studio Activities

If you choose to extend your instruction to include art making, the theme of Spirituality and the key questions you select as your focus can provide the basis for follow-up studio activity.

OBJECTIVES

- Students make artworks that express meaningful feelings or ideas.

- Students explore the potential and limitations of tools, materials, and processes within a particular medium.

- Students seek influences from other artworks.

- Students use texture to enhance the meaning and tactile quality of their work.

Select available media appropriate to the skill levels of your students. For example, you might choose tagboard construction, clay slab construction, or modification of purchased or found containers. Review the theme and key questions to help students transfer what they have learned to their own art making. For example, a student might make a special box to hold a meaningful personal object or to represent an idea that she or he believes is important. Students should seek art influences by viewing special containers made in diverse cultures in different eras (for example, medieval reliquaries, Native American ceremonial baskets, Northwest Coast carved chests, ancient Egyptian sarcophagi, etc.). Depending on the medium you choose, students can explore a variety of techniques to add texture to their containers (for example, with tagboard containers by gluing, added tagboard, or piercing; for clay slab boxes by carving, scoring, stamping, or clay attachments; for modified containers by piercing or gluing found objects, such as fabrics, lace, feathers, buttons, seeds, etc.).

Student Exhibition

Exhibit the Theme Title, Theme in Life, Theme in Art, and Key Questions with samples of student writing and artwork. You are invited to send samples of student work to hrcartprojects@asu.edu for possible publication on the Latino Art Community Web site, www.latinoartcommunity.org.

Interdisciplinary Transfer Potential

Social studies: comparative religion

Mathematics: measurement

Geography: sources of raw materials

History: traditions

Language arts: reading, oral reports, listening

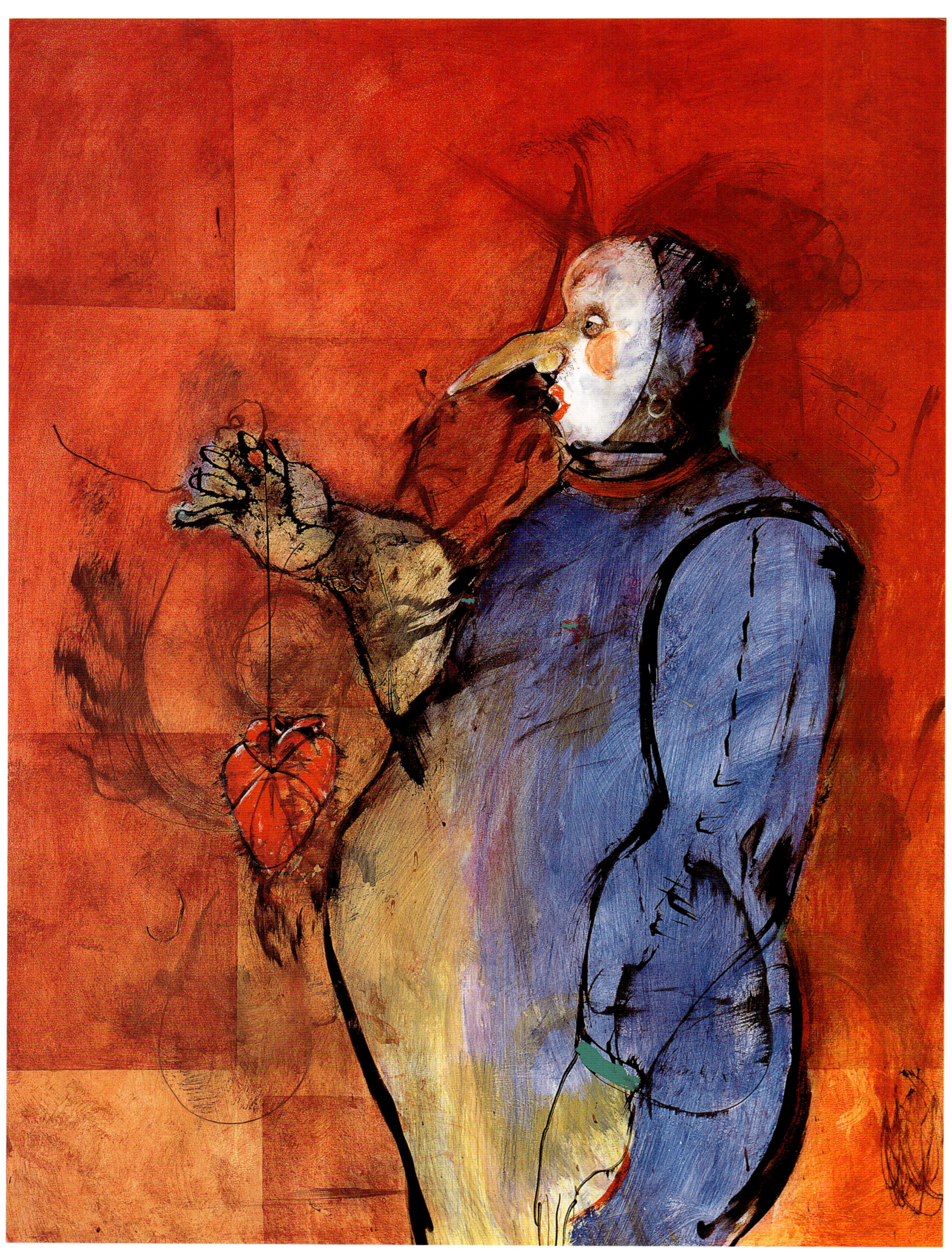

120 Maximiliano Pruneda III, *Recompensa del amor/The Reward of Love*, 1998-9, acrylic on Masonite, 48" x 36"

theme four:
meanings deeply felt or widely known

Theme in Life: We all seek meaning in our lives.

Theme in Art: Art can express both shared and individual meanings.

Introduction to the Theme

"Meaning" is a word we use to describe how we understand. From the time we are babies, we all try to make sense of the world we live in. As we grow, we remember experiences and find relationships among them. Because we live with others in a culture, we have shared meanings about certain events, activities, and experiences, such as holiday celebrations, religious observations, and family traditions. Sometimes members of a group or culture share symbols or other activities that carry special meaning to them but that others may not easily understand, such as a club emblem or handshake. Something meaningful to one person—a grandmother's quilt, a family's invented game, or a special song—may be meaningless to someone else. We need personal or cultural context to see the meaning in a discarded photo album or handmade toy. As unique human beings, we also develop individual meanings that are based on our experiences and the way we think about them. Art is one way to express meanings, whether they are shared or individual.

Key Questions

ARTIST'S INTENTIONS

Why did the artist want the artwork to look the way it does?

CULTURAL UNDERSTANDING

How is the artwork understood within the culture in which it was made?

VISUAL FEATURE

How did the artist use shape in the artwork? (Note: When three-dimensional, such as in sculpture, shape becomes form.)

THEMATIC ACTIVITIES

Introduce students to the Theme Title, the Theme in Life, and the Theme in Art. Ask students to read the Introduction to the Theme to help orient them to the general topic they will be studying. Read and explain that they will be using these questions to guide their investigation into the theme of Meanings Deeply Felt or Widely Known.

Students' Experience with the Theme

OBJECTIVES

- Students identify shared and personal meanings in their lives.

Use discussion starters such as the following to help students identify how the theme of Meanings Deeply Felt or Widely Known relates to their own lives:

- Think about your school culture. What ways of talking or dressing, gestures, and activities do you share with your classmates that others outside your school may not understand?

- Name some events in your life that are important to you, such as family reunions, religious observances, or school ceremonies. What other people participate in these events with you? Those who have similar experiences develop shared meanings about events. Others do not.

- Because every person is unique in some way, everyone has private or individual meanings about things as well. In a journal, make a list of things that have special meaning to you.

Artists express meanings in their art. The meanings may be broadly understood or deeply personal.

Student Discussion of the Theme in Chicana/o Art

OBJECTIVES

- Students interpret artworks as expressions of meanings that may be widely shared or individual.

In random order display *Requiem* by David Anthony García (PLATE 70), *In Memory of a Rabbit* by David Rosales (PLATE 69), *El Chuy* by Luis Guerrero (PLATE 82), *Con cariño, Lydia Mendoza* by Ester Hernández (PLATE 81), *Mariachi LP* by Frank Ybarra (PLATE 83), *Vigil* by Connie Arismendi (PLATE 72), *Héchale* (see note on the spelling of this title in the commentary on this work) by Eduardo Oropeza (PLATE 79), and *Young Bride* by Ana Laura De La Garza (PLATE 74). Begin the activity by asking:

- What are these artworks about? (Some are about music. Others, which may be more difficult to interpret, have personal meanings.)

Remind students that meanings in art can be broadly understood or individual. Post two thematic titles, "Widely Known Meanings" and "Deeply Personal Meanings," and ask students to vote which artworks go with which theme. Have students support their decisions and debate any split votes. As a possible extension, use the Internet or talk with people who know more about Chicana/o culture to investigate the subject matter and meanings in any of the artworks used for this activity.

Additional Inquiry Activities

The Introduction outlines an array of questions from which you might select specific directions to extend students' inquiry. Questions about the art maker's intention, about cultural understanding, and about shape are offered here as examples. Your curriculum may lead you to adapt or replace one or more of these questions.

Inquiry into Students' Experience

OBJECTIVES

- Students give examples of intentions and how they can be expressed.
- Students identify cultural understandings of events and activities.
- Students identify shapes in the world around them.

STUDENTS' (ARTIST'S) INTENTIONS

- What is an intention? (a goal or an aim)
- What do you intend to do when you finish your schooling? For example, you might intend to travel, find a job, get more education, join the military, or start a family.
- In addition to big goals for our lives, we have many small day-to-day intentions. What do you intend to do when you get home from school— or next weekend? Do you intend to play baseball or soccer with friends, do your homework, get a snack, watch TV with your family, listen to some music, or do something else?
- Give other examples of intentions that you or someone else might have; for instance, losing weight, improving grades, or being a better friend.
- What are some ways you can let others know your intentions?
- List nonverbal ways that people can show their intentions, such as through their actions.
- Have you ever failed to carry through on an intention? What kept you from succeeding?
- If others have ever misunderstood your intentions, consider sharing examples with the class.

CULTURAL UNDERSTANDING

- Give examples of events or activities that you and your family, classmates, sports team, or religious group share.
- What do these mean to your group or culture?
- Do you think that others outside the group or culture understand these events and activities as you do? Why or why not? Consider asking someone if you're not sure.
- Consider sharing your experience if you've ever had difficulty understanding what another group or culture is doing.

SHAPE

- What geometric shapes, such as circles and squares, can you name?
- Look around the classroom and identify as many geometric shapes as you can.
- Are all the shapes in the room geometric, or are there other kinds of shapes as well?
- Mathematicians have labeled some simple geometric shapes, but there are many other

shapes that don't have names. Point out other interesting shapes in the classroom.

- What do we call shapes that are not geometric? (natural or organic shapes)

- Find or draw a shape that is both geometric and organic.

Artists have intentions when making art, and their intentions help them make decisions about how the artwork looks. Because they share experiences and meanings, people from an artist's culture may have special understandings about the work of art. Most artists use shape or form in their artwork.

Inquiry into Chicana/o Art

OBJECTIVES

- Students identify artists' intentions.

- Students investigate how people understand art from within their culture.

- Students analyze how artists use shapes in their work.

ARTISTS' INTENTIONS

Explain that sometimes artists reveal more than they consciously intend in their artwork. At other times artists may intend to do something but not fully succeed. Thus, artists' intentions are not necessarily the same as what their artworks do or express. Still, what artists actually say about what they are trying to do can be useful in helping us understand their work.

Display *Self-Portrait* by Barbara Carrasco (PLATE 6) and *Southwest Pietà* by Luis Jiménez (PLATE 99). Ask students to look carefully at the subject matter and guess what stories the artists were intending to tell. Then ask:

- Which artwork tells the ancient story of Ixtaccihuatl (popularly known as "Ixta") and Popocatepetl ("Popo") who were turned into mountains by the gods?

- Which artwork refers to the artist's battle with the Los Angeles Redevelopment Agency over censorship of the artist's mural for the 1984 Olympics? (The mural included unfavorable scenes, such as the internment of Japanese Americans during World War II. In her self-portrait, Carrasco—or her work—faces obliteration by a paint roller approaching from the upper left. The large paintbrush in the image

reads "Siqueiros No. 1" in reference to the Los Angeles murals by Mexican artist David Alfaro Siqueiros that were painted over 50 years earlier.)

Assign students to groups to find additional information about the artists and artworks. As necessary, pose questions to encourage inquiry, such as "What Mexican, Native American, and U.S. symbols can you find in *Southwest Pietà*, and what do they mean?" or "What does the grid in the background of the Carrasco *Self-Portrait* mean, and why do you suppose the artist showed herself dressed as an athlete?" Have students share their findings before reading the following statements made by the artists about their intentions:

Luis Jiménez said that the image of Popo and Ixta in his *Southwest Pietà* "embodies a personal sense of loss over what actually happened when European culture collided with Native American culture" (conversation with Mary Erickson, August 19, 1997).

Barbara Carrasco said that "*Self-Portrait* is a reflection on my experience being censored as I created the mural *L.A. History: A Mexican Perspective* in 1982. Most of my work to that point had been public political statements; this serigraph [print] was a very personal statement" (conversation with Melanie Magisos, November 17, 2003).

- How do the artists' stated intentions help you understand more about their artworks?

CULTURAL UNDERSTANDING

Divide the class into two groups and distribute the following artworks:

La lotería: *El Santo* by Xavier Garza (PLATE 85), *The King of Things/El rey de las cosas* by Artemio Rodríguez (PLATE 77), *El Rocket* by Luis Valderas (PLATE 78).

La música: *El Chuy* by Luis Guerrero, *Con cariño, Lydia Mendoza* by Ester Hernández, *La serenata* by George Yepes (PLATE 80), *Mariachi LP* by Frank Ybarra.

Ask each group to begin by briefly looking at its set of artworks. Ask students what they think the artworks are about and have them record their initial responses to the question. Then ask students to examine their set of images and identify subject matter as fully as possible. Encourage their inquiry, as necessary, by asking questions such as "Who is Lydia Mendoza?" Depending on students' backgrounds and experiences, you may need to tell them that:

- *La lotería*, in this case, is not like the U.S. lottery. Rather, it is a picture game much like bingo.
- The skeletons in *Héchale* refer to *el Día de los Muertos,* the Mexican Day of the Dead. (For another example, see *Panchito y Tía Tita* by Antonio Rael [PLATE 19].)

Ask students to determine the significance or importance of their identified subject matter within Chicana/o culture. If possible, consult with Chicana/o students or others about the meanings of the works of art. You will find additional information about Chicana/o understanding of these works in the first part of this book.

After students have presented their findings, continue with a full-class discussion about the inquiry activity:

- Were there Chicana/o students in the groups? If so, how, if at all, did their knowledge and understanding of the artworks differ from those of the other students?
- Did either group consult with other appropriate individuals during the study? If so, what happened—or what might have happened if they had done so?
- What did you learn about Chicana/o art and culture from this activity?

SHAPE

Display *Requiem* by David Anthony García, *The King of Things/El rey de las cosas* by Artemio Rodríguez, *In Memory of a Rabbit* by David Rosales, and *Jugo de naranja* by Dolores Guerrero (PLATE 71).

- Are the shapes in these artworks mostly organic or geometric?
- What geometric shapes do you see?
- Why do you suppose the artists used more organic than geometric shapes? (Look at the subject matter.)

CROSS-CULTURAL ACTIVITIES

The theme of Meanings Deeply Felt or Widely Known as well as questions about the artists' intentions and about cultural understanding can guide students' investigation of art made in any culture. Divide the class into groups to locate reproductions of artworks from assigned cultures and to investigate that culture guided by each key question.

OBJECTIVES

- Students identify meanings in artworks.
- Students explain why artists make art (the artists' intentions).
- Students describe how people understand art from their own culture in ways different from the way others see it.

Assign groups to the following cultures:

- An African culture (for example, Yoruba or Dogon)
- A Native American culture (such as Cheyenne or Nez Perce)
- A pre-Conquest culture in Latin America (for instance, Mayan or Aztec)
- An Asian culture (such as Tibetan or Laotian)

Each group should look for explanations of the specific images and symbols used in art made in their assigned culture. They should find as much information as possible about the intentions of the artists in that culture. If they are unable to find statements made by artists about their work, students can gather information about the roles of art in their assigned cultures as a basis for speculating about artists' intentions. Finally, students should use what they learn about their assigned cultures as a way to more fully understand their art.

Groups should share their findings, illustrating their presentations with artworks from their assigned cultures. They should report on:

1. the meanings in the artwork
2. the artists' intentions
3. how people from that same culture understand the works

STUDIO ACTIVITIES

If you choose to extend your instruction to include art making, the theme of Meanings Deeply Felt and Widely Known and the inquiry questions you selected as your focus can provide the basis for a follow-up studio activity.

OBJECTIVES

- Students articulate and review their intentions throughout the art making process.

- Students make artworks that contain meanings that are broadly shared or personal.

- Students use geometric or organic shapes in their artworks.

- Students speculate as to how different cultural groups would understand their artworks.

Select media appropriate to the skill levels of your students. Review the theme and key questions to help students transfer what they have learned to their own art making. For example, ask students to think about something that is important to them that they could express through a symbol. Before beginning the studio activity, have them express their ideas, specify whether they have shared or personal meanings, and record their intentions for art making. Direct students to use geometric or organic shapes to make symbols, and encourage them to reflect on their original intentions as they work, making appropriate modifications as necessary. Have students decorate personal items, such as T-shirts or notebook covers, with their symbols. Ask students to share their symbols and their art making intentions and to speculate as to how different cultural groups would understand them.

Student Exhibition

Exhibit the Theme Title, Theme in Life, Theme in Art, and Key Questions with samples of student writing and artwork. You are invited to send samples of student work to hrcartprojects@asu.edu for possible publication on the Latino Art Community Web site, www.latinoartcommunity.org.

Interdisciplinary Transfer Potential:

Mathematics: geometric shapes

Music: Mexican and Chicana/o music, instruments, and musicians

Social studies: cultural understanding

Language arts: journal writing, oral reports, interviewing, reading, listening

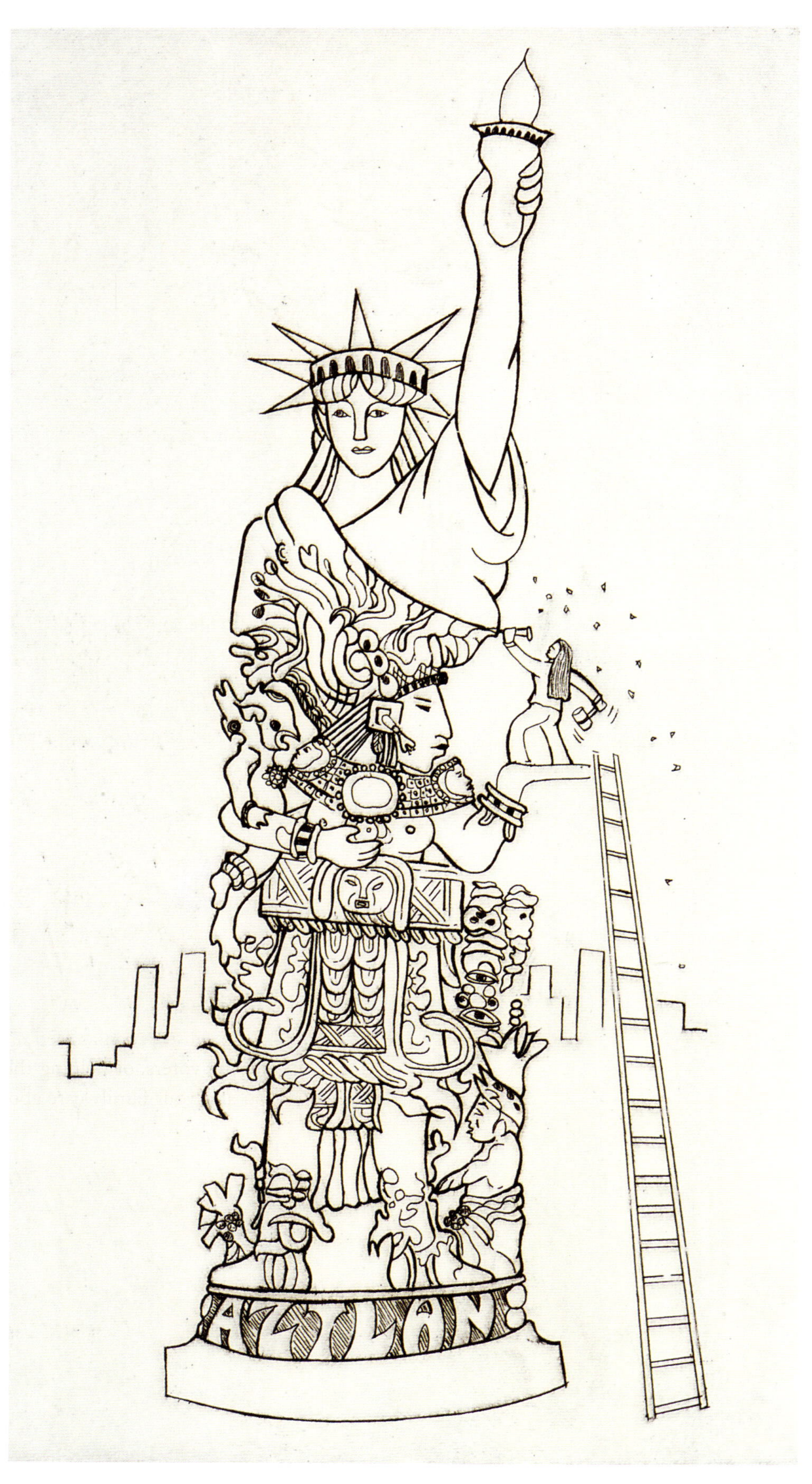

121 Ester Hernández, *Libertad* (Liberty), 1987, etching, 15" x 8"

theme five:
cultural icons

Theme in Life: We all respond to special people, causes, and the symbols that represent them.

Theme in Art: Art can call people together by representing important people, causes, and symbols.

Introduction to the Theme

Living in a family, in a neighborhood, and in a community puts us in contact with other people. Living together, we come to share common experiences and concerns. People may come together as a group to respond to a concern, and some people may come to be viewed as leaders because of their involvement. Groups frequently use symbols to represent themselves, their identity, or their concerns. Icons can also represent a group or a cause. An icon is an image or a likeness, and we sometimes understand the word to mean the best of something. Cultural icons represent heroes, aspirations, and achievements of a group.

Key Questions

ARTIST'S LIFE

What is the background and life experience of the artist?

FUNCTION

What does the artwork do?

VISUAL FEATURE

How did the artist use light and dark (value) in the artwork?

THEMATIC ACTIVITIES

Introduce students to the Theme Title, the Theme in Life, and the Theme in Art. Post and ask them to read the Introduction to the Theme to help orient them to the general idea they will be studying. Read and explain that they will be using these questions to guide their investigation into the theme of Cultural Icons in art.

Students' Experience with the Theme

OBJECTIVES

- Students identify heroes, causes, and symbols important to their families and community.

Use discussion starters such as the following to help students identify how the theme of Cultural Icons relates to their lives:

- Who are the role models or heroes that you and your family look up to?

- What have these people done, or what do they represent?

- What needs exist within your community? Who are the leaders and community members who have tried to address these problems?

- Which members of your community or culture would you like others to know about or remember? Why?

- What causes, such as feeding the hungry, registering voters, or helping the environment, do you and your family care about?

- What are symbols, and why do we use them?

- What symbols commonly represent ideas that are important to you and your family? Think about flags that represent national origin, symbols that identify religious beliefs, or graphics that identify a political campaign.

- What other symbols, such as team, university, or business logos, can you recognize in your school or community?

Sometimes artists use symbols or other imagery to represent important people and causes in their art.

Student Discussion of the Theme in Chicana/o Art

OBJECTIVES

- Students interpret artworks as expressions of important people, causes, and symbols.

Display *Frida's Messengers* by Alfredo Arreguín (PLATE 88), *Pancho Villa and the Cisco Kid* by Sam Zaragosa Coronado (PLATE 86), *Homenaje a César Chávez* by Ester Hernández (PLATE 89), *Posada y su hijo* by Artemio Rodríguez (PLATE 3), and *Sandra Cisneros* by César A. Martínez (PLATE 87). Assign each artwork to a group of students, asking them to identify the individuals depicted and their accomplishments or causes. (Make sure the group assigned the Ester Hernández artwork addresses the eagle symbol behind César Chávez.) After groups share their findings, ask:

- Why do you think the artists chose to feature these individuals in their artwork?

- As an extension, students might ask members of the Chicana/o community about these cultural icons.

ADDITIONAL INQUIRY ACTIVITIES

The Introduction outlines an array of questions from which you might select specific directions to extend students' inquiry. Questions about artists' lives, about function, and about light and dark (value) are offered here as examples. Your curriculum may lead you to adapt or replace one or more of these questions.

Inquiry into Students' Experience

OBJECTIVES

- Students investigate and report on the lives of people in their families or community.

- Students analyze the functions of familiar objects.

- Students identify light and dark (value) in the world around them.

ARTISTS' (AND OTHERS') LIVES

- Collect biographical information about friends, family members, or people in your community.

- Find out where they were born and whether they have lived anywhere else. Have they traveled to other parts of the country or world?

- Where have they gone to school? What work do the adults do?

- What interests do they have, and what do they like to do in their free time?

- What are some activities or events that are important to them? What causes are they interested in?

- Who are their heroes or role models?

- What big decisions have they made?

- What events have changed their lives?

- What hopes do they have for the future?

FUNCTION

- Make a list of objects in your home and school that you use regularly.

- What does each object do for you?

- Does your family have some objects, such as dishes, that you use every day and other similar objects that are saved for special occasions? How are the objects the same, and how are they different? What makes the special-occasion objects special?

- Give examples of how objects can be used for something other than their intended function, such as using a cup as a pencil holder or a milk crate as a stool. Why do we sometimes use objects for other purposes?

- What are some objects that have multiple functions, such as a cellular phone with a built-in camera or a stroller that converts to a car seat? Why do people create such objects?

LIGHT AND DARK (VALUE)

If possible, provide black-and-white photographs or photographic reproductions from books or newspapers for this activity.

- Identify the darkest and lightest areas in black-and-white photos. Where are the in-between areas? (If necessary, squint to see the different areas of value more easily.)

- Do the photographs have mostly dark areas, mostly light areas, or a combination of values (lights, mediums, and darks)?

- Now look for values—lights, mediums, and darks—in colors. (Paint chips from a hardware store are a good tool for this exercise.)

- Identify light, dark, and medium values in the classroom. Look at clothing, furnishings, and displays.

The backgrounds and life experiences of artists influence the artwork they make. Art can serve different functions, including honoring heroes and gathering people together. Artists use lights, darks, and mediums (values) in their work.

Inquiry into Chicana/o Art

OBJECTIVES

- Students investigate the lives of artists.

- Students identify the functions of works of art.

- Students analyze how artists use light and dark (value) in their art.

ARTISTS' LIVES

Display *Pancho Villa and the Cisco Kid* and *Guerrillera II* by Sam Zaragosa Coronado (PLATES 86 and 95), *Homenaje a César Chávez* and *Libertad* by Ester Hernández (PLATES 89 and 121), and *Southwest Pietà* and *Ball Rattlesnake* by Luis Jiménez (PLATES 99 and 100). Divide students into three groups and have each group investigate one of the artists. Ask them to prepare the following to share with the class:

- basic biographical information

- education or art training

- significant life experiences

- influences

- the relationship between the subject matter and the artist's life

FUNCTION

Engage students in a discussion and make a list of possible functions of works of art, such as providing decoration, teaching values, displaying cultural pride, recording history, or advancing political agendas. Display *Guerrillera II* by Sam Zaragosa Coronado, *Libertad* by Ester Hernández, and *One Little Indian Versus the Corporate Trolls* by Laura Molina (PLATE 91). As a class or in smaller groups, look at the title of each artwork, identify the subject matter, and try to determine its message.

- Which artwork "reconstructs" the U.S. Statue of Liberty? What do you think the artist is trying to say by changing its foundation?

- Which artwork challenges a U.S. entertainment icon? What is the significance of the dark-haired woman standing outside the gate with barbed wire around her neck?

- Which artwork shows a guerrilla fighter? How does the artist make sure we know he is referring to women as fighters?

Return to the list of functions that artworks can serve. Ask students what primary functions these artworks serve. Add functions to the list as necessary.

LIGHT AND DARK

Display *Libertad* by Ester Hernández, *Ricardo Flores Magón* by Carlos Cortez (PLATE 4), *Guerrillera II* by Sam Zaragosa Coronado, *One Little Indian Versus the Corporate Trolls* by Laura Molina, and *La Virgen de Guadaliberty* by Nephtalí de León (PLATE 113). Ask students to squint at the artworks to find the areas of lightness and darkness.

- Which two artworks have only light and dark areas? (*Libertad* and *Ricardo Flores Magón*)

- Which artworks have light, medium, and dark areas? (*Guerrillera II, One Little Indian Versus the Corporate Trolls, La Virgen de Guadaliberty.*) Find the lightest and darkest areas in each.

CROSS-CULTURAL ACTIVITIES

The theme of Cultural Icons as well as questions about the artists' lives and about function can guide students' investigation of art made in any culture. You might choose art from cultures identified in your curriculum or from cultures of local interest to replace those suggested here.

OBJECTIVES

- Students investigate and report on symbols in artwork.

- Students identify artists in another culture and investigate and report on their lives.

- Students investigate and report on the functions of art in a culture.

Group students into teams to locate reproductions of artworks from an assigned culture and to investigate that culture, guided by each key question. Assign each group to one of the following cultures:

- An indigenous group in the Americas (for instance, Zapotec, Inuit, Huichol, or Inca peoples)

- A cultural group in Africa (such as the Baule or Asante)

- A U.S. cultural group still strongly identified with its place of origin (for example, the Chinese population in San Francisco or Cubans in south Florida)

Teams should locate reproductions—or locally available examples—of artworks made in their assigned cultures. Each team should identify symbols used in the artwork and seek as much information as possible on the meaning and function of artwork within the culture. Also direct students to investigate how people become artists, whether artists work individually or in groups, and if individual artists are recognized by name.

Teams should share their findings, illustrating their presentation with artworks from their assigned culture. They should report on:

1. what symbols the artists use and what they mean

2. the lives and work of artists

3. the intended use of the artwork within the culture

STUDIO ACTIVITIES

If you choose to extend your instruction to include art making, the theme of Cultural Icons and the inquiry questions you selected as your focus can provide the basis for follow-up studio activity.

- Students make artworks that encourage others to take action.

- Students make artworks that convey messages that are meaningful to them.

- Students use symbols to reinforce the message of their work.

- Students use light and dark (value) in their artwork.

Select available media appropriate to the skill levels of your students. Review the theme and key questions to help students transfer what they have learned to their own art making. For example, students might make persuasive posters that encourage others to do something for the good of the community, such as vote on a school bond, pick up litter at a park, donate books to the library, participate in a food drive, or support a local event. Students should use symbols, words, and areas of light and dark to help convey their messages.

Student Exhibition

Exhibit the Theme Title, Theme in Life, Theme in Art, and Key Questions with samples of student writing and artwork. You are invited to send samples of student work to hrcartprojects@asu.edu for possible publication on the Latino Art Community Web site, www.latinoartcommunity.org.

Interdisciplinary Transfer Potential:

Social studies: political action, social systems

History: Mexican history

Language arts: journal writing, interviewing, oral reports, reading, listening, persuasion, biography

theme six:
beyond conventional imagery

heme in Life: Sometimes people do not do what we expect them to.

Theme in Art: Artists surprise us when they do the unexpected.

Introduction to the Theme

Conventions are sets of rules or customs that help people know what to do or how to behave. Greeting others is a good example. Depending on the culture, people may shake hands when they meet— or nod, kiss, bow, or salute. Cultures also have different conventions about eating. Some use chopsticks or forks, and others eat with their hands. Driving on the right side of the road is a convention that many countries follow, although England and some other countries have the convention of driving on the left. There are also conventions about reading. English and European languages, such as French and Spanish, are read from left to right; Arabic is read from right to left; and Japanese and Chinese are read from top to bottom. People within a culture expect others to follow their conventions, and they can be surprised or upset when that does not happen.

Art has conventions as well, and there are different art cultures called artworlds that have their own rules or conventions. For example, artists in different places and times have painted on different surfaces. In the nineteenth century (1800s), European painters worked on canvas while Chinese artists painted on silk. In other times and places, artists have painted on board, metal, glass, paper, or animal hide. Almost all artists learn the conventions of their artworld as part of their training, but some choose not to follow them. This may surprise others just as much as breaking conventions about eating with the right hand when visiting some African cultures or about removing shoes before entering a home in Japan.

Key Questions

ARTWORLD CONTEXT

What art traditions, movements, expectations, and training surround the artist?

STYLE

How does one artwork look like other artworks?

VISUAL FEATURE

How did the artists use space in the artworks? (Note: While artists can create the appearance of space in two-dimensional works such as paintings and drawings, they make use of actual space in three-dimensional sculptures.)

THEMATIC ACTIVITIES

Introduce students to the Theme Title, the Theme in Life, and the Theme in Art. Read or post the Introduction to the Theme to help orient students to the general topic they will be studying. Read and explain that they will be using key questions to guide their investigation into the theme of Beyond Conventional Imagery in art.

Students' Experience with the Theme

OBJECTIVES

- Students identify expectations and tell how they feel when the unexpected happens.

Use discussion starters such as the following to help students identify how the theme of Beyond Conventional Imagery relates to their own lives:

- Schools have many conventions about student behavior, from turning in homework to getting hall passes. Name some other school conventions.

- What happens when students do not follow conventions?

■ Students have expectations about what happens at school, as well. For example, students might expect to take tests, to get no homework before a school break, or to earn good grades if they work hard. List other expectations students have at school.

■ What are some expectations people outside of school might have? For instance, your family might expect your grandmother to make a favorite dish when you visit or your neighbor might expect her baby to start walking around his first birthday.

■ Things do not always turn out the way you expect, do they? Share examples of things that did not go as expected.

■ How do you feel when the unexpected happens?

Sometimes artists do the unexpected in their art.

Student Discussion of the Theme in Chicana/o Art

OBJECTIVES

■ Students differentiate between expected and unexpected subject matter.

Display *Atardecer/Dusk* by Silvia Capistrán (PLATE 106), *Chemism* by Mónica Aíssa Martínez (PLATE 110), and *Failing to Communicate* by Jerry De La Cruz (PLATE 107) along with *Héchale* by Eduardo Oropeza (PLATE 79), *First Aztec on the Moon* by Santiago Pérez (PLATE 48), and *La Virgen de Sandía* by Margarita "Mita" Cuarón (PLATE 59). Tell the students that all the artworks were made by Chicana/o artists. Lead a group discussion comparing and contrasting the works of art:

■ Do all the artworks seem to be alike, or are there differences?

■ Which works of art, if any, seem to go together?

■ Some people expect art to contain subject matter from an artist's culture. Point to subject matter that seems to relate to Chicana/o culture. (Depending on students' prior knowledge, they may need to know that the skeletons in *Héchale* refer to the Mexican Day of the Dead, that the imagery in *First Aztec on the Moon* refers to the ancient Aztecs who lived in the area that is now Mexico, and that *La Virgen de Sandía* is based on the much beloved Virgin of Guadalupe.)

After the discussion, assign groups of students to find the cultures (nationalities) and life dates of the following artists as well as reproductions of the designated artworks: *Impression, Sunrise* by Claude Monet, *Carnival of Harlequin* by Joan Miró, and *President Elect* (or *F-111*) by James Rosenquist. Ask the groups to present information about their artists, and then display the reproductions along with all of those used in the earlier activity. Ask students to group the reproductions together based on appearance.

■ Which artworks do *Atardecer/Dusk*, *Chemism*, and *Failing to Communicate* more closely resemble? Why?

■ Are Monet, Miró, and Rosenquist Chicano artists?

■ Why do you think the artworks by Capistrán, Martínez, and De La Cruz resemble those of Monet, Miró, and Rosenquist, respectively? Do you suppose the Chicana/o artists learned about the others in school or by looking at their art?

■ Does Chicana/o art have to include subject matter associated with Chicana/o culture?

■ How, then, would you define a Chicana/o artist or work of art?

ADDITIONAL INQUIRY ACTIVITIES

The Introduction outlines an array of questions from which you might select specific directions to extend students' inquiry. Questions about the art-world context, style, and space are offered here as examples. Your curriculum may lead you to adapt or replace one or more of these questions.

Inquiry into Students' Experience

OBJECTIVES

■ Students give examples of conventions they know or rules for particular kinds of activities.

■ Students discuss style in the world around them.

■ Students differentiate between actual space in three dimensions and the appearance of space in two-dimensional images.

- List some conventions you know, such as covering your mouth when you yawn or paying for your food before you eat in a fast-food restaurant.

- What activities do you know that have conventions, procedures, rules, or expectations about performance? Give examples, such as team sports, different types of dance, or musical performance. List some of the rules or expectations for one or more of the examples.

- What happens when you do not follow conventions or procedures? What kinds of results do you get, and how do others respond?

STYLE

- What does "style" mean?

- Besides clothes and hair, what kinds of things have styles?

- Describe the differences between two styles of music, clothing, or dance.

- What are some of the current styles in your neighborhood or school?

- What can somebody's style tell you?

- Do you think older members of your family had the same styles when they were your age? Ask them what clothes they preferred and how they wore their hair when they were younger. Look at old photos of them if you can. How do they look wearing different styles than you are used to?

- How do people respond when others do not follow current styles?

SPACE

- Imagine being outdoors looking at the space in front of you. Then imagine seeing a photograph or drawing of the same place. How are the place and the image of it different? Which has actual space, and which just shows space?

- What is the difference between two- and three-dimensional things? Find examples of each in your classroom.

- There is actual space in your classroom—you can walk *through* it. Look for pictures in your classroom or textbooks that *show* space but are actually two dimensional (flat on the surface).

Artists make use of real space when they make three-dimensional sculptures. Artists making two-dimensional works, such as photographs or paintings, can show space that is not actually there. This is usually easy to see in landscapes or artworks of outdoor scenes. Artists usually work in a style and follow the expectations of an artworld. Space is a visual feature artists can use to organize their artworks.

Inquiry into Chicana/o Art

OBJECTIVES

- Students identify features of the artworld that surrounds Chicana/o artists.

- Students identify style (visual similarities and differences) in art.

- Students identify overlapping used to suggest depth (space) in two-dimensional works.

ARTWORLD CONTEXT

Divide students into groups and assign each group one of the following artists: Mónica Aíssa Martínez, Jerry De La Cruz, Margaret García, and Marcus Zilliox. Ask students to investigate their artist and answer the following questions using printed information downloaded from the Internet or other sources:

- What training did the artist receive?

- What exhibitions and other art activities has the artist participated in?

- How have specialists in the artworld recognized the artist? For example, has the artist received grants or awards, or have critics or other art specialists written about the artist?

STYLE

Explain to students that art style refers to distinctive visual similarities and that multiple works of art from one artist may be done in the same style. Display the following reproductions in random order: *Still in Reverence* and *Reyna's Cantina* by Celina Hinojosa (PLATES 27 and 15); *Cocina jaiteca*, *Sofá So Good*, and *Once Juan Won One* by Larry Yáñez (PLATES 10, 11, and 13); *Nos ponemos como que tenemos calentura, bien sudaditos* by Juan Farias (PLATE 109); *Ancestral Roots* by Tlisza Jaurique (PLATE 103); and *Con Sapos, Nagual Mask* by Zarco Guerrero (PLATE 105).

- What three artworks were made by the same artist? How can you tell?

- What two works of art were made by another artist?

- Were any of the remaining artworks made by the same artists?

- How did you make your decisions?

Style can also refer to a culture or a time period, such as Egyptian, cubist, or impressionist art. If possible, look at art in one or more of these styles. To complete the lesson on style, display an array of reproductions from individual Chicana/o artists.

- Are these works of art done in one or multiple styles?

- Why might artwork made around the same time by artists from the same culture not share the same style?

- What beyond cultural identity may have influenced the artists' styles?

SPACE

Display *Atardercer/Dusk* by Silvia Capistrán, *Failing to Communicate* by Jerry De La Cruz, and *Recompensa del amor* by Maximiliano Pruneda III (PLATE 120).

- In *Failing to Communicate*, what appears to be closest to you?

- Why does it look as if the hand is in front of the person's face? The artist used overlapping, didn't he?

- When an artist uses overlapping (placing one thing in front of another), which object appears to be closer to you?

- Where do you see overlapping in *Recompensa del amor*? Does that look like a shadow behind the person? How does that help suggest space?

- Find the long pink line that goes across *Atardecer/Dusk*. Could that be the horizon line where the sky meets the earth? Find an example of overlapping here too. What is in front of the horizon line?

- When artists show space in their paintings, they can make it look deep (far away) or shallow (close by). Does the space look deeper in *Recompensa del amor* or *Atardecer/Dusk*?

CROSS-CULTURAL ACTIVITIES

The theme of Beyond Conventional Imagery as well as questions about artworld context and style can guide students' investigation of art made in any culture. Divide the class into two groups to locate reproductions of art from the assigned cultures and to learn more about those cultures.

OBJECTIVES

- Students identify where artists from two cultures learned about art and exhibited their work.

- Students group artworks by style.

- Students demonstrate that not all artists in the same culture work similarly.

Divide the students into two groups:

Spanish art: Salvador Dalí, Francisco de Goya, Joan Miró, Pablo Picasso, Diego Velásquez

Mexican art: Frida Kahlo, José Clemente Orozco, Diego Rivera, David Alfaro Siqueiros, Rufino Tamayo

Instruct students to find out where the artists in their assigned group were trained and who collected or exhibited their works. Direct the students to retrieve reproductions for each of their artists. At least three works for each artist should be typical of that artist's style. Challenge students also to find less typical examples that might indicate that the artist was trying something new or responding to other influences.

Have teams take turns presenting two reproductions, asking the other team to indicate whether or not the two works are done in the same style. Look at all the Mexican and Spanish examples, and conclude with a group discussion:

- Does an artist always work in the same style? What factors, such as changing times, important events, or exposure to new ideas, might influence an artist's individual style?

- Did you use subject matter to determine whether an artwork was Spanish or Mexican? If so, were you always right? And how did you decide when there were no clues in the subject matter?

- Is there one Mexican or Spanish style of art? Why do you think that is?

- What does that tell you about Chicana/o art? Are Chicana/o artists likely to work in only one style?

Groups should share their findings, illustrating their presentations with artworks from their assigned cultures. They should report on:

1. the artworld context in which the works were made

2. the styles of the works

3. any unconventional or surprising artworks

STUDIO ACTIVITIES

If you choose to extend your instruction to include art making, the theme of Beyond Conventional Imagery and the key questions you selected as your focus can provide the basis for follow-up studio activity.

OBJECTIVES

- Students work in (or deliberately break) a particular style.

- Students identify expectations that their artworks met (or did not meet).

- Students use overlapping to help suggest space in a two-dimensional project.

- Students participate in a (classroom) artworld to curate, present, and critique an exhibition.

Select media appropriate to the skill levels of your students. Review the theme and key questions to help students transfer what they have learned to their own art making. For example, you might post expectations for style in their imaginary artworld, such as muted colors, smooth lines, and repeated shapes. Ask most of the students to make collages according to the class style that also use overlapping to suggest space. Assign a few students to break at least one of the stylistic rules as they complete their studio activity. They could do that, for instance, by using bright colors or tearing edges to create jagged lines.

Have students research the following artworld roles: artist, curator, exhibition designer, museum educator, and critic. Direct them to take turns playing roles or to play them in sequence as they make art; select artworks for an exhibition; mount the artworks on a large craft-paper "wall"; prepare labels and write information about the art; and then write critical responses to the exhibition, including descriptions of the artworks and style.

Student Exhibition

Exhibit the Theme Title, Theme in Life, Theme in Art, and Key Questions with samples of student writing and artwork. You are invited to send samples of student work to hrcartprojects@asu.edu for possible publication on the Latino Art Community Web site, www.latinoartcommunity.org.

Interdisciplinary Transfer Potential

Social studies: cultural differences, social systems, conventions, and behavior

History: comparative history

Geography: location of countries

Language arts: journal writing, oral reports, reading, interviewing, listening

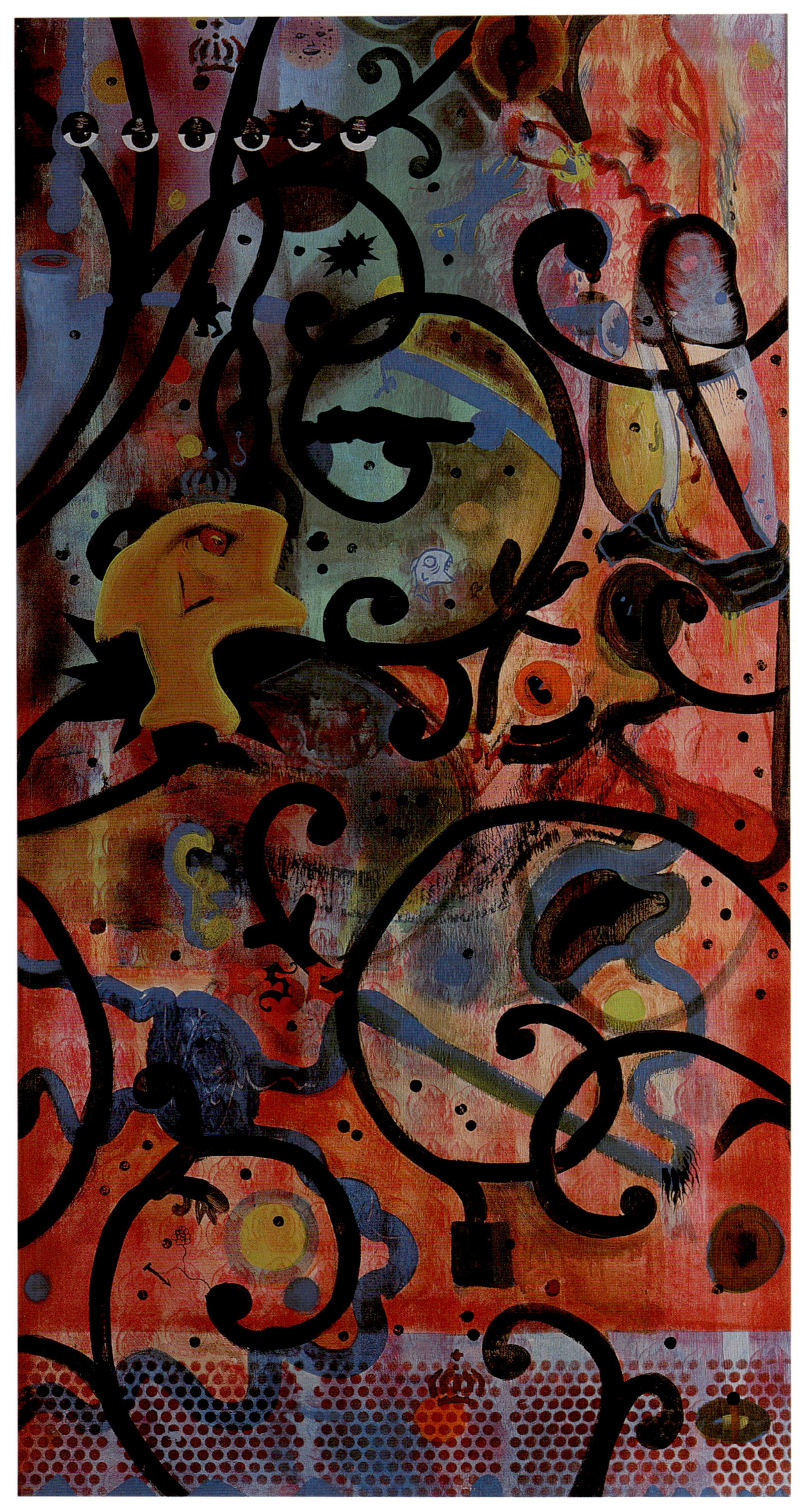

122 Marcus Zilliox,
*Wink and Jab
Ennui*, 1997, acrylic
on wood panel,
48" x 24"

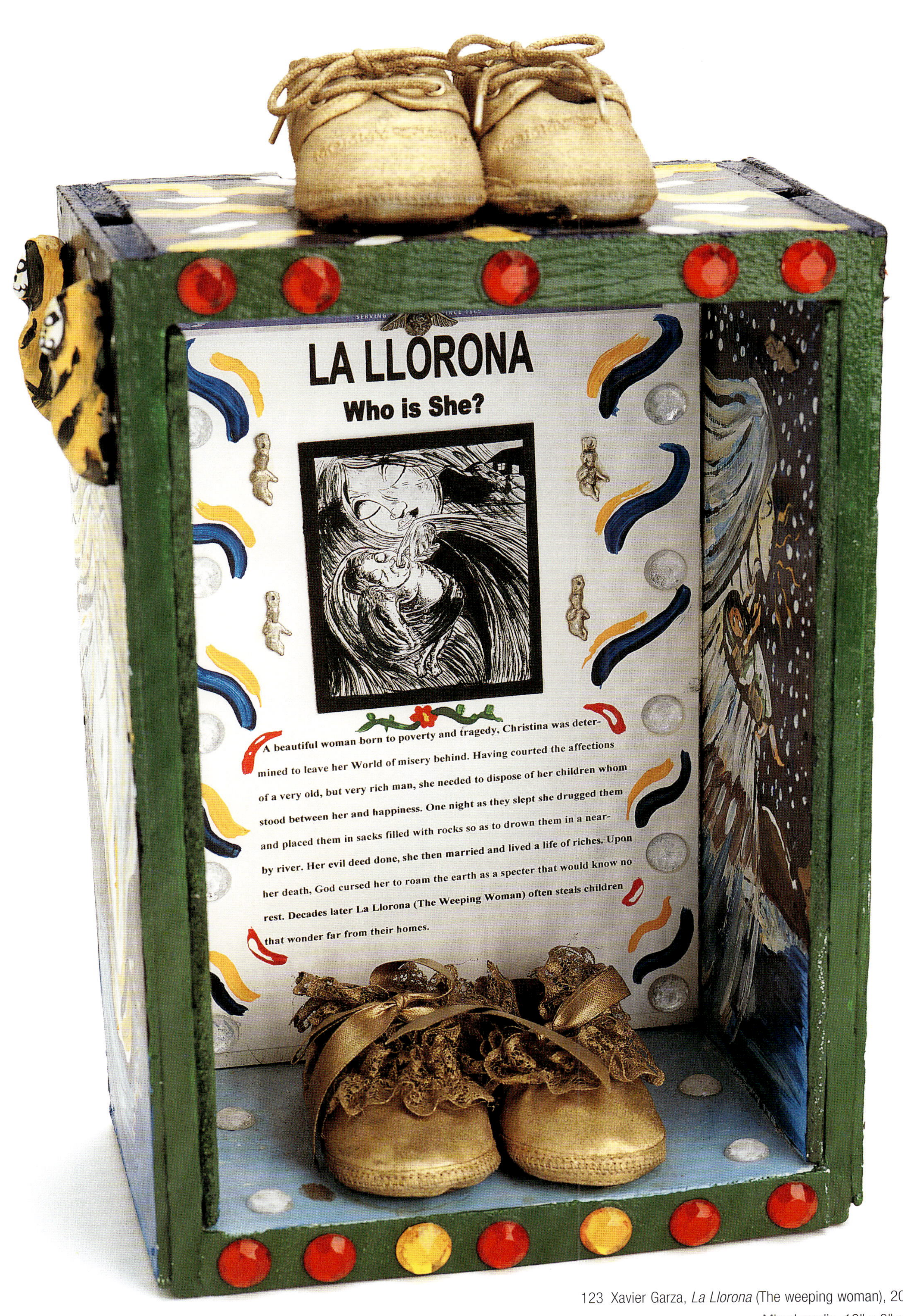

123 Xavier Garza, *La Llorona* (The weeping woman), 2002
Mixed media, 13" x 8" x 5"

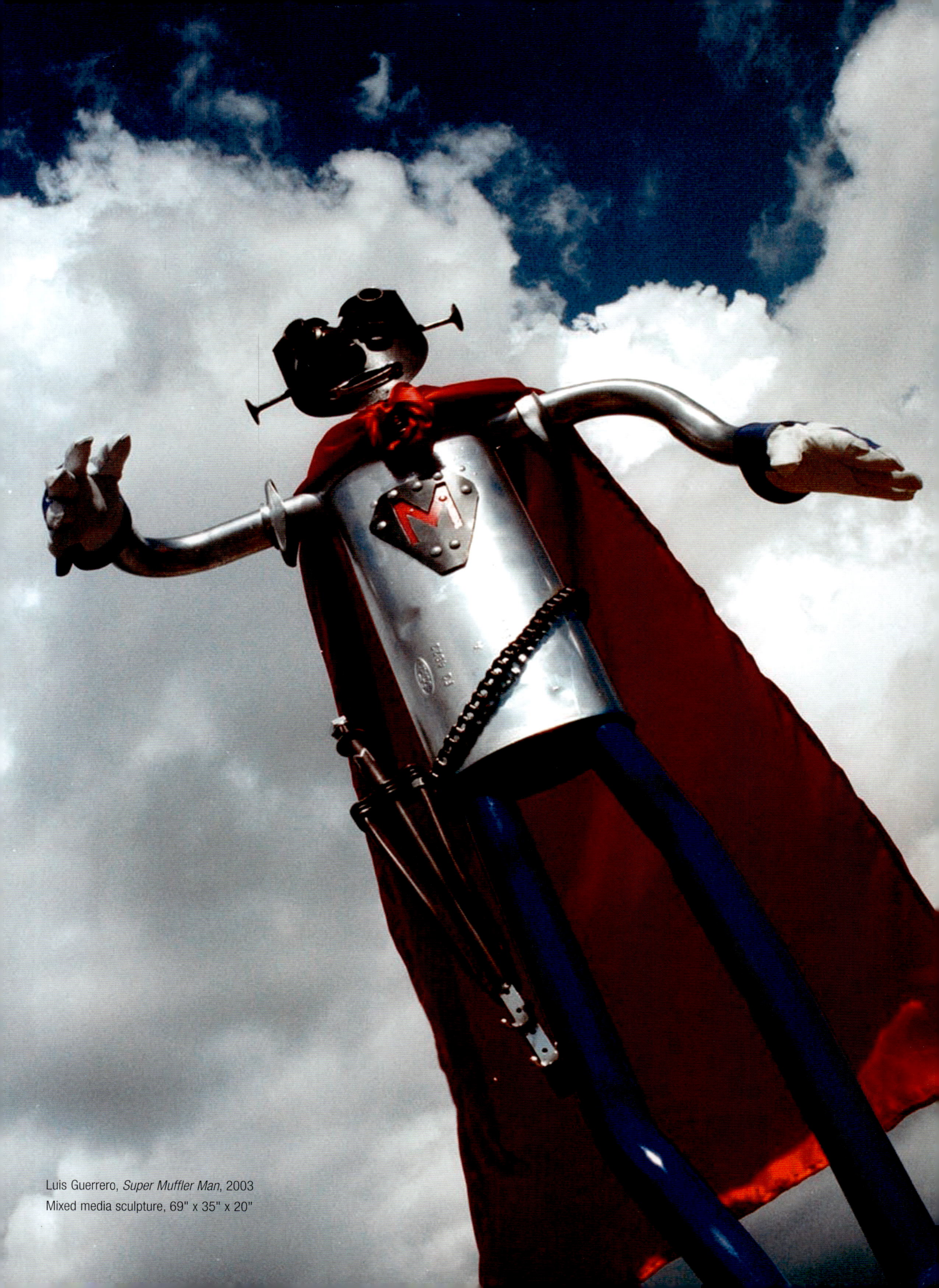

Luis Guerrero, *Super Muffler Man*, 2003
Mixed media sculpture, 69" x 35" x 20"

the authors and other contributors

PRINCIPAL AUTHORS

GARY D. KELLER is director of the Hispanic Research Center at Arizona State University and editor-in-chief of the Bilingual Press/Editorial Bilingüe. He is the author of over two dozen books and numerous scholarly articles encompassing both scholarship and creative literature. He was the 1992 recipient of the Charles A. Dana Foundation's major prize for "Pioneering Achievements in Education." Keller's curatorial activities have included exhibitions at annual conferences of the National Association for Chicana and Chicano Studies and exhibitions at Arizona State University, including solo shows by Sam Coronado, Boyer Gonzales, Ester Hernández, and Malaquías Montoya. He is the lead author of *Contemporary Chicana and Chicano Art: Artists, Works, Culture, and Education* (2002) and one of the principal developers of *Chicana and Chicano Space: A Thematic, Inquiry-Based Art Education Resource*, an online guide to Chicana/o artists and their work. He recently was awarded a grant from the National Endowment for the Arts to create a Latina/o visual artists' online community.

MARY ERICKSON is a professor of art at Arizona State University and an internationally recognized scholar and educator who has specialized in documenting the work of Chicana/Chicano artists. Along with Gary Keller, she was the lead developer of the important Web site *Chicana and Chicano Space: A Thematic, Inquiry-Based Art Education Resource*. She was the 1995 recipient of the National Art Education Association's Lowenfeld Award. She is editor of *Translations*, a publication of the National Art Education Association, and has published numerous articles in journals including *Studies in Art Education*, for which she served as commentary editor for four years. She is coauthor of *Art History and Education* (University of Illinois Press, 1993) and author of *Multicultural Artworlds: Enduring, Evolving, and Overlapping Traditions* (National Art Education Association, Reston, VA). She was a visiting scholar at the J. Paul Getty Center for Education in the Arts from 1994 to 1995, during which time she was also chairperson of the center's doctoral fellowship program. She is 2002 National Art Educator of the National Art Education Association.

PAT VILLENEUVE is associate professor of art education, arts administration, and museum studies and coordinator of graduate studies in art education at Florida State University. A former visiting professor and faculty associate at Arizona State University, she contributed to *Contemporary Chicana and Chicano Art: Artists, Works, Culture, and Education* (2002) and presented at the Arizona State University First Annual Latina/o Art Auction and Symposium (2003). She and Mary Erickson have coauthored "Ode to Mexican Artists," an instructional resource on Chicana/o art that appears in the May 2004 issue of the *Art Education* journal. She has presented and published extensively on art education and art museum education topics and is past editor of *Art Education* as well as a former commissioner of research for the National Art Education Association. With extensive experience as a museum education curator, she is currently preparing an edited book on art museum education. She directed a Fulbright-Hayes group project to Mexico in 2000, and in 1993 she was named Outstanding Art Museum Educator of the Year by the Kansas Art Education Association.

CONTRIBUTORS

MELANIE MAGISOS is senior project developer for digital initiatives at the Arizona State University Hispanic Research Center, where she has worked to develop Web sites, CD-ROMs, DVDs, and books on Chicana/o art and artists. In 2003 she produced a symposium and auction of Chicana/o art. As the executive director of the Center for Image Processing in Education in Tucson, Arizona, Ms. Magisos directed the development of more than twenty interactive CD-ROM and Web site projects for educators (many of them award winners), facilitated the delivery of professional development workshops to thousands of secondary science and math teachers nationwide, and directed a series of national imaging conferences. She has been the manager of a NASA planetary image library and an editor of a series of space science books. Ms. Magisos holds an M.A. degree in film and a B.A. in English from Ohio University and is an award-winning filmmaker.

AMY K. PHILLIPS received her B.A. in journalism from New Mexico State University in 1988. A published book author and editor, Ms. Phillips has focused on nonfiction. For several years, she worked as a liaison between book publishers and industry service providers and vendors. Before becoming involved in book publishing, she was editor-in-chief of a newspaper in Alaska, an editor of artist directories in New Mexico, a freelance features and arts writer for various newspapers, and an editor of archaeological gray literature in Arizona. She is currently a program coordinator at the Hispanic Research Center, Arizona State University, where she coordinates research and materials and assists on various writing and editing projects.

THOMAS H. WILSON is director of the Mesa Southwest Museum in Mesa, Arizona. Previously he was director of the Museum of New Mexico in Santa Fe; director of the Logan Museum of Anthropology and the Wright Museum of Art, as well as director of Museum Studies, at Beloit College; director of the Southwest Museum in Los Angeles; and deputy director of the Museum for African Art in New York City. Dr. Wilson earned a B.A. from the University of New Mexico in anthropology and his Ph.D. from the University of California, Berkeley, in Mayan archaeology. After two years as an assistant professor at the University of Nairobi, Richard Leakey hired him to be coast archaeologist for the National Museums of Kenya. Upon returning to the United States after seven years in Africa, Dr. Wilson worked in the Museum Program at the National Endowment for the Humanities, where he oversaw funding for significant museum programs nationwide. He received a J.D. from the University of Maryland and is licensed to practice law in New York.

ANGELICA M. DOCOG has been assistant director and curator of education at the Mesa Southwest Museum in Mesa, Arizona, since 2001. Ms. Docog is completing her Ph.D. at the University of Manchester, England, and is currently writing a dissertation on a child's life in early Pueblo Indian culture. She holds an M.A. degree in history museum studies from the Cooperstown Graduate Program, State College at Oneonta and the New York State Historical Association, Cooperstown, New York. Ms. Docog completed additional graduate work on the history of dress at the Courtauld Institute of Art, University of London, England. She earned a B.A. degree in 1983 in history and art history from Seton Hill College, Greensburg, Pennsylvania. Her scholarly interests include the representation and interpretation of Latino culture in museums; the representation of dress and textiles in portraiture; collections care and documentation; and women and children in Asian, Latino, and Native American cultures.

PHOTOGRAPHER

CRAIG SMITH, who photographed most of the art in this book, maintains a dual career as a professional photographer and an exhibiting artist. He earned his B.F.A. from the Kansas City Art Institute in 1985 and an M.F.A. in photography from Arizona State University in 1990.

index of artworks

This index is alphabetized using the word-by-word system. Definite and indefinite articles in Spanish (*el, la, los, las, un, una*) appear at the end of the title, like their English counterparts (*the* and *a/an*), except in the case of titles commonly considered as a unit: *El Chuy*, *La Llorona*, and *El Santo*.

index of artists

Alphabetization of artists' names generally follows standard Spanish practice (i.e., alphabetizing by the first surname), except in those cases where the artist is more commonly known by the second surname.

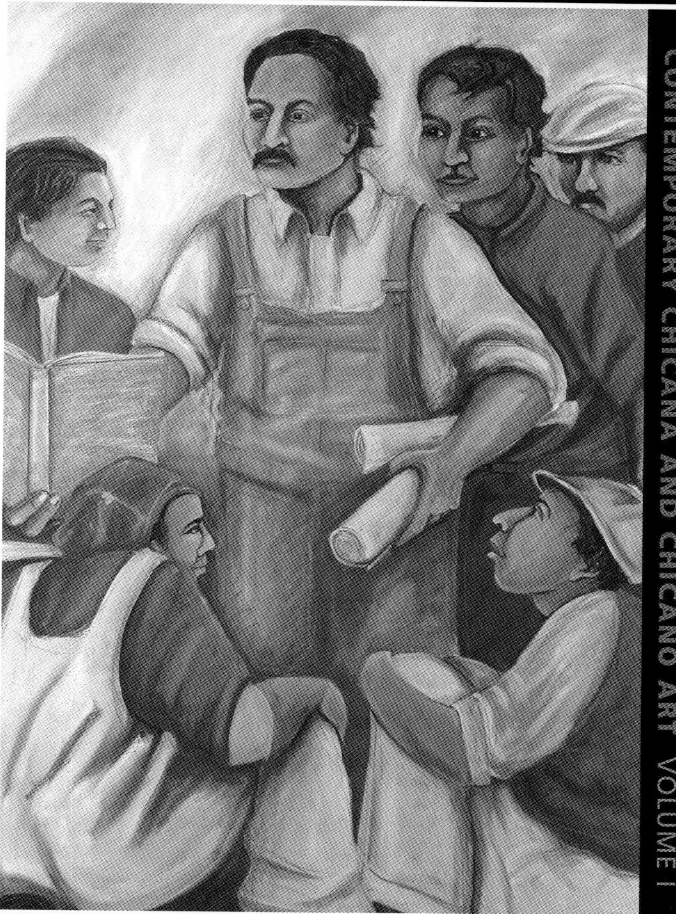

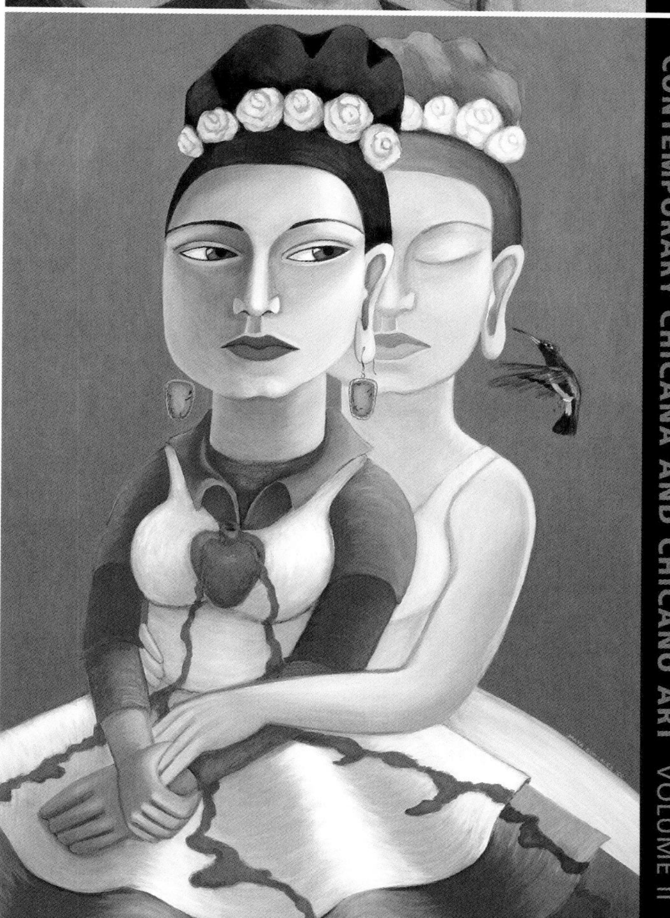

Cover art, top: Malaquías Montoya, *Un maestro pa'l futuro,* 1997;
bottom, Maya González, *The Love That Stains,* 2000

CONTEMPORARY
CHICANA AND CHICANO ART

Artists, Works, Culture, and Education

*by Gary D. Keller, Mary Erickson,
Kaytie Johnson, and Joaquín Alvarado*

WINNER, *Fine Art Category
2003 Independent Publisher Book Awards*

"A comprehensive, lavish and sophisticated
presentation designed to elevate the works
of Chicana and Chicano artists to a new level
of significance in the larger art world . . .
an unqualified success."

—*Southwest BookViews*

"The absolute bible of contemporary
Chicano art."

—*Cheech Marín*

"An original, two-volume publication that
will leave the most skeptical and jaded art
lovers impressed."

—*San Antonio Current*

"The work of the artists is world class.
This book, which is also world class, will
help bring attention to their art."

—*Rudolfo Anaya*

"This set represents a major attempt
to understand and provide access to
Chicano art."

—*Library Journal*

*Vol. I, 336 pages; Vol. II, 342 pages
Paper: $120.00/set; Cloth: $150.00/set;
Boxed Set (slipcased): $160.00/cloth set*

Phone orders: 480-965-3867
Fax: 480-965-8309
Email: brp@asu.edu
Web site: www.asu.edu/brp

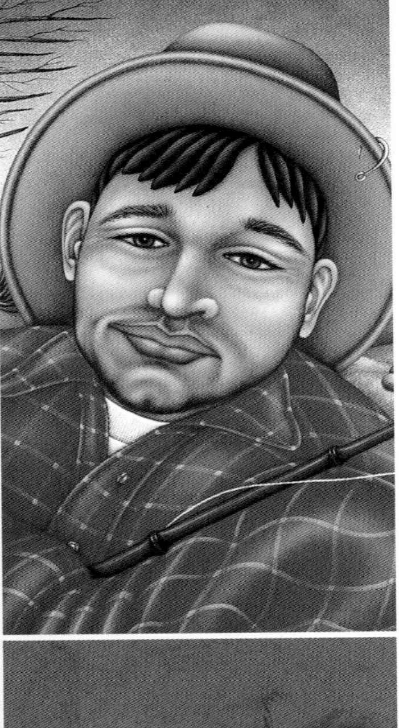

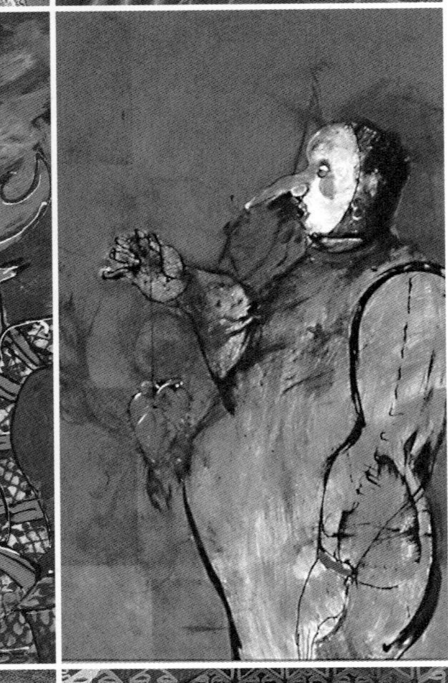

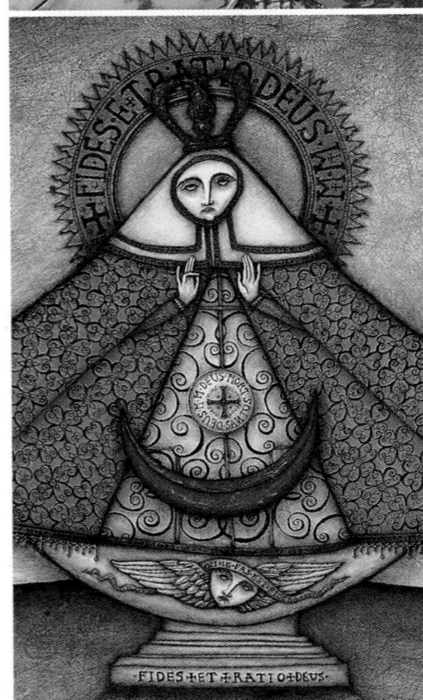

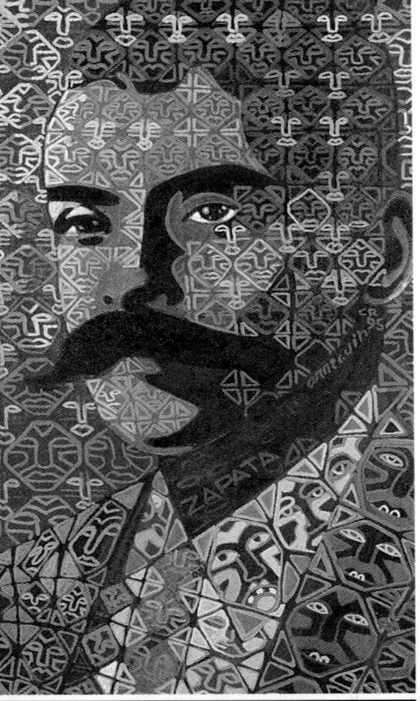

LATINA/O ONLINE
ART COMMUNITY

An Internet-based Home for Artists, Artwork, and Organizations

Designed to provide services to artists, galleries, museums, collectors, and information to the larger art-appreciating public, the Latina/o Online Art Community has as its twin goals connecting people committed to Latina/o art worldwide and introducing this art to new audiences.

Whether you are an artist or just interested in art, you can:

- List or find out about upcoming arts events in your area or nationally.
- Read about, contact, and see sample work by individual artists.
- Link to galleries or museums.
- Create your own Web page with samples of your art.
- View exhibitions on relevant arts topics.
- Study research materials.
- Read viewpoints by scholars and journalists.

Join Us! It's Free!

http://www.latinoartcommunity.org

Developed at the Hispanic Research Center at Arizona State University.

This project is supported in part by a grant from the National Endowment for the Arts.

Art, clockwise: Elizabeth Gómez, *Moths*, 1997; Celina Hinojosa, *The Lenten Harvest*, 1998; Maximiliano Pruneda III, *Recompensa del amor/The Reward of Love*, 1999; Alfredo Arreguín, *El joven Zapata*, 1995; Daniel Martín Díaz, *Fides et Ratio*, 1999; Aydee López Martínez, *New and Improved Coatlicue*, 2000